"In the evangelical tradition in which John Sanders works, his is a highly contested but also greatly needed view of providence. Sanders covers the fields of biblical theology, systematic theology and philosophy of religion with remarkable expertise, and has developed a strong argument for God taking risks in relating to human beings."
Adriö König, *professor of systematic theology, University of South Africa*

"Sanders's book is a benchmark treatment of the theology of providence. Future treatments of the topic will have to reckon with the succinct and arresting proposal developed with such care in this volume."
William J. Abraham, *professor of theology, Perkins School of Theology, Southern Methodist University*

"It is rare to see theological work that integrates biblical, historical and philosophical resources in so sophisticated a fashion. This is an immensely important book. . . . But let the reader beware: it may change the way you read the Bible or think of God or live the Christian life."
Terence E. Fretheim, *professor of Old Testament, Luther Seminary*

"Some people have gotten the impression that God is an unblinking cosmic stare or a solitary metaphysical iceberg, and they naturally have difficulty relating to God as a loving, interacting Person. This book will help them overcome such misconceptions and greatly advances the case for the openness model of God."
Clark H. Pinnock, *professor of theology, McMaster Divinity School*

"John Sanders marshals the most extensive survey available of the biblical and traditional warrant for the model of 'relational theism' in which God's freedom is seen precisely in God's willingness to accept the risks of authentic give-and-take with humanity. Readers will be impressed both by the seriousness of Sanders's exegetical and historical work and by the pastoral sensitivity with which he probes the implications of this alternative model of God's providential activity."
Randy L. Maddox, *Paul T. Walls Professor of Wesleyan Theology, Seattle Pacific University*

"A challenging and persuasive portrait of a dynamic and sovereign God. . . . By focusing first on the biblical text, Sanders forces us to think about what God has actually done, about how God actually operates, rather than how we think God should or ought to act."
Michael Holmes, *professor of biblical studies and early Christianity, Bethel College*

THE GOD WHO RISKS

A Theology of Providence

JOHN SANDERS

"The Risk Model" P340.

InterVarsity Press
Downers Grove, Illinois

InterVarsity Press
P.O. Box 1400, Downers Grove, IL 60515
World Wide Web: www.ivpress.com
E-mail: mail@ivpress.com

InterVarsity Press® is the book-publishing division of InterVarsity Christian Fellowship/USA®, a student movement active on campus at hundreds of universities, colleges and schools of nursing in the United States of America, and a member movement of the International Fellowship of Evangelical Students. For information about local and regional activities, write Public Relations Dept., InterVarsity Christian Fellowship/USA, 6400 Schroeder Rd., P.O. Box 7895, Madison, WI 53707-7895.

Scripture quotations, unless otherwise noted, are from the New Revised Standard Version of the Bible, copyright 1989 by the Division of Christian Education of the National Council of the Churches of Christ in the USA. Used by permission. All rights reserved.

Passage in chapter five reprinted from "Historical Considerations" by John Sanders in The Openness of God *by Clark Pinnock, Richard Rice, John Sanders, William Hasker and David Basinger. Used by permission of InterVarsity Press, P.O. Box 1400, Downers Grove, IL 60515.*

Passage in chapter six reprinted from "Why Simple Foreknowledge Offers No More Providential Control than the Openness of God" by John Sanders in Faith and Philosophy 14 *(January 1997): 26-40.*

Cover photograph: SuperStock
ISBN 0-8308-1501-5
Printed in the United States of America ♾

Library of Congress Cataloging-in-Publication Data

Sanders, John, 1956-
    The God who risks : a theology of providence / John Sanders.
       p.   cm.
    Includes bibliographical references and indexes.
    ISBN 0-8308-1501-5 (pbk. : alk. paper)
    1. Providence and government of God.   I. Title.
BT135.S26   1998
231'.5—dc21   98-24532
                                                                              CIP

| 15 | | 14 | | 13 | | 12 | | 11 | | 10 | 9 | | 8 | | 7 | | 6 | | 5 | | 4 | | 3 |
| 09 | | 08 | | 07 | | 06 | | 05 | | 04 | | 03 | | 02 |

Acknowledgments 7
1 Introduction 9
2 The Nature of the Task 15
   2.1 Metaphors and Models 15
   2.2 Criteria 16
   2.3 Anthropomorphism 19
   2.4 A Shared Context 23
   2.5 Two Objections 26
   2.6 Conclusion 37
3 Old Testament Materials for a Relational View of Providence
  Involving Risk 39
   3.1 Introduction 39
   3.2 The Creation and Its Divinely Established Conditions 41
   3.3 Freedom Within Limits 45
   3.4 The Implausible Happens 46
   3.5 God Suffers on Account of His Sinful Creatures
      but Will Not Abandon Them 49
   3.6 The Divine Purpose: Creating a Relationship of Trust 50
   3.7 God May Be Prevailed On 53
   3.8 Joseph: A Risk-Free Model? 54
   3.9 God Works with What Is Available 56
   3.10 Divine-Human Relationality in the Covenant 61
   3.11 Divine Goals with Open Routes 63
   3.12 Excursus on Divine Repentance 66
   3.13 Divine Wrath and Mercy in the Context of Covenantal Relationality . . . 75
   3.14 The Absence and Presence of God 79
   3.15 The Potter and the Clay: An Examination of So-Called
      Pancausality Texts 81
   3.16 Divine Love and Humiliation 87
   3.17 Conclusion 88
4 New Testament Materials for a Relational View of Providence
  Involving Risk 90
   4.1 Introduction 90
   4.2 The Baptism 91
   4.3 The Birth of Jesus and the Bethlehem Massacre 92
   4.4 The Temptation of Jesus 94
   4.5 Confession and Transfiguration 95
   4.6 Compassion, Dialogue and Healing Grace 96
   4.7 Gethsemane: The Pathos of Jesus 98
   4.8 The Cross of Jesus 104
   4.9 The Resurrection 107
   4.10 Grace, Judgment and Humiliation: Divine Love in Jesus' Teaching . . . 108
   4.11 Various Texts on Providence 112

4.12 Conclusion to the Life of Jesus 115
4.13 The Church as the Vehicle of God's Project 117
4.14 The Nature and Goal of the Divine Project 124
4.15 Eschatology and Providence 125
4.16 Excursus on Predictions and Foreknowledge 129
4.17 Conclusion 137
5 Divine Relationality in the Christian Tradition 140
  5.1 Introduction 140
  5.2 Some Early Fathers 142
  5.3 Augustine 147
  5.4 The Middle Ages 151
  5.5 From Luther to Wesley 153
  5.6 Contemporary Theology 158
  5.7 Conclusion 164
6 Risk and the Divine Character 167
  6.1 Introduction 167
  6.2 Summary of a Risk View of Providence 169
  6.3 The Nature of Divine Risk 170
  6.4 The Divine Character and Providence 173
  6.5 Excursus on Omniscience 194
  6.6 Conclusion 206
7 The Nature of Divine Sovereignty 208
  7.1 Introduction 208
  7.2 Types of Relationships 209
  7.3 Specific Versus General Sovereignty 211
  7.4 Divine Permission 217
  7.5 Human Freedom 220
  7.6 The Concept of Divine Self-Limitation 224
  7.7 Can God's Will Be Thwarted? 228
  7.8 Divine Purpose with Open Routes 230
  7.9 Conclusion 235
8 Applications to the Christian Life 237
  8.1 Introduction 237
  8.2 Salvation and Grace 237
  8.3 Evil 251
  8.4 Prayer 268
  8.5 Divine Guidance 275
  8.6 Conclusion 278
9 Conclusion 280
Notes 283
Bibliography 340
Indexes 357

Acknowledgments

Many people have had a hand in shaping my life experiences and my ideas about divine providence. It is with deep appreciation that I reflect back on all the stimulating discussions I had with my fellow students and professors during my college years. Though there are too many people to list, I would like to mention some former professors who were especially instrumental in helping me formulate my views on the subject of providence: Robert H. Thompson, Wayne Born and John Linton. Several people have been kind enough to read parts or all of the manuscript of this book and to offer advice, suggestions, criticisms and encouragements along the way. Readers included David Basinger, Chris Botha, Gregory Boyd, David Burrell, C.S.C., Rodney Clapp, Thomas Flint, Terence Fretheim, William Hasker, Mike Holmes, Alan Padgett, Clark Pinnock, Alvin Plantinga and Daniel Rieger. These folks sometimes agreed and sometimes disagreed with what I said. Their comments and criticisms served to sharpen the book. Also, I would like to thank the Center for Philosophy of Religion at the University of Notre Dame for granting me a fellowship that provided time for further research, writing and thought-provoking discussions among the members of the center. Special thanks go to Adriö König, under whose guidance I completed an earlier version of this work for my doctoral thesis in theology at the University of South Africa. Adriö provided excellent advice as well as spirited debate in order to improve this work. Finally, I wish to express my heartfelt appreciation to Dean Fredrikson, my teacher and dialogue partner for twenty years, who has shown me what it means to always be "becoming a Christian." To him this book is appreciatively dedicated.

ONE

INTRODUCTION

. . . .

The police car, lights flashing and siren wailing, sped past me as I was driving home. When I reached the stop sign at the corner, I could see several police cars and an ambulance up ahead at the scene of an accident. Because I was working for the local newspaper as a photographer at the time, I reflexively decided to take some pictures of the accident. When I reached the scene, I could see a semitrailer blocking the road, a motorcycle lying on its side and a white sheet covering something near the truck. Someone approached me and said, "You don't want to take any pictures here. Your brother Dick is lying under the wheels of that truck." The next few minutes are a blur in my memory, but I do recall getting home. I went to my room and prayed, "God, why did you kill my brother?" As I look back on that prayer, I am fascinated that I asked God such a question. I was a nominal Methodist at the time, and I did not believe that God caused everything that happened. Perhaps I had picked up from the broader culture the belief that God was the cause behind all tragedies ("acts of God," as insurance companies call them). In years to come many a Christian attempted to provide me with "good" reasons why God would have ordained my brother's death. Those discussions served to spur my reflection on divine providence for over twenty years.

The belief that God is the ultimate cosmic explanation for each and every thing, including all the bad things we experience, is quite widespread, at least in North America. About fifteen years after the death of my brother I attended the funeral service of a young child whose parents were close friends of mine. At the graveside service the pastor said, "God must have had a good reason for taking her home." Of course, "taking her home" is a euphemism for God's killing her. In a little while the euphemism wore off and the parents inquired as to why God killed their daughter. Several weeks later when I was visiting these friends, they had a question for me: "Why did God kill our baby girl?" They were angry with God but did not feel safe enough to cry out in lamentation at church. They had always been told that God's ways are best and that questioning God is a sin. In answering their question, I sought to provide them with a different model of God—the one that is explained in this book. Many people, both churchgoers and nonchurchgoers, feel anger and even hatred toward God. But their anger is directed at a particular model of God.

After talks had broken off between Iraq and the United Nations over the Iraqi invasion of Kuwait, UN Secretary-General Javier Pérez de Cuellar said, "War is now in God's hands." When President Gerald Ford heard this statement, he remarked, "I wish it were; I'd feel a lot better about it." Did de Cuellar's remark manifest faith in divine providence, whereas Ford's did not? No. But their remarks do reveal different understandings of providence.

There are many different views of divine providence. For the purposes of this study, all of them may be placed under one of two basic models: the "no-risk" view and the "risk" view. Either God does take risks or does not take risks in providentially creating and governing the world. Either God is in some respects conditioned by the creatures he created or he is not conditioned by them. If God is completely unconditioned by anything external to himself, then God does not take any risks. According to the no-risk understanding, no event ever happens without God's specifically selecting it to happen. Nothing is too insignificant for God's meticulous and exhaustive control. Each and every death, civil war, famine, wedding, peaceful settlement or birth happens because God specifically intends it to happen. Thus God never takes any risks and nothing ever turns out differently from the way God desires. The divine will is never thwarted in any respect.

But if God is in some respects conditioned by his creatures, then God takes risks in bringing about this particular type of world. According to the risk model of providence, God has established certain boundaries within which creatures operate. But God sovereignly decides not to control each and every event, and some things go contrary to what God intends and may not turn out completely as God desires. Hence, God takes risks in creating this sort of world. Although there are varieties of each basic model of providence, this study focuses on the two main views, emphasizing the family resemblances among the various members of each family.

Some theologians claim that only the no-risk model affirms divine sovereignty, which proves that there is only one model of sovereignty. These theologians attempt to win the debate simply by definition. For them, divine sovereignty can only mean exhaustive control of all things. Their claim is questioned in this work. It is not up to human beings to dictate the sort of providence God must exercise. Instead, we should try to discern what sort of sovereignty God has freely chosen to practice. The word *providence* refers to the way God has chosen to relate to us and provide for our well-being. Consequently, God may or may not have chosen to exercise no-risk sovereignty. We have to observe what God has chosen to do in history—based preeminently on the history of Israel and Jesus of Nazareth—rather than simply define the type of sovereignty God must exercise.

Many Western theists have held that God takes no risks in governing the world. After all, they reason, if God is a God of order, then there is no room for a God who, in the words of Einstein's famous phrase, "plays dice with the world." Yet scientists, philosophers and theologians are moving away from the idea of a deity who is the "will-to-power" to a God who is the "will-to-community," a God who desires to be in relationship to all his creatures and desires a personal relationship with humans. The task of this present work is to give a coherent account of what is involved in the divine-human relationship and to explicate, from within this view, the ways in which divine providence is risk taking.

The sensibilities of many people will be shocked by the notion that God is a risk taker, for the metaphor goes against the grain of our accustomed thinking in regard to divine providence. Theorists on metaphor, however, hold that a good metaphor is supposed to challenge conventional ways of looking at things and suggest an alternate perspective. Metaphors disclose a way of viewing life and relationships, but they may also conceal things from us. When certain metaphors (for example, God as king) reign for so long in theology, we risk being conditioned to overlook aspects of God's relationship with us. When this happens, we need new "iconoclastic" metaphors that reveal to us something that we overlooked. It is my contention that the metaphor of God as risk taker opens up new ways for us to understand what is at stake for God in divine providence: things that

biblical exegetes, as well as theologians and liturgists in their fields, may
have overlooked in the biblical record.

It should be pointed out that thinking of God as risk taker only makes
sense within a particular theological model: a personal God who enters
into genuine give-and-take relations with his creatures. Neither an
impersonal deity nor a personal deity who meticulously controls every
event takes risks. The portrait of God developed here is one according to
which God sovereignly wills to have human persons become collaborators
with him in achieving the divine project of mutual relations of love. Such
an understanding of the divine-human relationship may be called
"relational theism." By this I mean any model of the divine-human
relationship that includes genuine give-and-take relations between God
and humans such that there is receptivity and a degree of contingency in
God. In give-and-take relationships God receives and does not merely
give.[1]

Thus understood, relational theism encompasses a number of views
regarding divine omniscience. Views that affirm a degree of conditionality
in God come under this heading. Thus proponents of "freewill theism,"
simple foreknowledge, presentism (the openness of God) and some
versions of middle knowledge may be called relational theists. Although I
defend one view of omniscience in this book, the fact remains that
relational theism has given rise to a number of views that bear strong
family resemblances.[2] I argue that the key element in the debate over
providence is not the type of omniscience God has but the kind of
sovereignty God has decided to exercise.

In order to articulate the heuristic value of God the risk taker for the
Christian life, a model of God as a personal being who enters into
personal relationships with us must be established. This is done in the
various chapters of the book. Chapter two discusses various methodological matters important for assessing the success of the proposal. In
particular, the charge that my model entails an "anthropomorphic"
understanding of God is addressed. Chapters three and four examine the
Old and New Testament material supporting this model. These chapters
look at biblical texts that are commonly ignored or radically reinterpreted
in order to remove the element of risk from divine providence. I focus on
the nature of God and the divine project that this God has undertaken.
Chapter five examines the Christian theological tradition to retrieve certain
elements often overlooked in Western theology in order to show that the
model here proposed is in consonance with major themes of the tradition.

Chapter six seeks to give some philosophical clarification to the notions of God derived from the biblical material. How should we understand the nature of the God who undertakes the project of entering into reciprocal relations with his creatures? Sometimes the attributes of God are derived solely on the basis of the *dignum Deo* (what it is dignified for God to be according to natural theology) instead of by looking at the particular sort of project God is seeking to accomplish in history. In my opinion, philosophical theologians need to pay more attention to what God has actually decided to do in human history and need to be a little less sanguine about their own intuitions reading what a deity must be like. Then it becomes clear that the classical attributes of God need some revising. Chapter seven applies these ideas to the doctrine of sovereignty and explores the two basic models of divine sovereignty. Chapter eight spells out the practical implications of these views of divine sovereignty for the Christian life. Comparing and contrasting different views is one way of clarifying positions. To this end the risk and no-risk models of divine sovereignty are compared regarding several key areas of providence: salvation, suffering and evil, prayer, and guidance. It will be argued that one's view of providence makes a significant impact on one's devotional life. Issues such as whether or not the divine will may be thwarted in any respect and whether God's plan for the world is a blueprint or a general overall strategy will be explored.

This book consists of two major parts: biblical and theological/philosophical. Why include two different studies in one volume? Academic professionalism has encouraged scholars to work in very specialized areas, and consequently biblical scholars on the one hand and theologians and philosophers on the other often are unaware of what is being said in the other discipline. In my own work as a theologian I have benefited greatly from the detailed studies of biblical scholars that show precisely what the texts do and do not say. Sometimes theologians and philosophers use biblical texts to support or illustrate their views only to discover that the texts mean something else. And biblical scholars sometimes make theological/philosophical claims about providence and the divine nature without being informed of the current state of discussion regarding these topics in philosophical theology. Philosophical theology can lend clarity to concepts about the divine nature and providence that can be useful to the biblical scholars. It is my hope that this work will help bring people in these separate disciplines into fruitful dialogue with each other.

There are further reasons for combining biblical and philosophical theology. Since I have grave concerns about natural theology (attempts to discover what God *must* be like apart from any divine revelation), it is important to pay close attention to the biblical text to see just what sort of providence is being depicted. Sometimes philosophers do not pay much attention to what the Bible says on their topic and thus seem to simply create views of God out of their own imagination. Those who do interact with the Bible commonly interpret biblical texts that seem to disagree with the claims they are making by dismissing them as examples of "anthropomorphism." I shall have more to say on this in the next several chapters. A final reason for attempting to bring the separate disciplines together is that some Reformed thinkers are scandalized by the notion of divine risk taking taught by some contemporary theologians and philosophers. They believe that the Bible teaches nothing of the sort, so it is important to show in some detail that the biblical narrative actually affirms genuine give-and-take relations between God and humans (in which God not only gives but in some sense receives) such that God is depicted in the Bible as taking certain risks. For these reasons I think it important to incorporate biblical and philosophical theology into a single work.

At this juncture a number of qualifications may be helpful. To begin, this work is constructive. That is, it attempts to develop a particular theological model rather than critique a standard position. Although critiques occasionally are made, they are not the primary goal. Second, I am not writing a general treatise on the doctrine of providence covering all the topics normally examined in such works. Rather, I am examining providence through the lens of divine risk taking and am studying aspects of providence in order to see what should be said concerning a risk-taking God. This will lead some readers to judge the book "imbalanced." Third, I have no delusions that this study will settle all the disputed issues.[3] Fourth, though this work touches repeatedly on the subject of theodicy, it is not about the problem of evil. It is about a personal God who enters into genuine give-and-take relations with us. From this particular model of God implications may be drawn out for the problem of evil. Finally, my particular way of working out the details of the openness model of God in respect to relational theism is not the only way it can be done. The openness model is but one of several families making up the relational theism clan. And even within the openness model, family members are not identical. Proponents of openness, such as David Basinger, William Hasker, Gregory Boyd and myself, disagree at times regarding matters of emphasis, approach and detail. This is the case among proponents of any theological model (Calvinism, Molinism, Thomism, etc.), but I wish to call attention to the fact that what I say is not the only way it may be said by a member of the family.

TWO

THE NATURE OF THE TASK

· ·

Constructs

2.1 Metaphors and Models

A theological project on providence is worked out in a wider framework of beliefs involving questions that pertain to methodology, to the question of how we are to know what God is like and to the appropriateness of human language for speaking of God. This chapter discusses these sundry issues in order to acquaint the reader with the broader theological context in which the present study is done. In particular, I want to justify the approach to Scripture taken in the next two chapters.

The metaphorical and anthropomorphic language of the Bible is taken seriously because it is through the idiom of Scripture and its various metaphors that we understand and relate to God.[1] The language of Scripture is "reality depicting" in that what we understand to be real is mediated through its metaphors and images.[2] Metaphors help us make sense of things with which we are initially unfamiliar by making comparisons. When we assert that Elvis is the king of rock 'n' roll, we make a comparison between kingship and Elvis's relation to other rock 'n' roll singers. When we assert that God is king of the earth, we also make a comparison between kingship and God's relation to the world. Metaphors have the peculiar quality of saying that something both "is" and "is not." What is asserted is correct, but it is not the whole story.[3] Saying that God is a rock tells us something about God but not all that needs saying, for a variety of metaphors are required to adequately describe God and God's relationship to us. Metaphors (even those about God) are reality depicting in that they tell us of a real relationship between God and the world. If we claim that our language about God depicts nothing about God or portrays no genuine divine-human relationship, then our discourse about God will be severely restricted.

Models, whether in science or in religion, often embody a key metaphor or cluster of metaphors that guide our reflection and application to life. Certain metaphors function in a comprehensive way in that they come to "control" or "orient" our thought and life about particular subjects and so may be called *key models*.[4] Key models, or "root metaphors," offer sustained and systematic reflection on a topic and suggest comprehensive life applications. In this way they provide meaning to our experience and shape the way we live. Different key models embody different theologies.[5] Many of our theological disputes arise because we look at the "evidence" through different lenses. When we read the Scripture through the lenses of certain models, we tend to interpret Scripture from that perspective. Thus it is not surprising that someone affirming God as the immutable king would view the biblical texts on divine repentance as anthropomorphisms so that God never actually changes his mind.[6] Moreover, our models shape the practices of the Christian life (for example, petitionary prayer) we develop. Do our prayers ever affect what God decides to do? The way we view such practices discloses the model we affirm. Because models make a difference in how we read the biblical text, as well as in how we live out our faith, it is important to ponder these relationships. The model of a personal God who enters into genuine give-and-take relations with us—which entails divine risk taking—will be examined to see what impact this model has on important doctrines and practices such as divine repentance and petitionary prayer.

2.2 Criteria

All theological models attempt to have "public intelligibility."[7] Intelligibility, or rationality, is a communal affair, so I include the word *public*. In order to be "rational" a model must meet the rules of intelligibility established by the community in which one advances the proposal. In my view there are three general criteria for evaluating a theological model in the Christian tradition. The first criterion is *consonance with tradition*. Since theologians develop theological models and theologians are socially located in particular traditions, any proposed model must reach a significant degree of harmony with the authoritative sources of that tradition. In the case of Christian theology the primary standard, or norming norm, is the Bible. If the theological model does not resonate with Scripture overall and with the person and work of Jesus in particular, it cannot, with integrity, be called Christian.

Moreover, all theologians belong to particular traditions of interpretation of Scripture. We are Roman Catholic or Orthodox or Protestant, not to mention the various subtraditions in each of these communities. Any theological model must not only resonate with Scripture but must also find a place within the religious tradition of the audience to whom the proposal is being made.[8] The problems we select to address, the evidence we cite, the interpretation we give to the evidence and the rhetoric we use to communicate our proposals owe a great debt to the communities to which we belong. This does not rule out reforms, even significant ones, within our traditions, however, for they are not static.[9] From time to time barnacles and other encrustations need to be removed if the tradition is to make better headway in the world.[10] It is with faithfulness to the tradition and concern for it that the reforms discussed in this book are put forth. The Scriptures as well as historical theology are explored for elements that support the notion that God takes risks in governing the world.

The second criterion is *conceptual intelligibility.* In order for the model to make sense, the set of concepts that it entails must be unpacked and examined for internal consistency, coherence with other beliefs we affirm, comprehensiveness in covering the range of relevant considerations, and communicability. If a concept is contradictory, it fails a key test for public intelligibility, since what is contradictory is not meaningful. Furthermore, if concepts integral to the model are mutually inconsistent, the coherence of the model is called into question.[11] A model with too many internal tensions lacks cohesiveness. Regarding comprehensiveness, theological models highlight certain aspects of the faith while overlooking others. The more comprehensively a model covers the range of relevant considerations, the more satisfactory it will be. Vincent Brümmer puts it well when he says, "A systematic theologian is required to develop a suggested theological key model derived from the cumulative tradition, coherently and comprehensively, in order to see what it entails for the whole conceptual scheme of the faith: which elements of the tradition will be highlighted and which will be filtered out or overlooked?"[12] I would add that a proposed model may afford fresh insights into cherished aspects of the faith as well as relieve certain tensions regarding the faith inherent in a different model.

All models have costs in that they have strengths and weaknesses. The determination of what is "too costly" is influenced by the particular lenses through which the evaluator is looking. Thus, what may be considered a strength by one person or group may be viewed as a weakness by another. Concerning communicability, it may be said that all rationality presupposes communities of language users and people committed to the project of sense making. Rationality is never a merely private affair, for the standards of rationality depend on the traditions of specific communities. Christian theology has generally assumed that if you wish to communicate rationally to others, then you must do so with logical consistency and coherence; otherwise, you forfeit the right to claim public intelligibility for your model.

The third criterion is *adequacy for the demands of life*. The proposed model must be relevant to the real-life situations faced by the community. The theological model needs to help us in our relationships with God, others, the creation and ourselves. It must be useful in enhancing such activities as prayer, comforting the suffering and acting responsibly in the world. Not only must the model be judged as to whether it is adequate on the corporate level, it must also be evaluated on the individual level. Though all of us are situated within specific communities, we nevertheless have our own personal experiences and identities that shape our evaluation of any particular model concerning its adequacy for helping us cope with life. Thus everyone will not necessarily evaluate the model in the same way. Yet the fact remains that theological models have to demonstrate their value in the lives of the people of faith.

This work attempts to address the model of divine providence as risk taking in light of these three criteria. Thus it makes use of biblical, historical, systematic and philosophical theology. Chapters three and four seek to demonstrate consonance between the risk model of providence and the Bible (the foundation of our tradition). It is important for theologians not merely to reflect on the Bible but to actually examine in detail particular biblical texts. Historical theology—tracing what the tradition has said on the subject—is also important, and to this end chapter five is included (though there is interaction with the Christian tradition throughout the book). Regarding the development of theological ideas, it should be noted that the no-risk model has a head start of some several hundred years. Thus theologians employing it have had ample time to respond to questions of interpretations of various biblical texts and questions pertaining to the nature of God and the Christian life. It cannot be expected that the risk view of providence will be able to handle immediately all the questions thrown at it. Nevertheless, this study represents a sustained attempt to develop and substantiate the risk model of providence.

For some time now there has been a new wave of critical reappraisal and responsible reconstruction regarding the doctrine of God. Some older views of God are dying and others are seriously ill. This study is an attempt to bring healing to certain aspects of the God of classical theism.[13] Chapters six and seven as well as parts of others use philosophical theology to show the conceptual intelligibility of this model by looking at its internal coherence and answering questions regarding certain "problems" this view might be thought to engender. Finally, chapter eight draws on systematic theology to probe how this model affects other important doctrines and to see whether the model of a risk-taking God is adequate to the demands of the life of faith. It is important that all three disciplines function together, since biblical scholars may be unaware of theological or philosophical paradigms through which they view the text and theologians and philosophers may be unaware of what the biblical texts actually say about the matter on which they are reflecting.

It will be argued that the no-risk model of God has in some respects strayed from its scriptural moorings, has fallen into incoherence and has failed to meet the demands of the practice of faith. The project here undertaken develops the model of God as risk taker and explores the implications of such a model for the life of faith.[14] Because the arguments put forth are all situated in a contextual web of belief, those who do not share my larger web of belief are not likely to agree with my conclusions. Moreover, I make no claims of "proving" my case. This book is an attempt to offer what may be called a cumulative case in support of divine risk taking. It does not pretend to be the only model a Christian may be rationally justified in holding. But I do believe it is superior to the no-risk model of providence in having greater fidelity to the biblical story, a more coherent view of the nature of God and better approaches to life-application issues such as evil, prayer, guidance and a personal relationship with God. Some critics maintain that this view espouses a God who is "human, all too human" or an "anthropomorphic" deity. To this charge I now turn.

2.3 Anthropomorphism

Some may find something odd about applying human concepts to God. Is this not making God in our image? But all the language we employ to speak of God is human language and thus is tinged with anthropomorphism. Those who have found this situation quite troubling have sought an escape.[15] The desire not to speak about God anthropomorphically simply seems correct. After all, just about everyone takes the biblical references to the "eyes," "arms" and "mouth" (anthropomorphisms proper) of God as metaphors for divine actions, not assertions that God has literal body parts. But some go further, claiming that the anthropopathisms (in which God is said to have emotions, plans or changes of mind) are not actually to be attributed to God.

And others claim that all human language for God is improper, since it brings God down to our level and imposes human concepts and language on God. The prophet Isaiah is often cited in support of such views. After all, did he not chide his contemporaries for making idols of the incomparable God: "To whom will you liken me and make me equal, and compare me, as though we were alike?" (46:5; compare 40:18, 25). Later he says, "For my thoughts are not your thoughts, nor are your ways my ways, says the LORD. For as the heavens are higher than the earth, so are my ways higher than your ways and my thoughts than your thoughts" (55:8-9). This text has become the classic affirmation among theologians and philosophers down through the centuries of God's absolute transcendence. The Isaiah passages as well as other biblical texts declaring that God is "not a human being" (Num 23:19; 1 Sam 15:29; Hos 11:9) are often understood as biblical warrant for the disparagement of anthropomorphism.

Philosophers have long criticized the ascription of human characteristics to deity. Not long after Isaiah the Greek thinker Xenophanes railed against anthropomorphic deities, saying that "if oxen and horses or lions had hands, and could paint with their hands, and produce works of art as men do, horses would paint the forms of the gods like horses, and oxen like oxen."[16] Eighteenth-century philosopher David Hume, arguing against "natural religion," has one of his characters say that he is scandalized by the anthropomorphic character of natural theology's arguments for God: It is degrading to the deity to assume that the divine mind is just like a human mind. "So near an approach we never surely can make to the Deity. His ways are not our ways. . . . We are guilty of the grossest and most narrow partiality, and make ourselves the model of the whole universe."[17] In the nineteenth century Ludwig Feuerbach launched a trenchant critique against all anthropomorphism by claiming that Christendom had created a God in its own image. He says that humans create God by making God into our antithesis: "God is the infinite, man the finite being; God is perfect, man imperfect; God eternal, man temporal; God almighty, man weak; God holy, man sinful."[18] According to Feuerbach, this "God" is a purely human creation, a total anthropomorphism so that the attributes of the divine nature are really attributes of human nature. Thus theology is merely anthropology.

Since this book makes significant use of anthropomorphic language about God, it is important to respond to these objections. First, as Karl Barth points out, the Bible does teach the hiddenness and incomprehensibility of God. God is not knowable unless God makes himself known, and even then we do not possess a complete understanding of God. Barth goes on to say that this hiddenness is not due to the inadequacy of human language and thought for talk of God and not because of any metaphysical distinction between the abstract and the sensual. Instead, the incomprehensibility of God is based on the Creator-creature distinction that comes to us from divine revelation.[19] An additional reason for divine incomprehensibility is God's personal nature, for persons are not capable of being fully circumscribed by definition and language.[20]

Second, Hebrew Bible scholar Terence Fretheim notes two ironies in connection with the depreciation of anthropomorphism by theologians.[21] First, anthropomorphism is a distinction of Israelite religion, in contrast to the language of other ancient Near Eastern religions; in fact, anthropomorphic metaphors predominate.[22] If we dismiss them, we lose much of the Hebrew Bible. Indeed, behind the depreciation of anthropomorphism lies the notion that biblical language is unsophisticated or premodern and therefore misapprehends the nature of God. But are philosophically abstract and supposedly nonanthropomorphic understandings of God really more "advanced" than ancient Israel's view? Dietrich Bonhoeffer held that the "abstract concept of God is fundamentally much more anthropomorphic, just because it is not intended to be anthropomorphic, than childlike anthropomorphism."[23] The other irony surfaces when Christians disparage anthropomorphism, since Jesus is the consummate anthropomorphism. If Jesus is God incarnate, then it does not seem that God is especially concerned about having human characteristics predicated of him. Moreover, following Abraham Heschel, the charge may be reversed: God's concern for justice and love is not anthropomorphism; rather, our concern for justice and love is a theomorphism![24] Humans are created in the image of God, and so the human must be seen as a theomorphism. This is the stance of the Christian faith.

Third, humans, as sinners, are not consistently theomorphic because we fail to love, seek justice and forgive. This is precisely what Isaiah meant by "my thoughts are not your thoughts, nor are your ways my ways" (Is 55:8). Unfortunately, this text has for so long been understood as a philosophical timeless truth—God is ontologically and epistemologically wholly beyond us—that it is commonplace for contemporary theologians as diverse as Gordon Kaufman, John Macquarrie, J. I. Packer and Geoffrey Bromiley to use this verse as a general principle espousing human inability to understand the divine nature and activities.[25]

But Isaiah is not establishing axioms about transcendence. He is informing his people that they may feel safe in returning to Yahweh, despite their previous idolatry, because Yahweh is a God who pardons and shows mercy on sinners. He implores the Israelites to return to Yahweh *because Yahweh is not like us humans—he forgives!* (See also Hos 11:8-9.) It is because God's character is different from human sinfulness that God seeks genuine reconciliation and healing for the wounded relationship. This and similar texts refer to character differences between God and humans, not ontological and epistemological differences. For Isaiah, God is incomparable to humans in that he loves those we would not. Thus the real paradox is not between God as the absolute and God as anthropomorphic but between God's grace and human sin.[26]

Other biblical texts commonly used to support the teaching of an abstract transcendence and immutability also fail in this regard. Numbers 23:19 refers to God's steadfast loyalty to the people he brought out of Egypt. He will not change his mind and curse his people no matter what religious rites the prophet Balaam performs. In 1 Samuel 15:29, Samuel declares that God will not take back his decision to remove Saul's kingship. God will not change his mind about this matter. These texts pertain to specific divine decisions based on particular human situations. They do not describe an abstract transcendence.[27]

The fourth point is that the term *anthropomorphism* may have a narrow or broad meaning. The narrow, and customary, sense refers to speaking of God as having human characteristics such as emotions or eyes. Anthropomorphism, however, is sometimes used more broadly in the sense that all our language about God is *human language*. When speaking of God, whether we use abstract terms such as *necessity* and *aseity* or concrete terms such as *lover* and *rock,* we are inevitably predicating properties of God that are derived from human categories.[28] When humans use language, it is *human* language that we use to speak about anything— from God to black holes. As Herman Bavinck observes, "*All* scripture is anthropomorphic," and all so-called abstract names for God such as infinite, *actus purus,* omnipotence and Being Itself remain anthropomorphisms in that they are human words applied to God.[29] Consequently, if we are to talk of God, then our choice is between using anthropomorphisms (in this

Lest we forget the Bible is the Word of God. God Revealing himself to man.

broader sense) and being locked into the frozen silence of absolute ineffability. This does not mean, however, that theology is merely anthropology. Our language, anthropomorphic though it is, remains reality depicting. That is, there really is a being, God, to which our language refers.

Though the biblical writers criticize certain conceptions of God, they repeatedly use a wide array of anthropomorphisms for God.[30] God is said to hear, speak, see and smell. God is faithful, wise, long-suffering and loving. God plans, chooses, acts and experiences grief and joy, sorrow and delight. God is depicted in the familiar human roles of father, mother, husband, shepherd and king. God is also theriomorphized as lion, lamb and vulture and physiomorphized as fire, wind and fountain of water.[31] Nonetheless, all of these descriptions are by human authors, and so they are anthropomorphic in the sense of using human language to refer to God. Finally, these anthropomorphisms are vitally important, for they depict God in relation to us and cannot be rejected unless one desires to deny God's covenantal relationship with us.

We cannot escape using human language (anthropomorphism) when speaking of God any more than we can escape it when speaking of our dogs or our computers. Human words are all we have to speak about anything. The choice before us, argued the ancient skeptic Carneades, is that any notion of God will either be anthropomorphic or meaningless.[32] If, he says, we claim that God is unqualifiedly infinite, unlimited and immovable, then we do not have a being that we can know and thus the concept is meaningless. If we think of God as personal, living and *Jesus Christ* interacting with us, then we are speaking anthropomorphically.

This is a Biblical Counsel. Cornerstone.

2.4 A Shared Context

Speaking of God with human language (anthropomorphically) is legitimate if we have a proper understanding of where we stand in order to talk about God. South African theologian Adriö König points us in the right direction when he asserts that "we have no knowledge of God other than in and through his participation in our history."[33] Thomas Aquinas said that "we come to know and name God from creatures," meaning that all of our knowledge of God arises from within the created order.[34] Many centuries earlier Hillary of Poitiers said, "We must believe God's word concerning Himself, and humbly accept such insight as He vouchsafes to give. [We must believe] in Him as He is, and this in the only possible way, by thinking of Him in the aspect in which He presents Himself to us."[35] In a quite straightforward manner Hillary says that the Bible, with all its anthropomorphism, nevertheless presents God as he truly is.[36] John Calvin correctly notes that we should leave it to God to define himself as God does in Scripture and that "God cannot reveal himself to us in any other way than by a comparison with things we know."[37]

If God speaks to us through Scripture, then God knows how to use human language and concepts in such a way that they are adequate for understanding that which God desires us to know. This requires us to presuppose a shared context between God and the creation.[38] By context I mean the conditions of our existence, including our language, history and spatiotemporal world. This is our context, and the biblical revelation asserts that God enters into that context with us by being in relation to us. In relating to us, God communicates and acts in the created order. By being in relation to us, entering into our context, God makes use of human ways of knowing and speaking to communicate with us. The search for the God unrelated to creation, the God beyond God, leads us to a dead end. Asking the familiar question, What was God doing before he created the world? seduces us into searching for the unrelated God that we mistakenly think is the real God beyond God the Creator and Redeemer. However, we know only the Lord our Creator and Redeemer, the God who is in relation to us *(quoad nos)*. Faith can confess nothing less than that this is who God truly is in himself *(in se)*.

The creation *is* different from God, but no more different than God intended it to be.[39] The only way of knowing just how different we are from God is by God's revealing that to us. According to the Bible, God is a distinct ontological other from us: God is not the world. Yet we come to know this from God's relationship to us in the world. Fretheim remarks that "at least since the creation of 'the heavens and the earth, God has been related to the world from within its structures of time as well as those of space."[40] What we know of God is through his relationship to the creation—his involvement with us in our context. We believe that God existed apart from the world even though we only come to know that from within the world. As his creatures, we know nothing of God apart from God's relationship to the world. Does this mean that God has no being apart from the creation? No! It only means that *we* have no knowledge of God apart from the way he has created us and revealed himself to us. Brian Hebblethwaite writes, "If God creates a temporally structured universe, then, *whatever his own eternal being may be,* he must relate himself to his creation in a manner appropriate to its given nature, i.e. temporally."[41] Although the possibility exists that God's eternal being may be different from the way God relates to us, we have no way of knowing it is different and no reason to say it is different unless we wish to deny God's revelation to us in history. We know nothing of a God unrelated to us.

Does this imply that God is literally like us? Macquarrie observes that all talk of God, in terms of symbols, metaphors or models, ultimately returns to some core likeness between God and the creatures, or it lapses into agnosticism.[42] Does this mean that God shares some of the same (univocal) properties with creatures or only similar (analogous) ones?[43] Even those who defend the doctrine of analogy presuppose that in *some* respects similarities between God and us are univocal.[44] Aquinas, for instance, held that the "universal" terms, such as being, good and living, are not used metaphorically for God but "absolutely," "properly" and "literally."[45] Those who practice negative theology apply such predicates as incorporeality and immutability in a literal way to God. Perhaps what these Christians mean is that though God may be unlimited or "infinite" with respect to certain properties (for example, love and wisdom), God is not to be thought of as completely unlimited with respect to all properties, since such a notion is incoherent.

Although many Christians have used the terms *infinite* and *unlimited* with respect to God, they have not ordinarily meant to claim that God is completely infinite in the sense that God shares absolutely nothing in common with us such that all human language is inappropriate to God.[46] After all, the same Christian writers who said that God is infinite also said that God did not have a body and thus we could truthfully speak of God as a spiritual being. It seems that most Christians have used these terms in order to claim that God is never exhaustively known by us or to distinguish Christian orthodoxy from other views such as paganism or process theology.[47] Furthermore, thinkers as diverse as John Duns Scotus, William of Ockham, George Berkeley, William Alston, Richard Swinburne, Thomas Tracy and Paul Helm all agree that there must be a "hard literal core" or "univocal core" to our talk about God.[48] There must be some properties that are used of God in the same sense that they are used of things in the created order. Otherwise we will be back in the cave of agnosticism. Anthropomorphic language does not preclude literal predication to God. Of course, the question must be asked, What is it to which the anthropomorphisms refer? If God shares the same context with us by entering into relation with us, as the biblical revelation presupposes, then we have a basis for our language about God. What I mean by the word *literal* is that our language about God is reality depicting (truthful) such that there is a referent, an other, with whom we are in relationship and of whom we have genuine knowledge. Even though God may not be

exhaustively known by us, we can have actual knowledge of God, since
God enters into relationship with us.

What sort of terms qualify as part of this reality depiction? The most
basic one, according to the biblical portrait, is God as personal. God is
portrayed as a being who relates with other beings; who loves, suffers,
intends, enacts intentions, responds to others and so on. Minimally, we see
God as a personal agent. When God is said to be a husband, father and
friend, these metaphors depend on the reality of God's being a personal
agent.[49] Apart from personhood they make no sense. Saying God is
personal affirms anthropomorphism in the broad sense of the term-human
language is appropriate for speaking of God. If God is literally a personal
agent, then there is a shared context and anthropomorphism (human
language) is inescapable. At this point some fear that if we cannot escape
anthropomorphic language for God, then we will create God in our own
image. But this need not be the case, since anthropomorphism should not
be equated with anthropocentrism (the former is inescapable, whereas the
latter is not).[50] Moreover, there are numerous safeguards in the biblical
literature to help keep us from such idolatry.

Finally, it could be said that Jesus is the consummate anthropomorphism: the Logos became flesh and blood and tabernacled among
us (Jn 1:14); the person who has witnessed Jesus has seen the Father (Jn
14:9); Jesus is the exact representation of the divine nature (Heb 1:3) in
whom deity dwelled in bodily form (Col 1:15-20; 2:9). If the incarnation is
true and the divine Son experienced fully human life, then God in this way
relates to the world in precisely the same way we do. Jesus is the
consummate revelation of God in human form. The divine self-disclosure
in Jesus puts an end to the claim that being in the form of a human is
contrary to the divine nature. To overturn this, we would need a priori
knowledge that the divine nature is completely unlike human nature,
which would render an incarnation impossible.[51]

God is whole God & wholly man.

2.5 Two Objections

2.5.1 God as Wholly Other
The history of Western thought is replete
with people who have heaped scorn on the notion of God's sharing the
same context with us, for it raises the "scandal of anthropomorphism."
Some conservative (and some liberal) thinkers object to the view of God
expressed in this book on the grounds that God is "infinite" and so is
"wholly other" from us. The pre-Socratic philosopher Anaximander said
that the ultimate metaphysical principle necessary to make sense of our
lives cannot be found within the realm of existence. Instead, we must posit

Anselm - God is greatest possible being; that which nothing greater can be conceived. } How we must talk about God.

what he called the "unlimited," which is totally beyond anything we know. It is utterly ineffable because the unlimited has no predicates. Plato believed we have to ground our rationality in something other than our own existence. He dismissed the Greek poets' stories of the gods as anthropomorphic and searched for the perfect, the timeless and the immutable. This he found in the realm of the Forms, which exist outside our spatiotemporal world.[52] Aristotle posited an ultimate metaphysical principle (the unmoved mover): a consciousness thinking on itself that exists beyond the conditions of time. These thinkers set the stage in the Western tradition for saying both that "God" is wholly other and that we must *posit* such an idea because it *serves* a vital role in our metaphysics. Thus, assuming the existence of an ultimate metaphysical principle, or "God," is necessary for thought, even though the essence of this principle may be wholly beyond our understanding.

The Jewish thinker Philo of Alexandria located Plato's Forms in the mind of the Jewish God. Nevertheless, he affirmed that we cannot know God's essence or say anything about it, since to say something is to define it and to define is to *limit*. Because it would be unfitting to worship anything limited, we must not place any of the limitations of human language and thought onto God. Since God is unlimited, we are consigned to silence. Philo tried to escape this transcendental agnosticism by saying that though we cannot speak of the divine being itself, we can speak of its existence because we see the effects it produces as a cause of the world. A good number of Jewish, Christian and Islamic thinkers have followed Philo in saying that we cannot know the essence of God—who God really is—and that those who take the biblical portrait of God's love and anger as depicting the reality of the divine nature are guilty of "idolatry." The philosophical and theological attack on anthropomorphism assumes that we cannot know the essence of God. But we CAN know God, I can know His grace.

In the modern era, Immanuel Kant held that the noumenal realm of things-in-themselves is beyond our knowing. Since the concept of "God" belongs to the noumenal realm, God cannot be directly apprehended. Following the classical tradition, Kant says we must posit the existence of the noumenal realm as a ground for morality ("God" remains a useful concept for us). God is wholly other than we can know, but we must assume a transcendental ideal (the unconditioned condition) in order to explain our own existence. He holds that even though we cannot prove the existence of a supreme being, the concept of what it means to be "God" is still useful, since it necessarily excludes all limitations drawn from human experience. Again Kant is following tradition here when he says that anything "belonging to mere appearance (anthropomorphism in its wider sense) is out of keeping with the supreme reality."[53] By this Kant does not mean that we cannot speak of God, for he holds that the concept of God is by definition an "ideal without a flaw" and so possesses the transcendental predicates of necessity, infinity, unity, timelessness, omnipresence and omnipotence. Though God is free from all conditions of space and time, we can at least refer to such a being.

Kaufman and John Hick are heavily indebted to Kant in this regard, though they take the next step, which Kant was unwilling to take—the admission that humans are the ones who construct the concept of God. In taking this step, they claim to be following a maxim that has been significant in Western theism: The finite cannot contain the infinite. For Kaufman, the word *God* is the symbol for the ultimate mystery behind human existence.[54] He speaks of the "real God" (God-in-himself), which is completely ineffable, and the "available God" (God in relation to us), which is a human construct of our theological imagination. Although we are cut off from knowing anything about this mystery, we are forced to construct models of God in order to give meaning to our lives. Kaufman believes that God is totally infinite and thus all human language is anthropomorphic (in the broad sense) and inappropriate for speaking of God. Consequently, he heaps ridicule on any anthropomorphic conception of God—especially personalistic ones.

According to Hick, "God," or what he prefers to call the "Real," is outside all human experience and language. We cannot talk about the Real, for to do so implies that the Real is an object within human experience.[55] The finite cannot contain the infinite, so no human thoughts or words are able to grasp the being of God. There is simply no way of knowing what God really is, whether personal or impersonal, good or bad, knowledgeable or ignorant. Thus, says Hick, the major religious traditions are all attempts to express the infinite mystery behind the human phenomena we call religious experience. A common thread running through all these thinkers is the belief that there is an *infinite* qualitative difference separating divinity from humanity.

The appeal to God's absolute infinity argues that thinking of God as personal in a literal way overlooks the fact that the concept "personal" when used for God is actually a finite symbol for the infinite that lies beyond the personal. Depicting God in personal symbols, as in the Bible, limits God. J. N. Findlay charges that it is "wholly anomalous to worship anything *limited* in any thinkable manner."[56] According to this way of thinking, to speak of God making use of any human concepts is to commit ourselves to belief in a "finite" God and makes us guilty of idolatry.[57]

There are, however, some major problems with making God infinite and wholly other in this strict sense. To begin, what precisely is meant when people such as Philo say that "to define is to limit"? Why should we think that predicating love of God actually limits God? Does language have the capacity to limit the object, or is it merely our understanding that is limited? I see no reason to believe that my thoughts about God actually limit God any more than my conceptions of an ant limit the ant. It is true that *my* concepts about God will be limited, but so what? This is only a claim about our creatureliness, not the Creator. Moreover, the assertion that God is unlike anything in the world may be understood in at least two different senses: (1) God is not completely like anything in the world or (2) God is completely unlike everything in the world.[58] It is one thing to assert that God does not share all properties with anything else, but it is quite another matter to say that God does not share any properties with anything else. Clearly, I (along with the bulk of those in the Christian tradition) am rejecting this latter notion. Christians have generally held that although God is more than we can ever comprehend (exhaustively know), God is not totally beyond our knowing or our ability to be in relationship.

Furthermore, if "infinite" means without any predicates from within the confines of the conditions of our existence (all human language and conceptualizing), then we are committed to agnosticism about *anything transcendent*—not just God! Since all of our thought and language occur within this realm, we are cut off from that which is beyond it. Søren Kierkegaard understood that our "understanding cannot even think the absolutely different."[59] If the qualitative difference between God and humanity is absolutely *infinite,* then there is no correspondence between God and the creation, and this will preclude any notions of creation or revelation.[60] Thus it would seem that those who affirm that God shares no properties with anything in the created order are committed to silence concerning anything transcendental (despite their continued talk of it!).[61] If "the finite cannot contain the infinite," then all revelation of God in history, any incarnation, the possibility of a personal relationship with God and all knowledge of God within our existence are ruled out. The concept of God becomes Teflon to which no predicates will stick. One can put any property one likes into the pan of a Teflon God, but it will slide off into the fire, and we will be left with no sustenance for our lives.

Donald Bloesch correctly notes that "God is not 'absolute infinity' (as the older theologians understood it) because this would then exclude the possibility of fellowship with God within the structures of finitude."[62] Hick and Kaufman, of course, are more than willing to make such concessions. Yet Hick (but not Kaufman) still desires to claim that "the Real" exists. Feuerbach's criticisms are devastating at this point. He says that what is completely ineffable lacks predicates and what has no predicates has no existence: "The distinction between what God is in himself, and what he is for me destroys the peace of religion, and is . . . an untenable distinction. I cannot know whether God is something else in himself or for himself than he is for me."[63]

Feuerbach appropriately criticizes the long-standing distinction between God as he appears to us and God as he really is. There is no way for us to know a god beyond the God who comes to us in Jesus. In theology there is a long-standing distinction between the "revealed God," or God in relation to us (*quoad nos, Deus revelatus* and economic Trinity), and the "hidden God," or what God is like in and of himself (*in se, Deus absconditus* and immanent Trinity). Those scandalized by anthropomorphism align themselves with the tradition elevating the hidden God above the revealed God and attempt to discover the face of God behind the mask. This maneuver today elicits a strong reaction that God does not wear a mask. Rather, the God who reveals himself to us is the same God who remains hidden. Thus it is not surprising to find those who follow "Rahner's rule" that the economic Trinity is the immanent Trinity and vice versa or that God *pro nobis* (for us) is the God *in se* (in himself) and vice versa.

In my opinion, though the notion of the hidden God has been abused, it should not be completely rejected, for the reason that it is one way of affirming that God has being apart from the world and does not need the world in order to be fulfilled. Of course, even this arises out of our understanding of the Christian faith (*de dicto*), the doctrines of the relational Trinity and creation ex nihilo, not out of any supposed knowledge of God's being itself (*de re*). Though I agree that God would be God without a creation, *we* cannot know what God is like *in se* apart from us because all of our knowledge of God is embedded within the conditions in which God has placed us. All that is possible for us to know is what God is like in relation to us. God may be different in himself (*in se*) than God is with us (*quoad nos*), but we can have no knowledge of that difference. The Lord our Creator and Redeemer is what God is really like in relation to us. If God is different in himself we cannot say. Some may desire more than this, but I think the God who comes to us in Jesus is quite sufficient. We do not need to seek another God.

There is another difficulty with the appeal to infinity. How do those who claim that the finite cannot contain the infinite *know* this to be the case? It is logically possible that ultimate reality is beyond human knowing, but how does the person affirming this know that it is? Sallie McFague claims that all human language "applies properly only to our existence, not God's." How does she know this is the case?[64] Is she somehow able to discover the real nature of transcendence and inform the rest of us that we cannot speak about it properly? Such people claim both that something is unknowable and that they know something about the unknowable. If it is asserted that "human language and logic do not apply to God," on what basis can this assertion possibly be affirmed? The traditional answer states that it can be affirmed on the basis of a preconceived idea of God whereby we begin with a definition of God derived from what it is "fitting" for God to be. For many in the Western tradition, it has been judged fitting for God to be exempt from all spatio-temporal categories and to be beyond all human speaking and knowing. The problem with this tactic is that the conclusion is affirmed precisely on the basis of *human* language and logic! That is, we are using human language to speak about something so transcendent and so unrelated to us that it is totally ineffable. But if this is so, how can we say or know *anything*, including the existence, of this completely ineffable something or other? Paul Tillich sought to evade this difficulty by saying that God does not exist but is rather "Being Itself." Even this tactic fails, however, for the term *Being Itself* is still within the realm of human language and conceptualization and so seeks to predicate something about the transcendent.

These thinkers are attempting to arrive at a concept of the ultimate metaphysical principle that transcends all concepts. Kierkegaard scornfully described this quest as "the ultimate paradox of thought: to want to discover something that thought itself cannot think."[65] Frank Kirkpatrick correctly says that "an idea or concept of that which transcends all concepts is a contradiction in terms."[66] Brümmer asks, "If *none* of our concepts are applicable to God, how can we indicate who it is that we consider to be indescribable?"[67] According to Kaufman and Hick, it would seem that we cannot, and so Feuerbach's question returns: How do they know this something exists at all outside of their own imaginative constructs?[68]

Why would anyone posit something like divine transcendence outside the boundaries of human language and thought? Perhaps the most common answer is that many people believe that we need a transcendent ground or sufficient reason for our existence.[69] In this schema the idea of "God" is a functional concept fulfilling a felt human need. God the concept becomes the tree supplying the lumber for our transcendental building projects. A problem here is that our need for a transcendent ground does not necessarily mean it exists or does not exist, for we are not able to escape (transcend) our creaturely context to establish transcendence. Instead, God comes to us in order to establish a relationship with his creatures. But even accepting the need for a transcendent ground to our existence does not necessarily lead to conclusions about the nature of that ground. We are creatures who are different from God, but no more different than God intended us to be. In order to know just what the difference is, we would do well to pay attention to what God says and does in history.

If it is inappropriate to think of God as infinite in all respects, can it be appropriate to speak of God being "limited" (i.e., with qualities and properties) in any way? Yes. Feuerbach correctly says, "To the truly religious man, God is not a being without qualities, because to him he is a positive, real being. . . . The denial of determinate, positive predicates [to God] . . . is simply a subtle, disguised atheism. . . . Dread of limitation is dread of existence. . . . A God who is injured by determinate qualities has not the courage and the strength to exist."[70] The Christian tradition has commonly affirmed that we can make predications of God; the debate was over how we can do so. Because we are creatures, all of our thought and language assumes various types of limitations. If, for instance, we say that God is not the world but is ontologically other than the world, then we are expressing a conceptual limitation for our understanding of God because God is not then everything that exists. To speak of an "other" is to affirm ontological limitation.

Furthermore, our statements about God involve semantic distinctions. If we say God is unlimited in goodness and wisdom, it distinguishes God from being bad or unwise and so we affirm one property rather than another.[71] If we say that God is personal, then God is limited to not being impersonal. Anything we say about God, or God says to us, involves such limitations (in this strict sense of the term). If we hold that God is absolutely unlimited in an unqualified sense, then God is beyond any relationship with us and is thus unknowable. If we affirm that God is related to us, then God can be knowable but our language will express limitations. Consequently, the issue is not whether we must think of God by means of ontological and semantic limitations but which ones we shall use.[72] Those in agreement with Findlay's claim that we should not worship something "limited in any thinkable manner" will likely find the trinitarian God of the Bible disappointing, since the God of Scripture is not an idealized universal principle (idea) but a personal being who interacts with us in history. Christianity is not about an *idea* or principle but about a *personal God* who gets involved in his creational project. The triune God is a particular deity, and Jesus, God incarnate, is the particular Savior.

Those who affirm Lessing's "necessary truths of reason" will always be scandalized by such particularistic claims and will opt, instead, for the universal impersonal principle to which all "rational" minds can assent.[73] The Father, Son and Holy Spirit—the Creator and universal God—is nonetheless a particular deity who does particular actions in human history.[74] The particularity of this God will always be offensive to those such as Lessing, Hick and Kaufman who search for the ultimate metaphysical principle without substantive properties, infinite in all respects and beyond all particularity. Their quest is futile, however, for there is nothing to be found at the end of that road except total ineffability.

Even orthodox Christians who affirm divine revelation sometimes succumb to this same sort of problem when they claim that God had to "accommodate" himself to human language. It is commonplace for theologians to claim that biblical anthropomorphisms are "accommodations" on God's part to our limited abilities to understand.[75] Perhaps, but how do they know this is so? Have they found out the God beyond God? Sometimes appeal is made to what any being with the title "God" must be like. God, it is claimed, is a term for which only certain properties are "fitting" *(dignum Deo).*[76] Any God worth his salt must conform to our intuitive notions of deity or get out of the deity business. Since the biblical depiction of God does not, according to some people, measure up to what is fitting for God to be, the doctrine of divine accommodation is enacted to protect the Bible from charges of falsehood.

For instance, it was common for classical theists to maintain that God, as God, could not suffer. Thus all the biblical depictions of divine grief do not refer to what God is actually like but are only divine accommodations to our finite minds. Calvin, for instance, said that God "lisps" to us as does a nursemaid to a young child.[77] Of course, those making such a claim were somehow able to transcend their finite minds in order to know what God is really like. That is, they seemingly believed they could observe God using both lisping and normal discourse and were consequently able to tell the rest of us which forms of discourse were accommodations and which were literal. Though I do not wish to deny that God is in certain respects beyond our comprehension, I do want to point out that lurking behind the notion of divine accommodation seems to be the idea that some people *know* for a fact what God is really like and are thus able to inform the rest of us (to borrow an expression from Philo) "duller folk" that we are mistaken. Or perhaps what is meant by accommodation is that human language always corrupts divine speech to us. Because God must use our cultural-linguistic context, it is thought impossible for God to communicate to us who God really is. However, the one asserting this must first demonstrate knowledge that God cannot do this, that it is impossible for God to be involved with us such that we can adequately know and relate to God. I do not believe it possible to substantiate such a claim.

A fundamental Creator-creation distinction enables us to say that God "transcends" space, time and the other aspects of the boundaries of created being in the sense that God establishes the parameters for our existence. The doctrine of creation ex nihilo implies that God is ontologically distinct from the creation and not identical with it. Thus we may say that God is different from the world because God is not a creature. But, I would add, the creation is no more different from the Creator than God intended it to be. "The distinction," as Robert Sokolowski calls it, afforded by the Christian doctrine of creation allows us to affirm that God is the unique, self-sufficient, ontologically distinct, free Creator of all that is.[78] This does not, however, mean that God is beyond being. This sort of talk is self-refuting because it never escapes the language of being.[79] Our knowledge of God as Creator comes from "inside" the world. We do not reach from the inside to the outside. God reaches us as an insider. Our knowledge and language cannot go beyond the parameters God established for us as creatures. We cannot think and speak of God other than as a being in relation to us.

Those who claim that God is completely transcendent in the sense of being outside our boundaries—totally unrelated to us—are claiming more than is proper. Any statement we make about God and any statement God makes to us will be from within the conditions God established at creation. All this is to say that the assertion "God is infinite" (totally unlike us) is not a meaningful assertion and that arguments based on it should be viewed skeptically.[80] This does not mean that we worship a "finite god." It is only to claim that we cannot speak or think of God apart from the conditions God established for us at creation and that we should not suppose that these conditions preclude us from knowing, at least partially, who God is.[81] I now turn to the other main objection to the claim that we cannot think of or relate to God apart from the limitation of our creatureliness.

2.5.2 The Appeal to Antinomies   The second major objection to my view of the divine-human relationship occurring within a shared context arises from theologians who claim that this position ignores the role of paradox and antinomy in theological discourse. Evangelicals in the Reformed tradition, for instance, tend to claim not that everything about God is beyond us but only that *some* aspects of deity or the God-human relationship transcend human intelligibility. Regarding the topic of providence, such thinkers sometimes dismiss attempts to elucidate the relationship between divine sovereignty and human responsibility, claiming that it is simply a "mystery beyond human understanding." The subject simply transcends human reason. (Thus books such as this one are considered a waste of time.)

It is helpful to distinguish between paradox, mystery and antinomy. Paradoxes are puzzling remarks that go against our normal way of thinking, and mysteries are notions that are beyond our ability to fully comprehend. Yet neither paradox nor mystery is nonsense or self-contradictory. Antinomies, however, are statements that are either self-contradictory or inconsistent when taken together with other claims. Evangelical theologian Packer cites the following examples of this: the Trinity as three in one; the Incarnation, through which the infinite becomes finite or the eternal becomes temporal; and the sovereignty of God and human responsibility.[82] Antinomies are in the order of square circles and colorless red cars. Packer says that the biblical revelation contains several claims that simply cannot be reconciled in this world.[83] Donald Carson agrees: "For us mortals there are no rational, logical *solutions* to the sovereignty-responsibility tension."[84]

Some theologians claim that although antinomies are contradictions for us, they are not for God. They hold that doctrines such as divine sovereignty-human responsibility are only apparently contradictory or that they may be genuinely contradictory for us but not contradictory for God. It is sometimes said that human logic depends on time and space (the boundaries) and cannot be applied to the way God operates because God is outside of space and time. Even though we are unable to reconcile these truths, God knows how to do so. After citing the "my thoughts are not your thoughts" passage of Isaiah 55:8, Packer says of the biblical antinomies, "We may be sure that they all find their reconciliation in the mind and counsel of God, and we may hope that in heaven we shall understand them."[85]

Several points may be made in response to the appeal to antinomy.[86] Although the appeals to mystery and paradox are justified, the appeal to antinomy is illegitimate for several reasons. To begin, there is the problem of claiming that an antinomy is only an apparent contradiction. When we say that something is apparently contradictory, we mean that it looks but is not actually inconsistent for the statements in question can be shown not to be contradictory. If the doctrine of the Trinity is either a genuine contradiction or not contradictory at all, then it is not appropriate to call it an "apparent" contradiction.[87]

Moreover, the suggestion that certain doctrines are genuine contradictions for us but not for God is illegitimate because the claim is unknowable. Unless God informs us that such is the case, we have no way of knowing that it is. It has been widely accepted throughout the Christian tradition that God does not speak to us in contradictions.[88] Packer and Carson go against the tradition in this respect claiming that God has, in fact, told us about such antinomies in Scripture. For example, they hold that the Bible teaches both exhaustive divine control over all events and that humans remain morally responsible.

Most Christians understand the Bible to teach divine sovereignty and human responsibility. But they do not understand the Bible to define sovereignty or responsibility in ways that entail a contradiction. In order for there to be an antinomy, the terms have to be understood in a certain way. *Sovereignty* has to be defined as meticulous divine control of every single event (including human actions), and *human freedom* must be defined in "libertarian" (indeterministic) terms as the ability to do otherwise than even God desires. Only with something like these definitions could we arrive at a genuine antinomy. Carson and (I believe) Packer affirm exhaustive divine sovereignty, but they do not agree with this definition of human freedom. Instead, they opt for "compatibilism," which asserts that we are free as long as we act on our desires. Consequently, divine determinism and human responsibility are compatible. But if so, then there is no antinomy because meticulous divine sovereignty is reconcilable by human logic to a compatibilistic understanding of human freedom. Moreover, many theists accept libertarian freedom but understand the biblical teaching on divine sovereignty as "general providence" rather than meticulous providence.[89] Thus we have a difference of interpretation of Scripture, but neither view entails an antinomy.

Furthermore, even if there are antinomies in Scripture, where does it say in Scripture that such antinomies are not genuinely contradictory for God? How, for instance, does Packer know that the Trinity or the divine sovereignty–human freedom antinomies are not illogical for God also? On what basis does he claim to know that God's logic is different from ours? It may well be, but how does he know? The appeal to Isaiah 55:8-9 will not work. As Helm notes, it is "to be understood as referring to the power of divine grace, not to a logic-transcending omnipotence."[90]

A final point against the antinomy objection is that it seeks to escape the rules surrounding intelligibility. What philosophers call contradiction some theologians refer to euphemistically as antinomy, or logical paradox. But in doing theology, we simply have to "play by the rules" of the game, and one of these rules is that our discourse must make sense. Interestingly, theologians who claim the right to be inconsistent expect us to make sense of what they are saying. My position here does not rule out paradox and mystery (as defined above) or metaphors and riddles. It simply excludes discourse that lies outside the boundaries of consistency and coherence— that is, nonsense. Stephen Davis agrees: "Like it or not, we are stuck with these limited minds of ours; if we want to be rational we have no choice but to reject what we judge to be incoherent."[91] If theology and talk about God are supposed to be intelligible and intelligibility is defined, in part, by logical consistency, then antinomies are excluded from theological discourse.[92]

To be rational in the practice of theology is to enter the domain of public criteria for intelligibility. The exclusion of contradictions from theological discourse is not an idiosyncratic one, but a public one imposed by the community. To be intelligible we have to be able to communicate with one another. This means that we must operate within the boundaries in which God created us. We simply have no other choice but to think and speak within these limits. If we lapse into contradiction or incoherence, then we violate some of the conditions of the public criteria by which theology is considered meaningful. This does not mean that logic is the standard to which God is subject, but it is the standard for our meaningful discourse about God. I have no desire to be a rationalist, placing logic above God. There may be realities that are incomprehensible to us, lying completely outside our abilities to understand them. However, if God desires to communicate meaningfully with us, then he will have to do so within the conditions of his own creation. One of these conditions is that intelligibility excludes antinomies.

2.6 Conclusion

The appeals to antinomy as well as to God as wholly other or infinite in all respects fail to take seriously enough the conditions of our createdness. They are attempts to escape these limitations and say something meaningful about that which lies beyond our boundaries. Apart from revelation we cannot know that anything exists beyond our boundaries, and if, by revelation, we are informed of a transcendent existence, we can only understand it by use of our conditions. The quest to get outside our boundaries is an old one that has been attempted by both Christians and non-Christians. But if we take our status as creatures seriously, then we shall have to content ourselves with knowing and speaking about God within the conditions of our createdness. In other words, we must understand the God-human relationship as taking place within a shared context, and so the use of metaphors and anthropomorphic language (in the broad sense) when speaking of God is necessary. These are some of the limiting factors within which theological proposals must be set forth.

The Bible portrays God as a personal agent in a literal sense. This implies a shared context for both God and human agents. Consequently, we cannot escape the realm of anthropomorphism. This does not render God less worthy of worship or diminish his majesty, for the true majesty of God is revealed in Jesus, through whom we understand, that God adopts human language and experience to communicate with us. The purpose of this book is not to reduce God to the limits of human understanding, but to propose that from within the boundaries of our createdness God can be known and to propose a model of the divine-human relationship that reexplores old vistas for our understanding of God and deepens our appreciation of the freedom, love, wisdom and power of God. God has undertaken a project, and it is only from within this project in which God is related to us that we know God at all. If God decides to disclose himself to us as a personal being who enters into relationship with us, who has purposes, emotions and desires, and who suffers with us, then we ought to rejoice in this anthropomorphic portrait and accept it as disclosing to us the very nature of God. The personal God who undertakes the project of creation in order to achieve certain ends and enters into this project in a decisive way in Jesus is a God who is not afraid of anthropomorphism. The next two chapters will examine the divine project in light of the biblical narrative.

THREE

OLD TESTAMENT MATERIALS FOR A RELATIONAL VIEW OF PROVIDENCE INVOLVING RISK

. . . .

3.1 Introduction

Many theologians have developed a risk-free view of providence from Scripture. In this model God has a controlling relationship with the world such that everything works out in exhaustive detail just as God desired. Yahweh is the king over the whole earth who reigns over the nations (Ps 47:7-8). God is the potter and we are but clay in his hands (Is 29:16; Jer 18:1-6; Rom 9:21). God makes the rain to fall on the just and the unjust (Mt 5:45), God feeds the birds of the fields (Mt 6:26), and God ensures that none of them dies without his will (Mt 10:29). The metaphors of king and potter (understood in domineering ways) have been extremely influential in shaping the theological understanding of providence toward an emphasis on divine control with the resulting loss of any reciprocal relations between Creator and creature.[1]

Granted the pervasiveness of the traditional view, can a biblical case be made for a view of providence involving divine risk? Is there material in the Scripture, which has either been ignored or interpreted in favor of a risk-free view (due to preunderstandings), that would support an open model of God's relationship with his creatures? The purpose of the next two chapters is to give an affirmative answer to these questions by examining the nature of the divine project—what God is working toward and how God goes about accomplishing this goal—in the scriptural narrative. It is claimed that there is more than sufficient biblical data teaching that God does not exercise meticulous providence in such a way that the success of his project is, in all respects and without qualification, a foregone conclusion. Rather, God works with his creatures in flexible ways seeking to obtain the goals he has for them. God genuinely enters into dynamic give-and-take relationships with humans, loving them and providing for them but not forcing his will on them through overwhelming power. Instead, God works through the power of love, seeking to bring us into fellowship with himself and into collaboration with him in the divine project.

Due to space limitations it is not possible here to be exhaustive in covering the biblical material. Numerous texts will be discussed in order to substantiate the claim that the risk model enjoys biblical support. I will follow, somewhat, the order of the canonical narrative itself, though not necessarily a chronological order, developing selected texts in detail so that the reader gains a "feel" for what is actually going on in the narrative.

To date, few biblical scholars have addressed the topic from a truly relational perspective, let alone examined the concept of risk in the biblical material. The reasons for this are not hard to come by. First, theological presuppositions color scholars' approach to the biblical text. Vincent Brümmer comments that "Western thought has suffered from a systematic blind spot for relations."[2] The Western tradition desires, instead, an underlying metaphysical principle removed from all temporal and spacial relationality.[3] As was seen in the last chapter, it has been thought that a relational God would be a limited being and thus would not be worthy of the title "God." It is difficult to overcome such prejudices, even when reading the biblical narrative. Despite the tremendous respect given Abraham Heschel's works on God's relatedness to his creatures, many Old Testament scholars continue to work within the thought patterns of earlier theologies.[4]

Since the 1960s the discipline of biblical theology itself has been in a state of unsettledness, with no agreed-on methodology or purpose. In the current climate biblical scholars are hesitant to make theological claims from the text. Nevertheless, there are several important studies (especially studies of prayer and divine suffering) by biblical scholars that address the issue of genuine reciprocity in divine-human relationships. I will draw on them, freely adding my own material, to support the contention that God creates a world in which he sovereignly decides to experience genuine give-and-take relations with his creatures. In freedom, God chooses not to control everything and so takes risks in his providence!

So this means God is Reactive?

3.2 The Creation and Its Divinely Established Conditions

The doctrine of creation sets the stage for the doctrine of providence, so it is important here to take it into account. Broadly speaking, there are two main ways in which the biblical materials on creation (not just Gen 1—2) are understood: God as the Creator of *all* that exists and God as the victor over chaos.[5] Both of these ideas have important insights for the study of providence. The notion that everything except God has a beginning has led, in the history of the church, to the doctrine of *creatio ex nihilo* (creation out of nothing). Although I affirm *creatio ex nihilo,* I agree with most modern studies of Genesis 1 that this doctrine cannot be derived from this text (see instead 2 Macc 7:28; Rom 4:17; Heb 11:3). Genesis 1 can, however, legitimately be understood to refer to an absolute beginning in which God is prior to all else.[6]

Several implications follow from this understanding. First, just as we cannot, in principle, penetrate to grasp whatever may have existed prior to the big bang, so we cannot, in principle, fathom God apart from our relationship as creatures. We ought not speculate about what it means to be God. Instead, we must see what God actually decides to do in relation to the creation in order to know what it means to be God. God defines God. Second, the creation is due to divine grace. God did not have to create. It is the divine wisdom in freedom that brings into existence something that is not God. Since the creation is contingent, not necessary, one cannot draw conclusions about the Creator from the nature of the creation without further ado.[7] Third, God works within limits. For God to say yes to creating this particular world means that God had to say no (we think) to other possibilities. We believe that God could have made humans without material bodies, for instance. A single positive choice implies a self-chosen limitation with the negation of other options. God has sovereignly decided to create and work with this particular world rather than others. Fourth, God is the sovereign Creator, for there is no opposition to his act of creating. We must be careful in basing a doctrine of providence on this aspect of creation, since it is an open question (at this stage in our reading of the biblical text) whether God can and will sovereignly create beings over which he does not exercise total control.[8] We must wait to see what God actually decided to create.

The other way of looking at the creation texts focuses on "conflict and victory" or *creatio contra nihilum* (creation versus nothing/chaos).[9] This position notes that Genesis 1 does not actually say that God created everything, since darkness seems to already exist and other creation texts (for example, Ps 74:12-17; 104) refer to the time when Yahweh subjugated

the powers of chaos (Rahab, the sea, etc.) and established order.[10] These
beings stand opposed to Yahweh's way. According to Jon Levenson, these
powers of chaos are subjugated to Yahweh through conflict. Although they
are not allowed to retain control, they do acquire control from time to time
and so pose a threat to Yahweh's sovereign will. The "confinement of
chaos rather than its elimination is the essence of creation, and the survival
of ordered reality hangs only upon God's vigilance."[11] The emphasis of the
creation story is not on God's absolute sovereignty but on God's "mastery"
over his opponents.[12] The chaos forces were confined at creation but they
from time to time mount a challenge against God, so God has to subdue
them again and again. Some take this view to imply an initial dualism
where Yahweh is limited by chaos.[13] But, as Levenson points out, though
the Hebrew Bible sometimes affirms that God created chaos and other
times denies this, it is clear that Yahweh has the ability to overcome these
forces—even if he does not always do so.[14] There is "no limited God here,
no God stymied by invincible evil."[15]

These two understandings of creation share some important affirmations.
In each view God freely creates an environment and sovereignly establishes
boundaries that are "good" (that is, what God desires for our benefit). In
each God brings beings into existence and then names them. Such acts
testify to Yahweh's lordship *and* relationality. (To name something is to
respond to it.) In both views God stands against that which works to undo
us. God is "for us," and our well-being depends on Yahweh's faithfulness.
In both there is hope for the future despite our present experiences of
suffering. If God has brought new things out of nothing or has conquered
chaos in the past, then we may have confidence in God for establishing
new and greater things (for example, the new heaven and earth) and
triumphing over the forces of death and disorder in the future.[16]
Understood in this way, the doctrine of creation provides the backdrop for
genuine drama as the biblical story unfolds. As Creator, God established an
environment for various types of creatures with boundaries set around the
forces of chaos, which bring disorder, injustice and affliction. As Creator,
God has not finished being creative, for he continues to introduce new
things into history. The stage is thus set for what Levenson calls the
"dramatic enactment: the absolute power of God realizing itself in
achievement and relationship."[17]

Second, the doctrine of creation draws a strong distinction between God
and his creatures as well as a significant relationship between them. God
is distinguished from the creatures as a distinct other from them. God
creates a world different from himself, yet it is no more different than he

desires. The world is neither divine nor made from slain gods as in some of the ancient Near Eastern myths (for example, Enuma Elish).[18] Nevertheless, between God and his creatures there exists a dynamic relationship. In creation, Yahweh is the king enacting a covenant with his vassal.[19] By virtue of being the Creator, Yahweh has a prior claim on the creation. It is not free simply to do whatever it wants. Rather, it is to acknowledge its Lord and follow his instructions. As will be seen, however, despite Yahweh's almighty power in creating and his claim as king on the creation, the unfolding of the intended relationship is not guaranteed but is, given God's resourcefulness, a live option.

Third, God establishes structures in the creation over which humans have no control without thereby eliminating all freedom and development.[20] There is no a priori way of knowing these structures. If we want to know how the world works, then we must look to see how it functions rather than speculate about how the universe ought to be structured according to some humanly manufactured ideal. If the creation and the structures it contains are the result of divine freedom, then we cannot deduce from first principles the way the world ought to be. Emil Brunner is correct when he says that "never can thought of itself build up the idea of a contingent, non-necessary, freely-posited world."[21] Moreover, if we want to know what sort of relationship comes about between the Creator and the creatures, we must look to revelation to see what exactly God has decided to do. For, again, no preconceived notions of Creator or omnipotence or the most perfect being inform us what sort of relationship God actually chose to have with his creation.[22] God sovereignly establishes the conditions of the creation and what sort of relationship he will have with it. We cannot deduce our understanding of providence from some notion of God. Rather, we must look to see how God has actually decided to exercise providence. Furthermore, God retains his freedom, so that the exercise of providence does not have to be uniform or unchanging.[23] Only revelation informs us whether providence remains always the same or whether it is subject to changes.

What sorts of conditions and relationships does God establish with the creation? God creates beings that are not God and places them in relationship with one another. Various sorts of life forms are created that occupy different mediums (atmosphere, oceans and land). This is what God desired, for he says it is "good." Particular attention is given to the role of human beings in this creation. They are part of the creation but are given the special demarcation of bearing the image of God (Gen 1:26). Moreover, it is only with the creation of humans that a divine consultation ensues: "Let us make."[24] Terence Fretheim comments that the "let us" language refers to a divine consultation: "The creation of humankind results from a dialogical act—an inner-divine communication—rather than a monological one."[25] From the beginning God, even if viewed as king, is one involved in dialogue rather than monologue. Humans are fashioned after the image of this dialogical God who enters into genuine reciprocal relations with his creatures. "There are some twenty images of God the creator in these two chapters which, when seen in interaction with one another, provide for a more relational model of creation than has been traditionally presented."[26]

Take the image of God, for instance. However "image" is defined, it at least involves humanity in two sets of relationships, one with God and the other with creatures.[27] It is God who decides how similar to himself humans will be and what sort of relationship God will have with them. Humanity may be understood to be in relationship with God, since God places the responsibility of caring for the world in the hands of humanity. The divine mandate implies that God is the one ultimately responsible for dominion, for it is his to give. Dominion is not the right of humanity but the result of a divine gift. Consequently, humans are understood to be distinct others from God who exist in relationship to God. This relationship involves both gift and responsibility. God graciously provides an environment for the sustenance of the humans and calls them into the care of that gift, indicating that God desires our service and obedience. Not only does God choose to share existence, the fact that God delegates responsibility implies that God is willing to share power with humans. God sovereignly decides that not everything will be up to God. Some important things are left in the hands of humanity as God's cocreators such that we are to collaborate with God in the achievement of the divine project. For instance, the naming of the animals is left in the hands of humanity. Just as God creates names for things, so humans are allowed to create names for things. God grants to humanity something of his own creative power. God is not a power-hoarding deity. There is freedom for humans to be creative within the "rules of the game" God has established. The structure is not so rigid that it eliminates all movement and newness for either humans or God.[28] The creation was never intended by God to remain completely unchanged. After all, even God says that some "good" things were yet to be created, namely, woman (2:18). The man did not experience all the sorts of relationships God intended humanity to have, for there was no suitable collaborator for him (2:20). Once Adam realized this need, God worked to fill it, thus bringing to fruition the range of relations God purposed to create.

In summary, the creation stories depict divine providence as creating an environment for the sustenance of the creatures, granting divine blessing on them, establishing communities of relationships and bestowing tasks to be accomplished. The divine sovereignty has decreed that it should be this way rather than one of exhaustive divine control. God creates significant others and gives them "space" to operate. *yet He also defines how they will Relate to Each other. The "do" — Deut 10 Good*

3.3 Freedom Within Limits

Though God grants the creatures room to be genuine others, God desires that this freedom be used within limits. God establishes boundaries for humanity outside of which it is not good for them to be. God provides a garden for Adam's aesthetic enjoyment and physical nourishment (2:9). In this garden are located the tree of life and the tree of the knowledge of good and evil. A command is given that he may eat from all the trees except the tree of the knowledge of good and evil. Humans are not to decide on their own, apart from God, what is good—what is in their own best interests. God establishes the boundaries for creatureliness. If we break through these limits, we reject the divine wisdom, implying that God does not have our best interests at heart. We are not created to live our lives separate from God but in trusting confidence that God loves us and gives his commandments for our good. We honor God and keep the creation heading in the direction God intends when we acknowledge our creaturely limits.

Significantly, God does not grant the humans permission to trust God or not trust him as though trust in God were optional. Levenson remarks that "for all the language of choice that characterizes covenant texts, the Hebrew Bible never regards the choice to decline covenant as legitimate."[29] God says, "Trust me, do not eat of this particular tree." A negative consequence is stipulated if they do: death (definitely not a "live option"). The possibility of death introduces an element that is not intended by God's act of creation. The command and threat of punishment imply the possibility that God's intention for the creatures may fail.[30] God desires to bless humanity through a life of loving trust, which is manifested in obediently caring for the creation and abstaining from an attempt to get outside our limits.[31] At this point God expects humans to trust God and believe that he has their best interests in mind. God, in freedom, establishes the context in which a loving and trusting relationship between himself and the humans can develop. God expects that it will, and there is no reason to suspect, at this point in the narrative, that any other possibility will come about. A break in the relationship does not seem *plausible* considering all the good that God has done. Yet a *possibility* has been introduced by God's commandment. God now places an unavoidable decision before the humans (the earliest reference to the biblical theme of testing): Will they be faithful to live within the boundaries of their creatureliness?[32] Here we have the *sovereign risk!*

God sovereignly places humans in an environment for their good and expects them to respond appropriately. In this sovereignty God grants humanity space to be a significant other in relation to God. God provides some relational distance, as he does not smother them with his presence. By commanding them to trust and obey, God also acknowledges the possibility of mistrust and sin. Up to this point Genesis has been silent regarding any opposition to God. But in making creatures who should love him but may oppose him, God places the risk out in the open. Yet there is no reason to expect anything except love in return to the loving providence of God, for God has (so to speak) stacked the deck in his favor.

3.4 The Implausible Happens

In Genesis 3 the totally unexpected happens. The naked humans are exposed to a temptation that calls the divine wisdom into question. The issue at stake is whether the divine providence has granted humanity all that is good for them or whether God is keeping back something that would be truly beneficial. The opportunity for temptation comes from one of God's creatures, the serpent. There is no dualism in this text, in which something coeternal with God opposes God. Instead, it is from God's own creation that beings distinct from God seek to establish more distance from God than God ordained.

The serpent poses a question about what God has said: "Did God say, 'You shall not eat from any tree in the garden'?" (3:1). It is striking that the serpent does not use the expression "LORD God," which is common in the rest of Genesis 2—4. Gordon Wenham sees in this "a suggestion of the serpent's distance from God. God is just the remote creator, not Yahweh, Israel's covenant partner."[33] The serpent desires a dialogue about the words of God. Already, we see that God's work and words are open to being discussed; and if open to being discussed, then open to question; and if open to question, then open to being accepted or rejected. It is through this opening in the created order that the serpent seeks an advantage. "Here is the little opening in the tent of creation through which the camel's nose of sin may enter."[34]

The woman answers the serpent that they are permitted to eat from the trees in the garden except one. That one, she claims, cannot even be touched lest one die. Moreover, she adopts the serpent's expression, "God," instead of "LORD God." The woman has opened herself to probing God's command. The serpent takes advantage of that openness by suggesting a different possible future from the one God had proclaimed. Whereas God had said they would die on eating from the tree of the knowledge of good and evil, the serpent says they will not die. Instead, he suggests the half-truth that they will have a sort of divine wisdom regarding good and evil. In other words, the serpent implies that God has been holding back something good from his creatures. Does God have their best interests in mind?

This interchange demonstrates that God has made the world in such a way that it is possible to question the divine wisdom. God leaves enough space for trust to develop, but this also allows space for doubt. God leaves room in his universe for him to be challenged by his creatures. Why does not God either make the conditions such that challenges are impossible or annihilate the challenge as soon as it originates? The answer, I suggest, is that God has entered into an enterprise whereby he seeks the highest good of his creatures and desires to solicit the love of his creatures in freedom.

As we return to the narrative, the serpent's claim that their eyes would be opened is proved correct but not in the way they anticipated. In Genesis 3:22 God confirms the serpent's statement. The humans have gained new "knowledge" pertaining to good and evil, but the harmonious relationships that God had established for the humans are rent asunder. Both the God-human and interhuman relationships become alienated. For instance, when God questions Adam, the man responds with a tacit accusation that is directed at God: It is your fault for creating this woman (3:12). Adam claims that the woman through whom God intended to help Adam has failed him. Though both the man and the woman call into question the divine wisdom, claiming that God's providence is not very good, it is the man who claims that God's purposes have failed. Only God as Creator has a perspective that understands the created order as a whole and the needs of each part. But this is rejected in their act of mistrust. Their eyes have opened, and they do see the world differently. It is not, however, what God intended.

With the rejection of the divine wisdom, the implausible possibility occurred.[35] There was no good reason to reject God's blessing and provision. There was every reason in the world to trust the wisdom of the Creator for the well-being of the creature. There is never a good reason to sin, only rationalizations. When God inquires of the humans why they have done this, they respond with lame excuses. After all, what reason could possibly be given for rejecting divine grace? Sin is fundamentally irrational; there is no cause for it given the goodness of God's creation. In light of this Paul Fiddes suggests that human sin was "something strange to God" in that it was not planned. Now God has to adjust his project in response to this horrible turn of events.[36]

Sin is deceptive (Rom 7:11; Heb 3:13). The serpent acted on this when he told another half-truth claiming they would not die (that is, experience physical death). God had declared emphatically that they would die on the day they ate from the tree of the knowledge of good and evil. Again, the narrator has the serpent being shown correct and God wrong—sort of. The promised punishment of 2:17 has given rise to several different understandings, but only the two most promising will be discussed here.[37] Death could have a broader meaning whereby the humans experienced a breakdown in relationships and so, in a sense, "died." Sin is then punished through its distorting effects on all that humans enter into. The threatened "death" may also have its more straightforward sense of immediate physical death, that is, the death penalty. It often has this meaning in the Old Testament when the threat is from God or a king.[38] If it is interpreted as immediate physical death, then God does not follow through with the threat but rather expels them from the garden. In this case we have the first instance in the Bible of what will become a major theme: *divine relenting from negative consequences in favor of mercy.* God had threatened to terminate the relationship if the humans failed to trust God. But when God faces the sin, he cannot bring himself to fulfill this threat. A dire consequence—expulsion—is enforced, but God chooses not to end the relationship. Though I prefer the second interpretation, on either one it is clear that God does not simply walk away from his creation. God continues to work with his creatures, showing grace in the face of sin. God is faithful to his creational project and assumes the risks entailed in that commitment.

That God remains faithful to his creatures is manifested in several ways. To begin, although there will be an ongoing struggle with sin (symbolized by the serpent), humanity will eventually triumph by crushing its head (3:15). This is probably not a messianic prophecy, but it does suggest some hope for the future.[39] Second, God provides for their inadequate attempt to cover their nakedness by providing more durable clothing for them (3:21). God does not leave them exposed under sin but seeks to modify the situation so that they may cope with their new perspective on the world. Although God sends them out of the garden, he goes with them. He does not abandon them.[40] Finally, God cares for them in that he does not want them to eat from the tree of life and live forever in sin. The realm of sinful estranged relationships has already shown itself. Partaking of the tree of life under those circumstances would result in a never-ending existence in an unhappy state. In this case, God is still working for the best interests of the humans, and these divine actions may be understood as attempts to restore their trust in the divine wisdom and provision. Is God a fool? Will his attempts at restoration succeed? Only the history of God's activity and the human response to it will tell.

3.5 God Suffers on Account of His Sinful Creatures but Will Not Abandon Them

Despite God's continued efforts to work with his creatures, sin becomes ever more pervasive. Whereas in Genesis 1:31 God "saw" everything that he had made was very good, in 6:5 we are told that God "saw" that humanity was very wicked. Whereas God formed humans into life (2:7), humans form their thoughts toward evil. It is emphatically asserted that "every inclination of the thoughts of their hearts was only evil continually" (6:5). Clearly, "creation has miscarried."[41] God takes full responsibility for creating these beings who have turned toward sin, and this responsibility brings grief to God (6:6). God regrets his decision to go ahead with the creation in light of these tragic developments. He is extremely disappointed at how things are turning out. Despite all the blessings God has provided, humanity turns away from the divine love. This pains God in his very heart. The narrator says that human hearts are continuously evil, and the divine heart suffers the pain of rejection. God is open to and affected by what he has made. God forbears with the sin of humanity, but it takes its toll on the divine life. The cost to God is great in terms of personal suffering.[42] God cares, and caring leads to pain when it sees the beloved destroying itself. Philip Yancey suggests that in Genesis "God learns how to be a parent." Regarding God's heart being filled with pain, Yancey says that "behind that one statement stands all the shock and grief God felt as a parent."[43] Fretheim concurs: "God appears, not as an angry and vengeful judge, but as a grieving and pained parent, distressed at what has happened."[44]

God is involved in the situation and it affects him deeply. Whatever God decides, he will never be the same again. God now knows what it is to experience grief. It has entered into the very heart of God. The divine decision is to erase the creatures he has made, for he is sorry that he made them (6:7). The flood could reverse God's act of creation. If God destroys it all, then God seems to be giving up on his project. At first the judgment sounds complete. But then we read that "Noah found favor in the sight of the LORD" (6:8). This time God "saw" someone in whom he could take pride, someone who was going in the direction God intended. Consequently, God does not give up hope and will continue his project through Noah's family. In Noah God finds a possibility for a future that is open despite the pervasiveness of sin.

After the judgment God renews his commitment to Noah and the entire human family descended from him, saying that he will never again flood the earth and providing a sign as a promise (9:11-12).[45] God makes a covenant with his creation that never again will virtually everything be annihilated. The sign of the rainbow that God gives is a reminder to himself that he will never again tread this path (9:14-16). It may be the case that although human evil caused God great pain, the destruction of what he had made caused him even greater suffering. Although his judgment was righteous, God decides to try different courses of action in the future.[46]

3.6 The Divine Purpose: Creating a Relationship of Trust

In the course of his life Abraham develops a relationship with God. Abraham's faith in God matures by fits and starts, and God's confidence in Abraham grows. The divine goal of developing people who love and trust him in such a way that they collaborate with God toward the fulfillment of the project finds success in this patriarch.

God calls Abraham to leave his homeland and travel to a place not yet revealed so that God may grant him a land and a posterity and make him a blessing to the nations (Gen 12:1-3). But the land of promise holds no ease. Despite God's promised blessing, Abraham experiences famine, strife and war. Decades go by and he possesses no land and has no children. God appears to Abraham in a vision informing him that his reward will be very great (15:1). Abraham boldly questions God: You promised me children, but I have none. Are you going to do anything about this? (15:2-3). For the first time in the story we have dialogue between Abraham and God. God has made promises to Abraham but it is only through the dialogue and Abraham's petition—making his requests known to God—that the promise will come about. Prayer is important for God's activity in the world. God specifically states that children will come forth from Abraham's body and promises him innumerable descendants. Abraham's response demonstrates his faith. He believes God for a son. This expression of trust and confidence in God is precisely what God is looking for in people. Thus God proclaims that Abraham is in proper relationship to God (15:6).

The dialogue continues as God reiterates the promise of the land. Then

Abraham inquires what assurance God will give him that he will possess it (15:8). A trusting relationship with God involves questions. God does not consider these questions impertinent or doubting.[47] On the contrary, God answers his questions. Moreover, to this last question God puts his own life on the line by passing through the sacrificed animals (15:9-21): in his relationship with Abraham God proclaims, in effect, "may I be cut in two if I fail in my promises to you." This act of self-imprecation reveals just how committed God is to Abraham. God is willing to become vulnerable for the sake of his promise. God's way into the future for the blessing of the human race is bound up with this man.

In this vision God assures Abraham that God will be faithful to his promise. Nevertheless, God forewarns Abraham that rough times are ahead for his descendants (15:13-16). It should be noted, however, that God does not here speak with precision about who will cause them trouble, and the timing is ambiguously stated.[48] Apparently God wants Abraham to know that difficult times lay ahead but God will be faithful to his promise long after Abraham has departed from the scene.

In Genesis 16 Sarah comes to the conclusion that the divine promise is not going to come through her, so she gives her maid Hagar to Abraham to bear his child. Some interpret this maneuver as a lack of faith on the part of Abraham and Sarah, who scheme instead of waiting on divine providence. But this reflects a misunderstanding of how providence works. God has not told them through whom the child will come, so why should they not use the brains God gave them? God names the boy (16:11) and makes a promise to Hagar, "I will so greatly multiply your offspring that they cannot be counted for multitude" (16:10), using the same language God had used with Abraham. Thus one could reasonably conclude that Sarah was correct and the promised son would be Ishmael. There was nothing improper or faithless in their decision, for Genesis acknowledges that God works through human planning.[49]

In Genesis 17 God continues to clarify his will, saying that the promised line will come through Sarah. Abraham's response is twofold (17:17-18). First, he considers what God has to work with. Both he and Sarah are well past the childbearing years. Second, he petitions God to go with what is already available: Ishmael. Abraham would rather stick with what he has than risk some new venture. God reassures him that Ishmael will be blessed but makes it clear that God will establish his covenant with the son Sarah will bear. When Sarah hears of this, she considers it a pipe dream (18:12). The Lord responds by asking whether anything is too difficult for God to perform (18:14). This statement should not be abstracted into some sort of philosophical principle. The point of the question is that God expects them to have faith that God can perform what he has promised. Though God works with what is available in any given situation, humans are not to delimit the divine possibilities.[50] If God says it is yet possible for them to have children, then it is possible.

Abraham waited decades for God to clarify and then deliver what was promised, maturing in his faith. In light of this the reader is shocked to read that God puts Abraham to the test (chap. 22) to see whether he has faith.[51] The reader is informed at the beginning that this is a test, but Abraham is not. For him, the command to offer Isaac up as a sacrifice could mean that God has repudiated his promise. But Abraham has grown in his faith. God has overcome seemingly insurmountable obstacles in giving him Isaac. Now Abraham trusts God to provide a way into the future, fulfilling his promise despite this baffling command. His confidence in God is manifested in his statement to the servants that he and Isaac will return to them (v. 5) and in his answer to Isaac that God would provide the offering (v. 8). The long journey provides opportunity for second thoughts, and the reader wonders whether Abraham will follow through. But Abraham continues on, and just as he prepares to sacrifice Isaac, God prevents him from doing so. God desired to see whether Abraham trusted him and finally was able to say, "For now I know that you fear God, since you have not withheld your son, your only son, from me" (22:12).

God intends to test Abraham's faith, not to have Isaac killed (22:1). The test is genuine, not fake. Walter Brueggemann says that this test "is not a game with God; God genuinely does not know. . . . The flow of the narrative accomplishes something in the awareness of God. He did not know. Now he knows."[52] God's statement, "now I know," raises serious theological problems regarding divine immutability and foreknowledge.[53] Many commentators either pass over this verse in silence or dismiss it as mere anthropomorphism. It is often suggested that the test was for Abraham's benefit, not God's. It should be noted, however, that the only one in the text said to learn anything from the test is *God*. Abraham probably learned something in his relationship with God, but that is not the point of the text. If one presupposes that God already "knew" the results of the test beforehand, then the text is at least worded poorly and at most simply false.[54]

If the test is genuine for both God and Abraham, then what is the reason for it? The answer is to be found in God's desire to bless all the nations of the earth (Gen 12:3). God needs to know if Abraham is the sort of person on whom God can count for collaboration toward the fulfillment of the divine project. Will he be faithful? Or must God find someone else through whom to achieve his purpose? God has been faithful; will Abraham be faithful? Will God have to modify his plans with Abraham? In 15:8 Abraham asked God for assurance. Now it is God seeking assurance from Abraham. God had unilaterally made promises to Abraham, yet there was a conditional element, for God wanted Abraham's obedience in order to bring about the promise (18:19). It is clear that God's purposes require a faithful and trusting Abraham. There is risk involved for both God and Abraham. God takes the risk that Abraham will exercise trust. Abraham takes the risk that God will provide a way into the future. In the dialogical relationship God finds reason to have confidence in Abraham, and Abraham's confidence in God proves to be well placed. God does provide an offering.

After the test God renews his promises of land, descendants and blessing to all people (22:15-18). Twice God says that he will do this *because* Abraham has been faithful. These remarks continue to discomfit commentators due to later theological debates about merit. Abraham's obedience does not here merit the divine blessing, for that had already been given. Rather, as R. W. L. Moberly remarks, "a promise which previously was grounded solely in the will and purpose of Yahweh is transformed so that it is now grounded *both* in the will of Yahweh *and* in the obedience of Abraham."[55] God will work in the world but typically not apart from people of faith. Human faith and action make a difference to God in the fulfillment of his plans. In choosing to depend on human beings for some things, God takes the risk of being either delighted or disappointed in what transpires.

3.7 God May Be Prevailed On

God has bound himself to his creation. God makes himself available to his people. In being available, God provides access that people may call on him. Abraham prevailed on God in attempting to alleviate the destruction of Sodom (Gen 18:22-33). In this narrative God takes the initiative and, in the visitation of the three men, provides the opportunity by which Abraham may bring his case before God. The divine decision was yet open, and God invited Abraham into the decision-making process. God chooses not to exercise judgment without the human input of this man he trusts. In cases such as this it is clear that God considers others as having something significant to say. Because God desires a genuine relationship, he is open to his creatures, especially through prayer. Prayer serves, says Samuel Balentine, "as a microcosm of one of the Hebrew Bible's most important

theological claims: the relatedness of God and humanity."[56] Fretheim adds
that "prayer has to do with that which brings the human and the divine
factors into the fullest possible power-sharing effectiveness."[57] Through these
prayers we see that God sovereignly chooses not to govern the world
without our input. Whether it is wise for God to do so is another matter.

In a fascinating and mysterious text Jacob also prevails with God.[58] In
Genesis 32 Jacob is returning to his ancestral home in deep fear of what
Esau will do to him. When Jacob is alone, a man encounters him. They
wrestle all night long, neither gaining the advantage. Toward daybreak the
adversary requests that Jacob let him go. By now Jacob has guessed this
person's identity and so refuses to let go until he is blessed. Jacob's request
is granted. He is blessed and is given a new name, Israel: he who strives
with God. Afterward, Jacob acknowledges that he has been with God in a
rather extraordinary way. Jacob had wrestled with God and prevailed. God
did not overwhelm him with superhuman power but entered into the
match in such a way as to ensure a "fair fight." God wants to see what
Jacob is made of. Apparently Jacob is made of stout stuff, for God cannot
get away and so asks Jacob to release him. Jacob refuses to do so until
God blesses him. In this we understand that Jacob is not the superior, for
he seeks the blessing from the superior. Jacob understands that God is a
God who blesses, a God who is favorably disposed toward him, despite
the fact that Jacob is a scoundrel. Moreover, it was God who took the
initiative to engage Jacob. Jacob could not have wrestled with God had
God not desired it. God is truly gracious in making himself available to
both esteemed characters such as Abraham and scoundrels such as Jacob.

3.8 Joseph: A Risk-Free Model?

The story of Joseph's being sold into slavery and his eventual rise to
rulership in Egypt commonly serves as *the* paradigm in discussions of
providence. Actually, it is not the story but a particular *interpretation* of
Joseph's remarks to his brothers in Genesis 45:4-9 that has become
normative for understanding providence as risk-free. As a result many of
the texts discussed in this chapter are either ignored or dismissed as mere
anthropomorphism. I acknowledge that a risk-free reading of the text is
possible in which God arranges all the details in such a way that Joseph
inevitably rises to leadership and so saves his family and the Egyptians
from famine.[59]

Fretheim, however, points out several problems with a risk-free reading
of the Joseph narrative.[60] First, the text explicitly ascribes responsibility for
selling Joseph into Egypt to the brothers (37:28; 45:4-5). Second, Joseph's

remarks in Genesis 45 should be read in light of his more reflective comments in 50:19-21. There Joseph tells his brothers that they committed *evil* in selling him. They sinned against him (42:22). It is problematic, to say the least, to ascribe sin and evil to God.[61] The text says that the brothers want to kill him, but one of them persuades the others not to and has a plan for rescuing Joseph. Much in the story depends on the brothers' decisions, whereas God is absent from the text. Finally (50:20) Joseph suggests that what they intended for evil, God intended for good. I take this to mean that God has brought something good out of their evil actions. God was not determining everything in Joseph's life, but God did remain "with" him (39:2).[62] The divine presence does not mean the removal of famines, sibling hatred or personal betrayal. It does mean that God will be working from within the situations to redeem them.

How should Joseph's remarks that God "sent" him to Egypt and made him ruler of Egypt (45:5, 7, 9) be understood? First, it should be remembered that Joseph has used language like this before. In 43:23 he says that *God* gave the money back to his brothers even though Joseph admits that he had the money put in their sacks (see 42:25, 28). Furthermore, the remarks of 45:5, 7, 9 occur at a tense moment in the dialogue. Joseph's brothers are overwhelmed by anxiety, and they fear for their lives due the ruse Joseph has played on them. Moreover, Joseph is brought to tears in the presence of his brothers, desiring reconciliation. Now is not the time for condemning words. He desires to vanquish his brother's fears. Although he acknowledges that they sold him into Egypt, he suggests that everyone look on the bright side—what God has done through this. Their lives and those of the Egyptians have been spared the devastating effects of the famine.

Joseph plays down the human factor and elevates the divine factor in order to allay their fears. After reconciliation is assured, Joseph remarks that what they intended for evil, God intended for good, so that many people would live (50:20). It is the glory of God to be able to bring good out of evil human actions. But nothing in the text demands the interpretation that God actually desired the sinful acts. The text does not say that God caused or necessitated the events. In fact, the text is remarkably silent regarding any divine activity until Joseph's speeches. Until now, the events could have been narrated without reference to divine activity at all. In fact, unlike in the other patriarchal stories, here God is strangely absent. Joseph never invokes God! It is in retrospect that Joseph identifies God's activity in his life working for the preservation of human life.

3.9 God Works with What Is Available

The book of Exodus (much like the Joseph narrative) begins with God's working behind the scenes and making use of opportunities that arise through human agency. The king of Egypt, fearing the growing Hebrew minority, embarks on a plan to reduce their numbers. He first afflicts them with toil that breaks (1:13), making their lives bitter with forced labor. Then he orders the Hebrew midwives to kill baby boys at birth. The midwives, however, "fear God" and so foil Pharaoh's scheme. God uses the faith of these humble women to limit the evil of the mighty king. Finally, Pharaoh orders that the baby boys be thrown into the Nile River. Why the Nile? It was considered the divine source of life for Egypt, so Pharaoh may have beeen thinking, "Give them to the god of the Nile and let him be the judge whether they live or die." If so, we have the beginning of a contest between Yahweh and the gods of Egypt to see who is truly God.

The story then focuses on one Hebrew baby and his deliverance. Again, God works through women. One Hebrew woman does not want her baby drowned, so she places him in an "ark" and has her daughter stand guard by it. This mother does not "leave everything in the hands of God." Indeed, she takes active steps to ensure the well-being of her child. No doubt many Hebrew babies were drowned or eaten by animals in the Nile. This mother does all she can to prevent that from happening to her son. Again, God is not mentioned. But we know from the rest of the story that God makes use of the actions of this mother and daughter to eventually bring deliverance to the Hebrew people.

While the Hebrew daughter is standing guard, a daughter of Pharaoh comes to bathe at the spot where the basket has been placed. Did the Hebrew mother know about the princess's daily routine? She seems to be gambling on the Egyptian princess's having mercy on her son.[63] The princess, unlike her father, takes "pity" on the boy. She hires the boy's mother to nurse him and takes him into her own home to raise him as her son (2:9-10). Again, it is women who intervene to frustrate Pharaoh's decree. God uses the decisions of the Hebrew mother as well as Pharaoh's daughter in order to work against the evil king. But everything is not being worked out according to some divine blueprint. That would be reading into the story and would raise an insufferable objection: God wanted the oppression and the death of the Hebrew boys so that he could save *one* of them. The narrator does not ascribe any role regarding these matters to God in these first two chapters. Instead, the focus has been on human activity. But it will become clear later in the narrative that God makes use of the actions of these women to bring deliverance. Consequently, God takes a risk, since these people could have failed—they could have acted differently and let the boys die. If so, God would have to find another means of liberating his people and the story of Exodus would be different from what it is.

It can be difficult to read these first two chapters of Exodus without having the "rest of the story" in mind. Knowing that everything works out in the end, we may be tempted to read a divine blueprint into the narrative—where everything happens exactly as God desires. Since things turn out well in the end, we tend to forget the terrible suffering that occurred and that many Hebrew babies died. Why did God not prevent the oppression in the first place? Why do we read of the deliverance of only one Hebrew boy? Why not give Pharaoh a brain aneurism to prevent his horrible decree? After all, later on ·in Exodus God brings about the miraculous. Why not here? The only answer I have for these troubling questions is that God works with what is available in the situation. Even miracles depend on the context. God has chosen not to ride roughshod over his creatures but to work through the resources available in seeking redemption. That God is concerned is made clear in 2:23-25, as the cries of the Hebrew people make an impact on God. The cries for help stimulate God, and the death of the king of Egypt opens new possibilities for God and leads to the call of Moses.

In Exodus 3 we learn that God wants to work through Moses in order to deliver the Israelites. Despite being in the presence of God, Moses is able to resist the divine will, presenting five reasons why God's plan is not feasible. At the beginning of the dialogue it is not a foregone conclusion that Moses will work with God. The divine presence does not ensure that God will get his way. As the dialogue progresses, God seeks to answer each of Moses' concerns. Moses first remarks about his own inadequacy, to which God replies that he will be "with" him (a repeated theme in the patriarchal narratives). Moses, however, is not comforted, for he next requests that God reveal his name. In the ancient Near East it was commonly thought that knowing the name of someone—even a god—gave one a degree of power over that person. On this basis Moses calculates that God will not reveal the divine name to him.[64] The revelation of the divine name "Yahweh" (3:15) implies a certain intimacy in relationship that will allow Moses to prevail on God. In other words, God makes himself available and vulnerable.[65] God grants this request to Moses, repeats his concern for the Israelites and proceeds to inform Moses what will happen in Egypt. He instructs Moses to gather the elders of Israel together and inform them of what God has disclosed. Moreover, Moses is told that the elders will believe what Moses says. He is then instructed to take the elders with him to Pharaoh and request a time for sacrifice to Yahweh. Finally, God informs him that only after a struggle will the people be released.

This lengthy divine speech is usually understood to imply foreknowledge whereby God discloses precisely what will happen in advance. In light of what actually happens, however, not all of these statements come to pass exactly as "predicted." First, the elders (3:1B) are never said to appear before Pharaoh. Instead, Aaron takes their place (5:1). The reason why Aaron takes their place is stated in 4:14. God concedes to Moses' self-appraisal of being a poor public speaker. God's original plan was for Moses to be the negotiator. But God goes to "plan B" in order to help Moses, demonstrating divine flexibility in his plans and willingness to adjust to human requests. Second, whereas God had said the elders would believe Moses, Moses asks God, in effect, "What if you are wrong about this? What if they will not believe you sent me?" (4:1).

Brevard Childs remarks that some commentators have attempted to avoid the force of Moses' question.[66] Brueggemann correctly notes that Moses' statement that they will not listen to his voice "is a direct refutation of the assurance given by God in 3:18."[67] Instead of telling Moses that he has a false understanding of divine foreknowledge, God provides Moses with three signs for the purpose of convincing the elders that Yahweh has appeared to Moses. Apparently God thinks Moses has a legitimate point, for he gives him the signs to verify his commission (4:2-5). Attempts to escape this conclusion by claiming that the signs were solely for Moses' benefit ignore the fact that three times God says the signs are for the purpose of convincing the elders (4:5, 8, 9). Moreover, God concedes the possibility that Moses is right when God acknowledges that the first wonder may not compel belief. A reason is given for the second sign: "If they will not believe you or heed the first sign, they may believe the second sign" (4:8). Furthermore, God grants a third sign to be used *if* the elders do not believe the first two signs. "If" language implies a somewhat uncertain future.[68] In other words, God admits to Moses that he does not know for certain how things will go but graciously gives Moses special help to achieve the divine purpose.

What can be said of all this? First, God does not rebuff Moses for questioning the divine word. God takes his question seriously and is open to challenge. Second, we should understand that some of God's unconditional utterances about the future are open to being recast in light of new situations. If this is the case, then there is no contradiction between 3:18 and 4:8-9, one saying that they will listen and the other saying that they may not. God may make remarks about future human actions that are highly probable but not certain.

God's statement that Pharaoh will not let the people go without a struggle is based on his knowledge of the king's stubborn nature. It is not an inviolable future in which Pharaoh is without choice. It may be objected that the hardening of Pharaoh's heart implies that he can only do what God determines he will do. God simply decides the way things will go instead of working with the resources available. The hardening of Pharaoh's heart is commonly cited in discussions of divine sovereignty to demonstrate that God is in full control of even oppressive and disastrous situations.

There are problems, however, with such an interpretation of the narrative.[69] When we hear the word *harden* in reference to God, we normally think in terms of complete control. But the three Hebrew terms used in the narrative *(kabed, hazaq* and *qashah)* generally mean "to make something strong or heavy or to encourage (reinforce) someone."[70] The other occurrences of these words in the Old Testament do not carry deterministic overtones.[71] If it is deterministic, then one wonders why God must harden his heart more than once. "It is important to note," says Fretheim, "that an act of hardening does not make one totally or permanently impervious to outside influence; it does not turn the heart off and on like a faucet."[72] After all, God hardens the hearts of Pharaoh's advisers (10:1), yet they plead with Pharaoh to let the Hebrews go and serve Yahweh (10:7). The same divine activity (hardening) does not produce only one sort of reaction, for Pharaoh and his advisers are all hardened and yet they disagree with one another. Divine hardening does not remove their decision-making capacity or their ability to take a different course of action.

That the divine strengthening leaves Pharaoh with alternatives is indicated by the conditional language employed in 8:2, 9:2 and 10:4. God proclaims that particular judgments are coming *if* Pharaoh does not release the people. If, however, Pharaoh is so under divine control that he cannot let them go, then God's use of *if* is disingenuous, for the future is not open.[73] By uttering a conditional, God is saying to Pharaoh that he does not have to persist in his intransigence; he may repent. If, however, God is controlling Pharaoh such that Pharaoh cannot do otherwise, then God's speech is deceitful.

The narrative asserts that the purpose of God is to be glorified and that the Egyptians would "know that I am Yahweh" (7:5, 17; 8:10, 22; 9:14; 14:4, 18). Donald Gowan, following Walther Zimmerli, argues that this formula means more than intellectual awareness of a fact; it means to become oriented toward Yahweh in one's life.[74] God intends to bring about changes in the lives of Pharaoh and the Egyptians, not just with Israel. It hardly glorifies God if Pharaoh is not a genuine opponent but merely a puppet for God to manipulate. God and Pharaoh are involved in a real conflict, one that is not settled by overwhelming divine power.

Pharaoh repeatedly hardens his own heart before God ever hardens it. God is intensifying what Pharaoh has already decided on. Pharaoh is steadfast in his course of action, and God strengthens his resolve. But why, it may be asked, would God do such a thing, especially when Pharaoh is on the verge of letting the people go? I think that God is trying to push Pharaoh out of his comfort zone in the attempt to get Pharaoh to come to his senses and repent.[75] Pharaoh has positioned himself in a sinful state, so God "gives him over" to further judgment. God ups the ante in the increasing destruction of the Egyptian economy. Furthermore, the plagues are, I believe, directed against the Egyptian pantheon—showing the utter futility of the patron deities to protect Egypt.[76] Pharaoh is pushed by God to decide: either stick with his old deities and remain steadfast in his oppression, in which case he will suffer further judgment, or repent and call on Yahweh—the god whom he said he did not know (5:2). What God desires is the redemption of Pharaoh, and to this end the plagues are deployed.[77] However, as Gowan remarks, "all this destructive activity seems to have failed to accomplish the purpose that is emphasized so strongly throughout the passage, except that Israel was persuaded" (14:31).[78]

To adapt an illustration from Fretheim, Pharaoh is in a canoe heading down a swift river. As the river narrows toward the waterfall, it picks up speed. There are ample warnings along the way, such as the roar of the falls and the spray of water rising up from it. The canoeist either heeds the warnings and gets over to the bank or stays the course and suffers the consequences. There does come a point when it is too late to turn back. But such a doom was not in place from the beginning. Whether Pharaoh steers to the bank or goes over the edge, the Egyptians will know that Yahweh has done these things and so will glorify him.

In making use of the resources available, divine sovereignty does not exercise absolute control over the human order. God does not easily get his way with either Moses or Pharaoh. God persuades, commands, gives comfort and sometimes brings judgment in order to get humans to sign on to his project. God genuinely wrestles with his human creatures. Sometimes God gets everything he wants, and sometimes he does not. Regarding the nonhuman creation, however, the book of Exodus presents a very different picture of divine sovereignty, since in this realm there is little, if any, resistance to God.[79] The plagues, the crossing of the Sea of Reeds and the provision of food and water in the wilderness all testify to Yahweh's ability to make use of the created order. These forces do not appear resistant to the divine will as do human agents. God can make use of the processes in nature to produce some quite unusual events. Again, God makes use of the resources available in the created order. God elects to work in and through the world he made in order to deliver and provide for his people.

3.10 Divine-Human Relationality in the Covenant

God created in freedom. God elected to work with Abraham in freedom. In freedom God chose Isaac over Ishmael, Jacob over Esau and Israel over the other nations. In these cases divine election comes first, but election must be understood as resulting from the divine love for the sake of relationship. Consequently, a conditional element arises: Will the people accept divine election and be faithful to it? In election God freely takes the initiative and then freely binds himself by promise and covenant to creation, to Abraham and to Israel. God now establishes a covenant with the people. After Sinai "the entire history of Israel, as portrayed in the Bible, is governed by this outstanding reality. Covenant consciousness suffuses all subsequent developments."[80] While they are camped at Sinai, God institutes a covenant with the Israelites:

> You have seen what I did to the Egyptians, and how I bore you on eagles' wings and brought you to myself. Now therefore, if you obey my voice and keep my covenant, you shall be my treasured possession out of all the peoples. Indeed, the whole earth is mine, but you shall be for me a priestly kingdom and a holy nation (Ex 19:4-6).

In gracious freedom God establishes a covenant—a working arrangement with the people of Israel. In grace God delivered the people from their bondage in Egypt. In his mightiness he brought them to himself. This act is described metaphorically as an eagle's protecting its young (compare Deut 32:11-14) and a parent's carrying a child (Deut 1:31).[81] Both metaphors depict powerful help and concern for the people. The first words of the covenant are about God's gracious acts of deliverance and closeness ("brought you to myself"). Whatever follows in the covenant, its foundation is laid in grace. In the divine-human relationships grace is always first.

God expects people to respond to his grace by faithfully keeping the covenant. God desires obedience to his word. And God's commandments

have the people's best interests in mind, for they will be for their good
(Deut 6:24; 10:13). God desires that the people exercise trusting obedience
to his word. God is still in the work of developing people who love, trust
and obey him. God has already displayed his mighty love for them. Now
he wants a loving response from the beloved. Brueggemann comments,
"While Yahweh's initial rescue is unconditional and without reservation, a
sustained relation with Yahweh is one of rigorous demand for covenant."[82]
The bestowal of the covenant promise was solely Yahweh's prerogative
and was not conditioned by anyone. Human participation in the covenant
promise and the blessings it entailed were conditional.[83] God initiates the
relationship and intends for it to involve give and take. The covenant
involves reciprocity, but this is due solely to God's free decision.

Walter Eichrodt describes the covenant relationship as "bilateral."[84] He
acknowledges that it is not a covenant between equals, for God is the
superior partner. The covenant truly involves partnership, but *bilateral* is
perhaps not the best term for the divine-human covenant. Adriö König
prefers the term *monopluristic* because it emphasizes that the covenant is
one-sidedly established by the Lord yet also conveys the sense of mutuality
between God and the people.[85] God brings about the covenant in gracious
free love. God is not forced into this relationship. Inside the covenant
relationship exist boundaries and obligations for both the people and God.
God, the king, wants a relationship with the people, the vassal, not with
automatons who can do nothing but what the programmer designs. God
is dependent on the people to ratify and fulfill the covenant.[86] He expects
them to be responsible and to contribute (within the limits of their
createdness) to the relationship. God binds himself to the covenant people
and will do what is appropriate and legitimate (within the limits he has
established) for their well-being. God is deeply involved in history. Jürgen
Moltmann comments, "The more the covenant is taken seriously as the
revelation of God, the more profoundly one can understand the historicity
of God and history in God."[87]

Blessings are promised to the people as they faithfully trust the
covenant God: they will be a "priestly kingdom and a holy nation." The
text does not explain what this means. I suggest that it involves a ministry
on the part of the Israelites to the rest of the world. Through them, all the
nations of the world would be blessed (Gen 12:3). As God's "treasured
possession," they would serve to direct people to God. The question is
whether Israel will fulfill this calling. God places his project for the future
of the world into their hands. God will work with them, but God
sovereignly decides to make his project dependent on this people. They

cannot do it without God; God will not do it without them. Risk is involved, for God makes his redemptive work vulnerable: Will anyone faithfully keep the covenant? Will the people become a holy nation? Will they love God with all their strength (Deut 6:5), show love to their neighbors (Lev 19:18), care for the aliens among them (Lev 19:34) and care for widows and orphans (Deut 10:17-19)? A reading of the Bible reveals that, overall, God was very disappointed with Israel in this regard. The cultus failed to produce godly people. God sent prophets to them, but their messages went largely unheeded. After centuries of struggling with the people, God expresses his exasperation with them: "I was ready to be sought out by those who did not ask, to be found by those who did not seek me. I said, 'Here I am, here I am,' to a nation that did not call on my name. I held out my hands all day long to a rebellious people" (Is 65:1-2). One can almost picture God jumping up and down, waving his arms shouting, "Here I am!" so desirous is he of covenant relations.[88]

3.11 Divine Goals with Open Routes

The breaking and renewal of the covenant in Exodus 32—34 gives important insight into the divine-human relationship.[89] Especially significant in this regard are the prayers of Moses. The worship of the golden calf (Ex 32) constituted a grievous breach of the covenant. The event precipitates a rather heated and tense exchange between God and Moses. God's speech begins and ends with his telling Moses to leave him immediately (32:7,10). Moreover, God proclaims that the Israelites are Moses' people, thereby implying that they are not God's. Finally, God informs Moses of a new plan of action. God will destroy the people and start over again with Moses. Moses will then have a role similar to Noah's. "God is prepared to scuttle Israel as the promised 'great nation,' and to reassign and redeploy the great Abrahamic promise of Genesis 12:2 to Moses."[90] Certainly it is within the divine freedom to do this. By starting over again with Moses, God would remain faithful to his basic commitment while basing his specific options and responses at any one time on the unfolding events and human actions.

Moses, however, does not agree with God. Instead of leaving the divine presence as commanded, Moses risks divine wrath in order to intercede for the people.[91] He believes it possible to alter the divine word, and to this end he gives three reasons why God should not follow through on his threatened course of action (32:11-13).[92] First, he says that the people belong to God, for God is the one who just delivered them. Second, the Egyptians may ascribe "evil motives" to God.[93] Third, he reminds God of his promise to Abraham. God could have rebutted all of Moses' reasons: first, God delivered them, but he has no confidence in them; second, God does not care what the Egyptians think because he has healthy self-esteem; third, he is keeping his promise to Abraham because Moses is one of his descendants. Or God could have replied that he is sovereign and can do what pleases him. But God gives no such answers. Instead, the text simply says that God changed his mind and did not do what he said he would. Apparently, Moses has a relationship with God such that God values what Moses desires. If Moses interprets God's intentions in an unfavorable way and God values his relationship with Moses, then God must either persuade Moses or concede his request. It is unlikely that Moses presents God with new information.

The real basis for the change in God's decision comes from a forceful presentation by one who is in a special relationship with God. With Moses' prayer, the decision-making situation is now altered for God.[94] Being in relationship to Moses, God is willing to allow him to influence the path he will take. God permits human input into the divine future. One of the most remarkable features in the Old Testament is that people can argue with God and win. Fretheim comments, "Hence human prayer (in this case, intercession) is honored by God as a contribution to a conversation that has the capacity to change future directions for God, people, and the world. God may well adjust modes and directions (though not ultimate goals) in view of such human responsiveness."[95]

After Moses visits the idolatrous scene, he returns to Yahweh and continues his intercession (32:31-34). He requests that God forgive the people. This time, however, God does not grant his petition. Punishment will be meted out. Moses, despite his close relationship with God, does not receive everything he requests. Furthermore, God switches from plan A to plan B, saying that the divine presence will not accompany the people. Instead, God will send a messenger (angel). God is worried that if he dwelt in their midst, he would destroy them (33:3). Even in wrath God is concerned for their well-being and believes this will be a suitable arrangement. Yet verses 4-5 indicate that the issue is not finally decided. On hearing of God's decision to go with plan B, the people begin to mourn and show their concern by refraining from wearing their ornaments. God responds by approving this behavior and declaring that it should continue in order for God to finally make up his mind what to do with them. In essence, God is saying that he will consider returning to plan A if he observes appropriate changes in the people. Moses' next prayer consists of a complaint and a request. He complains that God has not revealed the identity of this "messenger" (an indirect way of requesting God to return to plan A). On the basis of his special relationship with God, he asks, "Show me your ways, so that I may know you and find favor in your sight" (33:13).

In response to Moses' complaint, God again changes his mind and says that his "face" (the divine presence) will go with the people—God returns to plan A. Apparently because of the people's repentant attitude and Moses' request, God changes his mind and goes back to his original plan. Moses is pleased with this and replies that if God himself does not go with them, then he does not want to go. For it is Yahweh's presence that distinguishes the people of Israel (33:15-16). It is not entirely clear what Moses is asking when he says, "Show me your ways." V. Cassuto suggests an intriguing interpretation.[96] What Moses desires, he says, is to know the criteria by which God decides when to forgive and when to punish. In this way Moses will be able to determine when he should intercede (knowing he will be successful) and when he should not attempt it. God does not address this request until Moses raises it again.

God acknowledges his special relationship with Moses, whereupon Moses seizes the opportunity to ask God, "Show me your glory" (33:18). Again, it is not clear what Moses desires. Perhaps it is the desire to be radically close to God—face to face. The divine response is to grant Moses insight into the divine goodness and the meaning of the divine name (Yahweh). God says that it is enough for Moses to know that God is gracious and compassionate (33:19). But the exercise of these qualities is, finally, up to God. Moses may request forgiveness for the people, but it is ultimately up to God's discretion to grant it. What Moses needs to know is that God is a God of grace and compassion. To this end God then provides Moses with a theophany—a revelation of the divine character. Yahweh is "merciful and gracious, slow to anger, and abounding in steadfast love and faithfulness." He forgives iniquity yet will not neglect needed judgment on sin (34:6-7).[97] These attributes characterize God in relation to his people. This is what humanity needs to know in order to live in relation to God. Informed of these divine characteristics, we may make our way in the world with God, his steadfast love renewing us, his justice challenging us and his mercy comforting us.

Moses does not get everything he requests in his prayers. Yet it is clear that God takes Moses' concerns seriously, even to the point of twice changing the divine plan. We are not told what God would have done had Moses failed to make these petitions. The text is clear, however, that Moses became a partner with God in shaping the future. Patrick Miller observes that Moses did not pray "thy will be done," for it is the divine will that we call on God and even argue against God.[98] There is no self-surrender on Moses' part. Through prayer he enters into a relationship of reciprocity. Gowan says,

> The picture of God presented to us throughout the Old Testament is that of a God who has chosen to work *with,* rather than just *upon* human beings, so that humans (in this case Moses) are given the chance, if they will accept the responsibility, to contribute to a future that will be different from what it would have been, had they remained passive.[99]

Prayer encourages dialogue, not monologue. By speaking up, Moses made an impact on God. God chooses not to leave the future solely in our hands, but neither does he decide that we should simply leave it in God's hands. God sovereignly decides that the route into the future will involve a genuine divine-human partnership. Balentine comments that

> prayer is a constitutive act of faith that creates the potential for newness in both God and humanity. Neither partner remains unaffected or unchanged after the discourse of prayer. . . . In [the] Hebraic understanding God is open and receptive to change . . . [grounded in] God's unrelenting commitment to be in relationship with humanity.[100]

3.12 Excursus on Divine Repentance

The biblical references to God's changing his mind have created no small controversy in the history of interpretation.[101] Such texts raise a number of issues. One concern is whether divine repentance implies that God is fickle or untrustworthy. If God *can* change his mind, can God be trusted? Yes. As the biblical narrative progresses, it becomes clear that God remains faithful to his overarching goals. For instance, in Exodus 32 whether God destroys the Israelites and begins again with Moses or decides to continue working with the people, God remains faithful to his promise to Abraham and his project of developing a people of faith.[102] But God has different options available, and the one that he will choose is not a foregone conclusion. Sometimes God allows human input in regard to the option that is realized. As God permitted Abraham's intercession for Sodom (Gen 18:16-33), so now God allows Moses incredible access to him. With or without human input, God remains faithful to his project of redemption. God shows steadfast love and sticks to his overarching goals, which he has made known through his promises. God remains unchangeable in his commitment to this project of redemption but remains flexible regarding precisely when, where and how it is carried out.

Another concern is that the divine-repentance texts create tensions with the notions of divine immutability and foreknowledge. Theologians from Philo to John Calvin have asserted that it is *impossible* for the divine mind to change. For Calvin, God can no more change his mind than he can be sorrowful or sad.[103] Biblical texts about God changing his mind, according to Calvin, do not describe God as he truly is but only as he appears to us. It simply is not appropriate for God to be described as repenting or being sorrowful, for that would imply "either that he is ignorant of what is going to happen, or cannot escape it, or hastily and rashly rushes into a decision."[104] Any of these options make God look foolish and are not fitting ascriptions to a transcendent, omnipotent, omniscient and immutable deity. The repentance texts are thus mere anthropomorphisms, in which God accommodates himself to us as a nurse lisps to a young child.[105] Reformed philosopher Paul Helm distinguishes between "the anthropomorphic and the exact language of Scripture" so that the "statements about the extent and intensity of God's knowledge, power and goodness must control the anthropomorphic and weaker statements."[106] Otherwise, we make God in our image.

Norman Geisler distinguishes between "which passages must be taken literally (metaphysically) and which should not," since "the same text [1 Sam 15] speaks of God as repenting and not repenting, thus making it necessary to interpret at least one of these instances as non-literal."[107] Those who think it impossible for God to change his mind typically appeal to one of two criteria in order to distinguish the literal from the nonliteral passages of Scripture regarding divine repentance. The first criterion, as expounded by Geisler, is that since it can be demonstrated by "extrabiblical propositions" (that is, philosophical arguments) that God is wholly immutable and completely unconditioned by creatures, then "God literally cannot change his mind."[108] For Geisler, philosophical arguments are normative for controlling the reading of the Bible. The second criterion seeks, instead of a philosophical measure, a rule from within the Scripture itself for distinguishing anthropomorphic from literal texts. Bruce Ware, following Calvin's suggestion, says, "A given ascription to God may rightly be understood as anthropomorphic when Scripture clearly presents God as transcending the very human or finite features it elsewhere attributes to him."[109] If the Bible in one place predicates a change of mind with respect to God but elsewhere proclaims that God cannot change his mind because "God is not human," then the texts predicating a change of mind in God are to be taken as anthropomorphic expressions that are not literally true of God.

There are numerous difficulties with these criteria. First, how do Calvin, Helm and Ware know that God is "accommodating" himself to us as a nurse lisps to a young child? In order to know that the nurse is lisping and not speaking "normally," one would have observe the nurse in both forms of discourse. This is a problem especially for Calvin, as he denies that we have access to the way God (the nonlisping deity) really is apart from God's self-revelation. If the Scripture is God's lisping discourse to us and we have no means of observing God's nonlisping discourse, then on what grounds do we claim that God is indeed lisping to us? How would anyone know, since we cannot observe God's "normal" discourse? On what basis do these thinkers claim that these biblical texts do not portray God as he truly is but only God as he appears to us? How can they confidently select one biblcal text as an "exact" description of God and consign others to the dustbin of anthropomorphism? Geisler uses philosophical reasoning to establish a priori what is appropriate for a deity to be like *(dignum Deo)*.[110] Since it is not "proper" for a deity to change his mind, biblical assertions to that effect must be revised to say something else.[111] But someone who agreed with this method of determining what a "perfect being" is might still disagree with the content of what is "proper" for God. After all, it could be argued that it is "fitting" for the most perfect being to change in response to human beings; to not change in relation to us would be imperfect.

There are problems with the second criterion also. Ware admirably attempts to locate the criterion for distinguishing the exact language of Scripture from anthropomorphic language in Scripture itself. He identifies texts that explicitly deny that God has certain human characteristics as the transcendent ones. Passages saying that God will not change his mind because he is *not human* (Num 23:19; 1 Sam 15:29) describe God as he really is and force a reinterpretation of the repentance texts to mean something other than what they say.[112] Unfortunately Ware does not justify his preferring negative statements about God over the positive ones. On what grounds should his criterion be accepted? Is it really the case that negative terms give us the truth about God and positive ones do not? Where is this principle found in Scripture? Moreover, Ware's own criterion becomes problematic when put into use because Hosea 11:8-9 says God repents because he is *not human*. According to Ware's own criterion, when the Bible predicates something of God and this predication is accompanied by the "transcendent" ground that God "is not human," then we have the literal truth about God. Following Ware we have a real problem on our hands because the Bible teaches both (1) that God cannot change his mind because he is not human and (2) that God literally does change his mind because he is not human.

What is the provenance of the second criterion, if not the Bible? Calvin's discussion of the matter is similar to Ware's.[113] Calvin says we "ought not to imagine any commotion" or change of mind in God. And why not? Here Calvin does not give a scriptural reason. He bases his assertion on the belief that any change in God would be a change for the worse, and this would imply imperfection in the divine being. That is, Calvin does not seem to be following his own sound advice that we allow God to reveal himself to us in Scripture as he really is instead of grounding our knowledge of God on a philosophical principle.[114] Instead, he succumbs to Plato's dictum of perfection: Any sort of change in God would be a change for the worse.[115] Consequently, the second criterion actually reduces to the first. A particular preconceived notion of God is allowed to adjudicate what the biblical text will be allowed to say. Distinguishing the texts that mean what they say from the ones that mean something other than what they say is dependent on the theological control beliefs of an immutable and wholly unconditioned deity.[116]

Even if it were granted that divine repentance is "anthropomorphic" (in the narrow sense), the question remains regarding its meaning. What do such texts intend to teach us if they do not mean what they say? If God knew all along, for instance, that King Hezekiah was not going to die, then what was God doing when he announced that Hezekiah would die shortly? Was God lying? Claiming that biblical texts asserting that God "changed his mind" are merely anthropomorphisms does not tell us what they mean. If, in fact, it is impossible for God to change his mind, then the biblical text is quite misleading. Asserting that it is a nonliteral expression does not solve the problem because it has to mean something. Just what is the anthropomorphic expression an expression of? Thus classical theists are left with the problem of misleading biblical texts, or, at best, meaningless metaphors regarding the nature of God.

Another problem with this approach is that it seems to abstract the "will not repent" idea from the contexts in which they occur. The two texts asserting that God will not repent refer to specific situations in which God refuses to reverse a particular decision. In one case God refuses to allow Balaam to change the divine mind and curse Israel (Num 23:19). In the other case God rejects Saul's pleas to keep the kingship in his family (1 Sam 15:29).[117] The 1 Samuel passage is especially instructive. God informs Samuel that he "repents" that he made Saul king (15:11 RSV). Samuel responds by praying all night for God to repent of this repentance. But God refuses Samuel's intercession. Subsequently, Saul begs that the divine decision be rescinded. In response, Samuel says that God will not repent of his repentance. In this instance, he assures Saul, God will not change his mind (15:29). And the story concludes by reiterating that God repented making Saul king (15:35). Consequently, sandwiched between two declarations of God's changing his mind (15:11, 35) is the remark that God will not change his mind (15:29).[118] This chapter says both that God changes his mind and that God will not change his mind. In its context the teaching is clear: God reserves the right to alter his plans in response to human initiative, and it is also the divine right not to alter an alteration. Consequently we need not follow the suggestion that one set of texts is literal while the other is anthropomorphic, since both sets portray God in dymamic relations with humans.

God had originally planned to establish Saul's household as a perpetual kingship in Israel (1 Sam 13:13-14) but then changed his mind. Despite Samuel's intercession, God proclaims that he will not change his mind about this change of mind he has had. Taken in their literary and historical contexts, these "I will not change my mind" texts are not abstract propositions about divine immutability. Rather, they speak of God's steadfastness in certain concrete situations to reject the human petition.

Yet some do understand divine predictions to be immutable truths,[119] asserting that texts such as "Has he spoken, and will he not fulfill it?" (Num 23:19) and the test of a prophet (Deut 18:21-22, in which a prophet is judged by whether or not the event comes to pass) imply that whatever God speaks as a prediction will happen. In the instances just mentioned God decides to go with one particular option. But in many other instances God does indeed speak and does not perform it due to divine repentance. An examination of three divine repentance texts may help make this clear. Perhaps the best-known example occurs in the book of Jonah. The prophet announces the destruction of the Ninevites in categorical terms. His message of judgment includes no conditional element to the effect that Nineveh will be destroyed unless there is widespread repentance on the part of the people. The very reason Jonah refuses to announce his message is that he wants the Assyrians to be destroyed. But he knows that Yahweh is a God who is "ready to relent from punishing" (4:2). Jonah knows that Yahweh is able and willing to change his mind and so refuses to preach. Jonah is convinced that God may indeed speak and not perform it.

Another instructive instance of divine repentance occurs in the story of King Hezekiah (2 Kings 20). When the king falls mortally ill, the prophet Isaiah comes to announce that the king will die shortly. Isaiah makes this announcement in categorical (not conditional) terms with the familiar refrain "thus says the LORD." The force of these words is intended to drive home the certainty of Hezekiah's imminent death. Amazingly, however, the king does not take the prophet's words to imply a fixed future, for Hezekiah prays to God, giving God reasons why he should live longer. Before Isaiah is out of the palace, the word of Yahweh instructs him to return to the king with a new message. Again Isaiah begins with "thus says the LORD." But now God has changed his mind *because of* Hezekiah's prayer (20:5). God declares that Hezekiah will recover from this illness and will live another fifteen years. The words "thus says the LORD" announce the first message and the second message, which reverses the first. Yahweh is free to change his mind in response to human beings. Not even the authoritative "thus says the LORD" can prevent Yahweh from repenting if he so decides.[120] God, using his wisdom in conjunction with input from the human relationships, freely decides when he will carry out the prediction and when he will alter it. Either way, the decision remains faithful to his redemptive project.

The third illustration of God's repenting of his "word" occurs in connection with the priest Eli and his sons. God had said that Eli's descendants would have a perpetual priesthood in Israel. Upon observing the wickedness of Eli's sons, however, God changes his mind, cutting off Eli's household from the priesthood (1 Sam 2:30). God's initial promise was apparently made without a conditional element, but it is within the divine province to make it conditional on what comes about in the course of the divine-human relationship. This is precisely the teaching Samuel gives to King Saul: Yahweh would have established Saul's line for perpetual kingship, but in light of Saul's disobedience God turns to another (1 Sam 13:13-14).

Of course, that God's word may be alterable does not imply that it is always or easily changed. The prophet Nathan announced the "word of the LORD" to David that the child born to him and Bathsheba would die. In response David fasted and cried to the Lord to let the child live, believing that God might be gracious to him and change his mind pertaining to the divine judgment (2 Sam 12:14, 22). David did not accept the word of the Lord as unalterable. Nevertheless, in this case God refused to be moved by David's prayers and fasting. Divine repentance is a biblical teaching, but it is not a guarantee.

The traditional approach to the repentance texts involves yet another problem. Many today admit that God experiences changes in emotions but continue to affirm foreknowledge. They claim that God knows from all eternity that, for instance, Saul will disobey God at a particular point in history. God nevertheless experiences a genuine change in emotion from joy to grieving over Saul. It is questionable whether it is coherent to affirm both that God has always known of this event and that God now has changing emotions about that event. Furthermore, Fretheim identifies a moral problem with this view: "For God to say, for example, 'I know that I will be provoked to anger by the sin of David with Bathsheba' runs into tough moral ground. God should immediately be angry at the point of God's *knowledge* of the sin, and not just at the point of its occurrence. But the texts say that God was provoked to anger at a particular historical moment, not that some previous divine provocation was realized."[121] The notion of change in God is problematic for the doctrine of foreknowledge.[122] This is, in part, the reason why Calvin (along with many others) affirmed a strong doctrine of divine impassibility (God cannot be affected by others) and rejected the doctrine of foreknowledge in favor of the doctrine of foreordination.

A better approach to the divine-repentance texts is to acknowledge that they are metaphorical in nature.[123] Metaphors do not provide us with an exact correspondence to reality, but they do provide a way of understanding reality. No single metaphor captures the biblical God. Rather, a number of metaphors are used in order to build up a portrait of God. In the Bible some metaphors are more pervasive and are used to qualify others. For instance, God as loving both pervades and qualifies other metaphors. God is not just any king or father or hen, he is a loving one. Fretheim refers to these pervasive and qualifying metaphors as "controlling metaphors." The metaphor of divine repentance signifies God's ability to remain faithful to his project while altering his plans to accommodate the changing circumstances brought about by the creatures. In other words, divine repentance expresses the divine wisdom, faithfulness and love. Just as the metaphors regarding God's eyes or hands signify divine awareness and ability to act, so the metaphor of divine repentance informs us that God is responsive in his relations with us—a very meaningful metaphor indeed. In this approach, then, all biblical metaphors are to be taken seriously. None are dismissed as mere anthropomorphisms because they are part of the divine revelation.

Several points of evidence demonstrate that divine repentance is a significant controlling metaphor in the biblical narrative.[124] First, the metaphor of divine repentance is pervasive in the Old Testament. At least thirty-five times God is said to repent or not repent (this includes only passages in which *niḥam* occurs, not all passages that depict a change in God).[125] God is said to repent of something he has already done, such as creating (Gen 6:6) or making Saul king (1 Sam 15:11, 35). God decides *not* to repent about certain matters, for instance, electing David king (1 Sam 15:29) or judging sin (Jer 15:6). God sometimes repents of what he said he would do or has already begun to do (Ex 32:14). In these cases God changes his mind either because the people repent, or because someone intercedes (for example, Moses) or simply because the divine compassion overrides the divine anger.[126] The prophets learned that God is free to change his mind. In the words of Heschel, "[They] had to be taught that God is greater than His decisions."[127] God can neither be compelled to repent nor be prevented from repenting, for divine repentance is neither automatic nor predictable. Whereas Moses succeeded in persuading God to change his mind, Samuel could not persuade God to let Saul remain king, despite interceding all night long.

Second, "divine repentance is in fact found within a variety of traditions, northern and southern, early and late: Jahwist/Elohist; David-Zion; Deuteronomic History; eighth- and seventh-century prophets; exilic and post-exilic prophecy; psalmody."[128] The theme cannot be dismissed as belonging to some small band of esoteric teachers. It pervades Israel's history. Third, the repentance metaphor also occurs in a wide variety of genres, including divine speech (where God says "I repent") and creedal statements. Basic creedal affirmations call attention to what is most important for Israel's faith. Two such statements say God "is gracious and merciful, slow to anger, abounding in steadfast love, and relents from punishing" (Joel 2:13; see also Jon 4:2). Divine repentance is included with divine grace and love as a key characteristic of God. David Allen Hubbard remarks, "So dominant is this loyal love, so steeped in grace . . . and mercy . . . that it encourages Yahweh to stay open to changes in his plans. . . . God's openness to change his course of action . . . has [in these two passages] virtually become one of his attributes."[129]

It may be objected that divine repentance is literally impossible, since God has exhaustive foreknowledge of future events. In a later chapter I will argue that perhaps one version of foreknowledge does not necessarily rule out divine repentance. Here I only wish to establish that there is sufficient biblical warrant for affirming that the future is in some respects indefinite even for God. God is not following a blueprint in working with us. Although some of God's future actions are determined by him and thus are definite, others remain open or indefinite. In his book *The Suffering of God* Fretheim details a vast amount of evidence from the Old Testament that this is the case.[130] Here I have space only to summarize his main points and list a few of the Scriptures he discusses.

That the future is open (at least partially indefinite) is indicated by four types of divine speech acts. First, there are the occasions where God says "perhaps" the people will listen to my prophet and "maybe" they will turn from their idols (for example, Ezek 12:1-3; Jer 26:2-3). God says, "I thought Israel would return to me but she has not" (see Jer 3:7; compare 32:35). In these texts God is explicitly depicted as not knowing the specific future. God himself says that he was mistaken about what was going to happen. Second, God makes utterances such as "*if* you repent then I will let you remain in the land" (see Jer 7:5-7). Such "if" language—the invitation to change—is ingenuine if God already knew they would not repent.[131] God gave King Zedekiah two possible courses of action with a resulting outcome of each (Jer 38:17-23). The text indicates that the future was as yet undetermined. If God knew it was already determined, then why give Zedekiah options? Similarly, God repeatedly sent Elijah to call King Ahab to repent, but the king refused to do so. Was God playing a cat-and-mouse game with Ahab? If God foreknows from the moment he gives the invitation that it will be pointless, then God is being deceitful by holding out a false hope. On the other hand, if God is genuinely inviting the people to change, then the future is not yet definite.

Third, God "consults" with certain people of faith in deciding the course of action God will take, such as Abraham (concerning judgment on Sodom, Gen 18) and Amos (regarding judgment on Israel, Amos 7). God, in freedom, decides not to decide without consulting these figures of faith. In the case of Moses (Ex 32), he decides to change his decision in response to Moses' intercession. Finally, God asks questions that are not merely rhetorical. God agonizes over what to do with his sinful people (Hos 6:4; Jer 5:7). When God asks, "What am I going to do with you?" God is seeking a response from the people. God desires dialogue. If the people will join in dialogue, reconciliation is yet possible. By asking such questions, God puts a decision to the people; judgment is not yet inevitable.

That the future is partially indefinite has already been demonstrated in connection with the testing of Abraham, as God learns ("now I know") that Abraham really trusts him (Gen 22), and in connection with Moses' challenge to a divine "prediction" that the elders would believe him (Ex 4:1). God acknowledges that Moses was correct in stating that the elders might, indeed, not believe him. Moreover, biblical characters do not seem to believe that divine forecasts are inevitable. Even though God told Rebekah that "the elder shall serve the younger" (Gen 25:23) in reference to Jacob and Esau, she nevertheless feels compelled to take some risky actions (Gen 27:5-17).[132] The text does not suggest that the oracle fixes the future for her sons. She certainly did not leave this "prediction" in the hands of God. The oracle expressed what God desired in the matter, and God enlisted Rebekah's help to this end (a risk God takes in the patriarchal culture). The common assertion that Rebekah's actions (and Sarah's in Gen 16) were sinful reflects a docetic view of divine activity in the world. On the contrary, God has sovereignly chosen to work through his creatures, allowing their actions to be significant to the divine project.

Joseph's dreams are often taken to indicate a revelation of divine foreknowledge, since everything comes to pass as was "predicted." For instance, Joseph dreamed that his brothers and parents would "bow down" to him (Gen 37:6-10). But neither Jacob nor the brothers believe they have to do what the dream describes (37:8, 10; Joseph's parents never do bow down to him).[133] It is commonly overlooked by proponents of foreknowledge that some predictions in Scripture either do not come to pass at all (for example, the account of Jonah; 2 Kings 20) or do not come to pass exactly as they were foretold (for example, Gen 27:27-40, in which Jacob's blessing is qualified by Esau's blessing; Acts 21:11, in which it is incorrectly predicted that Paul would be bound by the Jewish authorities and handed over to the Gentiles).[134] One would think that a God with foreknowledge would get such details straight.[135]

The view of omniscience, known as the openness of God (or presentism), can explain both scriptural passages in which the future is sometimes definite and passages in which it is indefinite, even for God.[136] Texts indicating that a future event is definite suggest that either the event is determined by God to happen in that way or God knows the event will result from a chain of causal factors that are presently in place. Passages in which God does not know the future indicate that God has not decided what will be. The matter is open for both God and creatures. Both sets of texts have straightforward explanations, and there is no need to call one sort of biblical passages the "literal" truth about God while labeling the others "anthropomorphic." Although I affirm that the future is partly definite and partly indefinite for God (that is, the openness of God), the most important issue here is the affirmation of relational theism, in which God enters into reciprocal, give-and-take relations with creatures. If proponents of exhaustive foreknowledge can coherently accommodate this into their theology, then so be it. However, I do not think the biblical material supports their position.

3.13 Divine Wrath and Mercy in the Context of Covenantal Relationality

God is described as caring deeply about his covenant relationship with his people. God becomes angry at times and shows mercy at other times. Heschel's monumental study *The Prophets* wonderfully brings out these twin themes. He eloquently describes the passion of the divine-human drama with all the ebb and flow this relationship involves. Heschel's remarks on the divine wrath and how it relates to mercy have deeply influenced this section, and I might add, much of my thinking on God.

Philo and many of the church fathers were appalled at biblical references to divine wrath, since they did not consider it appropriate for God to be angry.[137] Consequently, references to divine wrath were either allegorized or equated with punishment. Either way a volatile emotion was kept out of the divine nature. It should be acknowledged that human wrath can be a dangerous emotion that has the power to undo us, and so reservations about ascribing it to God are understandable. But Scripture unashamedly does just that. Exodus 32 demonstrates that Yahweh is a God who gets angry. But Heschel is right in holding that wrath must be understood as an aspect of the divine pathos—it is a distancing of the relationship. For Heschel, pathos means that God is concerned for, not apathetic toward, us. In other words, divine wrath must be discussed in connection with the divine-human relationship. As part of God's pathos toward us, wrath is an instrument in the divine hands, not an attribute of God. It is always a secondary pathos toward us. God's wrath concerns the divine displeasure at a particular situation in history, not an essential attribute. It is not the Creator's fundamental stance toward his creation. In this way of thinking all attempts to balance wrath (or justice) with love as equal attributes of God are misplaced.

Even as lawgiver, God is not expounding a moral code of sheer justice. The covenant stipulations pertain to righteousness, or the right ordering of relationships. Heschel writes, "Righteousness goes beyond justice. Justice is strict and exact, giving each person his due. Righteousness implies benevolence, kindness, generosity."[138] Crime in Israel is not primarily a violation of a law but a sin against the living God. It is a breaking of the fundamental relationship between creature and Creator. Consequently, justice and righteousness must be understood within the divine-human relationality that God established.

God is judge over his people but not in the Western legal sense of being a neutral, dispassionate decision maker. Judges in Israel were advocates for the people, displaying concern for the needy and the oppressed. Deborah, Gideon and David sought to liberate the people and put societal relationships in the state God intended. Judges in Israel were to emulate the divine judge, "God of gods and Lord of lords, the great, the mighty, and the terrible God, who is not partial and takes no bribe. He executes justice for the fatherless and the widow, and loves the sojourner, giving him food and clothing" (Deut 10:17-18 RSV). God is a judge who loves his creatures and desires their well-being.

Even when the divine judge pours out his wrath, there is love behind it. This idea is aptly summed up by Heschel: "The secret of anger is God's care."[139] Divine wrath bespeaks divine concern. God cares deeply about his beloved—the creatures he made. He is not indifferent toward them. God cannot stand to see the beloved ruin herself, so he actively seeks her renewal. When those efforts are rejected, God becomes angry. The divine wrath is a response to being dismissed by the one he loves. The break in relationship brings grief to the heart of God.[140] God is personally involved. He has made himself vulnerable, and that vulnerability has been betrayed. The breaking of the relationship is like a divorce, and its impact on God is real; it changes him.

As grief turns into anger, God takes steps to change the situation. Divine suffering results in attempts at reconciliation. God brings punishment on his people in order to move them toward reconciliation (Hos 6:1). There is purpose in the divine anger, and once this purpose is achieved it may vanish in an instant. Heschel explains: "The anger of the Lord is instrumental, hypothetical, conditional, and subject to his will. . . . Far from being an expression of 'petulant vindictiveness,' the message of anger includes a call to return and to be saved."[141] The purpose of God's wrath is to open a future for the broken relationship. God sometimes imposes great suffering on his people as a means of discipline. "The Lord is long-suffering, compassionate, loving, and faithful, but He is also demanding, insistent, terrible, and dangerous."[142]

But beyond the dangerous wrath of God lies his mercy. God is ever ready to repent in response to his people's repentance. These ideas are wonderfully portrayed in Judges 10:6-16. In this passage the Israelites worship other gods, forsaking Yahweh. In response Yahweh delivers them into the hands of foreign oppressors who mistreat the people for eighteen years. Finally the Israelites cry out to Yahweh, confessing their sin. That God is still angry at them is made clear by the divine speech to them. God says that he has taken care of them and has repeatedly protected them from enemies, "yet you have forsaken me and served other gods; therefore I will deliver you no more. Go and cry out to the gods whom you have chosen; let them deliver you in the time of your distress" (10:13-14 RSV). Yahweh has had it with these people; he will no longer deliver them. He challenges them to seek help from their adulterous lovers. God is here depicted as a wounded lover speaking strong words of rejection. Yet the people of Israel do not believe that the divine rejection is final, for they immediately put away their idols and serve Yahweh. Even though God has cast them off, they persist. They do not take the divine wrath as the final word. And indeed it is not, for when "Yahweh could bear the misery of Israel no longer" (10:16) he raised up Jephthah to deliver the people he so emphatically said he would never deliver.

That God's wrath is real yet subsumed under mercy is brought out repeatedly in the Prophets. Hosea speaks of the inner turmoil God goes through in relation to the faithlessness of his people: "How can I give you up, Ephraim? How can I hand you over, O Israel? . . . My heart recoils within me; my compassion grows warm and tender. I will not execute my fierce anger; I will not again destroy Ephraim; for I am God and no mortal, the Holy One in your midst, and I will not come in wrath" (11:8-9). God is not like us in that his compassion is more fundamental than his anger.

The Old Testament understanding of divine wrath and mercy develops progressively. The Decalogue in Exodus proclaims the divine wrath toward idolatry before it mentions God's lovingkindness (20:4-6). Although the extent of lovingkindness is greater than that of wrath, divine love is extended to those who love God. God revises this statement later in Exodus after Israel's apostasy with the golden calf. Several changes are made, which reflect a greater emphasis on the divine love (34:6-7).[143] To begin, the order is reversed; divine love is placed before mention of punishment of sin. Second, the conditional is removed, calling attention to God's unconditional love. Third, many new elements are added in describing the divine nature: God is compassionate and gracious, slow to anger, and abounding in lovingkindness and faithfulness, and he forgives iniquity, transgression and sin. The reference to judging follows this statement, and it is not included in the list of divine attributes.

These affirmations are again modified in the creedal formulations of Joel 2:13 and Jonah 4:2.[144] God is still gracious and compassionate, slow to anger, abounding in lovingkindness. But a new element is added: God repents of his judgments on sin. Also, the reference to not clearing the guilty has been dropped from the formula. The entire idea of visiting iniquity on future generations is explicitly repudiated in Ezekiel 18:14-20. From all this we see that as God works toward the achievement of his project, a clearer picture emerges of who God is in relation to his people. Divine wrath exists and it can be terrible, but it serves a purpose: bringing the people back from a life of death. God puts before the people the ultimate choice. "I have set before you life and death, blessings and curses.

Choose life so that you and your descendants may live, loving the LORD your God, obeying him, and holding fast to him; for that means life to you" (Deut 30:19-20). Again we see the divine risk: will anyone love, obey, and hold fast to him so as to have life? The divine project is to give genuine life to his creatures. God's wrath and mercy are not arbitrary, but elements in bringing that project to fruition.

3.14 The Absence and Presence of God

"The Lord used to speak to Moses face to face, as one speaks to a friend" (Ex 33:11). "How long, O LORD? Will you forget me forever? How long will you hide your face from me?" (Ps 13:1). Some biblical writers speak of intimacy with God, whereas other writers can't seem to find God. Some texts refer to God's great provisions for the people, whereas others call divine providence into question.

Fretheim distinguishes three aspects of divine presence in the Old Testament:[145] (1) the structural or general presence, by which God is never absent from his created order; (2) the accompanying presence, by which God stays with his people throughout their journeys (even into exile) and (3) the tabernacling presence, by which God chooses to dwell in a specific place among his people. To these I would add a fourth: God's acts of deliverance or special provision by which people experience the divine presence in miraculous providence. This last type of presence usually occurs when God is beginning a new work (notice the cluster of miracles in Exodus), validating the commissioning of a prophet (Ex 4:2-9) or demonstrating Yahweh as the true God (1 Kings 18; 2 Kings 18—19). All four types of presence are due to divine grace and reveal God's desire to be present in an intimate way with his creatures. God makes himself approachable. God is holy and transcendent, but these terms must be understood within the divine relatedness to his people, not as some abstract "wholly other."[146] The holy God is one who may be approached by his creatures—even "face to face." Holiness pertains to the way in which God establishes his presence among the people, not some otherworldly transcendence.

Presence has to do with relationship. The distance between those in the relationship decreases as they freely share themselves. Becoming close means being available and vulnerable. The relationship may backfire. One may be taken advantage of and hurt. In this regard it is not surprising that the divine presence is affected by human action. Although God is never considered entirely absent in the Old Testament—those who ask where God is expect God to hear their question—God may withdraw his special presence from individuals or from the temple (Ezek 8:6). Sometimes God's presence is removed in order to test someone (for example, Hezekiah in 2 Chron 32:31, and Job). At other times the divine absence is a response to sin: God "hides his face" (Mic 3:4) from the evildoers. But this is certainly not true of every case where God is felt to be absent. In the complaint Psalms there is no mention of sin, and God's absence is considered irrational.[147] The supplicant is simply dismayed that God has withdrawn (for example, Ps 44). Such texts are another reminder that we are allowed to question God. One's relationship with God is not so unambiguous as to prevent all skepticism.[148] Many a biblical writer faulted God for not acting and attempted to prod God into action. Brueggemann believes that in these laments "the petitionary party is taken seriously and the God who is addressed is newly engaged in the crisis in a way that puts God at risk."[149] God is vulnerable to being misunderstood by his failure to act. Such misunderstanding leads to tension in the relationship between God and the petitioner.

Another kind of complaint asks why the wicked prosper (Jer 12:1). If God is so almighty and is so concerned about widows and orphans, then why does God not act? The "lament tradition" does not ask God for strength to cope with the situation; it cries out for divine action to change it. This tradition asks where the divine presence is in oppressive situations.[150] To such questions no definitive answers are given. A possible answer is that God is slow to anger but will eventually bring judgment about. Or the resources through which God wants to bring judgment may not yet be available.

The prophet Habakkuk complains bitterly about God's absence in the midst of the violence and injustice of his day (1:1-4). He demands the divine presence to do something about it.[151] He will not silently accept the status quo as having been ordained by divine providence. God responds to him by revealing that the Babylonians will invade Israel as a punishment for sin (1:5-11). God has been waiting for the Babylonians' military might to grow so that he can make use of them. Habakkuk is dismayed and upset that God would use a people more wicked than the Israelites to punish the Israelites. He rebukes God for such an outrageous plan and accuses God of approving evil (1:12-17). God responds by asking Habakkuk to trust him and by giving him a vision in which God condemns the evil practices of both Israelite and Babylonian (2:2-20). Habakkuk, armed with a better understanding of God's hatred of sin, prays that God will remember mercy in wrath (3:2). The book concludes with Habakkuk's saying that he is terrified about the coming invasion, for it is going to be rough. Nevertheless, he confesses his trust in God his Savior. He believes that the divine wisdom in bringing judgment on the people is for their redemption—God has their best interests in mind. Habakkuk acknowledges that the divine absence as well as the divine presence in judgment are aspects of God's redemptive project.

3.15 The Potter and the Clay: An Examination of So-Called Pancausality Texts

"Just like the clay in the potter's hand, so are you in my hand, O house of Israel" (Jer 18:6; compare Is 29:16). The Old Testament describes God as directing the paths of people and kings (Prov 16:9; 21:1), of making dumb and deaf, seeing and blind (Ex 4:11) and of bringing calamity on the people of Israel (Is 45:7; Amos 3:6). The simile of potter and clay, along with the pancausality texts just cited, are typically used to claim that every single thing that happens should be ascribed to God, for God gets exactly what he wants.[152] This idea is so taken for granted that it goes largely unexamined. The evidence we have already surveyed indicating that God is in a dynamic give-and-take relationship with humans and in which God sometimes does not get what he wants is overturned. The verses just mentioned are identified as the "clear didactic" passages, whereas the others surveyed are mere anthropomorphisms. The verses interpreted as affirming divine pancausality of everything tell us the truth of the matter! Is this so?

A significant problem with this approach lies in hermeneutical malpractice on the part of many commentators and theologians. They jump from particular statements to universal statements. For instance, Calvin, after citing the texts about God's sending wind to feed Israel with birds and causing Jonah's ship trouble, says, "I infer that no wind ever arises or increases except by God's express command."[153] Moreover, after citing some particular divine blessings and judgments on the Israelites, he claims that not a single drop of rain falls without God's explicit command.[154] That God made use of wind and rain in his relationship with Israel is clear, but these particular actions in historical situations must not be turned into universal principles. This common practice of extracting a universal idea from a particular historical statement is used to overturn the pattern of the divine-human relationship we have discussed above. But our survey of Scripture showed that God has sovereignly decided not to "control" everything and his purposes can be rejected. This pattern of open relationship discloses the divine character and the project God desires to accomplish.

How should these so-called pancausality texts be understood? Fredrik Lindström's *God and the Origin of Evil: A Textual Analysis of Alleged Monistic Evidence in the Old Testament* provides a careful and detailed study of these texts. Lindström began his study to confirm a certain thesis: Old Testament writers believed that everything which happened was specifically controlled by God. In the process of working through the texts, however, he came to the opposite conclusion, that none of the passages cited as affirming divine causality of all good and evil do, in fact, teach this. The basic problem, he says, is that commentators rush to assert a universal principle instead of placing the texts in their literary and historical contexts. Also, they fail to conduct semantic field studies on the key terms.[155] Although Lindström's study covers a large number of texts, only the ones most commonly cited in support of divine pancausality will be examined here.

Isaiah 45:7 states, "I form light and create darkness, I make weal and create woe; I the LORD do all these things." Does this mean that God is responsible for every single act of good and evil in the entire cosmos? Not at all, for as Lindström observes, the entire section pertains to Yahweh's dealings with Israel, not the entire cosmos. This is evidenced by the terms used. "Light" (*'ôr*) is not used in Isaiah 40—55 to refer to cosmic creation. Rather, it is used as a metaphor for political liberation from the Babylonians (Is 42:6; 49:6; 53:11). The same is true of "darkness" (*hōšek*), which is a metaphor for misfortune and captivity (42:7; 47:5; 49:9). The creation verbs (*ysr, br'* and *'śh*) are used in this section to depict God's bringing about the impending liberation of Israel. Opinions differ about the particular historical event to which "darkness" refers. König believes that it refers to Israel's experience of the exile.[156] Their deportation to Babylon is the calamity that Yahweh brought on them. Lindström, however, sees here an antithetical reference: "the *positive* phrases 'who forms light' and 'who makes weal' have to do with Yahweh's saving intervention on behalf of his people, whereas the *negative* phrases 'who creates darkness' and 'who creates woe' refer to Yahweh's destruction of the Babylonian empire."[157] In either case the conclusion is the same: Isaiah 45:7 refers to the specific experiences of Israel in exile and not to divine pancausality. "I the LORD do all these things" alludes to the promise of the return from exile, not to every single event that happens in life.

"Does disaster befall a city, unless the LORD has done it?" (Amos 3:6). This is sometimes taken to mean that any and every calamity—every earthquake or terrorist bombing—that happens in the world is due to God. But this is not Amos's meaning, for he has a specific historical occasion in view. The prophet asserts that it is Yahweh who is bringing calamity on Israel.[158] The people were unwilling to recognize the Lord's hand against them (4:1-6; 9:10). They refused to believe that God would punish them for their sins, so they sought other explanations. Amos declares that God reveals his judgments on Israel to his prophets (3:7). The people should make no mistake: it is Yahweh who stands against them. Despite the fact that insurance companies refer to all natural disasters as "acts of God," this verse is not a general principle about divine pancausality. If it were, then we have some genuine problems, for "what sense would there be in God's punishing an evil action which he was himself in the last instance the cause of? What, for example, are we to gather from the fact that YHWH will punish the Ammonites for having ripped up pregnant women in Gilead (Amos 1:13) if the exegetes are correct in assuming that the ultimate cause of all evil is YHWH himself (3:6)?"[159]

Moreover, if God is thought of as "the ruler of history" such that all events in world history flow from his hand and if it is asserted that the biblical writers assumed this, then it makes no sense to say that the prophets proclaim that God is *now* bringing about this or that particular event because all events, in fact, are brought about by God (even if by secondary causes). If God is the cause of everything, then why single out certain things as being "from God"? If God foreordains every detail that happens, then it is incredible that things go so badly and so absolutely contrary to God's stated will. Is God inauthentic or perhaps even schizophrenic? Amos 3:7 asserts that no calamity befalls a city unless God reveals it to his prophets. If this were a universal statement, then we would expect God to give us advance notice of terrorist bombings. If Amos 3:6 is used to support divine determinism of all urban disasters, then, according to 3:7, there should be prophetic revelations concerning them. I am not aware of any such modern-day revelations, from the Oklahoma City bombing to the massacre of several children in a Scotland gymnasium. Problems such as these do not arise, however, if Amos 3:6 is understood as a particular pronouncement of divine judgment on the sins of Israel.

The same line of interpretation holds true for Lamentations 3:38, which reads, "Is it not from the mouth of the Most High that good and bad come?" Although many take this to refer to disasters in general rather than the calamity of the Israelite exile, Lindström's study demonstrates that a contextual analysis shows that only a singular historical event is in view. The verses immediately prior to 3:38 assert that the "bad" that has come on Israel is a consequence of sin. There is no arbitrary judgment or capricious action by God here. The context of 3:38 follows the sequence of ideas contained in Deuteronomy 30:1-3, the covenant treaty. Deuteronomy 28—30 refers to blessings and curses, life and death depending on whether the covenant people remain faithful to God. The book of Lamentations alludes to these treaty curses with statements that passersby will shudder (Lam 2:15; 3:46; Deut 28:37), that parents will eat the flesh of their children (Lam 2:20; 4:10; Deut 28:53) and that wives will be ravished (Lam 5:11; Deut 28:30). Consequently, Lamentations 3:38 asserts that the specific historical calamity of the exile, not all calamity in general, is brought about by God.

Proverbs 16:9 declares that "the human mind plans the way, but the LORD directs the steps." Proverbs 21:1 says that "the king's heart is a stream of water in the hand of the LORD; he turns it wherever he will." A couple of points may be made about these verses. First, these sayings, along with all the others in Proverbs, should be understood as guidelines for godly living rather than universal principles that always hold true. Taking every proverb as a universal principle results in contradictions (for they simply cannot all be practiced at the same time, for example, 26:4-5) and inaccuracies (for example, it is not always true that a quiet answer turns away wrath, 15:1). The proverbs about human plans and the Lord's purposes should be seen in terms of the book's call for seeking the covenant God's wisdom in our planning. The God of Israel desires that his people seek his input instead of doing what they (on their own) think is best. Just as with Adam in the garden, so for the people of Israel. No one can chart a wise course through life without trusting in divine wisdom (20:24). God directs his people's steps (16:9) and guides the king of Israel (21:1) when they seek God's wisdom. When they do not, God stands against them. Though some kings "did right in the eyes of the Lord" (for example, 2 Chron 20:32; 25:2), others, such as Saul, did not (for example, 1 Sam 15:11; 2 Kings 16:2; 2 Chron 28:1).

If we take Proverbs 21:1 as a universal statement, then we have the problem of explaining why God became angry with the Israelite kings who broke the covenant, when they were only doing what God wanted. How could the Lord want people to break his covenant? The very idea is blasphemous. Those who universalize this text to include all kings everywhere must conclude that all the evil they ever committed in history is exactly what God wanted from them, since they, like water, could not but go in the direction God's hand determined.

In Exodus 4:11 God responds to Moses' protestations of personal inadequacy by saying that he is the creator of the human mouth and is responsible for the dumb and the deaf, the sighted and the blind. Some interpret this to mean that every single case of physical defect is specifically brought about by God. They "are not merely the product of defective genes or birth accidents. Those things may indeed by [sic] the immediate cause, but behind them is the sovereign purpose of God. . . . No person in this world was ever blind that God has not planned for him to be blind."[160] Others, however, interpret this verse as a statement that because God created Moses, God can use him despite this weaknesses. God created human sensation, and God takes full responsibility for creating a world in which such gifts might be defective. This is a general statement that such things happen in God's world. Fretheim observes: "The text does *not* say, however, that this divine activity is *individually applied,* as if God entered into the womb of every pregnant woman and determined whether and how a child would have disabilities."[161] Evangelical commentator Walter Kaiser writes, "While God was not to be blamed for directly creating any defects, his wise providence in allowing these deprivations as well as his goodness in bestowing their ordinary functions mirrors his ability to meet any emergency Moses might have suggested."[162]

God gave the created order, and especially the human order, integrity and otherness. Although the creation owes its being to God, God grants it space to be different. In working with his creatures, God sometimes seems to act alone, demonstrating his special providence, for instance, at the crossing of the Sea of Reeds, the capture of Jericho (for which God gave ridiculous military instructions) and the feeding of the multitude in the wilderness. Normally, however, God "feeds" the people through their wise agricultural practices and grants them victory over enemies (for example, Ai) by exercising sound military strategy. Although God occasionally takes center stage (usually at the beginning of a new work) doing things for the people, normally God provides the wisdom that humans need for living properly in the created order. Even miracles make use of resources available in the created order (for example, wind parted the Sea of Reeds and locusts destroyed crops). Some texts say that God directly controls the natural elements, whereas other texts ascribe to them a degree of autonomy (for example, Hag 1:10-11).[163]

Like other metaphors for God, such as hen, rock and father, the potter metaphor says something true about God's relationship with his people. But it does not explain the whole truth or even the only truth. There is an element of truth in describing God as a mother hen, but it is not the sole truth, and not every aspect of "henship" should be attributed to God. Similarly, in certain respects God can rightfully be described as a potter, but God is not a potter in all respects. To the Western mind, clay is inanimate and cannot resist the potter. It is thus not surprising that this metaphor serves as a controlling metaphor in many theological discussions of providence, since it comports well with the notion that God meticulously controls everything. We are simply clay in the potter's hands. In the words of G. C. Berkouwer: "Scripture nowhere suggests that God's work is limited by human activity."[164]

The use of the potter and clay metaphor in the Bible does not, however, sustain such a conclusion.[165] In Isaiah 29:15-16 and 45:9-13 the metaphor occurs in a debate about whether God has the right to perform certain actions. Some people, far from being passive "clay," were claiming that God was doing things he had no right to do. Isaiah responds by saying that God, as Creator and potter, is fully within his rights in these cases. If God, in sovereign concern for his people, decides it is best to bring judgment on them, that is his prerogative.[166] In Jeremiah 18 it is also a question of divine prerogative. Does not God have the right to change his plans regarding Israel? Cannot God change his mind about a prophecy he has given if the people's behavior warrants such a change (18:7-10)? The metaphor of potter and clay leads some people to expect a clear assertion of God's complete control of Israel. But such is not the case. Jeremiah repeatedly speaks of the conditional ("if") in connection to both the clay (Israel) and the potter (God). If Israel repents, then God will relent. If Israel is recalcitrant, then God may change his mind regarding the promised blessing (vv. 7-10). Brueggemann refers to this as "Yahweh's responsive sovereignty."[167] The fact that Israel can take initiative violates the metaphor, since clay cannot take initiative. So the relationship between Yahweh and Israel is not exactly like that of a potter and clay.

For Jeremiah, the word of the Lord does not foreclose the future but opens up new possibilities. The people are called to a decision that will affect the future for both God and themselves. In this respect God is like a potter. When the clay does not turn out as anticipated, the potter changes his mind and works to reshape the clay into something else. But why would the clay not turn out the way God intended? Either because God is not a skilled enough potter, or because there is some defect in the clay. If God exercises meticulous control over his clay, then the problem is definitely with God. The texts using the potter metaphor, however, place the blame on the clay, which resists the will of the potter. Neither Isaiah nor Jeremiah consider the clay (the people) to be inanimate objects incapable of resisting the divine potter. Rather, the divine potter desires to shape the human clay into a particular type of vessel: one that responds to the divine love with trusting obedience—a kingdom of priests. God is carrying out the project of creating a people who are holy and loving. The potter wants a vessel that redounds to his glory. But this particular clay has rejected the divine project. The people do not want what God wants. Hence, the potter-clay metaphor must be understood in terms of the give-and-take relationship that God has sovereignly established. It should not be understood as teaching total divine control over all things, since the biblical writers do not make use of this aspect of the metaphor.

To sum up, God does bring about particular blessings to his people as well as particular calamities in response to their breaking the covenant. But God is not behind every single event that happens in life. When some biblical figures attributed adverse events to God, they were in error (for example, 1 Sam 23:7; 2 Sam 4:8; 18:31).[168] The so-called pancausality texts refer to specific actions of God and must not be understood as generalizations about divine action. Moreover, God is indeed a potter and a king but one whose clay and subjects sometimes cooperate with and sometimes rebel against divine initiatives. At times the rebellious subjects even kill the king's messengers. The clay refuses to be shaped in the direction the potter desires. In response, God sometimes brings events to a determined head and at other times allows events to go their way. This results in a messy view of providence. Deism and pancausality offer more straightforward perspectives in which God uniformly does nothing or uniformly does everything. But God has sovereignly decided to providentially operate in a dynamic give-and-take relationship with his creatures.

3.16 Divine Love and Humiliation

God loves his creation. Out of this love, God takes steps to redeem creation when it goes astray. God sovereignly makes himself vulnerable because he cares for his creatures and gets involved with them. Even wrathful judgment expresses this divine love. God does not stand idly by and watch his beloved ruin herself. The love God has for his people is neither indifferent nor soft. It is a powerful love that acts in the best interest of the beloved. Several metaphors are used to describe the depth of this love. God carried Israel in his arms as a parent carries a child (Deut 1:31). Israel is God's firstborn son (Ex 4:22), whom God birthed and nursed as a mother does (Is 49:15). God longingly remembers the period of his betrothal to Israel (Jer 2:2). Finally, Hosea calls on an intimate metaphor from human experience: God is Israel's husband.[169]

God's love and concern take preeminence in the theophany given to Moses (Ex 34:6-7) and in two of Israel's creedal statements (Joel 2:13; Jon

4:2). As God continued to work with his people, love took center stage as the key characteristic of God.[170] Yahweh loves with an "everlasting love" (Jer 31:3) and so continues in his faithfulness. Hosea says that despite such faithful love, God's beloved committed adultery and thus inflicted anguish on God. Israel's faithlessness is inexplicable. Despite her turning to prostitution, God seeks her out and desires her restoration. God is willing to humiliate himself by taking back this disreputable woman as his wife.[171] Hosea describes God as a husband. But the typical human husband would divorce his wife, wanting nothing more to do with such a harlot. It is difficult to imagine a human husband who would do what God does, for it would mean self-humiliation in the face of one's community. God, however, is the true husband whose ways are not our ways (Is 55:8). God suffers the humiliation and risks taking back his unfaithful bride in the hope that the relationship can develop into one of mutual love and respect.

3.17 Conclusion

The Old Testament shows that God has, in sovereign freedom, decided to place himself in fundamental relatedness to his creation. It is a world in which he grants integrity to his creatures and singles out human beings for a special relationship involving genuine give-and-take dynamics. The divine-human relationship is to be one of reciprocal love. God loves his creatures and desires to bless them with all that is in their best interest. In return, God expects people to trust him and manifest that trust by collaborating with him toward the fulfillment of the divine project. Despite human rebellion God remains faithful to his project of seeking restoration of the broken relationship. God initiates new developments but is open to input from his creatures. God has a goal but remains flexible as to the details of its accomplishment. Sometimes God's plans do not bring about the desired result and must be judged a failure. The covenant history records many disasters and setbacks for God. Nonetheless, God resourcefully tries out different paths in his efforts to bring his project toward a successful completion. God's activity does not unfold according to some heavenly blueprint whereby all goes according to plan.[172] God is involved in a historical project, not an eternal plan. The project does not proceed in a smooth, monolithic way but takes surprising twists and turns because the divine-human relationship involves a genuine give-and-take dynamic for both humanity and God.

The type of relationship God offers his people is not one of control and domination but rather one of powerful love and vulnerability.

God establishes the relationship in such a way that he risks the possibility of rejection. The divine project of developing people who freely enter into a loving and trusting relationship with God lacks an unconditional guarantee of success. Will anyone trust God? God expected positive results, but all things have not gone as God desired. God nevertheless continued to invest himself in the project in the hope of regaining what was lost. The Old Testament reveals God's actions and God's incredible persistence in seeking to bring his project to fruition. The New Testament witnesses the continuation of God's providential risk taking, and to this I now turn.

FOUR

NEW TESTAMENT MATERIALS FOR A RELATIONAL VIEW OF PROVIDENCE INVOLVING RISK

. . . .

4.1 Introduction

In this chapter I do not attempt to cover all of the New Testament in demonstrating that God enters into genuine give-and-take relations with humans—relationships in which God takes risks. Rather, I focus on the person and work of Jesus, for it is in Jesus that God does something radically different in terms of the divine-human relationship. Earlier God had spoken through the prophets, and now he speaks through the Son (Heb 1:1-2). It is in Jesus that God comes to us in a most distinct and revealing way. In Jesus, God incarnate, we have the ultimate anthropomorphism. Becoming human is a most scandalous thing for God to do. Gregory of Nyssa remarked that the incarnation and the cross of Jesus manifest the transcendent power of God in a more luminescent way than miracles or the vastness of the creation.[1] If Jesus is *the* ultimate revelation of who God is and what humans are supposed to be in relationship to God, then we should pay particular attention to the way divine providence works in the life of Jesus.

Strangely, most studies of providence say little or nothing about the words and works of Jesus. They typically pay a lot of attention to the relationship between the ideas of omnipotence and goodness while ignoring the revelation of providence in the life of Jesus. Karl Barth criticized Protestant orthodoxy for being "blatantly 'liberal'" in deriving the doctrine of providence primarily from the concept of absolute omnipotence rather than from Jesus Christ.[2] When the Bible is used, the Joseph story (understood from a risk-free model) functions as the paradigm for understanding providence. Not only does the classical tradition fail to begin with Jesus, it also, as T. J. Gorringe observes, passes over the Old Testament motifs of God as servant and as sufferer in favor of the metaphors of king and lord understood by "direct and non-inverted analogy with earthly rulers."[3] The task of a Christian doctrine of providence is to understand the "foolishness of God" in the life of Jesus.

According to the Gospel of John, Jesus is the divine word who became human and tabernacled among us, displaying his glory (1:14). Moses requested to see the divine glory, but God denied his request and instead allowed Moses to experience the proclamation of the divine name (Ex 33:18—34:7). In Jesus, however, we have the divine glory and the divine name itself in human form; one who has seen Jesus has seen God (Jn 14:9). Jesus Christ in his humanity is constitutive of the very nature of God, for he is the definitive self-revelation and self-communication of God to us. Taking a close look at the life of Jesus can show us how providence is exercised. We can learn to appreciate the power of faithful love when we understand that everything is not unfolding according to some eternal movie God produced. In Jesus we see the genuine character of God, who is neither an omnipotent tyrant nor an impotent wimp.

In this chapter I examine Jesus' life and teachings to see what providence entails before moving on to other passages in the New Testament. Though there are few New Testament studies of providence from a relational perspective, E. Frank Tupper's *A Scandalous Providence: The Jesus Story of the Compassion of God* is quite helpful.[4] Tupper examines several episodes in the life of Jesus (primarily from the Gospel of Matthew) in order to see what is being said about providence. I summarize his discussion and then look at God's attempt to unite Jews and Gentiles into one body in the church, since this project sheds light on the nature of divine providence.

4.2 The Baptism

"This is my Son, the Beloved" (Mt 3:17). Tupper begins his study with the baptism in order to clarify the type of relationship Jesus had with God.[5] Jesus is described as the "beloved" Son, a filial relationship akin to Abraham and Isaac's. Moreover, Jesus prayed to the "Father" and taught his disciples to do the same (Mt 6:9), revealing that God intends for us to have a filial relationship with him. From the beginning God intended to bless his creatures with his presence. Yahweh brought his presence near to the people of Israel in various ways. Through Jesus we can experience the divine presence as *Abba,* or Father.[6] It is not some remote deity of justice or a distant creator who comes to us but the heavenly Father who desires to bless us through Jesus. The king of creation does not intimidate us or dominate us, as in the traditional monarchical model of providence. Instead, the king sends his son in order to reconcile us, making us children of the king and siblings of Christ. God is indeed King and Father, though an atypical king and father.

4.3 The Birth of Jesus and the Bethlehem Massacre

Matthew 1—2 and Exodus 1—2 contain several parallels that link the birth stories of Jesus and Moses. In both there is a royal decree, parents who actively respond to the decree, fearful kings, slaughter of male babies and people on the run from the authorities (exile). In Exodus God chose to work through, and so became dependent on, weak persons (Hebrew and Egyptian women) in that situation. God became genuinely dependent on the women and did not merely work through them in the sense of "secondary causes." It is the same in the New Testament. Commentators customarily emphasize God's unilateral intervention—he was completely independent of all human agency—when speaking of the incarnation.[7] But such is not the case. In the Gospel of Luke an angel informs Mary of God's desire to bless her with a special child (1:26-33). Mary, however, does not simply acquiesce. She does what her Old Testament counterparts did, pondering the angel's words and asking a question (1:29, 34).[8] She is not condemned for questioning a divine plan; she is given an explanation. Satisfied, she grants her consent to participate in this activity of God. God does not unilaterally achieve his goal of incarnation by forcing his will on Mary. God brings it about with Mary's active participation. If Mary had declined or if Moses' mother had let her son drown, then God would have sought other avenues. After all, it is doubtful that there was only one maiden in all of Israel through whom God could work. God is resourceful in finding people and then equipping them with the elements necessary for accomplishing his purposes.

Mary needs God's resourcefulness, since she is engaged to Joseph. When Joseph finds out that Mary is pregnant, he assumes that she has been unfaithful and decides to divorce her. Perhaps because Davidic sonship is conferred on Jesus by Joseph, God intervenes in an attempt to persuade Joseph that Mary is righteously participating in an act of God. Joseph asks no questions and consents to cooperate in this event. Even with their cooperation, God's entry into the world is surrounded by scandal. In fact, the lineage of the Messiah is robed in sexual scandal. In the genealogy Matthew lists four women: Tamar, Rahab, Ruth and Bathsheba. Tupper observes that each woman was involved in some sort of sexual scandal and that all were active participants in their respective situations.[9] In bringing the Messiah into the world, God seeks the cooperation of people of faith, but he does not draw back from situations lacking public respectability. Mary and Joseph are placed in a predicament in which they may either reject God's desires and keep their public respectability or trust God and subject themselves to possible lifelong disfavor. They place their confidence in God and consent to the risk this entails. God places his trust in them, giving his consent to the risks involved. The incarnation does not come about through sheer overwhelming power but through the vulnerability of being genuinely dependent on some Jewish peasants.

The Magi visited the family in Bethlehem and probably had several conversations with Joseph. One can imagine Joseph's shock when he was informed what the Magi had told Herod. Referring to this baby boy as the "king of the Jews" in front of Herod is tantamount to signing his death certificate. Joseph and the Magi would no doubt be troubled by this turn of events. Working with the resources available now that the danger is known, God warns the Magi and Joseph of the danger they are in through dreams. Tupper observes that the dreams in Matthew 1—2 are grounded in human awareness of the situation. This new information makes it possible for God to provide the needed warning. In response, Mary and Joseph trust God and flee to Egypt.

When Herod's soldiers arrive, they kill children aged two years and younger, producing great mourning in the village. Matthew then quotes Jeremiah 31:15, claiming that this text is "fulfilled" (2:17-18). Questions flood out of this story. Why does God not warn the other parents?[10] Does God not care for the other children? Does God play favorites? What of God's intended blessing for these children and their families? Did this happen according to some predetermined plan? Tupper provides some needed responses.[11] First, divine providence is exercised "in conjunction with and conditioned by the historically defined context of time and place, the participation of human agents, the extent of the development in the situation, and the limits and possibilities available."[12] According to the knowledge of Joseph and the Magi, Jesus was the only child in danger. The angel had warned that Herod was looking for only this child. Working within the limits of the context, a warning to all Bethlehem would not make sense. Second, I do not believe Matthew understood Jeremiah 31:15 to be a prediction of a far distant event. Rather, it was seen as a reaction to the exile. Thus this verse from Jeremiah is "fulfilled" in the sense that what had happened before is being repeated.[13] It was neither predicted nor desired by God. The Bethlehem massacre was not the will of God and was not planned beforehand by God. Instead, it reveals that the will of God in its fullness may not be fulfilled in all situations.

4.4 The Temptation of Jesus

Just as God tested Abraham and Israel in the wilderness to see whether or not they trusted him, so now the Spirit drives Jesus into the wilderness to be tested by the devil (Mt 4:1).[14] Leaving aside the debate about whether or not Jesus could have failed the test, I wish to focus on the sort of messiahship the temptation narratives disclose.[15] That Jesus is the Son of God is not doubted by either the devil or by Jesus. The issue in the temptations is the proper role of Jesus as the Son of God, the Messiah.[16] In Genesis 2—3 we saw that God's word was open to interpretation, an opening that the serpent exploited. With all the messianic speculation going on in second-temple Judaism, there were various understandings of what the Messiah would do. The devil uses this state of unsettledness to see what path Jesus will take. Will he use his privileged status to turn stones into bread in order to feed not only himself but others? Will he apply certain Scriptures to himself to the effect that the Son of God cannot be harmed physically? Both of these would meet common messianic expectations and would carry tremendous political weight. The Messiah was expected to rule the world. Would Jesus take the devil's path in achieving this end? The world in which Jesus lived was one of brutal military repression, ruthless political and religious leadership, poverty and lack of shalom. Jesus had the power to overcome all this rather quickly. Some of Jesus' contemporaries understood the Old Testament to warrant such a path.

In the end all authority will be given to Jesus (Mt 28:18), but the path to his victory led through death and resurrection. The way of God in Jesus will not be achieved through overwhelming power or invulnerability. Jesus acknowledges his place as a creature of God dependent on divine provision, which entails the possibility that he shall go hungry and be susceptible to injury. Jesus accepts the finite conditions of existence as a blessing from God. Consequently, he does not accept the Old Testament "prediction" that the Messiah would be immune from bodily harm (Ps 91:11-12) as applicable to himself. Jesus trusts in the same providence that covers all humans. This involves acknowledging the risk and vulnerability we experience in life. Providence does not mean protection from the vicissitudes of life. Jesus chooses the path of faithful trust in God the Father in the midst of life's uncertainties. "What does it mean to worship and serve the *Abba* God?" asks Tupper. "It includes the renunciation of dominating power and overwhelming force as the way to accomplish the will of God."[17] The way of God in the world is not a display of raw omnipotence—a love of power—but the power of love. It is in this that Jesus trusts.

4.5 Confession and Transfiguration

Wherever Jesus travels, people are discussing his identity. In Matthew 16 Jesus asks his disciples what the word about him is on the street. Most believe that Jesus is some sort of great prophet. When he asks his disciples for their opinion, Peter declares that Jesus is the Messiah, the Son of the living God (16:16). Jesus informs Peter that he is correct and orders the disciples not to reveal his identity to others. Moreover, he begins to instruct them that as the Messiah he will suffer, be rejected, be killed and be raised to life again (16:21). Jesus repeats this message several times on his way to Jerusalem, but the disciples fail to grasp it. Their preunderstanding of what a messiah should be and do filters Jesus' words. The Messiah was to be an invincible, dominating ruler, rendering the pagan gods impotent and forcing the pagans to acknowledge the only true God. The Messiah would rid Israel's temple and land of pagan pollution.[18] That the disciples held this belief firmly is witnessed by the testimony of two disciples on the Emmaus road. They *thought,* mistakenly, that Jesus was going to be the "one to redeem Israel" (Lk 24:21). It is not until long after the resurrection that the disciples began to radically modify their preunderstanding of messianism. There is certainly enough material in the Old Testament to support their preunderstanding (but there is also enough room for God to decide to take a different path). It is not surprising, then, that Peter openly rejects the notion of a vulnerable, suffering Messiah (16:22). Who desires that sort of risky road? For Jesus, the way of the Messiah will involve vulnerable love, not political might. This was hard for the disciples to grasp, given their particular reading of Old Testament messiahship. (It is also difficult for us to accept, given our views of omnipotence.)

Matthew follows up this story with the transfiguration episode. Commentators regularly point out the numerous linkages in this story to the life of Moses.[19] Jesus is portrayed as the new Moses leading a new exodus (see Lk 9:31). The imagery might have led the disciples to conclude that their views of what the Messiah will do were correct: Jesus will overthrow the oppressive foreign regime in liberating the people. In fact, Jesus will do this but not in the *way* they thought. There will be another exodus but with some key differences. There will be a killing of the firstborn son, only this time it will be God's son rather than the sons of the oppressors. There will be liberation from the power of sin and death rather than immediate liberation from tyrannical political power. The new exodus will take place through the weakness of God on the cross rather than through the powerful yet destructive plagues. The new exodus is the old exodus in reverse. Although Jesus is the new Moses and the prophet par excellence, God is going about things in a quite different fashion.[20] During the transfiguration God says again that Jesus is his beloved Son with whom he is pleased and that we should listen to him (17:5). God approves of the way of Jesus in the world, a way of trust in the loving Father despite the vicissitudes of life. In Jesus, God is going about things in a new way even while being faithful to his purpose; we do well to pay attention.

4.6 Compassion, Dialogue and Healing Grace

The Gospels record a variety of miracles that Jesus performed. He healed many, but certainly not most, of the sick in Israel. Jesus showed concern for those around him. At one point after teaching and healing for three days in a remote place, Jesus said, "I have compassion for the crowd, because they have been with me now for three days and have nothing to eat; and I do not want to send them away hungry, for they might faint on the way" (Mt 15:32). Thus Jesus' miraculous feeding of the four thousand does not occur out of thin air. The people involved in the miracle have entered into relationship with Jesus, and Jesus works to enlarge the resources available. Divine providence occurs within historically contextualized settings. Miracles such as this do not just happen anytime, anywhere for any reason. The messiahship of Jesus is being demonstrated, and the people are open to this message. God works through this setting and the available resources to bless them.

Many healings result from dialogue with Jesus, showing that a willingness to enter into relationship with Jesus is an important element in the healing. In one such story a Canaanite woman beseeches Jesus to have mercy on behalf of her daughter (Mt 15:21-28). Jesus does not immediately address the woman, but she persists and causes a scene. Finally, Jesus tells her that his mission is to Israelites alone. She refuses to accept this answer and bows before him, begging for help. Jesus says that it is not good to give the children's bread to the dogs (15:26)—his mission is to the Israelites. The woman refuses to give up, however, and comes back with a rejoinder that acknowledges the propriety of Jesus' mission but still seeks a blessing. "Yes, Lord, yet even the dogs eat the crumbs that fall from their masters' table" (15:27). Like Jacob wrestling with God, she refuses to let Jesus go until he blesses her daughter. In response, Jesus grants her petition, and her daughter is healed. Although Jesus initially resisted giving her what she desired, she persuaded Jesus that her request did fit into his mission. Jesus here evinces an openness even to Gentile women.

Other healings exhibit Jesus' openness to others even to the extent that he changes his plans. In Luke 8:43-48 Jesus is on his way to heal a young girl. A woman in the crowd who is ritually unclean according to the Levitical code reaches out and touches him. When Jesus inquires who touched him, she remains silent, for she knows that anyone she touches is made ceremonially impure. Finally she confesses her deed and explains her motive. After she enters into dialogue and expresses trust in Jesus, Jesus responds, "Daughter, your faith has made you well; go in peace" (Lk 8:48). Commenting on this story, Jürgen Moltmann says that Jesus "grows from the expectations of the sick and in this atmosphere learns what the kingdom of God in its reality is."[21] On another occasion some friends bring a paralyzed man to Jesus, but they cannot get close to him because there is a crowd in the house (Mk 2). Undeterred, they go up on the roof, dig a hole in it and let their paralyzed friend down in front of Jesus on ropes. No dialogue takes place in this encounter, but their actions speak louder than words. In light of *their* faith Jesus heals the man. In this story it is the faith of the man's friends that seems to have an effect on Jesus. The faith of the community seems to have a role in shaping what God actually decides to do.

People's faith, or lack of it, deeply affected Jesus and his ministry. Mark says that Jesus could not perform many miracles in Nazareth due to the lack of faith by the people in the community (6:5-6). Their unbelief did not completely tie God's hands, but it seriously altered what Jesus would have done had they been more receptive to his message.[22] Not only did the response of the community affect what Jesus did, it also disturbed him. "Apparently Jesus had not anticipated the reaction of the people,"[23] for "he was amazed at their unbelief" (6:6). Oftentimes what God decides to do is conditioned on the faith or unbelief of people. As James says, we have not because we ask not (Jas 4:2).

In these stories some people believe that God is doing something special in Jesus and so are willing to enter into trusting relationship with him. At times Jesus does not seem interested in granting their requests or, in the case of the paralytic, is busy teaching. Jesus did not intend or plan to heal the woman with the hemorrhage or the daughter of the Canaanite woman.[24] Nevertheless, Jesus shows himself flexible and open to what arises in the situations, making use of them in trusting service to his heavenly Father. The particular acts of providence manifested in the ministry of Jesus are dependent on the attitudes and responses of the people he encounters. Sometimes what God wants to accomplish is brought about only when others enter into a relationship of faith. Jesus was unable to do some of the things he wanted to do because of a lack of faith in the community. In light of these stories we begin to see that everything is not following a predetermined plan.

Jesus' healings reveal God's opposition to sickness. The people Jesus healed were not made ill by God in order to identify Jesus as the Messiah. Jesus is not going around "cleaning up" the diseases God has spread (as is the case if one affirms divine pancausality). Jesus and the Father stand against that which destroys the health that God, as our Creator, intends for us.

4.7 Gethsemane: The Pathos of Jesus

The Gospels record that Jesus celebrated the Passover with his disciples before going to the garden. During the meal he claims that one of the disciples will "hand him over" (*paradidomi* does not mean "betray") to the temple authorities (Mt 26:21; Lk 22:21; Jn 13:21). Each disciple thinks that Jesus is referring to himself and none thinks of Judas. Because Judas has come to symbolize villainy, we tend to think Jesus' words are clear and that everything is working out according to some foreordained plan. But such is not the case.

William Klassen's exegetical study of the Judas narratives demonstrates that Judas was not "betraying" Jesus.[25] Judas was an apostle, a recognized member of the twelve disciples. He was on friendly terms with Jesus, who washed his feet at the last supper and sanctioned his mission of handing him over. According to Klassen,

> Judas became convinced, after discussion with Jesus himself, that an opportunity to meet with the high priest and those in authority in the Temple needed to be arranged. Jesus' own teaching had stressed that when a fellow Jew sins, one speaks to him directly about it (Matt 18:15-20//Luke 17:3). . . . Had the time come for him to confront the high priest?[26]

Judas may have thought that Jesus and the high priest could resolve their differences and bring about needed reforms. Jesus, no doubt, had his own agenda in mind for such a meeting. Regardless, Jesus instructs Judas to carry out this mission—"Do quickly what you are going to do" (Jn 13:27). Klassen finds it dubious that this injunction implies that Jesus "allowed his fellow Jew to write a passage ticket to hell," for it "would have violated a fundamental rule of Judaism if Jesus had told Judas to go out and deliberately commit a sin."[27] In this light it is clear that Judas is not betraying Jesus and that Jesus is not issuing any prediction of such activity.

It is not necessary to follow Klassen's interpretation to rule out a prediction about a betrayal. Jesus undoubtedly had plenty of discussions with his disciples in small groups and individually as they traveled about. Jesus and Judas (the treasurer of the group) would have had opportunity to discuss and debate the role of the Messiah. Perhaps Judas had a staunch commitment to a traditional nationalistic understanding of messiahship. Jesus, who had chosen Judas in good faith to be his disciple (he did not choose him to be a betrayer), would undoubtedly seek to transform Judas's view of the matter. Jesus had not been overly successful in reshaping the disciples' understanding messiahship in general, and Judas was apparently no exception.

But Jesus does not simply give up on Judas. It seems likely that at the Passover meal Judas was given the place of honor to Jesus' left (Jn 13:26).[28] Moreover, Jesus' act of dipping the bread into the bowl and giving it to Judas would have been seen as an act of friendship without any negative intentions.[29] Through such gestures Jesus was reaching out to Judas, seeking to change his direction. One can envision Jesus looking Judas in the eye, probing him, bringing him to a point of decision. After this moment Jesus says, "Do quickly what you are going to do" (Jn 13:27). Jesus here pushes Judas to show his cards, to make up his mind regarding what sort of messiah he desires Jesus to be. A risk is involved here, since there is no guarantee which way Judas will decide. Judas does "lay down his cards" and takes steps that he believes will force Jesus to show his hand. Judas gambles on his hunch that being confronted by the authorities will force Jesus to take on the role of political liberator and thus become a "genuine" messiah. None of this was predetermined.[30] Genuine options face both Jesus and Judas. The actual course of divine providence works itself out through and in response to these specific human choices. Jesus sought to change Judas's mind but apparently without success. Judas leaves the group and goes to the high priest.

At any rate, Jesus had reason to be deeply troubled. He leaves the meal and goes to the garden of Gethsemane, asking Peter, James and John to stay near him and pray. Jesus, deeply troubled (*agōnia*, Lk 22:44) about coming events, needs to pray about them and wants his friends pray for him and for their own testing in this time of crisis.[31] But his closest friends, failing to grasp the gravity of the situation, fall asleep. Jesus prays alone.

Three times Jesus prays the same prayer: "My Father, if it is possible, let this cup pass from me; yet not what I want but what you want" (Mt 26:39). This prayer is remarkable for several reasons. First, Jesus prays to his Father (*Abba* in Mk 14:36), not some distant and unconcerned deity. Jesus has an intimate relationship with God the Father and assumes that God is concerned. Second, he does not want to drink from the "cup" about which he has been telling the disciples he must drink. The cup is Old Testament imagery for the divine wrath (Is 51:17, 22; Ezek 23:32-34).[32] Jesus understands that he is being asked to experience death—the reward for sin. Like Habakkuk, he peers into the depths of the silence of God, into divine judgment, and is terrified by what he sees. He knows that just as in the Old Testament divine wrath was exercised for redemptive purposes, so it will be this time. Even though the love of God is the driving force behind the divine wrath, it does not make the experience of the wrath less painful.

Tupper observes a third aspect to this prayer: "The prayer is not the simple petition: 'Give me the strength to drink this cup.' Rather, he prayed: 'Remove this cup from me.'"[33] Although Jesus has repeatedly attempted to instruct his disciples about the particular path he, as Messiah, will take, he shows some hesitancy now. Is the path set in concrete? Must Jesus go this route even if he has misgivings? Matthew has Jesus say, "*if* it is possible" (26:39), and Luke reads, "*if* you are willing, remove this cup" (22:42). In Mark it is proposed that it is possible for the Father to do this because "all things are possible" for him (14:36). Yet Jesus finishes his petition with "not what I want but what you want." The prayer of submission is often seen as discrediting the prayer of petition. But Jesus presented this petition three times and requested not the strength to travel the path but an alternate route. His petition, "let this cup pass from me," is not empty rhetoric but a serious effort to determine the will of God. Jesus wrestles with God's will because he does not believe that everything must happen according to a predetermined plan. Even the Son of God must search and seek for the Father's will, for the Son is not following a script but is living in dynamic relationship with the Father. Together they determine what the will of God is for this historical situation. Although Scripture attests that the incarnation was planned from the creation of the world, this is not so with the cross. The path of the cross comes about only through God's interaction with humans in history. Until this moment in history other routes were, perhaps, open. Picking up again the illustration used in God's dealing with Pharaoh, it can be said that Jesus is in the canoe heading for the falls. There is yet time to get over to shore and portage around the falls. Jesus seeks to determine if that option meets with his Father's favor. But the canyon narrows even for God.

Isaac asked Abraham where the lamb was for the offering. Jesus is wondering whether his Father will supply a lamb. God stopped Abraham from offering Isaac, but God will not stop himself from offering his Son. Jesus is the lamb supplied. Providence has taken many a strange and twisting turn on its road to Calvary. In Gethsemane Jesus wonders whether there is another way. But Father and Son, in seeking to accomplish the project, both come to understand that there is no other way. Tupper writes,

> In Gethsemane Jesus learned with utmost clarity the limitations within the commitments of the identity of God, the limits that inhere in the freedom of God's love. . . . Now the Kingdom of God arriving with Jesus collided with the limitation of God in the dying of Jesus. The cross of rejection proved inevitable for the incarnation of the Kingdom. So God could not save Jesus from the cross and be who the *Abba* God is.[34]

After his session of wrestling with the Father Jesus no longer questions which path to take. Will this gambit work?

The notion that the cross was not planned prior to creation will seem scandalous to some readers. Scriptural and theological objections may be raised against the notion that the crucifixion was not set in stone prior to the creation. Texts such as Psalm 22:16, Ephesians 1:4, 1 Peter 1:20, and Revelation 13:8 and 17:8 are alleged to conflict with such an understanding. However, it is interesting that the New Testament writers do not make use of Psalm 22:16, although the church has made great use of it. Since the time of Justin Martyr Christians have used this verse to prove that the crucifixion was predicted. The Hebrew text of the Psalm reads "like a lion at my hands and feet," hardly a prediction of the crucifixion. But with a subtle change in Hebrew the text may be rendered, as many of our modern translations do, "they pierced my hands and my feet," which some take to imply foreknowledge of the crucifixion.[35] The Hebrew of this verse is not entirely clear and has occasioned much discussion. The reference to the crucifixion in it is doubtful. What is clear, however, is that many Christians have used this verse to justify belief in divine foreknowledge.

First Peter 1:20 says that God foreknew Christ and thus can be understood as affirming that the cross was foreknown from eternity. But this verse does not necessitate such an interpretation, and so there is no problem for the relational model. All that is required is that the incarnation of the Son was decided on from the beginning as part of the divine project.

Ephesians 1:4 says that God chose us in Christ beforehand, and Revelation 17:8 says certain names have been written in a book from the foundation of the world.[36] Again, this is no problem if taken to refer to something like "corporate election," whereby God elects a course of action and certain conditions by which people will be counted as "in Christ." According to corporate election it is the group—the body of Christ—that is foreordained from the foundation of the world, not specific individuals selected by God for salvation.[37] Moreover, Revelation is an apocalyptic genre that suffers from an overly literal interpretation. John's point is to assure the audience that God is on their side and that they are safe with God.

Revelation 13:8 is a bit more problematic.[38] Translators disagree about the syntax of the verse. What was it in particular that happened before the foundation of the world? Should it be understood, as is 17:8, that it is our names that were written in the book before the foundation of the world? Or should it be understood that the Lamb was slain before the foundation of the world? The NASB and NRSV say it is our names, whereas the KJV and the NIV say it is the slaying of the Lamb. The latter view is so ingrained in evangelical thought that either exhaustive foreknowledge is taken for granted (God always foreknew about sin and the cross) or divine determinism (God decided all this would happen) is assumed.[39] But neither view, foreknowledge or foreordination, interprets Revelation 13:8 *literally*. Jesus was not literally slain prior to the creation, since he was crucified during the reign of Pontius Pilate.

The model of omniscience defended in this book is consistent with either translation. Perhaps God knew the possible outcomes (what might happen if sin did come about or did not come about) and planned a different course of action in each case. Each one included the incarnation, but it took on a different rationale depending on which case came about.[40] Hence it could be said that God planned from before the foundation of the world that the Son would become incarnate. But God did not know which of the rationales for the incarnation would be actualized until after sin came on the scene. In any event it is not necessary to conclude that God was caught off guard.

Another option is to understand the language of Paul and John as praise for God's long-standing wisdom in accomplishing salvation for sinners. Hence "from the foundation of the world" is a way of referring to the extremely long time that God's wisdom has been working toward the salvation of his sinful creatures.

Paul Helm, a Reformed philosopher, raises a theological objection to this line of reasoning when he argues that the Fall must be presupposed in order to make sense of salvation, for if there had been no fall into sin, the incarnation would have been unnecessary. He believes that without human sin and Christ's redemption from it, God's character would not be fully manifest.[41] Colin Gunton responds to this objection with the "Scotist view," arguing that "had there been no fall, it would still have been the Father's good pleasure to come into personal relation with us through the incarnation of his Son."[42] This view, which was widely discussed in the Middle Ages and held by such notable figures as Albert the Great and John Duns Scotus, affirms the incarnation as necessary to the intended perfection of the creation, the climax of God's presence with his people, for the praise of the Creator.[43] Hence, the incarnation is not a contingency plan for redeeming fallen humanity but a means of accomplishing the type of relationship God always intended with his creation. Though God had always intended the incarnation, it took on additional significance in light of sin. The "Scotist" position on the incarnation is compatible with divine foreknowledge of the Fall, since it only maintains that God had a purpose for the incarnation antecedently to the Fall. The more traditional view, that the incarnation was not planned until after God learned (in his foreknowledge) about the Fall, implies that although Christ may *now* be the decisive turning point for human history, he was *not* so in God's original plan.[44] Hence, a major readjustment in God's purposes must be posited in that the incarnation becomes a *contingent* matter (contra supralapsarianism). My own view is that the incarnation was always planned, for God intended to bring us into the joy and glory shared among the triune Godhead (Jn 17:22-24). Human sin, however, threw up a barrier to the divine project, and God's planned incarnation had to be adapted in order to overcome it.

Acts 2:23 says that Jesus was handed over to the Jewish leadership according to the definite plan and foreknowledge of God. This verse is commonly taken to refer to the "paradox of divine sovereignty and human responsibility."[45] There is no paradox here, however. It was God's definite purpose (*hōrismenē boulē,* a boundary-setting will) to deliver the Son into the hands of those who had a long track record of resisting God's work. Their rejection did not catch God off guard, however, for he anticipated their response and so walked onto the scene with an excellent prognosis (foreknowledge, *prognōsei*) of what would happen. The crucifixion could not have occurred to Jesus unless somehow it fit into the boundaries of what God willed (*boulē,* Acts 2:23; 4:28). But this does not mean that humans cannot resist the divine will. Luke says that the Jewish leaders "rejected God's purpose *[boulēn]* for themselves" (Lk 7:30). God sovereignly established limits within which humans decide how they will respond to God.[46] In this sense God determined that the Son would suffer and die and sent him into a setting in which that result, given the history and character of the covenant people, was quite assured.[47]

4.8 The Cross of Jesus

Historically, most discussion of the cross has considered its effect on humanity. More recently the discussion has broadened to consider its effect on God. Moltmann asks, "What does the cross of Jesus mean for God himself?"[48] Through the cross the incarnate God, Jesus, did something that changed both human history and divine history in such a way that neither was ever the same again. In the cross of Jesus the divine-human relationship is affected on both sides. It is a decisive act in which God defines himself in his relationship to sinful creatures.[49]

What impact does the cross have on humans? Early on, it dashed the disciples' hopes against the rocks. They had thought that Jesus was the Messiah (Lk 24:21), but a crucified messiah was an oxymoron for them. A crucified person was accursed of God (Deut 21:22-23), whereas the Messiah was the anointed of God. How could the Messiah be godforsaken? It made no sense to them, given their interpretive framework of what messiahship meant. A crucified God was an oxymoron for Greeks as well.[50] A real king, a genuine messiah, a true Son of God would have come down from the cross, demonstrating his omnipotence (Mt 27:42-43). The cross struck everyone looking on as utter folly.

But "God's foolishness is wiser than human wisdom, and God's weakness is stronger than human strength" (1 Cor 1:25). There is profound mystery in what God was doing on the cross, and I do not pretend to understand it.[51] However, I am certain of one thing: God loves sinners and desires to destroy the evil that enslaves them. The cross expresses how God seeks to accomplish this. The cross did not transform the Father's attitude toward sinners from hatred to love. The Father has always loved his creatures—in spite of sin—and makes himself vulnerable to them, as the Old Testament demonstrates. The God who said to Abraham, "May I be cut in two if I break my promise" (Gen 15), is the God who dies on the cross to fulfill his promise. There is no single way of capturing the meaning of the cross because an array of images is required, but this much is clear: the cross is God's answer to sin and evil.

The multifaceted nature of Christ's work on the cross is demonstrated in the variety of metaphors and explanations that New Testament writers use to explain what Jesus did (for example, propitiation, redemption, justification and reconciliation). No single theory of atonement can do justice to the diversity of images connected with Jesus' act. Without taking a stand on any particular theory, I wish to make some observations. First, I understand sin to primarily be alienation, or a broken relationship, rather than a state of being or guilt.[52] This damaged relationship has produced mistrust, and we cannot compel God to love us. Furthermore, there is nothing we can do to merit God's love. Similarly, God cannot compel us to reciprocate his love, for that would not be love. In order to win our love, God forgives us the injury done to him. God considers the breach in our relationship a greater evil than the harm we have caused and so desires reconciliation.

But forgiveness comes with a price: the suffering of the one who has been sinned against.[53] The injured party must suffer the pain, forgoing revenge, in order to pursue reconciliation of the broken relationship. In this respect forgiveness is not "unconditional," since the person forgiving must fulfill this condition.[54] Calvary demonstrates that God is willing to pay the cost of forgiveness and to work to bring about reconciliation. Vincent Brümmer writes, "Christ's suffering is not merely the paradigmatic *revelation* of God's atoning forgiveness. Such a revelation is also a *necessary condition* for this forgiveness."[55] God has humbled himself and has met this painful condition necessary for the restoration of the personal divine-human relationship. In Jesus, God overcomes the estrangement and provides a way for us to repent and to be reconciled.

Second, just before the crucifixion Jesus celebrates the Passover with his disciples and institutes the "new" covenant through his blood (Lk 22:20). He makes himself out to be the new Passover lamb sparing the people from the angel of death. In the Old Testament Yahweh suffered because of, with and for the people. Now Jesus does the same. He suffers because of our sins. He identifies with our suffering. He suffers for us in order to restore us to a trusting relationship with God. The death of Jesus is the victory of sonship. He trusts the Father—despite the agony and uncertainty —obediently doing what he and the Father had agreed on. Who will trust in God? Jesus will! Jesus shows us that we can trust the Father even into death. Jesus' filial relationship with the Father gave him the confidence to follow through with his mission.[56]

But what of Jesus' lament: "My God, my God, why have you forsaken me?" (Mt 27:46)? It is intriguing that the Gospel writers even record this cry, since it is a scandalous outburst for the Messiah to make![57] In quoting Psalm 22, Jesus identifies with the lament tradition, which testified to uncertainty and even betrayal in the midst of trial.[58] In this lament Jesus identifies himself with our experience of being godforsaken. For Jesus, it was a terrifying experience because he had always been close to the Father. He was alone and cried out in abandonment. Yet Jesus, like his Old Testament predecessors, exhibits an element of faith as he cries out to his Abba, the God of the covenant community, and expects to be heard and answered. Jesus is still speaking to God, and he has not lost his faith. The disciples had deserted him, being unable to trust God that this was the way of the Messiah. Even Jesus found it difficult to trust in God as he trod this path. Is this really the way of wisdom? Will vulnerability and exposure lead to victory for God?

The Old Testament shows that God has been walking this path ever since he created our world. God has known suffering for a long time, but now he experiences it from our side through Jesus. Jesus becomes the victim but is not rendered impotent, for he demonstrates the way to victory: "Father, forgive them" (Lk 23:34).[59] The victim refuses to be vindictive. It is through the seeming weakness of forgiveness that Jesus overcomes the sin of the world. To cite the famous words of Dietrich Bonhoeffer: "God lets himself be pushed out of the world on to the cross. He is weak and powerless in the world, and that is precisely the way, the only way, in which he is with us and helps us. . . . Only the suffering God can help . . . . the God of the Bible, who wins power and space in the world by his weakness."[60] From a human perspective a messiah or Son of God dying on a cross is sheer folly and weakness. But it is through this "weakness" that God demonstrates genuine power—the power of love. As Moltmann writes, "Thus suffering proves to be stronger than hate. Its might is powerful in weakness and gains power over its enemies in grief, because it gives life even to its enemies and opens up the future to change."[61]

The cross made a difference to both God and humanity. Through the cross God defeats the "powers" arrayed against his project of establishing a trusting relationship with humans. God is a God of self-giving love, and the cross bluntly discloses this. The cross is the exemplification of the power and wisdom of God—the way of God in the world. It remains, however, a way of vulnerability and risk, not of overwhelming might and guaranteed results. Will this strategy of being resourceful, receptive and responsive succeed? Will the disciples come to trust in God's way? Will their lives be turned around? Will other people come to trust God through Jesus? Will reconciliation come about? Is God crazy to take this path? As the rest of the story unfolds in the New Testament, it becomes clear that God does succeed in building a people of faith. This he accomplishes through the resurrection of Jesus.

4.9 The Resurrection

How does the resurrection of one individual solve anything? Second-temple Judaism did not look for a dying messiah and certainly had no expectation of the Messiah's being resurrected. Tom Wright points out that for first-century Jews the term *resurrection* meant

> the raising to life of all the righteous dead, as part of the dramatic moment, within history, at which Israel's god would return to Zion and restore the fortunes of his people. Now it must be said clearly that at first sight the coming to life of a single dead body . . . would be, though of course exceedingly striking, quite insufficient to make Jews of the time declare that the longed-for redemption, the eventual release from exile, had in fact occurred. . . . It would not at all justify a claim that the person to whom this odd event had happened was therefore the saviour of the world.[62]

The Jews were looking for a general resurrection (Jn 11:24), not a dying and rising messiah. The cross had shattered the disciples' hopes, and the resurrection did not immediately alter this state of affairs. Although the raising of Jesus revived the disciples' hope, it did not fulfill it. Thus they ask the risen Jesus if he is now going to restore the kingdom to Israel (Acts 1:6). The problem was making sense of the scandal of a crucified and resurrected messiah, given their interpretive framework of providential expectations. They lacked a proper model for explaining the events in a way that connected them to God's project. A new framework had to be hammered out on the forge, and that took time.

Eventually the disciples and the New Testament writers came to see the resurrection of Jesus as the Father's ratification of Jesus' Abba experience and the victory of the way of love over the way of hatred and death. In the course of achieving this understanding, they had to modify or even reject familiar readings of the Old Testament and develop new understandings. The "resurrection" had to be reinterpreted to apply specifically to Jesus. The long-standing expectation of what God would do providentially had to be reshaped to fit what God had actually decided to do. The exact route taken by divine providence did not line up with their predictions. In freedom and in connection to the historical situation of the day God decided on the path of death and resurrection. Once the path of God became clear, then the cross and resurrection became God's definitive answer to human suffering, sin and death. In the resurrection God overcame death with life, despair with hope and sin with salvation. God did not avoid pain and death; he overcame them. God did not give up on his project when people crucified his Son. Rather, he brought something good out of evil. The resurrection of Jesus is the divine ratification both of

Jesus' experience of God as Abba and of his loving way with his fellow humans. Suffering, hatred and death do not have the last word. The resurrection gives hope that transforms our relationships, our societies and, ultimately, the entire cosmos. It is the sign of the new covenant and the promise of a new creation. Paul says that in light of the cross and the resurrection, nothing, including our own suffering and death, can separate us from the love of God in Christ Jesus (Rom 8:38-39). In hope, we look forward to God's ultimate victory over death (Rev 21:1-4).

The cross and resurrection allow us to draw three major affirmations regarding providence. First, Barth is correct when he affirms that God keeps true to his purpose in election but is free to vary the way in which he carries out his purpose.[63] Even with revelation we cannot presume to know how God will fulfill his promises. In wisdom God decided to fulfill his promises through the particular path Jesus took. In wisdom God decides how he continues to fulfill his promises, and the divine wisdom takes the changing circumstances of the world into account. Consequently, God is faithfully free to act providentially in the way he sees fit in response to the decisions his creatures make. God is free to do new things and so identify himself in new ways.

Second, despite our inability to forecast divine providence, in light of the cross and resurrection we have solid grounds for trusting that God has our best interests in mind, since he did all this to demonstrate his love toward us (Rom 5:1-11). Moreover, Jesus continues to work on our behalf in the presence of the Father (Heb 2:18; 9:24). God has been faithful in the past, so we look forward to his faithfulness in the future. Third, as we look to the future we should expect providence to follow the path definitively revealed in the life of Jesus. That is, we should not look forward to overwhelming power but to the way of sacrificial love. In Jesus we learn that God has chosen this way in the world—the way of cross and resurrection, which is also normative for the Christian life.

4.10 Grace, Judgment and Humiliation: Divine Love in Jesus' Teaching

The teaching of Jesus also brings out the way of God's love toward a world of sinners. God does not overlook our sin; it must be dealt with in order to bring about reconciliation. Jesus sounds like Yahweh in the Old Testament when he says, "Jerusalem, Jerusalem, the city that kills the prophets and stones those who are sent to it! How often have I desired to gather your children together as a hen gathers her brood under her wings, and you were not willing" (Lk 13:34). Jesus purposed to forge an intimate bond between Israel and God.

This purpose, however, does not find immediate fulfillment, because Jesus gets himself into trouble with the religious authorities. They do not accept the way of Jesus as the way of God with sinners (Lk 15:1-2). The term *sinner* in Judaism was a term of exclusion, referring to Jewish people who ignored the covenant God. Those who kept the covenant assumed that "sinners" had no place in God's grace and could not be God's people. The Pharisees considered such people outside of God's kingdom and thus took exception to Jesus' eating with them, since sharing a meal implied acceptance. In response, Jesus tells the parables of the lost sheep and the lost coin, which inform us that God is actively seeking his lost creatures.

Yet it is the story of the prodigal son that provides the most powerful description of the depths of God's love and grace.[64] In this parable the youngest son says, in effect, to his father, "I wish you were dead so I could get my inheritance now." This son shows no gratitude or respect for his father and disregards his father's concern for his well-being. He thinks his father is holding out on him. Jesus' audience would be outraged at such a request, for it is truly scandalous. The Middle Eastern listener expects the father to loudly denounce this son and expose him to public shame. Amazingly, however, the father grants his request! The father seems unwise in doing this. Perhaps he is taking the risk that his son will come to his senses and repent if he lets him experience life on his own.

The son quickly departs from his father's providence and settles in a far country. After a time the son finds himself in destitution and decides to return to his father, not as a son but as a hired hand. The Middle Eastern listener expects the son to be publicly shamed both by the villagers and by his father when he returns to the village. Not so. Jesus says that "while he was still far off, his father saw him and was filled with compassion; he ran and put his arms him and kissed him" (Lk 15:20). The father does not expose the son to the villagers' scorn. In fact, the father *humiliates* himself by running to meet the son—an undignified act in that culture. When the son begins to grovel in front of him, the father stops him and orders him to be decked out in finery and throws a party in his honor. These acts would confirm to the villagers that the father had completely accepted him back as a *son*. The father humiliates himself in order to exalt this wayward son.

When the elder son returns from the fields and hears the party going on, he remains outside. He would have been expected to go in and fulfill his culturally defined responsibilities of helping his father entertain guests. This son's relationship with the father is troubled also. The father again culturally humiliates himself by going outside the house to meet with this son. When the eldest son addresses his father, he insults him again by failing to use a title of respect. Moreover, the expression "this son of yours" implies that the older brother does not consider the sinner to be his *brother*. Pharisees, remember, did not regard sinners as God's people. Nevertheless, the father ignores these insults and tenderly answers, "My child," thereby showing his acceptance of this son also.

In this parable God is depicted as a father. But what an unusual father he is! Both sons publicly insult the father; but the father, in grace, humiliates himself and seeks reconciliation with his children. In terms of providence, both sons fail to trust the divine wisdom and love. God does not force his will on either son but practices love and forgiveness to win them back. As head of the household, the father could have resorted to overwhelming power to secure compliance. But God, seeking the reconciliation of both sons, chooses a different path, one of vulnerability and risk. The agape love of God is unselfish and nonmanipulative. God gives of himself for our well-being, even though it costs him to continue in such a loving relationship with sinful humans.

This same accepting love is found even in Jesus' teaching on judgment.[65] Jesus tells the formal parables of judgment during the last few days before the crucifixion. Consequently, they must be interpreted in light of the ministry of grace he was on his way to perform, which shows that the judgment is for reconciliation—not a settling of scores. Moreover, these parables bring out the teaching of inclusion before exclusion, grace before wrath, acceptance before rejection. No one is excluded from God's grace who was not already included in it. The parable of the king's son's wedding in Matthew 22 illustrates this.

Clearly, Jesus feels that the religious authorities have rejected his messiahship and tells them that the kingdom of God will be taken away from them (Mt 21:28-46). The broader background for this parable is the messianic banquet spoken of in Isaiah 25:6-9, which says that Jews and Gentiles will eat together in God's presence.[66] By New Testament times, however, Isaiah's encompassing vision had been curtailed so that Gentiles were largely excluded from the messianic banquet.

In the parable Jesus says that the king sends out his servants to inform those who have been invited that it is time to come to the party. But for some reason those invited refuse to come. The king ignores this insult and sends out other servants to ask those invited to come. But again they refuse. Some turn to their business affairs, and others openly brutalize and even murder some of the servants. Jesus is saying that just as the Old

Testament prophets had been rejected, so now the king's son is being rejected. The religious leaders refuse to come to the messianic banquet if Jesus is the Messiah. They do not want that sort of messiah. They do not believe Jesus is manifesting God's way in the world.

The king is rightfully enraged at bring snubbed and destroys those who spurn his invitation. (There is divine wrath in the New Testament.)[67] Jesus is telling us that there comes a time when the rejection of grace is dealt with. When grace is refused and the king's servants are murdered, what else is left? Judgment ensues on those who despise the grace of God. The king invited these people out of his own magnanimity. Jesus invites them to participate in the newness of life that he brings. If the life Jesus offers is refused, what can be left but deadness? The messianic banquet is only for the living.

The parable does not end here. The king is determined to have a party, so he sends out more servants to invite anyone and everyone to the feast. The invitations include "both good and bad" (Mt 22:10). God does not invite the good and snub the bad. He calls all, including the sinners, to trust in his gracious love. And the people do come—so many, in fact, that the banquet hall is *filled* with guests (22:10). Here we see God depicted as a king—but what an unusual king! What ancient Near Eastern king would invite common people and even strangers to his son's wedding?

A problem arises when an individual thinks he can come to the wedding on his own terms. When the king arrives, he finds one guest not dressed in wedding clothes. The king requests an explanation, but the man remains silent, refusing to accept the king's grace by entering into dialogue. Consequently, he is excluded from the party, for there is never a good reason for rejecting grace.

For our purposes it is important to note that the first invited guests as well as the guests invited as replacements are all recipients of the king's undeserved favor. Nobody in the parable is outside the king's favor. Everybody starts out with the king's acceptance. No one is excluded except those who rule themselves out by refusing to trust in the king's provision.

Jesus taught that God is serious about accomplishing his project. In fact, God brings the project to a climactic moment in the life and work of Jesus. These parables teach that God is gracious and is willing to humiliate himself and to be vulnerable, all the while working to bring us to a point of decision (judgment). God wants us to trust him and become his reconciled children. God wants a filial relationship with us grounded in his agape love. Instead of using his power to enforce compliance, God has taken the path of vulnerable, humiliating love, giving of himself to us in our wretchedness. The vulnerability of this love raises questions for us. Will we trust his providence or will we leave for the far country? Will we, like the younger son, return to the Father and experience his agape love? Will we reject God's way in the world (displayed in the life of Jesus) or accept the gracious invitation to the wedding? These are genuine questions for us as well as for God. They expose the risk God experiences along the route he has sovereignly established to take.

4.11 Various Texts on Providence

Besides Jesus' acts of healing and his telling of parables, there are several teachings of his which are usually mentioned when discussing providence. Sometimes these verses are used to justify the claim that God is micromanaging every tiny detail that occurs in life.

In Matthew 6:25-34 Jesus tells his disciples not to worry about their clothes or food because God provides for the birds of the air and the grass of the field. He states his case in absolute terms without qualification.[68] Does Jesus mean to say that humans should not plant crops or produce clothes (vv. 26, 30)? If we plant, reap and store crops, are we acting against divine providence? Hardly. Such actions are called for in the covenant regulations (Lev 19:9-10). And the birds of the air do not simply sit with their mouths open, waiting for food to drop into them.[69] Jesus says that God provides food for us. The question is *how* God does this. The expressions "birds of the air" (v. 26) and "grass of the field" (v. 30) seem to hark back to the creation account in Genesis.[70] Moreover, the lilies do not "toil" (v. 28), and we are not to be "anxious." This possibly alludes to the curse (Gen 3:16-19). If so, then Jesus, in announcing his Father's kingdom, acknowledges the limits of our creatureliness as well as our plight. He assures his disciples that the Father remains faithful to his own plan of creation and work of redemption. In Jesus, God has already inaugurated the coming kingdom, and we are to seek first his kingdom (v. 33).

Jesus is not denying the validity of farming or household duties and is not teaching people to expect a carefree existence spent waiting for God's provision to fall into their lap.[71] He is teaching that God's provision of life's basic needs frees his followers to pursue the kingdom of God. Jesus knows that we do not live by bread *alone* (Mt 4:4). We need bread and we are to produce it, but our physical needs must never distract us from our part in God's larger project. The coming kingdom does not ensure that the disciples of Jesus will never go hungry or naked. But just as God cares for the grass, even if it is burned tomorrow, so God cares for us, even if we experience droughts from time to time (6:30). Providence does not mean protection from the vicissitudes of life, but it does mean that God will be with us through them.

In Matthew 10:24-33 (compare Lk 12:1-12) Jesus tells the disciples not to fear those who can kill the body. Followers of Jesus may fall prey to serious harm and even murder. Nevertheless, they are not to fear murderers. Rather, they are to fear God, who will exercise eschatological judgment (10:28). Jesus' disciples are not to worry about such things. They may be persecuted and killed for following Jesus, but they should not be anxious about what happens to them. Even if they die for his sake, their heavenly Father cares for them. After all, God cares for the sparrows and knows the number of hairs on our heads (both insignificant details of life). Does this mean that God keeps a ledger of sparrows and hair follicles? Or does it mean that no sparrow dies and no hair falls out without God specifically decreeing that it be so? Although some take it in this sense, it does not seem to be what Jesus meant.[72]

In sending out the Twelve on a mission, Jesus wants them to be encouraged despite the difficulties they will encounter. The issue is a familiar one: Does the suffering of God's people mean that God has been defeated? Jesus does not provide an explanation to the problem of evil. He gives two different responses to evil, both of which arise out of the Old Testament.[73] First, a coming eschatological judgment will reveal the truth (Mt 10:26-27). Things are not always what they appear to be, and God's eschatological judgment will vindicate the sufferings of Jesus' disciples. Second, Jesus appeals to the wisdom tradition in emphasizing the inability of humans to understand life in its totality. But God knows even the insignificant details of life, such as the number of hairs on someone's head. Hence, we are not in a position to pass judgment on God for failing to deliver us from suffering. Jesus calls for his disciples to trust God in the face of suffering. He does not say, however, that the suffering is ordained by God. He says that just as God is concerned for sparrows and the hairs on each head, God cares about the disciples even in their persecutions. They are not to doubt God's concern for them, even in the midst of such horrible experiences. Again, providence does not mean being exempted from suffering. But nothing can separate them from God's concern. In this way the disciples are encouraged to hope in God's future and to trust in God's care, which frees them from fearing what others will do to them.

In Jesus' day some people thought that all suffering was a direct punishment for sin. The Old Testament wisdom literature discusses this issue without reaching any conclusion. Although Job, Ecclesiastes and the individual complaint psalms call into question the belief that all suffering is due to sin, it seems that many people continued to affirm it.[74] In Luke 13:1-5 Jesus is informed about some people whom Pilate had killed while they were presenting sacrifices in the temple. These were God's people offering their worship in the way God had prescribed, yet they met a horrible death. These worshipers of the true God were slain by a pagan ruler. Did God care for them? Or were they inauthentic worshipers whom God foreordained to be killed in their act of hypocrisy? Jesus asks the question whether they were wicked "sinners." He uses the term reserved for Jews who paid no attention to God's covenant. Many would have assumed that they were such sinners because of the circumstances surrounding their death. But this seems unlikely, since in presenting their offerings they were fulfilling the covenant.

In the same passage Jesus also speaks of a tower that fell on eighteen people and killed them. Was this an accident? Or was it God's punishment for their sins? The word on the street held that it was divine punishment. But Jesus refuses to attribute either tragedy to the sins of the victims.[75] God did not foreordain their deaths. That God does not intend such events is made clear in the ministry of Jesus as he stands opposed (in solidarity with the Father) to human suffering. Jesus uses these tragic events to call on his audience to seek God: no one knows when death may come, so place your trust in God now (compare Lk 12:20).

The same question is raised when Jesus is asked about a man born blind (Jn 9:1-5). Was his blindness to be attributed to his sin or to his parents'? It was assumed that there must have been some moral cause for his blindness. Some people thought God punished children or grandchildren because of distant sins (Exod 20:5, even though this teaching is overturned in Ezek 18:20). Others believed that the fetus was capable of sinning.[76] Jesus, following the Old Testament, rejects the doctrine that the man's blindness (or any defect in the created order) is the specific result of sin. This man's blindness was an opportunity for God's glory to be manifested in compassion and healing. God overrules this "faulty creation" by restoring the man's sight. Jesus stands with God against disease and deformity, since they are not what God intends. Jesus is not "cleaning up" the sickness that God has spread. And in restoring the man's sight, Jesus challenges his audience with their own "blindness" and their need to place their trust in Jesus, the light of the world.

Finally, in that most familiar of prayers, the Lord's Prayer, Jesus instructs us to pray that the Father's will be done on earth as it is in heaven (Mt 6:10). Requesting that God's will be done recognizes that God's sovereignty has not been realized yet. There is an eschatological element to the divine project, for not everything happens on earth as the Father desires. We are to work and pray for God's will to be done in our lives now and in the age to come. But it is not yet a complete reality in our world—this Jesus well knew.

4.12 Conclusion to the Life of Jesus

First, God in Jesus tabernacled among us, displaying God's way in the world. Jesus is *the* model for understanding God's relationship to the world. In Jesus we see what God is most truly like and what sort of relationship with us God desires. God is intimate and near, not remote or disengaged.

Second, the way of Jesus is compassion, sacrificial love and a strong desire for the sinful humans to be cured of their rebellion. Jesus stands against the sin that ruins the beloved and wants to eradicate it, transforming them into godlike creatures. In standing against sin Jesus, nevertheless, stands with the sinner. Jesus experiences alienation and death in order to reconcile us to God. If Jesus is the paradigm of providence, then God is fundamentally opposed to sin, evil and suffering.[77] If Jesus were cleaning up the mess that God had caused (for example, disease and suffering), then Jesus would be opposing God. But if Jesus is God manifest in the flesh, then never again can God be understood as ordering the destruction of a people, for God is the God of the Gentiles also (Rom 3:29). In Jesus God identifies with our sufferings and temptations.

Third, Jesus, like Yahweh in the Old Testament, asserts power over the physical creation by miraculously healing the sick, calming storms and feeding people. Like Yahweh, Jesus does not have an easy time persuading humans to do the will of God. Humans are much more resistant to divine purposes than the rest of the created order. Jesus desires to protect Israel as a hen gathers her chicks (Mt 23:37), but the people are unwilling to be gathered. Luke explicitly claims that the Pharisees and lawyers "rejected God's purpose for themselves" (Lk 7:30). Such texts fly in the face of G. C. Berkouwer's remark that "Scripture nowhere suggests that God's work is limited by human activity."[78] On the contrary, the teaching of Jesus stands opposed to the theology that everything happens just as God decrees it should and that God's purposes are never frustrated.[79] Furthermore, in Gethsemane Jesus did not get everything he wanted. Sometimes the desires of God are stymied. But God is resourceful and faithfully works to bring good even out of evil situations. God needs to be resourceful, since the providence God exercised in the life of Jesus was dependent on human choices and responses. Divine providence took the particular path it did in response to the actions of humans such as Mary and Joseph, the disciples and the religious authorities. The ministry of Jesus displayed openness and flexibility in response to others. He maintained his purposes but was open to modifying his plans in response to the requests of people. In Jesus we come to see God's way as responsive to his creatures, receptive to what they say and do and eminently resourceful in working with what is available to him in any given situation.

In Jesus we see the divine humiliation and vulnerability brought into clear focus. God is not the all-determining power responsible for sending everything, including suffering, on us. The way of God is love. "Jesus Christ is both the consummation and the explicative history of 'God is love.'"[80] This love is even willing to humiliate itself in the hope that we may be redeemed. The life of Jesus demonstrated service to and suffering with people rather than domination over them. The Son of God did not "regard equality with God as something to be exploited, but emptied himself, taking the form of a slave" (Phil 2:6-7). In him we understand that God does not have a "compulsive retention of power."[81]

Christology is the great stumbling stone to the classical view of omnipotence. Our views of divine power, providence and sovereignty must pass through the lens of Jesus if they are to come into focus regarding the nature of God. Metaphors such as king and potter must be interpreted in the light of Jesus rather than our normal understanding of kings and potters. After all, in the book of Revelation a search is made for one who can open the seals of a book (Rev 5:1-14). No one is found worthy to open the book until, at last, the Lion of Judah appears—the one who has overcome (5:5). This is what the disciples expected of the Messiah, and it is what we, with our traditional understandings of divine power, expect. Amazingly, however, the author changes metaphors. It is not the Lion that actually opens the book but an immolated Lamb (5:6). It is the slain Lamb, which explains the kind of Lion God is: God has "overcome" sin and death. This is not what anyone expected—this way of overcoming through suffering, death and resurrection. This way of God is risky (some would even say foolhardy), yet God, as Philip Yancey remarks, was courageous enough to risk it.

> It took courage to endure the shame, and courage even to risk descent to a planet known for its clumsy violence, among a race known for rejecting its prophets. A God of all power deliberately put himself in such a state that Satan could tempt him, demons could taunt him, and lowly human beings could slap his face and nail him to a cross. What more foolhardy thing could God have done?

"Alone of all the creeds, Christianity has added courage to the virtues of the Creator," said G. K. Chesterton. The need for such courage began with Jesus' first night on earth and did not end until his last.[82]

4.13 The Church as the Vehicle of God's Project

The book of Acts and the epistle to the Romans provide insights into divine providence as God seeks to develop the Jesus movement into a more inclusive body. My comments will focus on Acts 10—15 and Romans 9— 11, which I take to address a pivotal time in God's attempt to direct his people toward his vision of what the church should be. The main issue concerns the inclusion of the Gentiles into God's project without their first having to convert to Judaism.

4.13.1 Acts 10—15   God desired to complete his project of forming a people of faith from every nation, race, gender and economic status. Given the disciples' traditional understanding of the kingdom of God, this was no easy task for providence to accomplish. In Acts 10—15 God tries to teach the disciples that the divine project is to include Jews and Gentiles together in one people of faith. At this point in history the church is essentially Jewish and is led by Galileans. The disciples believe that God's project is for Israel alone (Acts 1:6). In Acts 6 a significant number of Hellenistic Jews join their native cousins in the church. The integration of these two groups causes some initial friction and leads to a reorganization of church leadership. But nothing prepares the disciples for the broad program God has in mind.

In Acts 10—11 Luke describes God's attempt to show Peter that Gentiles should be welcomed into the church as Gentiles. Up to this time anyone wishing to become a Christian had to practice the public Jewish observances of sabbath, circumcision and dietary regulations.[83] Christianity was considered solely a Jewish phenomenon. Before bringing Gentiles directly into the church, God selected a Gentile who worshiped Yahweh (a "Godfearer" acceptable to Jewish religion) to be the strategic bridge to full-scale, unconditioned acceptance of Gentiles into the church. Cornelius, a Roman centurion, was given to prayer and caring for those in need (Acts 10:2). An angel informs him that his prayers have made a difference to God (10:4) and that he should send for Peter. At the same time God grants Peter a vision of ceremonially unclean food and commands him to eat it (10:9-16). Peter refuses, reminding God he keeps the covenant regulations. This vision is repeated three times, but it is clear that God is not yet successful in teaching Peter the message (10:16-17). After the vision Peter accompanies Cornelius's servants back to his house, where the entire extended family and slaves have been assembled. Peter then understands that God is accepting Gentiles who have faith (10:34-35). He explains to them that the crucified and resurrected Jesus is the Messiah in whom they should place their trust for the forgiveness of sins. At that time the gift of the Holy Spirit is given to all those who are listening to the message (10:44). On seeing this phenomenon, Peter and the Jews with him decide it is permissible to baptize these Gentiles into the Christian community (10:47). When Peter returns to Jerusalem, however, certain Jewish Christians take issue with him (11:2). After he explains the situation to them, they conclude that God has accepted the Gentiles into the Christian community (11:18). Despite this initial victory for God, there were yet many obstacles to overcome.

In Acts 13—14 Paul takes center stage with his missionary journey. Some Jews and many Gentiles come to faith in Christ. However, certain Jewish Christians began to inform these Gentile Christians that they could not be genuine Christians unless they practiced the law of Moses (Acts 15:1). Paul and Barnabas strongly disagree with these fellow Christians, precipitating "no small dissension and debate" (15:2). It is decided to take the matter to the leadership at Jerusalem, where the debate breaks out afresh between Paul and some of his fellow Jewish Christians. It is important to keep in mind that this is a debate among Jews who have accepted Jesus as the Messiah. The Christian community is attempting to discern the leading of divine providence in this controversial matter—a potent controversy that threatens to derail, at least temporarily, God's intentions for the church. After all, was not Paul guilty of blurring the lines between the covenant people of God and those who were outsiders? Where does the divine presence rest?

In order to answer such questions a meeting is called that is marked by debate (15:7). During the meeting Peter recounts what God did in the household of Cornelius; Paul and Barnabas speak of God's signs and wonders among the Gentiles; and James cites a passage from Amos to claim that these events are part of God's project to bring the Gentiles into the community of faith. James suggests certain minimum behaviors that Gentiles should observe in order for Jews and Gentiles to fellowship together as the people of God. Those at the meeting agree to this and send out a letter stating this, accompanied by representatives to the churches where the debate has been raging.

God's plan of developing both Jews and Gentiles into a unified group of people exercising faith in Jesus furnishes several examples of providence. First, to accomplish this plan God was dependent on the people involved, especially Peter and Paul, to correctly interpret God's actions in these events. Obviously, not all Jewish Christians understood it the same way. God had difficulty in getting the apostolic church to follow his direction in this matter. But through discussion, debate and reflection they came to agreement. The letter sent by the Jerusalem leadership says, "It has seemed good to the Holy Spirit and to us" (Acts 15:28). In other words, they claimed that the conclusion they reached through argumentation was the will of God for their particular situation. The will of God was not mysteriously written on the wall of the room, but it came through debate and dialogue. God worked through and was dependent on the debating process in a way that the outcome was not guaranteed. In being dependent on the leaders of the early church, God took the risk that they would rightly ascertain the path God was leading.

Although God's plan of including the Gentiles in the body of Christ apart from the Mosaic law met with initial success, God did experience some setbacks. In Galatians 2:11-21 Paul refers to the "Antioch incident."[84] The Jerusalem council had sent its letters to the churches. At Antioch—Paul's home base—Jews (including Peter) and Gentiles were eating together, a sign of fellowship without religious barriers. However, Peter and Barnabas retreated from this practice when some Jewish Christians sent from James in Jerusalem came to Antioch. After that the Jewish Christians separated themselves from the Gentile Christians. For Paul, this destroyed the unity of the church and derailed God's providential work.[85] Peter's failure in this incident is particularly troubling, since he had been the first apostle to promote the inclusion of the Gentiles. It seems that God's original intention was to work through Peter in this matter. In the end, however, Peter fails, and God, resourcefully, turns to Paul to be the stalwart in this mission. It is similar in some respects to an Old Testament situation: God had thought Saul would be a good king, but in the end he had to turn to David.

God is resourceful, but God did not achieve everything he wanted to accomplish regarding his covenant people. Though Paul brought some to faith in Jesus, the primary response of his countrymen is to reject his message and force him to flee for his life (Acts 9:23-25; 13:45; 14:5, 19). The story in Acts is, in this respect, a tragic one: just as the promises to Abraham are beginning to be fulfilled, Israel rejects God's way of fulfillment.[86] The book of Acts ends with a speech by Paul to the Roman Jews (28:25-28). Robert Tannehill observes that this speech "cannot represent a satisfying ending for the author of Luke-Acts. The quotation from Isaiah 6:9-10 shows that the Jews' refusal to see and hear is anticipated in Scripture, but the fulfillment of this Scripture means that the 'hope of Israel' (also found in Scripture) is *not* being fulfilled."[87] God had worked so long to build a covenant people who would trust him into the future, but his project seems to be falling apart in his hands because the divine intentions for Israel are not being completely realized. But God does not throw in the towel! In response to this reaction by his countrymen Paul decides that his primary mission will no longer be to the Jews but to the Gentiles (13:46; 28:28). It is Paul's belief that God's providence is following this route in order to stir Israel to faith through faithful Gentiles (Rom 11:11).[88]

Does this modification of plans represent a "failure" on God's part? Clearly, God is not achieving everything he desires. On the other hand it could be said that God is being flexible and resourceful in altering his plans in order to achieve his purposes. Jesus was sent to the lost sheep of the house of Israel, and the early church focused its attention on persuading Jews of Jesus' messiahship. What else is God to do if the Jewish people, overall, reject his Messiah? God's vision—of forming a people of God from every race centered around his Son Jesus—takes a very winding path and certainly meets with a degree of success. The church did develop from an introversionist Galilean sect into an international conversionist group that was cosmopolitan and universal in nature.[89] Nevertheless, God's goals were not entirely met. The fact that the church came to include Gentiles at all means that God accomplished this purpose. The fact that the church became almost exclusively Gentile means that God did not achieve all he wanted. In fact, the predominantly Gentile makeup of the church could call into question God's faithfulness to his covenant people. This is an issue Paul takes up in one of his letters.

4.13.2 Romans 9—11   Paul's epistle to the Christians at Rome addresses the issue of Jewish-Gentile relations within the body of Christ. Paul wanted to use Rome as his new base of operations, and he wanted to be sure the Romans understood his perspective on the Jewish-Gentile question lest the Roman church go the way of the Antioch church in failing to understand God's way. I will concentrate on chapters 9—11, since they play an important role in discussions of providence. A failure to grasp this historical debate embroiling the apostolic church has led, in my opinion, to a misunderstanding of Romans, especially chapter 9. Some North American evangelicals still cite Romans 9 as the classic text for predestination of individuals and divine pancausality.[90] Other biblical scholars, however, see something quite different in the letter and arrive at a rather different understanding of Romans.[91] Currently there is controversy among New Testament scholars regarding the background and interpretation of Romans. I cast my lot with those who identify the central issues in the epistle as Jewish-Gentile relations and God's plan for the world. According to this view, Paul is not debating the eternal salvation and reprobation of individuals in chapters 9—11. His concern, rather, is whether God's election of Israel has turned out to be a failure, since the majority of Jews were not accepting Jesus as the Messiah. The danger was that a predominantly Gentile church, placing its faith in Jesus, would become arrogant, would regard ethnic Israel as hopeless and would find a mission to the Jews unnecessary.[92]

The covenant faithfulness of God is the topic of Romans 9—11. Paul argues that God has kept his promise to Abraham and is faithfully accomplishing his project. Paul is emphatic that God's project, overall, has not failed. Rather, the majority of his countrymen have misunderstood God's project. Although this misunderstanding is centered in the messiahship of Jesus, it has antecedents in the Old Testament. From time to time, Israel refused to acknowledge God's work in their midst (for example, Amos 3:6-7). Now they refuse to acknowledge God's work in Jesus and also refuse to include the Gentiles among the people of God apart from observing the public badges of covenant membership (sabbath observance, circumcision and food laws). According to Paul, God is accomplishing a new work that was promised from the beginning. The long awaited inclusion of the Gentiles is happening, but not in the way his Jewish brethren thought appropriate.

Paul claims that simply being a member of ethnic Israel does not add up to proper standing with God (Rom 9:6-13). God freely chose Isaac and Jacob rather than Ishmael and Esau to be the people through whom he would fulfill his promised redemption. Israel, of course, placed its trust in God's election of them but misunderstood both their status in this election and God's purpose—to bring the "nonelect" into his project. Is God not free to accomplish his task in the way he sees fit? Did God not reveal to Moses that it was solely God's decision when and to whom God would show mercy? Paul's point is that if God wants to show mercy to the Gentiles by bringing them into the people of God simply by faith in Jesus and without the badges of covenant membership, God is free to do it (9:15-16). C. E. B. Cranfield notes correctly that Paul is not thinking of an arbitrary and unqualified will of God but of God's merciful will, which desires the salvation of both Jew and Gentile.[93] Furthermore, God strengthened Pharaoh's heart in his rebellion in the hopes that it would help him come to his senses and repent. In the same way God now is hardening Israel in its rebellion in hopes that it will repent and so be redeemed (Rom 11:7, 25). The passages which Paul cites from the Old Testament reveal that God has done this to lesser degrees previously—bringing judgment on the nation in order to restore Israel. As Cranfield notes, the "power" that God exercises on Pharaoh and Israel is consistent with the power of God as described by Paul in the rest of the epistle: it is God's *saving power.*[94] God is seeking to accomplish his redemptive purposes, which involve bringing Jews and Gentiles together as the new-covenant people based on faith in Jesus.

Jeremiah drew on the potter metaphor to claim that God was free to bring judgment on Israel, and Paul does the same (Rom 9:20-22). James Dunn notes that the purpose of divine judgment is to correct all flaws in the vessels the potter is making.[95] God does not wish to leave Israel in this state of mistrusting God's purposes. Paul draws on the Old Testament themes of divine forbearance—granting time for repentance—and divine hardening—bringing things to a head.[96] But ethnic Israel now has the role previously played by Pharaoh—refusing to acknowledge God's ways. The covenant people stubbornly resist the potter's will. They refuse to collaborate in the divine project. The potter metaphor is useful in pointing up God's directing purpose, but it does not explain why the clay resists the potter's desires (unless it is simply asserted that God is a deficient potter). The relationship between God and Israel is not *completely* or solely like that between a potter and clay. God is not like a potter in all respects, and Israel is not like clay in all respects. God, although wishing to direct his people in a particular way, does not manipulate them. Israel resists the will of the potter by refusing to follow the path divine providence has chosen at this juncture in history. Paul is not arguing for divine pancausality here. This misunderstanding occurs when Romans 9 is divorced from its historical setting and universalized into a timeless truth.[97] Paul is not arguing about abstract principles of providence but about a specific historical situation between God and Israel. Clearly, Paul is not defending a doctrine of pancausality.

God had always planned on including the Gentiles and is now accomplishing this goal (Rom 9:23-33).[98] This is not a new plan for God but the bringing to fruition of his plan from the beginning. God did not foreordain Israel's rebellion (9:22). Yet God uses this situation to further his goal of bringing the Gentiles to faith in Jesus. Although God did not cause Israel's unbelief, he is resourceful enough to utilize Israel's rejection in order to bring about something good.[99] This reveals the awesome resourcefulness of God in that he is able to bring good things even out of a bad situation.

Does God's hardening of Israel mean that Israel cannot come to faith in

Jesus? Not at all. Divine hardening in Exodus did not render one unable to change. Paul explicitly says that hope is not lost regarding his kindred people, for God is seeking to use the conversion of the Gentiles to provoke Israel to faith (Rom 11:11-27). Trust in God's way is all that is required of them (10:1-13). God intends to reclaim them, and they may yet call on his mercy: God has shut up all in disobedience that he might show mercy to all (11:32). Thus God's overarching purpose is mercy.[100] Paul concludes this section by praising the ways of God; no one anticipated that God would bring about his merciful salvation to the world in the way he has done it (11:33-36).

Did Paul win the day with this argument? Did his fellow Jews accept Jesus as the climax of the covenant? Did he secure equal standing for Gentiles within the church apart from the badges of covenant membership? Did the salvation of the Gentiles stimulate Israel to trust in Jesus as the Messiah? God seemingly achieved some of what he desired but not all. On the one hand, Paul certainly won the day regarding Gentile salvation. The enormous growth of the church among the Gentiles and its transnational character testify to God's outstanding success here. On the other hand, the predominantly Jewish makeup of the early church was lost as fewer and fewer Jews placed their trust in Jesus. God wanted to redeem the nations through Israel but ends up attempting to reach Israel through converted Gentiles. In this we see divine resourcefulness in God's switching to alternative routes in order to keep his project going.

Nevertheless, God did not get everything he wanted. He banked his strategy on the Gentile church, and it has not, overall, been the agent God desired it to be in relation to Israel. This does not mean that God has given up on his goal of uniting Jews and Gentiles into one people of faith through Jesus Christ. But it was God's desire that the way Christian Jews and Gentiles lived in community in the church was to be the visible manifestation of the divine wisdom inaugurated in Jesus. God was seeking to use this body of believers to demonstrate his wisdom to the rulers and authorities (Eph 3:10-11). Today we see signs of hope as numerous congregations of messianic Jews are springing up and various organizations of Jewish and Gentile Christians are forming to promote the Jewish roots of Christianity and to demonstrate that a Jew can become a Christian without becoming a Gentile. If the predominantly Gentile church is getting over its anti-Jewish sins, then perhaps God will use these new initiatives to bring to fruition his intention of saving all Israel (Rom 11:26).[101]

To sum up this section, God has achieved some of what he desired, but not everything. God took the risk of working through the disciples and others in the early church. Some apostolic Christians understood the direction divine providence was going, whereas others (for example, Paul's detractors) did not and worked hard against it. The goals God accomplished were not easily achieved, yet the fact that God was able to overcome the disciples' deeply embedded preconceptions regarding messiahship demonstrates that God is victorious in getting people to follow him. In his providential work God encounters conflict and opposition to his project, and in seeking its fulfillment he experiences both victory and defeat.

4.14 The Nature and Goal of the Divine Project

> By this the love of God was manifested in us, that God has sent His only begotten Son into the world so that we might live through Him. In this is love, not that we loved God, but that He loved us and sent His Son to be the propitiation for our sins. Beloved, if God so loved us, we also ought to love one another. (1 Jn 4:9-11 NASB)

God's project is to develop people who love and trust him in response to his love and manifest their love of God in effective action to others. God takes the initiative of love toward sinners. God is gracious toward sinners, and this gracious love enables us to turn from our sin and place our trust in God. Furthermore, the divine love transforms our hearts to be concerned about the well-being of others. Salvation brings us into a personal relationship with God, and we actually begin to become godlike in our character. This transformation anticipates God's eschatological transformation of things in the new heaven and earth.

The New Testament writers see Jesus both as the one who brought divine love to us and as the model for the way we should live. The book of Hebrews speaks of Jesus' working to bring many children to glory (Heb 2:10). God desires to give us a place in his household. On our way to glory we are faced with temptations to turn from God's way, hence the exhortations not to commit apostasy (Heb 3:12; 4:1, 6). The author of Hebrews holds Jesus up as our model. He faced temptations and overcame them, so he is able to help us overcome ours (2:18). Despite difficulties and even death, Jesus remained faithful to God's project (3:2). We are to follow his example, not the example of the Israelites who refused to trust God, desired to return to Egypt and died in the wilderness (3:7-19). God was not proud of this generation. He had reached out to them repeatedly, but they continually refused to trust God with their well-being. Hebrews 11, however, cites people of whom "God is not ashamed to be called their

God" (11:16 NASB). God is still seeking people who will trust him despite hardships. The recipients of the letter were going through tough times (10:34), and the author encourages them to fix their eyes on Jesus (12:2) in order to remain faithful to him. God has not changed his purpose, for God remains faithful to his promise (6:17-18). The hope that we have does not mean that our lives will be comfortable or that nothing bad will happen to us. In 11:32-39 the author explains that although some people in the Old Testament were successful (by human standards), others were not. Whereas some were victorious in battle others were killed, some were miraculously delivered but others were martyred. Nevertheless, all these people gained God's approval, since they trusted God whether good or bad happened to them (11:39). God was as pleased with those who conquered kingdoms as he was with those who went hungry or were tortured. Providence does not allow us to predict what people of faith will experience in life.

God's Son, Jesus, was faithful, yet he suffered rejection and death. If we begin with Jesus as the model for experiencing divine providence as well as the goal of humanity—what we are meant to be—then our understanding of the role of providence changes dramatically. When people hear the word *providence,* they tend to think of power and control over all life circumstances. But if we look to Jesus and if we understand that he is what God wants to produce in us—a holy people—then we will not occupy ourselves with seeking power over others or making our lives more comfortable. Instead, we will seek the way of God, faithfully following his love, pursuing sanctification and cooperating with God no matter what befalls us. Paul saw himself as God's fellow worker (1 Cor 3:9) and encouraged Christians to see themselves as working together with God (2 Cor 6:1) to fulfill the divine project. According to Paul, God has chosen to be somewhat dependent on us to accomplish the ministry of reconciliation (2 Cor 5:18-20), for God desires our collaboration in this task. God is seeking to create a people of whom he is proud to be their God. This is the project God has had in place from the creation of the world. God has never given up on that project despite our sin. God has demonstrated his faithfulness through all the twists and turns providence has taken.[102] And God is not finished yet.

4.15 Eschatology and Providence

God is yet working to fulfill his promises and bring his project to fruition. The eschaton will surprise us because it is not set in concrete; it is not unfolding according to a prescribed script. Adriö König distinguishes between prophecies (or promises) and predictions (or forecasts).[103] He points out two basic differences. First, whereas predictions come about only once, promises are fulfilled repeatedly. There are very specific predictions of future events that come to pass (for example, 1 Kings 13:2-5). "But these predictions have a limited value, exerting no particular influence on salvation history. Distinct from these are prophecies and promises which are repeatedly fulfilled and which decisively influence the unfolding of salvation history."[104] König cites several examples of divine promises that the biblical writers claimed were fulfilled on several occasions and in a variety of ways. A prophecy such as "the day of the LORD" (Amos 5:18-20) "finds repeated fulfillment: in the fall of Jerusalem (586 B.C.; Ezek. 13:5; Lam. 1:12; 2:1, 22), in the ministry of John the Baptist (Mark 1:2; compare Mal. 3:1-2), in Jesus' earthly ministry (Luke 4:16-21; cf. Isa. 61:1-2), in the outpouring of the Spirit (Acts 2:16-21; cf. Joel 2:28-32), and in Jesus' second advent (2 Pet 3:12; Rev 16:14)."[105] Prophecies or promises continue to be fulfilled because God is not yet finished with his project.

Predictions are very specific forecasts of what is to occur, whereas prophecies allow room for God to fulfill them in a variety of ways—ways that we cannot anticipate. God fulfills prophecies or promises repeatedly, bringing out new aspects of them in conjunction with the new historical situation. Despite the messianic prophecies, no one anticipated the sort of messiahship that Jesus exhibited. The book of Acts (2:16-21) claims that the promised outpouring of the Spirit on the day of the Lord in Joel 2:28-32 occurred on the day of Pentecost, although most of the specific "signs" mentioned by Joel did not occur. If this is a prediction, it must be explained why things did not come about as predicted. But if it is a prophecy, then God is free to bring it to fulfillment in a way befitting the new situation.[106] Acts 15:15-18 cites the fulfillment of Amos 9:11-12. Whereas Amos had prophesied of Israel's return to political glory and rule over Edom, James claims in Acts 15 that this prophecy has been fulfilled by the inclusion of the Gentiles into the people of God. James understands that Israel will "rule" over the Gentiles through faith in Jesus.[107] If this was a prediction, then it was a failure, for Israel has not ruled Edom. But if it was a prophecy, then it was open to fulfillment in the way the wisdom of God saw fit.

Who would have anticipated such fulfillments? Who could have expected that God would fulfill his ancient prophecies in the way the New Testament writers claim God has done? A. van de Beek comments that "the way of God to Christ was not an established road. It is a way which can only be read in retrospect in the light of Christ, not guaranteed in advance."[108] The promises made to Abraham regarding a land, a seed and a blessing to the Gentiles are fulfilled in various ways in the Old Testament. In the New Testament these promises are qualified and universalized. Jesus is the seed of Abraham who climaxes what God intended from the beginning (Gal 3:16). Through him, Gentiles can become children of Abraham by faith (Gal 3:29). The people of God look forward to inheriting a "better country" (Heb 11:16), a "new earth" and a "new Jerusalem" (Rev 21:1-2). Clearly God is sovereign over his prophecies and can bring them to fruition in the way he deems best fitted to the particular historical circumstances.

The promises of God should be understood as part of the divine *project* rather than as some eternal blueprint, a project in which God has not scripted the way everything in human history will go. God has a goal, but the routes remain open. According to König, God is working in the world according to the covenant rather than to a meticulous plan. He objects to the idea of the plan most importantly because it casts a shadow on God, since it implies that God fights against (to the point of giving his only Son) that which he wanted all along as part of God's plan.[109] It is better to see God as working with us in history in order to bring about the fulfillment of his promises as part of his project of developing people who reciprocate the divine love and come to trust God. Tupper uses the analogy of a master weaver in this regard.[110] The master weaver utilizes the possibilities open at any given time in order to weave his purposes into the tapestry. The tapestry is not finished, and God is weaving alongside us to produce it. This is an eschatological model of God's relationship to the world: God is going to do more, but it is not possible for us to predict the precise way it will go. What we do know, through Jesus, is the direction in which God is moving: producing a Christlike people (Rom 8:29) to inhabit the new Jerusalem (Rev 21).

The trials of life may obscure God's working in our lives toward this project. But in Romans Paul gives three reasons why we should maintain our confidence in God amid trials. First, God can use the difficult times in our lives to produce Christlikeness in us. Paul says that tribulations can produce patience and build character. Seeing tangible evidence of the Spirit's work in our lives, we should expect even more growth (Rom 5:3-5). Second, "in all things God works for the good of those who love him, who have been called according to his purpose" (Rom 8:28 NIV). Paul does not say that all things do in fact "work together for good" (contra NRSV and NASB) but that God is working to accomplish good in all things.[111] John Stott observes that "all things do not automatically work themselves together into a pattern of good."[112] Sometimes even people of faith are worn down by trials. Tribulations do not always strengthen people's trust in God. Just because God is at work in our lives does not assure his victory. James H. Evans Jr. comments, "Providence refers not only to God's *acts* in history but more accurately to God's work in history. . . . God, in African-American religious experience, *works* in history. To work is to accomplish something in spite of resistance."[113] The purposes of God meet with resistance, and even God does not always get what he desires. Furthermore, the verse does not say that God specifically sends the trouble into our lives.[114] Rather, God makes use of the sin, evil and tribulations—which he has not ordained to come about—attempting to bring good out of evil. Paul is not saying that God does evil that good may come!

The third reason Paul gives for having confidence in God despite trials is that nothing in creation and not even death itself can separate us from God's love in Jesus (Rom 8:38-39). For Paul, circumstances such as nakedness, danger or personal injury tell him neither that God has abandoned him nor that he has sinned. Instead, he allows the life, death and resurrection of Jesus to be the foundation of his confidence in God's disposition toward him. The Father of Jesus, who raised him from the dead, does not allow death to have the last word over us for we are, in Jesus, his children. Death itself cannot withstand the coming kingdom of God—the divine project—for God is victorious over death.[115]

God is not yet finished with his project. Even after God's definitive work in Jesus there is still much sin and suffering. Things are not automatically put right. Van de Beek points out that "the time between the resurrection and the eschaton is also the time of the Holy Spirit. . . . What the Spirit does is to make known in the world, by way of human agents and human history, the decision that has been made in Christ. That takes time."[116] Furthermore, the way of the Spirit, like God's way to Christ, is not predictable or uniform. No analytic truths or principle of sufficient reason determine the path the Spirit must take, for the Holy Spirit is sovereign and free to work the way the divine wisdom deems best. The Spirit is not a computer program designed to follow a prescribed path. The Spirit is resourceful, flexible and patient in seeking to accomplish the divine project in the world.

But is the Spirit being successful in this effort? Is the world being saved? The television news seems to suggest otherwise. But much more is going on in the world than the networks consider "newsworthy." People are being affected by the work of the Spirit and do make transitions in their lives by responding to the divine love. Although God is not succeeding with everyone, the biblical witness is clear that God has made substantial progress in building a people of whom he is proud to be their God (Heb 11:16). Though the church has failed repeatedly, God has made use of it to spread his love to others. We have reason to hope in the Spirit, for the work of the Spirit is not yet done and the way into the future is not closed and sealed. The Spirit is active and seeking those who worship God in spirit and in truth (Jn 4:23). Though the Spirit may not get everything he desires, we have reason to hope because we have a God with a proven track record of successfully navigating the vicissitudes of human history and redeeming it. We have confidence that God will bring his project to the fruition he desires because God has proven himself faithful time and again.[117] He does not give up on us; we have good reason not to give up on him. God has achieved some of what he wants, but much more remains to be accomplished.

4.16 Excursus on Predictions and Foreknowledge

Whereas theology has traditionally emphasized the abstractions of omniscience and foreknowledge, the biblical writers stressed the wisdom and knowledge of God, which enabled God to be of help.[118] God has depth of knowledge (Ps 139:1-6) and breadth of knowledge (Job 28:23-24). At times God declares what will be (Is 44:6-7). But what the biblical writers value most is God's wisdom in his dealings with people (Rom 11:33). In Jesus are hidden all the treasures of wisdom and knowledge (Col 2:3). For the biblical writers, God's knowledge of the future is less important than his promises and his faithfulness to them.

The classical theological tradition, however, has not always shared this biblical emphasis. Instead, exhaustive foreknowledge has often been considered as one of the key defining attributes of God.[119] Gorringe, however, is more in line with Scripture when he writes, "What makes God God is not prediction but promise, God's *ḥesed* or covenant faithfulness."[120] Nevertheless, the idea of foreknowledge and the predictions assumed to be based on it are taken for granted today and must be addressed. In another place (6.5) I discuss why foreknowledge is useless for predicting the future or for guaranteeing the end from the beginning. Here I limit the discussion to biblical "predictions" and how a view known as "presentism" (God knows all the past and present but there is no exhaustively definite future for God to know) might account for them.[121]

The word *foreknowledge* occurs seven times in the New Testament (the verb *proginōskō* in Acts 26:5; Rom 8:29; 11:2; 1 Pet 1:20; 2 Pet 3:17; the noun *prognōsis* in Acts 2:23; 1 Pet 1:2).[122] Five times it is used for divine knowing in advance, and twice it refers to humans' having foreknowledge.[123] Obviously, if the term is applied to humans, then the mere use of the word *foreknowledge* does not settle our dispute, since (1) no human has exhaustive knowledge of the future and (2) the issue is the nature and content of the divine prognosis. When God is said to have foreknowledge, the object of the divine knowledge is either Jesus Christ or the people of God (as a group).[124] Hence God "foreknows" the incarnation as well as his decision to elect a people of God.[125] Neither of these requires exhaustive foreknowledge of future contingencies, only knowledge of what God chooses to do.

Many traditionalists focus on scriptural predictions and their fulfillment for apologetic purposes, proving either that Jesus was the Messiah because he fulfilled all the messianic prophecies or that the Bible is divinely inspired because the predictions are thought to be precisely fulfilled.[126] This is a rather curious claim given the fact that the disciples as well as others did not see Jesus fitting into their understandings of messianic predictions. Some claim that predictive prophecy requires divine control of "every atom" in the universe.[127] Others hold only that the predictions demonstrate God's exhaustive foreknowledge of the future. In his book *The Only Wise God* William Lane Craig provides a helpful summary of the biblical texts commonly used in this regard.[128] Although the passages he cites are compatible with the affirmation of foreknowledge, they do not *require* it. Claims to divine foreknowledge go beyond what the texts actually say. For instance, that God declares "the end from the beginning" (Is 46:10) can be interpreted harmoniously with either divine fore-knowledge or the present-knowledge model defended here. It all depends on the content the interpreter gives to the expression. I think God is declaring the "end" (exile and restoration) before it happens. But this does not entail exhaustive foreknowledge, only the ability of God to bring it about. The psalmist says that before a word is on his tongue God knows it (Ps 139:4). This may be explained by divine foreknowledge or by God's knowing the psalmist so well that he can "predict" what he will say and do. The psalmist expresses this idea in typical poetic fashion.

Craig correctly notes the scriptural assertion that God "discloses the future." But this does not explain whether disclosing a future event requires exhaustive foreknowledge or whether it may be explained in some other way. Richard Rice provides an overview of how such disclosures of the future may be understood by the present-knowledge model.[129] Sometimes God simply discloses what God is going to do irrespective of creaturely decision. God can bring some things about on his own if he decides to do so (Is 46:9-11). But this does not require foreknowledge, only the ability to do it.[130] Many of the biblical predictions commonly cited as requiring foreknowledge actually only require foreordination. In this respect Calvinism and presentism are in agreement: God foreknows what he determines to do.

Another explanation that accounts for some predictions is that they are conditional.[131] God declares that something will happen *if* certain factors come about (Jer 18:7-10). God discloses what "will" happen, but this is dependent on human response. For instance, God may declare that judgment will come on people if they do not repent or that blessing will come if they demonstrate trust in him. Sometimes, as in the case of Jonah, God leaves the conditional element left unstated. This is the usual way of accounting for "failed" predictions, in which God's statement of what would happen did not come about. For instance, in 1 Samuel 23:9-13 David asked God if Saul would come to the town of Keliah, and God said he would. Then David asked God if the people of the town would hand him over to Saul. Again, God said this would happen. But David was not handed over to Saul because he fled the area. In these cases proponents of exhaustive foreknowledge claim that if what God says will happen does not come about, then the conditional element should be assumed. I agree, but it should be noted that even "successful" predictions may have been conditional also. It is common for proponents of foreknowledge to apply the category of conditional prediction *only* to failed predictions and to view all fulfilled predictions as manifestations of exhaustive foreknowledge. But some divine statements regarding the future that came to pass were just as conditional—just as dependent on human response—as those that were unfulfilled. This was discussed in some detail in the section on divine repentance in the previous chapter. A problem arises regarding conditional promises, which proponents of exhaustive foreknowledge need to explain: How can a conditional promise be genuine if God already foreknows the human response and so foreknows that he will, in fact, never fulfill the promise?

A third way of explaining some predictions according to presentism is to see them as statements about what will happen based on God's exhaustive knowledge of the past and present. In other words, given the depth and breadth of God's knowledge of the present situation, God forecasts what he thinks will happen. In this regard God is the consummate social scientist predicting what will happen. God's ability to predict the future in this way is far more accurate than any human forecaster's, however, since God has exhaustive access to all past and present knowledge. This would explain God's foretelling Moses that

Pharaoh would refuse to grant his request. Nonetheless, this does leave open the possibility that God might be "mistaken" about some points, as the biblical record acknowledges. For instance, in Exodus God thought that the elders of Israel would believe Moses, but God acknowledges that Moses is correct in suggesting the possibility that they may not believe him (Ex 3:16—4:9).[132] God also thought the people of Jeremiah's day would repent and return to him, but they did not, to God's dismay (Jer 3:7, 19-20).[133]

This understanding of omniscience has the advantage of being able to explain in a straightforward fashion both the texts that depict God as knowing the future and those that portray God as not knowing the future in a definite manner. Some biblical texts speak of the future as foreknown and determined by God, whereas others refer to the future as open and unknown by God (in a definite sense). The traditional approach has been to affirm one type of text and deny the other any validity. For instance, proponents of exhaustive foreknowledge discount all the texts that depict God as having an open future in front of him in his relations with humans—where God does not know for sure what we shall do. Process theologians, on the other hand, reject passages that portray the future as definite and even determined by God. In the openness model of omniscience, however, both sorts of texts are valid and reveal aspects of God's relationship with us. In this model the future is in some respects open and in some respects closed. Hence, there is no need to dismiss any of the biblical texts.

The notion that God could be dismayed or wrong about anything may not sit well with some people, so perhaps some qualifications may be helpful. First, what is meant by the word *mistake*? Strictly speaking, God would make a mistake if he declared infallibly that something would come to pass and it did not. God would never be mistaken so long as he never said that *X* (for example, Adam will not sin) would infallibly come to pass and it did not. Using the term more loosely, we might say that God would be mistaken if he believed that *X* would happen (for example, Israel in Jeremiah's day would come to love him) and, in fact, *X* does not come about. In this sense the Bible does attribute some mistakes to God. Second, in either sense of the term conditional prophecies that did not come to pass would not constitute "mistakes" on God's part, since they are conditional and God was not claiming that such and such would happen regardless of anything that transpired. Third, it should be remembered that God can simply declare unconditionally that he is going to do something and do it. (The issue then is divine power not divine knowledge.)

Finally, even if we affirm that God is sometimes "mistaken" in the sense that God believed something would happen when, in fact, it does not come about, there is a question as to how often this happens. The biblical record gives a few occasions, but we are in no position to judge just how many times this occurs with God. Even if it happens regularly, this does not imply that God is helpless in the face of the future, since the real question is whether or not God has the wisdom, love, power and faithfulness to continue working with his project until he brings it to the fulfillment he intends. And this is answered in the affirmative, based on God's track record, regardless of one's view of the type of omniscience God has.

In summary, the present-knowledge model holds that divine predictions may be accounted for in one of three ways: as statements of what God, unconditioned by his creatures, intends to do; as declarations that are conditioned by the creatures of what God will do or of what will happen; and as inferences based on God's exhaustive knowledge of the past and present. When God provides a prediction regarding the future, a key consideration is whether God has the ability to bring it about. Presentism affirms that God does have such power (Is 43:13). Yet God is free to change his path based on his own purposes and his dynamic relationship with the creation.

Other factors that must also be considered include the distinction between prophecy, or promise, and prediction. Prophecies undergo multiple fulfillments and are not stated with a high degree of specificity. Who, from reading the Old Testament, could have predicted exactly what the Messiah would be like? The biblical literalists of Jesus' day rejected him as an impostor—not the true messiah "predicted" in the Hebrew Bible. Some evangelicals believe that anyone could have read the Old Testament and understood that the Messiah would be crucified and resurrected. But, as was shown above, this was not the case in Jesus' day. There is nothing specifically said in the Old Testament that would have led one to predict a dying and raised Messiah. Paul does claim (Acts 13:32-35) that the raising of Jesus is the "fulfillment" of the ancient promise, but it must be remembered that the term *resurrection* here has undergone a transformation of meaning. It is only in light of what happened to Jesus that the New Testament writers are able to reformulate their understanding of the Old Testament. Berkouwer is correct in stating that it is only after the fact, through faith in Jesus, that the believing community reads these prophecies.[134]

What do the New Testament writers mean when they claim that something Jesus did "fulfilled" an Old Testament passage?[135] For instance, when Matthew cites Hosea 11:1 as being "fulfilled" by the return

of Mary, Joseph and Jesus from Egypt, he is well aware that the passage in
Hosea is not a *prediction* of the future at all (Mt 2:15). Rather, it is a
reference to the exodus of Moses' day. For Matthew, such events are not
the fulfillment of ancient predictions about the Messiah; they serve to show
Jesus having similar experiences to those of Israel or individuals in the Old
Testament.[136] Matthew goes on to say that Jesus' being from Nazareth
fulfilled what was written in the Prophets (2:23). M. Eugene Boring, who
has a helpful discussion of Matthew's view of prophecy, comments on this
verse: "The fact that Jesus came from Nazareth generated a 'prediction' in
2:23."[137] It is in retrospect that the New Testament authors read the Old
Testament for parallels or recapitulation between the life of Jesus and Old
Testament events.

Some may object citing Matthew's claim that things must happen in a
certain way so that the Scriptures might be fulfilled (Mt 26:54; compare Mk
14:49). Yet Jesus does not specify *what* it is that must be fulfilled and *which*
prophecy he is alluding to. Moreover, Matthew attributes to "prophecies"
meanings they would not have had originally. In fact, Matthew modifies the
wording of many Old Testament texts in light of what he has experienced
in Jesus.[138] The Word of God is reinterpreted in light of what God is presently
doing. The conviction that God's project came through the life, death and
resurrection of Jesus shaped the way the New Testament writers read and
quoted the Old Testament. Boring says that it "does not mean that the
prophecies are a prewritten script that Jesus must dutifully act out, but that
the Scriptures represent the plan and will of God, to which Jesus willingly
and trustingly submits."[139] Jesus is not referring to some predetermined plan
of God but to his understanding of the way of the Messiah gleaned from the
Old Testament.

How are the predictions that Jesus himself made to be explained, since
these are sometimes understood as implying exhaustive foreknowledge?[140]
Jesus made several predictions, including some concerning his passion and
resurrection, the destruction of the temple and Peter's denial. Regarding his
passion and resurrection several points should be made.[141] First, the initial
disclosures were veiled, and the one that is quite detailed (Mk 10:33-34)
"contains no features which would not be generally known in capital
proceedings in Palestine at the time of Christ."[142] As the time draws nearer,
Jesus becomes more explicit. Although his predictions would later identify him
as a prophet, they do not require exhaustive foreknowledge. Raymond Brown
doubts that Jesus' initial predictions were all that clear, since "the disciples who
are supposed to have heard these predictions do not seem to have foreseen
the crucifixion even when it was imminent nor to have expected the

resurrection (Lk 24:19-26). . . . One may attribute this failure to the slowness of the disciples, but one may also wonder if the original predictions were as exact as they have now come to us."[143] Brown's suggestion has some merit, since the Gospel writers did clarify Jesus' words and actions so that their respective audiences would understand the meaning. Things became clear after the events. Nonetheless, even if Jesus' predictions of his passion were veiled, they were still made, and so one must account for them.

Jesus said that the temple would be destroyed and that not one stone would be left upon another (Mt 24:2; Mk 13:2; Lk 21:6). Brown comments, "If anyone would propose that this represented an exact foreknowledge of what would happen in 70, he need simply be reminded that the gigantic blocks of the Temple foundation are still standing firmly one upon the other in Jerusalem."[144] Many commentators pass over this prophecy in silence, or say that it is fulfilled in essence even if not in detail or claim that the foundation is not considered part of the temple.[145] Actually, foreknowledge could still be affirmed if one allows that Jesus is using hyperbole. Nevertheless, I think Jesus is basing his statement on what he believes will happen as a consequence of Israel's refusal to trust God. In my opinion, this was a conditional prophecy, not set in concrete. If the Jewish people had come to faith in Jesus, then this would not have happened.

Regarding the prediction of Peter's denial, several things should be noted. To begin, the announcement takes place after Jesus knows that Judas has left to turn him over to the authorities. Thus Jesus knows that the forces arrayed against him will also come against his disciples. According to Luke, the disciples have just had a dispute among themselves as to which one of them was the greatest (22:24). This reveals that the disciples are not in the best spiritual position for coping with the coming events. Furthermore, Jesus informs Peter of an impending spiritual attack on his faith: Satan wants to test him (22:31). Jesus is quite aware of the formidable demonic forces ready to put his disciples to the test. It is on the basis of Jesus' knowledge of the situation that he makes his prediction regarding Peter's denial. The prediction does not come out of the blue but arises out of the context of the relationships between Jesus and the disciples. Upon hearing the announcement, Peter strongly denies that it will come about. Like his Old Testament counterparts and despite his belief that Jesus is the Messiah, Peter does not view such predictions as predetermined to occur: He says that Jesus is wrong in this matter. This is a very interesting point. Against it one could claim that Peter held a deficient view of foreknowledge or foreordination, but it seems more likely that he held to the same view presented in the Old Testament—that even with God the future is open and the "prediction" is conditional.

The above interpretation of Jesus' prediction regarding Peter is not the only one available to the proponent of presentism, however. Lorenzo McCabe, for instance, suggests that Jesus is attempting to teach Peter a lesson concerning the importance of spiritual preparedness.[146] Hence if one wanted to say that the the three cock crows and the three denials of Peter were explicitly foreknown by Jesus, then one could simply assert that in this particular case God orchestrated events in order to drive home a point to someone God intended to be a leading apostle. In this case the "foreknowledge" is due to foreordination, which is compatible with presentism.

Immediately after this dialogue Jesus encourages the disciples to pray in order to resist temptation (Mt 26:40-41). But they fall asleep and so render themselves more vulnerable to the possibility of failing to trust God during the coming crisis. In light of these factors I understand Jesus' prediction of Peter's denial to be a conditional one based on his knowledge of Peter's spiritual state and the situation at hand.[147] In this case the "prediction" serves as a warning to Peter: Unless he takes some important steps, he will fail. Jesus knows both the forces arrayed against him and his disciples as well as the disciples' spiritual unpreparedness for the forthcoming crisis. If Peter and his fellow disciples had followed Jesus' instruction to pray, they would have been prepared for temptation and the prediction might not have come about.[148] However, Peter failed to pray and did succumb to temptation, so the conditional prediction was fulfilled.[149]

To sum up, God can predict the future as something he intends to do regardless of human response, or God may utter a conditional statement that is dependent on human response, or God may give a forecast of what he thinks will occur based on his exhaustive knowledge of past and present factors. The predictions of Jesus may also be understood in these ways. I am not claiming that the theory of exhaustive foreknowledge fails to explain biblical predictions, just that biblical predictions do not require this theory for their explanation. It may seem to proponents of exhaustive foreknowledge that the explanations of various scriptural texts discussed above are strained and unconvincing. But that is the way those who affirm presentism regard the explanations offered by proponents of foreknowledge on other texts such as divine repentance. "The crucial question," says David Basinger, "is whether the idea is faithful to the overall biblical portrait of God."[150] The preceding two chapters have sought to show that the present-knowledge model is indeed faithful to the biblical portrait of a God who enters into genuine give-and-take relations in which God is, at times, dismayed or delighted, upset or joyful and in which God even changes his mind. At other times he makes pronouncements regarding specific future events. The future is partly open or indefinite and partly closed or definite. Which is which depends solely on God's sovereign choices.

4.17 Conclusion

This survey of the biblical material pertaining to God's relationship to the world has sought to show the nature of the divine project as one in which God sovereignly enters into a relationship with his creatures in a way that involves risk for both God and his creatures. The almighty God creates significant others with freedom and grants them space to be alongside him and to collaborate with him. God expects this collaboration to proceed toward the fulfillment of his goal for creation. God loves us, provides for us and desires our trust and love in return. We see this most fundamentally demonstrated in the life of Jesus, who came not to dominate others but to reconcile rebellious creatures through the power of love. In the New Testament material we find continuity with many Old Testament themes but with some significant clarifications. In the life of Jesus we see both the goal God has for us (Christlikeness in the new heaven and earth) and the means of providential care God provides in the attainment of the goal. Jesus trusted his Father, accepting his place as a creature with all the vulnerability this entailed. Moreover, the work of God depends on the resources available in any given situation and the cooperation of humans. God resourcefully works with human attitudes, values and character, seeking to accomplish his project.

The life of Jesus shows that he is able to exercise greater control over the nonhuman world than over humans. Miracles, in part, are dependent on the social context and the relationships people had with Jesus. In these relationships Jesus showed himself flexible and open to adjusting his plans in response to the concerns of others. The way of providence in the life of Jesus did not occur by some predetermined plan. Everything is not being worked out according to some eternal script. God responds to his creatures and gets involved in the give and take of life. God remained faithful to his original commitment while working to fulfill it in ways the covenant people did not anticipate.

Furthermore, in Jesus God demonstrates his love toward us. The cross and resurrection are God's measured response to sin and evil. Through agape love God gives of himself in Jesus to sinful creatures and so experiences suffering and humiliation. Such love is nonmanipulative and unselfish, seeking the greatest well-being of the creatures. Divine love pays the cost of forgiveness and overcomes evil. This is the way that God displays his wisdom and seeks to win our trust. God is seeking to build a people of whom he is proud to be God. This is the divine project, established at creation, to which God has remained faithful. Yet the path of providence has taken many a winding turn, and no one can predict precisely what God will do. But a couple of things remain clear. In Jesus we see the very face of God, and so we can no longer doubt that the way of God is a love that desires the eradication of the sin which ruins the beloved. Yet, this love does not force its will on the beloved. Rather, it comes to us in passionate vulnerability. Furthermore, in contrast to the no-risk model, Jesus did not go about cleaning up the mess caused by the disease, disasters and misery that his Father had caused. In Jesus we find that he and the Father stand fundamentally opposed to sickness, chaos and evil. Our views of providence must be grounded in what God actually decided to do in history instead of deducing a normative understanding of providence from eternal principles buttressed with some proof texts.

The other thing that is clear is that God is not yet finished with his project. Jesus promised that the Holy Spirit would help us (Jn 14:16-17, 26). The divine presence is still with us. In the Old Testament the divine promise that God would be "with" his people normally occurred in times of danger. God usually did not remove the danger but promised to be with his people through the danger. Likewise, Jesus promised to be "with" us to the end of the age (Mt 28:20). The promise is that the divine presence stays with us even in difficult times. The Spirit who helps is still working. History has already witnessed the fruit of the Spirit, and we hope for more. The Spirit has not achieved everything that God desired, but God is making progress in reclaiming rebellious humans in love and faith. This is witnessed in God's success in overcoming the disciple's preconceived notions of messiahship; they did reorient themselves to the divine way of Jesus. The people God redeems are to participate in the covenant, working to enlarge the kingdom. God is working but has chosen not to work without us: we are to be collaborators with God. Consequently, humans have been given significant responsibility in the accomplishment of God's project. The exact way God decides to go as well as the degree of fulfillment God achieves in reaching his goal depends, in part, on us. God's initial risk has not proved a failure, since we see evidence of God's work in history. We look forward to God's work in the future, when he will abolish death and subject all things to himself (1 Cor 15:26-28). We have reason to hope, since God has repeatedly proven himself faithful in history. Because of the life and work of Jesus we have a solid basis to place our confidence in God's amazing love, faithfulness and resourcefulness. God is wise and competent in carrying out his project, and we look forward to its completion.

Having developed from the Old and New Testaments a relational model of divine providence in which God takes risks, it is now necessary to examine the Christian tradition to see if there are elements in it that may be retrieved in support of this model.

FIVE

DIVINE RELATIONALITY IN THE CHRISTIAN TRADITION

. . . .

5.1 Introduction

The way of reading the Bible described in the previous two chapters resonates well with the piety of many believers throughout the history of the church. The notion that God enters into reciprocal give-and-take relations with us and genuinely responds to our prayers permeates the sermons, prayers and devotional literature of Christians throughout the ages. This is important, since one of the criteria for evaluating a theological proposal is consonance with the tradition. Nevertheless, many readers will find themselves at odds with some of the interpretations advanced in the last two chapters. For instance, biblical commentators have long understood texts that speak of God's changing his mind as "anthropomorphisms," which do not depict God as he really is (see 3.12). Theological reflection on the nature of God has often claimed that God, being perfect, could not do such things. In the Christian tradition this has led, in my opinion, to a tensive relationship between what is affirmed about God in the piety and prayer life of many believers and what is affirmed about God in theological reflection. Although Christian philosophers and theologians never intended to downplay or reject a "relational theism," whereby God enters into truly personal relations with us, they sometimes forfeited or curtailed important biblical understandings of God such as those developed in the previous two chapters. This seriously hampered the development of a genuinely relational concept of God.

Certainly the element of divine risk taking has been neglected. In this book I intend to develop a model of God that is in full agreement with the canons of Scripture, the devotional life of the Christian tradition and some, but not all, aspects of the theological tradition. Since certain aspects of theological tradition challenge my proposal, I shall address it to see whether there are elements in it that may be retrieved toward the establishment of relational theism. I will argue that the model of providence defended here finds agreement with the intentions and functions, though not always the material content, of the theological tradition.[1]

According to the classical theist H. P. Owen, "So far as the Western world is concerned theism has a double origin: the Bible and Greek philosophy."[2] Classical theism is the product of the "biblical-classical synthesis."[3] Despite different attitudes taken by the church fathers toward philosophy, the influence of Greek philosophical notions of God is pervasive, even among those who "repudiate" philosophy. The fathers had several noble reasons for making use of Greek thought. As they sought to overthrow the gods of paganism, they found in philosophy some helpful critiques of the polytheistic gods. Moreover, they desired to show that the God of biblical history was the universal God rather than a tribal deity, that this God was compatible with the best thinking of their day and that the Christian God was the fulfillment of the God sought by the philosophers. In this light they sought to protect the Christian understanding of God from anything thought to be unworthy of deity, as was the case with the myths about the Greco-Roman pantheon. The fathers did critique certain aspects of the Hellenistic worldview. They did not believe that it had the total truth about God—otherwise there would have been no need for Jesus. On the other hand, though the fathers do retain many important features of the biblical God, they sometimes do not allow these features to call into question the philosophical understanding of the divine nature.

In seeking to accomplish these objectives, the early fathers did not sell out to Hellenism, but they did, on certain key points, use it to both defend and explain the Christian concept of God to their contemporaries. Classical theism, the product of the biblical-classical synthesis, has become so commonplace that many people today simply assume it is *the* correct scriptural concept of God and thus assume that any other alleged biblical understanding of God (such as the one proposed here) must be rejected. The classical view is so taken for granted that it functions as a preunderstanding that rules out certain interpretations of Scripture, since they do not "fit" with the conception of what is thought "appropriate" for God to be like. Nevertheless, certain elements in the theological tradition that buttress my contention that the model of providence developed here is in consonance with the tradition may be retrieved in support of relational theism.

5.2 Some Early Fathers

According to second-century writer Justin Martyr, God is unchangeable, eternal, incomprehensible, impassible, noncorporeal and anonymous. The ineffable God is nameless: Not even terms such as God, Father, Creator or Lord actually apply to God.[4] But Justin is careful not to allow these ideas to totally overthrow the biblical portrait of God as patient, compassionate and loving. He rejects the Epicurean notion that the gods do not concern themselves with human affairs when he declares that though there are no passions in God, he does care for us: God, after all, is "not a stone."[5] Justin also addresses the issue of divine foreknowledge and human freedom. He argues for a libertarian definition of freedom as the mark God bestowed on humanity that distinguishes them from the rest of creation and by which God can hold humans morally accountable for their choices.[6] Yet he also believes that God foreknows all the decisions humans will make, which explains the prophecies in Scripture. This does not, he believes, lead to determinism because God only foresees the free choices of individuals and bases his election on their choices.[7] In this respect God's decisions are in some sense dependent on human choices. Consequently, God is "responsive" for Justin. It is vitally important to note that Justin was struggling with the issue of how God could enter into genuine give-and-take relations with his creatures while retaining a strong sense of divine otherness. He believes God is in some respects conditioned by the decisions humans make, which is of fundamental importance for a relational theism. He affirms that God comes to us in Jesus Christ, getting involved in our history. Justin avoided either attributing any undesirable passions to God or saying that anything is forced on God without divine consent, while holding that God genuinely responds to us.

The picture is much the same in the important book by Irenaeus, *Against Heresies.*[8] Yet Irenaeus advances the discussion in a couple of significant ways. First, he explains the concept of divine wrath on evildoers in the sense that the evil deed is its own punishment (5.27.2). In this way, there would be no angry passions in God to disturb the divine blessedness. Second, and more importantly, he rejects the Neoplatonic need for intermediaries between God and creatures: God can deal directly with his creation.[9] This is significant, for it means that the otherness of God does not imply the impossibility of direct divine involvement in human life. Regarding the divine-human encounter he affirms libertarian human freedom and rejects any predetermination on God's part concerning human decisions (4.37.1-2). Though he does not want to allow what he deems negative passions in God, Irenaeus believes God gets involved personally with us.

Tertullian sought to do away with all attempts at combining Christianity with various philosophies. To his credit he affirmed that God can change his mind, as is clearly seen in God's repentance of his intention to destroy Nineveh.[10] He sought to break free of the limitations of the doctrines of immutability and impassibility to more easily allow for a reading of the biblical text that affirms divine *responsiveness* to changes in the world.[11] God's will can change in response to human decisions. For Tertullian, God has many feelings in common with us, but God has them in a way that is "fitting" for God so that the divine nature remains unaffected by them.[12] Moreover, he is willing to speak of the "crucified God" who suffered on our behalf.[13] God, he says, is not in control of everything that happens because he has chosen to grant humans free will by which they may participate with or fight against God's purposes. God foresaw the evil that would happen in the world but did not rescind the liberty he had granted at creation. Instead, he has chosen to respond with blessings and punishments, depending on human actions.[14] God is affected by what we do, but the effect is not imposed on God by us. Rather, God's way of being affected is different from the way we are affected. Perhaps more than any other early Christian theologian, Tertullian emphasized key elements of relational theism: God in responsive, resourceful engagement with us.

The third-century Alexandrian theologian Origen stepped up the tension between the biblical language about God and the Greek philosophical notions of God. Origen believes that God is impassible, immutable, uncreated, simple, all-powerful and all-knowing.[15] He holds that because God has foreknowledge of the free choices humans will make, God has providentially prearranged his responses. Via foreknowledge, God atemporally acquires the knowledge of what creatures will do in the future, and then God plans what he will do in response. He steadfastly maintains that God's foreknowledge of human decisions is not their cause and does not necessitate what will happen. For Origen and the fathers before him, foreknowledge does not preclude conditionality in God. Interestingly, some friends asked Origen why they should pray if God foreknows everything or if he has predestined all things. In response he rejects predetermination of all things, upholds human freedom and insists that prayer is still valuable even though God foreknows our prayers, since God did not foreordain them.[16] God merely foreknows our requests and has already prearranged his responses.

In a couple of famous homilies he stretches the bonds of classical theism when he affirms that God rejoices at human conversion and experiences sorrow for human sin. Moreover, the Son of God felt compassion for us in our sin and so condescended to take on human flesh and suffer on the cross for us. He even claims that God the Father experiences the human emotions of suffering, pity and love. It seems that Origen desired to defend a genuine relationship between God and humanity, but he found it difficult given the constraints of Hellenic thought. For he goes on to say that God is truly passionless and experiences uninterrupted happiness. All of the scriptural references to the passions of God (for example, anger and joy) are anthropomorphisms and cannot be taken literally.[17]

He similarly explains away biblical references to the repentance of God. They must be figures of speech, he says, because God is immutable and knows the future. God only appears to be joyful or angry and only seems to repent, but in actuality God never does such things, for if he did it would reflect negatively on the worth of the deity. What then of the incarnation? If Jesus is truly God, then did he not suffer and experience change and emotions? Origen struggles with this issue and ends up repeating, like those before him, that only the human side of Jesus suffered; his divinity remained untouched by the incarnation and temporality.[18] Though Origen sensed the tension in his thought here, he was unable to resolve it. He claims that God is genuinely responsive to our actions and prayers (God is conditioned by us for some things), but he has difficulty seeing how divine repentance does not detract from the perfection of God.

One writer of the third century made a significant attempt at qualifying the philosophical understanding of divine immutability and impassibility in light of the biblical narrative. Supposedly written by one of Origen's students, named Gregory, the text claims that though God cannot be forced to suffer, he can voluntarily choose to suffer for the sake of human salvation.[19] But even this sort of suffering is not genuine suffering, since God is not subject to suffering but only wills to share in sufferings. Since God chose to suffer of his own free will and was successful in obtaining redemption, it can be said that his nature remained impassible. The breakthrough here is seen in the affirmation of the divine freedom to sovereignly do things we might deem incompatible with deity. God is free to enter into relationship with us in such a way that God may experience suffering. Of course, it is suffering as only God can suffer, but it opens the door wider for understanding a more responsive deity who enters into give-and-take relations with his creatures.

Lactantius, a Latin writer, also criticized the supposed impassibility of God, producing a treatise on God's anger in which he defends the reality of divine emotions.[20] Arnobius, Lactantius' teacher, held that God is impassible in such a way that our prayers make no difference to God; they are merely for our benefit.[21] Lactantius responds by claiming that our prayers and worship do make a difference to God and that God's blessedness does not exclude the experiences of joy, benevolence, anger or pity.[22] If you remove these from God, he says, you remove any genuine religion and relationship with God. To those who claimed that God is perfectly impassible and at rest, Lactantius replied that to be perfectly at rest is to be dead.[23] God is impassible, but in a way befitting the God who enters into personal relations with us.

In his response to the Arians, who denied the full divinity of Jesus, Athanasius claimed that we have to begin with the historical salvation accomplished in the incarnation of the Son of God, not with a discussion of the being of God.[24] It is God himself, he claimed, who comes to save us in Jesus. This was an important methodological move, for it placed the divine revelation of what God has actually done and disclosed about himself as primary for our knowledge of the nature of God. If God comes to save us in Jesus, then Jesus is fully God. If that means that we have to revise our preconceived notions of deity, then so be it.

In the creeds the full divinity of the Son becomes formalized. The councils of Nicaea and Constantinople affirmed that the divine Son shares the same being as the Father, the two having an internal relation in the Godhead. Robert Jenson points out two important modifications of the philosophical God concept implied in these declarations. First, "to be God is to be related. With that the fathers contradicted the main principle of Hellenic theology." Second, if the Son is "begotten," then "to be God is not only to give being, it is also to receive being. And there went the 'rest of Plato.'"[25] The notion that God is truly Father and Son and Spirit means that God has internal relations. And so the notion that God has genuine relations with the creatures should not be inimical to deity.

In the East the Cappadocian fathers (Basil, Gregory of Nyssa, Gregory of Nazianzus) argued against Eunomius, who claimed that God was a simple essence (not composed of any parts) and so the Son and Spirit could not be fully God: God is devoid of internal relations. In response, the Cappadocians claimed that the terms "Father" and "Son" referred to the *relation* between the Father and the Son. In so doing they held that person, not substance, was the ultimate metaphysical category and thus, in opposition to Eunomius, they could claim that God was supremely relational.[26] The Father can beget the Son because the Father, as personal, has self-emptying love for another. God is then not alone, in isolation from relationships, but eternally related within the Godhead as Trinity. God is then not an "in-itself," apart from others, but the epitome of love in relation.

Moreover, the Cappadocians had a different understanding of God's external relation to history and the created order.[27] For them, the creator is radically different from the creature. But this does not mean that God is distant, since to be Creator is to be actively related to the creature. This is especially evident in salvation history, in which the *activity* of the Father, Son and Holy Spirit is the essence of God! Regarding God's relationship to time, Gregory of Nyssa chastises the Arians for defining God's being as having no beginning (ungenerate) rather than as having no end. He holds that the unending God is Lord over history, which provides genuine hope.[28] In fact, Gregory claims the Arian's timeless God is inactive whereas his God keeps things moving. This understanding of God as involved with time and as a relational being (both internally and externally) was a tremendous break with Hellenic thought.

Thus the fathers affirmed God's dynamic, responsive relationship with creatures. The God who responds is in some respects conditioned by the creatures. That God is affected by the creatures is, however, solely on the basis of the divine freedom—no one imposes it on God. Although the fathers adopt the vocabulary of Greek philosophy, they are attempting to articulate what it means for God to be the free Creator and the gracious Redeemer. The fathers intended to (1) protect God from appearing to be unworthy of worship (as was the case with the pagan gods); (2) uphold the notion that the Christian God is the universal God by virtue of being the Creator of all that is; and (3) affirm that God is the living God who enters into loving, responsive relations with us.

In faithfulness to the Bible they upheld God's love and grace. They sought to affirm God's faithfulness and moral constancy and to safeguard God from compulsion or force. They maintained that God enters freely into relationship with humanity and in grace saves us. The doctrines of immutability and impassibility were intended to safeguard divine freedom and prevent anyone from confusing the Christian God with the fickle gods of the pagan religions. In addition they understood the incarnation as a decisive action of God in human history that dramatically altered the course of world history. Finally, for the most part, they held that God freely created ex nihilo, denying the eternality and necessity of the world.[29] God would still be God even without a creation.

That their formulations were not always fully satisfactory (whose are?) should not detract from their noble intentions. In fact, I agree with their intentions even if I cannot fully agree with the material content of their formulations. It seems to me that they consistently desired to affirm that God enters into genuine personal, responsive relations with us. Is there any divine risk involved in such relations? The fathers do not seem to clearly address this question, though it seems to me entirely consistent with their understandings of sin being contrary to the divine will and God being, in some respects, conditioned by the creatures.

5.3 Augustine

The great African writer Augustine made a tremendous departure in regard to the nature of the divine-human relationship. Augustine's views on this matter have profoundly shaped Western theology, even to this day. In his early writings Augustine sought to make a place for human freedom and divine responsiveness to the creatures, but his mature thought repudiated such notions. It could be argued that for Augustine, immutability is one of the most important divine attributes because it cannot be removed without placing his entire conception of God in jeopardy. "Whatever is changeable is not the most high God" and "that is truly real which remains immutable."[30] Of course, the important issue is how immutability is defined and applied. According to Augustine, divine immutability means that neither the divine knowledge nor the divine will ever changes in any respect. All of God's thoughts are fixed from eternity, and God never has any alteration in his will. Hence God can be said to know but cannot be said to plan, for planning implies a yet uncertain outcome. Moreover, God cannot be thought to enter into give-and-take relations with us, for any receptivity in God would imply a change, rendering the deity less than perfectly immutable. Augustine made God's immunity to time, change and responsiveness to his creatures axiomatic for much of Western theology.

Yet a case can also be made that what Augustine is seeking to protect by such assertions is that God, as Creator, is not a creature; thus the categories of creaturely being do not apply to God. That is, since God is the Creator of time, time does not apply to God, so human terms such as *planning* or *thinking* do not properly apply to God. There seems to have been a popular question in the early church concerning what God was doing before he created the world. In one place Augustine facetiously replies, "Making hell for those who pry too deep."[31]

But he also gives a theologically developed response. He declares that God did nothing before he created the world because time was not created until the world came into being.[32] Hence the word *before* has no meaning when applied to God. It only concerns creaturely existence. Augustine connects divine timelessness to the immutability of God's knowledge and will. God does not will one thing now and another later because he wills once and for all everything that he wills.[33] If it were not so, then God would be mutable and hence would not be eternal and simple. Furthermore, God cannot be said to know one thing now and another thing later, since he knows everything, including all future events, in one eternal moment of "spiritual vision."[34] Though the notion of divine timelessness may leave room for divine responsiveness to creatures, we would have difficulty explaining it because our language is tensed. Nevertheless, Augustine applied divine immutability pervasively in his theology, and this made any responsiveness by God problematic.

This can be seen in his discussion of divine foreknowledge and human freedom.[35] If God does not know the future, then he is not God. God knows what is going to happen, but his knowledge is not the cause of those future events. God simply sees what is going to happen.[36] Such remarks sound as though Augustine agreed with the fathers before him that God's knowledge of what the creatures do is conditioned by the creatures. This would make God in some sense dependent on the world. Elsewhere, however, when discussing the nature of election, he makes clear that there is no conditionality in God.[37] The fathers had taught that God uses his foreknowledge to see who will have faith and then elects those who will. In this respect they thought we had the freedom to become Christians. Augustine, however, rejects such a belief for two reasons: his anthropology and his doctrine of God. The sort of freedom necessary to respond positively to God was lost, he says, in the fall of Adam, so God must choose who will become believers. And if God's predestination for salvation depended on his foreknowledge of who would come to Christ, then God's will would be dependent on humanity, and that would be a violation of the divine immutability and impassibility. God is not dependent in any respect on anything or anyone, however, so the gift of salvation must be totally independent of human agents.[38] Human wills cannot interfere with God's decisions, for "the will of the omnipotent is always undefeated."[39]

It is from such a perspective that Augustine interprets the texts about God's desiring all people to be saved (for example, 1 Tim 2:4) as meaning either that no person is saved unless God wills his or her salvation or that "all people" refers not to every individual but to some individuals from all classes and ranks of people (for example, kings and slaves).[40] God cannot be thought to actually desire the salvation of each and every sinner because it would mean that God willed something that did not come about. It would imply a risk and failure on God's part, for God would not get everything he wanted. Augustine reasoned as follows: (1) God's will is never thwarted in the least detail, for it is an omnipotent and immutable will. (2) Scripture asserts that not all will be saved. (3) Therefore, God must not really want each and every sinner to be saved. If God wanted them saved, then they would be saved. Hence, the biblical passages that seem to assert that God wants them saved must only appear to teach this while not really asserting it.

Augustine applied the same logic to the question of the perseverance of the saints. For instance, what about those people who for a time profess faith in Christ but do not hold it to the end of their lives? According to Augustine, some people, though confessing Christians, are not genuine Christians, since God has not granted them persevering faith. Unless God willed from eternity that a believer in Christ (even a pastor) persevere to the end, then that person was never truly predestined for salvation.[41]

Augustine seems to affirm "specific sovereignty," according to which each and every event that happens is decreed by God to occur. For instance, regarding infants who suffer or die, he says that God has good reasons for such events. "Perhaps God is doing some good in correcting parents when their beloved children suffer pain and even death."[42] Though God's will is immutable, he always acts justly in the circumstances of life. Thus we should never question God's judgment.

Regarding divine repentance, Augustine is well aware of the numerous biblical texts that speak of God's "changing his mind," but such texts are written for "babes" and do not properly refer to God.[43] There are, he says, a few texts in Scripture that truly describe God's nature, namely, the ones that say he does not change. Augustine knows what is fitting for God to be *(dignum Deo)* and uses this understanding to filter the biblical message. Augustine maintains that divine repentance is literally impossible, since God's knowledge and will are immutable and are so from eternity.[44] When God "changed his mind" by removing the kingship from Saul and giving it to David, God did not change his will but only his "work."[45] In other words, the effects of what God has eternally willed change, but the will of God remains immutable. An immutable God may act on but not *interact* with others. Thus God cannot truly be said to respond to creatures.

Augustine treats the divine "passions" similarly. When God shows pity, his heart is not changed, and when God displays anger, his will remains the same. God experiences no emotion of pity or anger despite the fact that his work effects salvation and punishment.[46] The Bible, when speaking of divine wrath, anger, love and mercy, must not be taken literally. After all, God has known from all eternity who would be punished and who would be saved, so it would make no sense to ascribe temporal upset to God.[47] All change is to be explained as a change in us, not God. He says that people who develop eye problems may no longer be able to tolerate the light of the sun—but the change is in them, not the sun. Likewise, when people sin and experience the effects of God's judgment, it is they who have changed and not God.[48]

The same line of thought can be applied to God's love and mercy. Though God begins to be our Father when we are regenerated by his grace, there is no change in God. God's love can be defined as his activity by which he causes us to exist and some of us to be regenerated.[49] God's mercy is his eternally foreknown and predestined grace to the elect. The biblical references to divine love, mercy and wrath refer only to God's works and not to any emotions or any change in God's relationship to us and certainly not to any change in God's substance. For Augustine, the divine love is reduced to mere beneficence, and all possibility of reciprocal relations is excluded.

But, it may be asked, does not the creation of a world imply a change in God? How then can God be said to be Lord over creation when there was no creation? Must not God in some sense *become* Lord when he creates? Augustine's reply is that being Lord does not belong to the nature of God; otherwise the creation would have to be eternal. God may be said to "become" Lord, but that is only an "accidental" relation and does not affect the being of God.[50] It seems here that Augustine is (rightfully) seeking to protect the idea that God would remain God without any creation. A problem arises, however, since he maintains that neither internal relations (among Father, Son and Spirit) nor external relations (with creatures) involve the essence of God; God has no "real relationship" with any other, including creation. God's relationship to us in the economy of salvation is not constitutive of what God is. God remains unaffected by every "relation" between God and the creature.[51] Neither the triune love nor the creation seem to make any difference to the divine life. The divine essence, for Augustine, is defined, as Jaroslav Pelikan notes, "in relation to absoluteness and impassibility rather than on the basis of the active involvement of God in creation and redemption."[52] It is important to affirm that God has being and would remain God apart from a creation. But Augustine's thought goes too far by not allowing that God freely enters into reciprocal relations with the creation—relations in which God sovereignly opens the divine life to being affected by what transpires in his beloved creation. Though it is not his intention, he makes God a remote deity, perilously close to being impersonal.[53]

Augustine's ideas have had a profound effect on Western thought. His understandings of creation, psychology, anthropology, soteriology, politics and history have influenced both Christian and non-Christian thinkers alike. On some issues Augustine traces out more fully the views of the fathers, and on other issues he brings about innovations. His understanding of grace, faith and God's "relationship" to creation are seen in mechanistic terms rather than in personalistic and covenantal categories. His emphasis on divine immutability takes precedence over God's suffering love and faithfulness and rules out any possibility of God's having give-and-take relations with us (let alone the notion of divine risk taking). He quotes the Bible extensively but interprets it within the Neoplatonic framework.[54] His consistent rejection of any sort of changeability or conditionality in God leads to problems in understanding the nature of God's love for his creatures and how God can have any sort of covenant relationship with them. "The immunity of God to all 'real relationship' with creation will become axiomatic in scholastic theology."[55]

5.4 The Middle Ages

Prior to Augustine the fathers had taught that God entered into give-and-take relations with us. God was thought to be responsive to our actions and to be conditioned by us in certain respects. This was especially so in the case of sin, for God responded to it by deciding to work toward our redemption from sin. After Augustine, however, such divine responsiveness is largely denied in Western theological discourse. I will not comment much on the theologians of the medieval period except to highlight a couple of points pertinent to this study. For the most part, Augustine's view that God does not enter into authentically reciprocal, give-and-take relations with us is taken for granted by those in the West who followed him.

John Scotus Erigena (b. 810), whose main authority was Pseudo-Dionysius, said that biblical descriptions of God are for the simpleminded.[56] In truth the infinite God is unknowable, for to know is to define and to define is to limit. In fact, God does not even know himself. God is absolutely immutable and impassible: "God neither acts nor is acted upon, neither moves nor is moved, neither loves nor is loved."[57] The Bible, he says, "shouts on all sides" that this view is false but, he argues, the Bible must be taken metaphorically whereas the method of what is fitting for God to be *(dignum Deo)* gives us the literal truth. Hence God is said to love because he is the cause of all love and is said to be loved because all things long for him. God is completely removed from all genuine relationships with humanity.

Thomas Aquinas, at the apex of medieval theology, sought to harmonize the biblical-classical synthesis he inherited from the Christian tradition with the newly discovered works of Aristotle.[58] Hence Aristotelian ingredients are blended into the Neoplatonic-Christian recipe. Aquinas believed that God is pure actuality containing no potentiality. That is, there can be no "becoming" for God because he is eternally actualized. The best name for God then is "He who is," for God is the only one whose essence it is to exist. Because of this, the categories we use to conceptualize and speak about things do not, in any straightforward sense, apply to God.

Regarding predestination, Aquinas took up Augustine's view that divine election of individuals to salvation does not depend on his foreknowledge, as that would make God dependent on the creature.[59] Instead, God simply chooses those he will save without regard to his foreknowledge of their lives. God is, in fact, so radically independent that his knowledge of the world is not caused by the world.[60] God knows the world by knowing himself. This knowledge is direct and involves no deliberation or reasoning from premises to conclusion, as either of these options entails transition from ignorance to knowledge. Moreover, if God's knowledge of what will happen in history depended on the creature, then God would be dependent and passive, which would contradict God's pure actuality. God is completely independent, immutable and impassible. This, of course, makes God's "relationship" with the world suspect. For Aquinas, the creatures' relationship with God is "real," whereas God's relationship to the creation is only "logical." What he meant by this is that the very being of God is not altered by the creation, since God would remain God without a creation. Fair enough, but it seems that when he compares the divine-human relationship to that of a stone-human relationship, it becomes difficult to think of the relationship in personal terms. God, he says, is like a stone column to which we stand in relation. The column may be on our right or our left, but the relation to the column is always in us and not the column. Moreover, his views on predestination make it clear that God does not enter into give-and-take relations with us. Our prayers can never affect God, he says. Rather, God has ordained our prayer as a means of bringing about whatever the divine will has decreed. As the zenith of medieval thought, Aquinas epitomizes the tensions of the biblical-classical synthesis in attempting to reconcile the God of historical action depicted in the Bible with the Hellenic deity beyond the categories of history.

5.5 From Luther to Wesley

In many respects the Reformers were able to reorient theology toward the experience of salvation through the cross of Christ. What God has done in salvation history, they said, must be the source of our knowledge of God. Martin Luther instigated a tremendous revolution in theological method when he began with the "God for us" of redemptive history instead of the God known by purely by rational thought *(dignum Deo)*. According to his so-called theology of the cross, there is no God beyond the God revealed in Jesus. He boldly asserts that in Jesus of Nazareth, God suffered and was crucified. He is well aware that this is an affront to both philosophical thought and human political experience, as kings do not voluntarily suffer for their subjects.[61] Luther's theology of the cross allows him to return to the "fatherhood" of God by which he contrasts the God of the Bible with the God of Greek metaphysics. On the one hand, there is God in himself, the absolute God apart from the world. On the other hand, there is the God of Israel, who reveals himself to us, binds himself to his Word, manifests himself in Jesus and limits himself to our understanding. All this is done *for us*, thus emphasizing God's loving relationship with his creatures.

Luther's breakthrough is seen in his insistence that the source for our knowledge of God is found in Jesus. Yet even with the disclosure of God in Christ there remains the "hiddenness of God." Luther scholars tend to distinguish two different senses of divine hiddenness in Luther's writings.[62] First is the idea that God remains hidden *in* his revelation: divine strength is manifested in weakness, and God gives life through death. God is who he declares himself to be in the cross of Christ, but this is only perceived through the eyes of faith. Yet even in this divine revelation not all of God is disclosed, for what we see is, following the imagery of Exodus 33:23, God's back *(posteriora Dei)*. The other sense of divine hiddenness for Luther surfaces in his debate with Erasmus. Here God remains hidden *behind* his revelation. Behind the God revealed in Jesus lurks a God who is completely unknown to us—God in himself. Luther says we must flee from this God to the God of the cross. But there remains a problem, for the "unknown God" has an inscrutable will that may be in opposition to the will of the revealed God. Erasmus had claimed that God does not desire the death of the sinner. Luther responded by saying that God "does not will the death of the sinner—that is, in His Word; but He wills it by His inscrutable will."[63] Though the Father of Jesus says he wants to save all, the God behind the God of Jesus does not want to save all, for he predestines only some to salvation and damns the rest.

Luther follows Augustine in arguing that God's will is the sole reason for individual salvation for two reasons. First, human wills are so depraved that they cannot choose the good, and thus God must choose for them. Luther thought that humans are still responsible for their actions, however, because he held to a compatibilist, or soft-determinist, definition of freedom. Accordingly, freedom means the ability to do what you want to do. Since we all want to sin, we are free to sin; and since none of us desires God, we are not free to seek him. We cannot change our desires. Only God can do that. We are like donkeys that go where the rider bids but cannot choose the rider. Second, "God foreknows nothing contingently, but that He foresees, purposes, and does all things according to His own immutable, eternal and infallible will."[64] God gets whatever he desires, which includes every human circumstance and eternal destiny. God's will is the ultimate cause for everything. Even God's foreknowledge is a function of the divine will so that God cannot be said to "respond" to human sin.[65] God wills what is to happen, and that is the cause of his foreknowledge. Consequently, individual salvation and damnation is solely up to God and not humanity.

Luther wanted to prevent any notion of human merit from creeping into his soteriology and may have overstated himself in doing so. He rightfully sought to claim that there is more to God than we can know. Nevertheless, there remains a tension, if not a contradiction, in the heart of Luther's theology. Whereas he began by claiming that there is no knowledge of God apart from that revealed in Jesus, he proceeds to inform us that there is a God behind this God whose inscrutable will overturns statements about God's universal salvific will in Scripture. Is Jesus actually God's final word on anything or not? Brian Gerish claims that we witness "the collapse of Luther's doctrine of God at this point. . . . Granted that *Christ* speaks nothing but comfort to the troubled conscience, who knows how it stands between me and *God in heaven?*"[66] According to Alister McGrath, Luther's appeal to a hidden will of God behind the will revealed in Jesus and Scripture "makes theology an irrelevancy," for any statement in Scripture may be overturned on the basis of the hidden will.[67] Luther scholars debate how these various strands of Luther's thought should be understood, but most agree that they cannot be fully harmonized. Though Luther often spoke of God's fatherly relationship with us and could, on occasion, speak as though God entered into give-and-take relations with creatures, there remains the other side of his thought, which seems to rule out reciprocal relationships with God.

Like Luther, John Calvin sought a return to biblical theology, away from speculation. Calvin uses the Bible extensively in his writings, seeking to develop an edifying and practical theology. He often speaks of God's great compassion and fatherly love for the saints. In speaking of the attributes of God, Calvin prefers to make use of biblical terms: eternal, wise, kind, merciful, good, just, powerful and truthful.[68] However, like Augustine and Aquinas, he understood God's knowledge and will to be absolutely independent of the creation. God does not look ahead and see what is going to happen, for that would make God dependent on what the creatures decide. God does not decide what he will do in response to anything the creatures do. All that God knows and wills is not in relation to the creation but simply in relation to his own will. This effectively denies any sort of mutual relationship between God and his creatures. It is all a one-way street, or better, a novel in which the characters do exactly what the novelist decides. Calvin's God exercises exhaustive control over absolutely everything: "Nothing happens except what is knowingly and willingly decreed by him."[69]

Regarding predestination, Calvin asserts that God's election of individuals to salvation is based solely on his will. Calvin follows Augustine in claiming that though there are statements in Scripture that seem to affirm God's universal salvific will, they cannot really mean this for if they did, then all would be saved. But we know that not all will be saved, so God must not actually desire the salvation of all. The reason that all are not saved lies completely with the divine will. He repudiates the notion of the early church fathers that God foresees faith in humans and then elects them. On the contrary, God "foresees future events only by reason of the fact that he decreed that they take place."[70] God knows the future because he determines the future. In fact, God decreed even the fall into sin. Yet Calvin seeks to deflect the charge that God is then responsible for sin by defining human freedom in compatibilistic terms and by making use of the Scholastic notion that God worked through secondary causes. As long as God does not directly determine events but only establishes the causes by which they come about, God is thought to be absolved of blame.[71] Furthermore, whatever God wills is right because his will is the criterion of justice. Lastly, Calvin says that we are not to question God's will in such matters (Rom 9:20-21). Whatever happens to us in this life, even a mother's lack of breast milk for her child, God has good reasons for bringing about.[72]

When discussing the origin of evil, God's providential use of the wicked and the double decree, Calvin appeals to a "hidden will" of God.[73] However, he denies that there are two wills in God. It only appears to us that there are two wills. Even with the revelation of God in Jesus, God has his secrets. The secret is not that God elects some for salvation and others for damnation. The mystery is why God so elects. Calvin admits the decree is "horrible," but says it nonetheless comes from the "abyss" in God, which ought to be reverenced.[74]

It comes as little surprise that Calvin believes God incapable of changing his mind. Repentance of any decision would contradict God's immutable and impassible will, as well as his foreknowledge. In his commentary on Genesis Calvin remarks on 6:6, where it is said that God repented and was grieved, that the text cannot mean what it says because such activities are impossible for God. "Certainly God is not sorrowful or sad; but remains for ever like himself in his celestial and happy repose." Calvin's hermeneutic presupposes that sovereignty means domination, and so biblical texts that go against this understanding are read differently.[75] Calvin's high view of Scripture did not prevent him from denying the obvious meaning of the text. God, he says, uses such anthropomorphisms because "we cannot comprehend him as he is." God graciously accommodates himself by "lisping" to us as does a nursemaid to a young child.[76] Of the numerous texts referring to divine repentance Calvin says that they do not reveal the truth of God and must be taken figuratively.[77]

Calvin identified two biblical texts that teach in a literal (truthful) way the immutability of God (Num 23:19; 1 Sam 15:29). Of course, one may ask how *Calvin* acquired the correct knowledge of the God beyond the scriptural revelation in order to know that God was accommodating himself to us. It may be the case, but how does Calvin know, if not by divine revelation? If he claims it is taught in Scripture, where does he get his criterion for claiming that texts saying that God "will not change his mind" (for example, 1 Sam 15:29) refer to the way God really is, whereas texts saying that God "will change his mind" (for example, Jer 18:8) refer to the way God appears to be to us?[78] Calvin does not say, but his approach effectively eliminates any possibility of God's responding to us.

An interesting tension in Calvin's thought, of which he was apparently unaware, is that when he discusses the nature and value of prayer he speaks a very different language, as though God does, in fact, respond to our prayers, is receptive and enters into reciprocal relationships with his creatures.[79] Calvin seemed to have a rather dynamic and relational understanding of the Trinity. His view of the triune life could have led to quite a different conception of the divine-human relationship had Calvin integrated his doctrine of election with his relational understanding of the Trinity.[80] Perhaps Calvin could have made room in his theology for God to have reciprocal relations with creatures, but he did not. Though Calvin speaks of the fatherhood of God in our lives, it is not a Father to whom our concerns, joys and sorrows make a difference. If they did, then God would be affected by us, which would imply some degree of conditionality in God. Emil Brunner concludes that in Calvin's theology "the personal relation between God and Man became a causal relation: God the cause, faith the effect."[81]

The sixteenth-century Reformed theologian Jacob Arminius follows Calvin in many respects but initiates a decisive break concerning the nature of God.[82] Arminius returns to an idea of the pre-Augustinian fathers: God's foreknowledge of what will happen is conditioned by what the creatures freely decide to do, not on God's immutable will. God uses his prevision of who will, through grace, come to Christ as the basis for divine predestination. Consequently, God genuinely *responds* to his creatures. Divine sovereignty grants the creatures genuine freedom. Arminius thus reintroduces into Western theology a degree of conditionality in God that allows God to enter freely into covenantal, reciprocal relations with creatures.

The eighteenth-century British preacher John Wesley came independently to some of Arminius's conclusions. Drawing on his reading of the Eastern church fathers, Wesley was able to develop a truly relational understanding of God and the divine-human relationship as he debated the issue of predestination with Calvinist teachers in the Church of England.[83] Contrary to popular belief, his disagreement with the Calvinists centered in the doctrine of God rather than in anthropology. Wesley thought that predestination, Calvinistically understood, (1) was incompatible with God's justice (distributive justice) and mercy, (2) rendered God insincere in offering salvation to all sinners and (3) was inconsistent with God's universal love and goodness.[84] He thought it reflected badly on the moral and loving nature of God, as taught in Scripture, to unconditionally save some and damn others. A key metaphor Wesley employed in this discussion was God as a loving parent. Whereas potentates may dispatch their subjects as they desire, God is typically portrayed in Scripture as a loving father. What loving father would withhold redemptive help from his children? Foremost in his understanding of the divine nature was love. God loves sinners and, short of overriding their integrity as persons, does all in his power to deliver them from sin.

Wesley's theology was relational: to know God and to be saved meant to be in a loving personal relationship with God and with others.[85] Personal relations cannot be coerced, and hence the grace God gives to empower sinners toward conversion cannot be irresistible. God is wise and loving, not simply powerful. If God simply overcame human rebellion by removing human freedom, "it would imply no wisdom at all, but barely a stroke of omnipotence."[86] The wisdom of God is displayed in working with humans as personal beings in the divine image, not as senseless stocks and blocks. God enters into genuine reciprocal relations with creatures. In this regard Wesley deliberately returned to the teaching of the fathers prior to Augustine regarding conditional election, according to which God foresees human faith in Christ and elects to save us on that condition. Consequently, some of what God knows and what God wills is conditioned by creatures.[87] God is a responsive God who enables sinful humans to respond to the divine love.

Wesley did not believe that sinners returned to God "on their own" apart from empowering grace. But he did believe that this enabling grace could be rejected. Although we cannot be saved without God's help, God will not save us without our participation. In Wesley's thought, the unchangeable holy love of God is the preeminent divine attribute, for only love is given such a regnant place in Scripture (1 Jn 4:8). And love seeks reciprocation from the beloved. Wesley evinces a truly relational theology. Although he does not directly address the issue of divine risk taking, it is implied in this theology. For example, he believes that God's redemptive love may be rejected by us, which would mean that God risks losing some he desires to save.

5.6 Contemporary Theology

5.6.1 Three Views Modern theology has witnessed a remarkable reexamination of the divine-human relationship as well as of the attributes of God. The contemporary scene manifests a wide spectrum of views on the subject. On the one hand are those who deny that we can have a personal relationship with God at all. Others claim that though we can have a relationship, it cannot be reciprocal. Next are those who maintain that God is necessarily dependent on creatures for what God wants to achieve. Finally, some affirm that God freely enters into reciprocal relations with us. These views will now be examined, with the bulk of the discussion given over to those who affirm reciprocal relations in the divine-human relationship.

The first view holds that we cannot enter into personal relations with God at all. Paul Tillich is an excellent representative of this perspective. He used classical theism's teaching on the ineffable and unnamed God to arrive at his designation for God: "Being-Itself."[88] For Tillich, God is the answer to the metaphysical question, What is being itself? The God that explains all being is not *a* being existing alongside other beings, as that would make God finite. All existing beings are a mix of being and nonbeing. But God is infinite, containing no potentiality or mutability. God, as Being-Itself, does not even exist, since to exist is to experience estrangement and to possess nonbeing, which are obviously inapplicable to deity. Interestingly, Tillich's understanding of God as fully immanent in the cosmos arrives at a conclusion held by many classical theists who emphasized divine transcendence: God can have no external relations with creatures. To think of having personal relations with God or being his partner in action is impossible if God is Being-Itself, since to have such a relationship is to posit two beings existing alongside each other. "It is an insult to the divine holiness to treat God as a partner with whom one collaborates or as a superior power whom one influences by rites and prayers."[89]

Though Tillich often denigrates biblical personalism, he sees the need to speak of God in personal terms, since "man cannot be ultimately concerned about something which is less than he is, something impersonal."[90] Though God as Being-Itself is beyond the categories of personal and living, Tillich repeatedly speaks of the "living" God, utilizing personal terms. Tillich applies biblical descriptions such as personal, living and acting to God in a symbolic sense only. They are not the literal truth about God but are pragmatic means for making life meaningful. The one nonsymbolic statement about God is that God is Being-Itself.

In line with the classical tradition, the true God is the God of abstract reflection who is beyond predication, not the biblical (symbolic) God. This is what Tillich meant by the "God above God." But a question arises at this point. It is one thing to claim that a statement such as "God carried Israel in his arms" is symbolic of the action of a personal God. It is quite another to say that the "action of a personal God" is symbolic. Of what is it symbolic? For Tillich, the living, forgiving, judging God seems to be a description of *our* participation in Being-Itself. God is not a separate being acting in and on the world but is immanent within our living and acting. Concerning prayer, he says that "we can only pray to the God who prays to himself through us."[91] Tillich's thought does not allow for any conditionality in God, divine risk taking or reciprocal personal relations between God and creatures.

The second option on the contemporary scene follows the thinking of Augustine and Calvin in asserting that though we can have a relationship with God, it cannot be a reciprocal one. This view is strongly held by many evangelicals in the Calvinist tradition. According to this position, God cannot in any way be conditioned by the creatures, as this would diminish God's absolute independence from the world. Regarding prayer, it is asserted that it is impossible to change God's mind or even to affect God, as this would impugn the divine nature. Petitionary prayer does not affect the divine will. Rather, our petitions are ordained by God and are followed by God's eternally ordained "answer." God could not change his will in response to something we requested, for he has always known what he was going to do. "All change," as A. W. Tozer says, "must be on our part."[92] In his book on prayer, W. Bingham Hunter claims that texts such as Exodus 32:9-14, which asserts that God changed his mind in response to a human prayer, are simply anthropopathisms.[93] Such texts simply cannot mean what they seem to say.

God exercises *exhaustive* control over each situation, which means that only what God purposes to happen in that particular time and place to that specific creature will happen. God does not take risks in governing the world because God micromanages every detail. According to this model of providence, there is a specific divine reason for ordaining each and every particular occurrence of evil and suffering. According to Paul Helm, since "God works everything for good" (Rom 8:28), there are no such things as accidents and there are no real tragedies in life.[94] If a three-year-old child contracts an incurable and painful bone cancer, suffering terribly until death, it is because God specifically ordained this to occur. Like clay in the hands of a potter, so everything occurs just as God desires.[95] Obviously in this theology God cannot be said to take any sort of risks.

Carl Henry, a leading evangelical theologian, argues that God is timeless, immutable and simple and that divine omniscience is not dependent in any respect on the creation. God foreknows because he foreordains. Consequently, prayer cannot affect God or change God's mind. Scriptures that indicate otherwise are anthropopathisms. Following Plato, he says that "God is perfect and, if perfect, can only change for the worse."[96]

This is not the whole picture within evangelical Calvinism, however, for its hymnody and piety often speak of God's genuine relationship and response to us. Clergy and laity alike assert that petitionary prayer can change God's mind (while at the same time affirming all the classical attributes). Nonetheless, these notions are clearly incompatible with the idea that God is completely unconditioned in all respects by the creatures. There is no room in this theology for genuine give-and-take relations with God. God gives but never receives. These thinkers profess to "personal relations" between God and humans, but such claims are inconsistent with their view of God. A truly relational theology and, of course, divine risk taking are eliminated.

The third alternative, process theology, affirms that all things are essentially or necessarily related. God and the world are involved in an ontologically interdependent relationship. Process theology criticizes classical theism for its overemphasis on absolute transcendence, immutability and impassibility. Instead, it argues that God should be understood as an ever-changing being evolving toward the perfection potentially his. God is creative only in the sense that God "creates" as *we* act, since this God cannot unilaterally act on the world. God does not coerce us but "lures" the world by love *(eros)* toward his purposes.

Process thought tends to stray from any biblical moorings and substitutes the metaphysics of change for the metaphysics of static substance and ends up with a God that, if personal at all, cannot act in history.[97] What sort of personal relationship can we have with a God who cannot act or communicate clearly? If process thought is a version of relational theism, it is a seriously deficient one, since a personal relationship with God is undermined. The God of process thought is pervasively conditioned by the creatures. It could not be otherwise because the God-world relationship is not of God's choosing. God is necessarily and ontologically dependent on the world: God would not have being or be who God is apart from the world. God needs the world in order to be God. The lack of a proper trinitarian theology as well as the denial of *creatio ex nihilo* has led process theism to an ontologically needy God.[98] The God of process theism cannot be said to take risks because God is not responsible for creating the world or establishing its conditions and does not have the ability to unilaterally make things other than they are.

5.6.2 Relational Theism in Contemporary Thought What I call "relational theism" affirms that God freely enters into reciprocal relations with creatures. There is significant diversity within this category, aside from

a general agreement that God, though ontologically distinct from creation (contra process theology), enters into genuine give-and-take relations with his creatures and is resourceful, creative and omnicompetent instead of all-determining and completely unconditioned by creatures. This has to be understood, however, as God's free and sovereign choice to create this state of affairs. It is not forced on God, as in process thought. God has made significantly free creatures upon whom he conditions some of his actions. God is truly involved in human history, opening up new possibilities in overcoming sin.

From the evangelical tradition James Oliver Buswell Jr. calls for a major shift in our understanding of God when he rejects the ideas of divine timelessness, immutability, impassibility and God as pure act. "We should," he says, "shake off the static ideology which has come into Christian theology from non-Biblical sources."[99] Buswell's plea has not gone unheeded. Serious philosophical attention has been given to divine temporality and passibility by Nicholas Wolterstorff and Stephen Davis.[100]

Evangelicals advocating a more open view of God break decisively with theologians who "cannot bring themselves to admit that anything God does can be conditioned by man or can be a reaction to something in creation. This sort of thing is regarded as a contradiction of sovereignty. As sovereign, God must always *act* and never *react*."[101] But God does react and enters into genuine responsive relationships with his creatures. In his relationships God is faithful, but God can change his mind and sometimes does. Evangelicals especially see the opportunity of affecting God in prayer. Of course, this is only because God makes himself open to our prayers, not because we can force our will on God.

Prayer is, according to Richard Foster, genuine dialogue with God.[102] In a particularly forthright declaration Foster says, "We have been taught that everything in the universe is already set, and so things cannot be changed. And if things cannot be changed, why pray? . . . It is Stoicism that demands a closed universe not the Bible. . . . In fact, the Bible stresses so forcefully the openness of our universe that . . . it speaks of God constantly changing his mind in accord with his unchanging love. . . . We are working with God to change the future!"[103] Echoing similar sentiments, Donald Bloesch holds that through prayer "God makes himself dependent on the requests of his children."[104] This dependency and openness of God result from, according to Gabriel Fackre, the fact that the divine love does not force its will on the creatures. Instead, God makes himself vulnerable by taking the risk of being rejected.[105] A growing number of evangelicals, such as Clark Pinnock, Philip Yancey, Henry Knight III, Gilbert Bilezikian, Greg Boyd,

John Boykin, Harry Boer and others, affirm a relational theism that makes room for genuine divine responsiveness.[106] Pentecostal piety has expressed such views.[107] Moreover, African-American theologian Major Jones asserts that in black spirituality and theology

> the content of God's consciousness is not so fixed that it cannot—if God will it—be constantly changing to include future events, as yet unknown in their non-being. We [in the black Christian tradition] believe human actions to be truly free, such that whereas God's knowledge of the past is total and absolute, God's knowledge of future events is not yet complete, particularly so far as acts of human freedom are concerned. The perfection of divine omniscience, then, must be construed to be God's always perfectly increasing knowledge taking in, with the passage of time, all knowable reality as it expands. Not to know as real and sure what is, as yet, neither sure nor real, is not imperfection; to know the unreal and the unsure as uncertain and still forming is to know perfectly whatever is to be known.[108]

From the mainline and Roman Catholic traditions several notable theologians also see the need for understanding God in more relational terms. Especially helpful are the works of Terence Fretheim, who demonstrates the openness of God from the biblical texts.[109] Thomas Torrance speaks of the "openness of God" to his creatures.[110] Thomas Oden, drawing heavily on the fathers, says that God has a name, enters into history, has emotions, responds to us and takes new initiatives.[111] Paul Fiddes's *The Creative Suffering of God* is a first-rate work discussing passibility and conditionality in God.[112] Theologians such as Jürgen Moltmann and Wolfhart Pannenberg see God's actions in the incarnation of Jesus as paramount for understanding the essence of God.[113] For them, Jesus reveals that God is involved in history and is willing to become vulnerable and even suffer because of and on behalf of us. God is a subject who acts in history and who involves himself in genuine relations with humans in time. Robert Jenson is highly critical of the biblical-classical synthesis, replacing it with a dynamic trinitarianism.[114] The theologies of Emil Brunner, Karl Barth, Thomas Finger, Eberhard Jüngel, Colin Gunton and C. S. Lewis manifest a movement back toward an understanding of God as personal and relational.[115] Especially significant are the works of contemporary Dutch Reformed thinkers such as Vincent Brümmer, Hendrikus Berkhof and Adriö König. For them, God sovereignly enters into reciprocal relations with his creatures and freely wills to be, for some things, conditioned by us.[116]

Roman Catholic feminist theologians Catherine Mowry LaCugna and Elizabeth Johnson demonstrate marvelous sensitivity to the classical tradition while evincing a truly relational and responsive trinitarian God.[117]

Some Catholics who wish to remain close to the Thomistic tradition nevertheless attempt to allow for divine responsiveness.[118] In this regard W. Norris Clarke says God

> is one who enters into deep personal relations of love with His creatures. And an authentic interpersonal relation of love necessarily involves not merely purely creative or one-way love, but genuine mutuality and reciprocity of love, including not only the giving of love but the joyful acceptance of it and response to it. This means that our God is a God who really cares, is really concerned with our lives and happiness, who enters into truly reciprocal personal relations with us, who responds to our prayers—to whom, in a word, our contingent world and its history somehow make a genuine difference.[119]

For Clarke and William Hill, God changes in his relations with us, but God's being never changes, as process thinkers claim.

The Eastern Orthodox have never followed the Augustinian conceptions of sin and salvation and thus have retained room for a responsive God.[120] On election, the Orthodox affirm the view, held by the early fathers, Arminius and Wesley, that God foresees the faith of believers and so elects them to salvation. Election, then, entails some conditionality in God wherein God responds to the choice of humans. The free choice of sinful humans to exercise faith in Christ does not, however, come about without the enabling grace of the Holy Spirit. The Orthodox view is summarized well by Bishop Kallistos Ware:

> The grace of God invites all but compels none. In the words of John Chrysostom: "God never draws anyone to Himself by force and violence. He wishes all men to be saved, but forces no one." "It is for God to grant His grace," said Saint Cyril of Jerusalem (died 386); "your task is to accept that grace and to guard it." But it must not be imagined that because a man accepts and guards God's grace, he thereby earns "merit." God's gifts are always free gifts, and man can never have any claims upon his Maker.[121]

In the Orthodox tradition there are genuinely reciprocal relations between God and humans in the salvation process.

Finally, a number of influential contemporary philosophers of religion affirm the full openness of God (a version of relational theism), including Richard Swinburne, William Hasker, J. R. Lucas, Peter Geach, Richard Purtill, A. N. Prior, David Basinger and Keith Ward.[122]

5.7 Conclusion

The theological tradition is not uniform when it comes to the question of conditionality in God. Whereas the early fathers, Eastern Orthodoxy,

Arminius, Wesley, Pentecostalism and a good number of contemporary theologians and philosophers provide a place for divine conditionality, Augustine, Aquinas, Luther and Calvin either reject any conditionality in God or are inconsistent on the subject. Clearly, relational theism is not new to the theological scene. Those affirming divine conditionality have not always addressed the notion of divine risk taking. But they all maintained that God may not get everything God desires (for example, some may be lost), thus implying divine risk taking.

Only the proponents of theological determinism consistently ruled out any place for divine conditionality and risk taking. Though such voices have at times dominated the Western theological scene, they have never found a place in the Eastern church. But certain luminaries in the Western tradition, such as Justin, Wesley and Barth, made room for give-and-take relations between God and his creatures. Even certain Thomists are finding ways of allowing for God to have reciprocal relations with creatures. Although these relational theists would not agree with all aspects of the model of providence proposed here, the model does find significant agreement with both Eastern and Western theological traditions. In the previous two chapters it was argued that the risk model of providence was in harmony with the Scriptures, and in this chapter it has been shown to be in consonance with a major thrust of the theological tradition.

Of course, the risk model sometimes finds agreement with the intentions and functions rather than the material content of certain theological formulations. For instance, applying terms such as *impassibility, immutability, timelessness* and *simplicity* to God was intended to protect the Christian conception of God from certain impure conceptions inherent in pagan religions. Though this was a noble motive, it did make it difficult to speak of relationality within the Godhead. The god of Greek thought is anonymous, self-sufficient, alone (unrelated), invulnerable, self-thinking thought, changeless and egocentric. The triune God of the Bible is "named" (as Yahweh to Israel and then as Father, Son and Spirit through Jesus), is God for others, makes himself vulnerable and is self-giving love. This God, as Nicaea established, is essentially related among Father, Son and Spirit. Since the creation the Trinity enjoys genuine external relations with us creatures. This personal God uses the divine freedom to enter into relationships of love involving reciprocity and mutuality. Though the tradition, with good intentions, employed immutability and impassibility in order to protect God's perfection, those traits were at times pushed so far as to leave no room for speaking of divine openness, in which God, in vulnerability, binds himself to others in love.

Chapters three, four and five have demonstrated that the risk model of providence finds substantial agreement with the Christian tradition. Hence the first criterion for evaluating a theological model has been met. Now it is time to address the criteria of conceptual intelligibility and adequacy for the demands of life. The next two chapters will examine the coherence of the model, and chapter eight will address its usefulness for the Christian life.

SIX

RISK AND THE
DIVINE CHARACTER

· ·

6.1 Introduction

In this study the overarching theological model has been that of relational theism: A personal God enters into loving reciprocal relationships with human persons. A key image employed to elucidate this model is that of risk taker. As does any image, it says something about the subject but not all that needs to be said, since a variety of images and metaphors are required to give a full picture of the subject. Nevertheless, the image of God as a risk taker has been underemployed in the Christian tradition despite the significance of this idea in the biblical narrative. Although divine risk taking is implied by certain formulations of, for example, the freewill defense, it has been overlooked in many philosophical discussions. The present chapter explores certain attributes of God in relation to the concept of risk taking. The next two chapters examine the impact divine risk taking has on doctrines such as sovereignty and various Christian practices.

The criteria for evaluating a theological proposal (discussed in chap. 2) are (1) concordance with the tradition, (2) conceptual intelligibility and (3) adequacy for the demands of life. As demonstrated in chapters three and four, God's involvement in personal relationships that entail risk taking is consonant with the primary norm of Christian theology, Scripture, especially in light of the person and work of Jesus. Chapter five argued that the history of Christian thought witnesses an attempt to speak of God in terms of personal, give-and-take relationships even as the element of divine risk taking in these relationships has been neglected. Consequently, the proposal here developed seeks to be faithful to the concept of a personal relationship with God, a common feature of tradition, while finding it necessary to modify certain other elements of the theological tradition in order to bring consistency to the model.

The present chapter focuses on the conceptual intelligibility of the proposal. Does it make sense? Is it self-consistent? Does it cohere with other well established doctrines? Does it shed light on some old problems? Does the model of a personal God taking risks in his interpersonal relationships "fit" within the Christian understanding of the divine nature? The goal here is not the production of a natural theology whereby the transcendental truth of providence—the sort of providence God *must* have—is established apart from the scriptural revelation. Rather, it is the much more modest use of philosophical theology, attempting to see whether or not the proposal meets the standards of rational discourse for *meaningful* assertions. That is, the view of God and providence developed in the preceding two chapters will now be examined for conceptual intelligibility. If a theological model contains self-contradictory assertions, then the model pays the price of conceptual incoherence. Although the third criterion, adequacy for the demands of life, is touched on in this chapter, it will be more fully discussed in chapter eight.

Finally, a word about definition. From the biblical material it was shown that God freely creates a world and gets involved with its affairs. There develops a give-and-take dynamic interpersonal relationship between God and humanity in which God does not always get what he desires. Nevertheless, God is victorious over the course of history in bringing his project to fruition. God is resourceful and adaptable in working to fulfill his plans. In some respects God makes himself dependent on humans for the achievement of his desires. God is not yet finished with his work and has more "up his sleeve."

What sorts of conditions must be met for an adequate understanding of providence? A Christian doctrine of providence must affirm (1) God's loving care for the creatures wherein he seeks their greatest well-being, (2) God's involvement with us in the flow of history and (3) God's intended goals for the creation. These conditions must be explained in light of what God has actually decided to do in history as revealed in Scripture, especially in Jesus. The model of God as risk taker in attempting to achieve his goal of creation through personal relationships affirms these conditions. The biblical narrative depicts God's persevering love in working to achieve his goals for the divine project and in attempting to bring us into a loving relationship with himself. The divine wisdom involves the ability to anticipate human responses. God acts to introduce new factors into history that direct it toward ends not otherwise attainable. God has ultimate goals that he refuses to change even as he remains flexible in seeking to accomplish them. H. H. Farmer was on track when he defined *providence* as "the adequacy of God's wisdom and power to the task with which he has charged himself."[1]

6.2 Summary of a Risk View of Providence

Farmer's definition of *providence* focuses on God's wisdom and power to accomplish the divine project. God's project involves the creation of significant others who are ontologically distinct from himself and upon whom he showers his caring love in the expectation that they will respond in love. God grants humans genuine freedom to participate in this project, as he does not force them to comply. Love is given freely and is received freely. Prior to creation, even if God had no warrant to believe anything would go amiss, there existed the "implausible possibility" that resistance to the divine purpose might arise. Despite this possibility God decided to enter into real give-and-take personal relationships with his creatures. God not only gives, he receives. God freely chooses to be affected by his creatures—there is contingency in God's relation with creation. Moreover, God is the sovereign determiner of the sort of sovereignty he will exercise. God is free to sovereignly decide not to determine everything that happens in history. He does not have to because God is supremely wise, endlessly resourceful, amazingly creative and omnicompetent in seeking to fulfill his project. In the God-human relationship God sometimes decides alone what will happen; at other times God modifies his plans in order to accommodate the choices, actions and desires of his creatures.

In grace God created and embarked on this program and in grace God invites us to participate as significant partners with him in bringing about the eschatological glory he intends for the creation. By his free sovereign will God enables us to become his lovers (Hosea) and friends (Jn 15:15) toward the establishment of his kingdom.[2] It is God's desire that we worship and enjoy him forever in a relationship of love. In the words of Hendrikus Berkhof, "The God who is free uses his freedom to establish communion. The sovereign one gives himself away. . . . Apparently he wants to be able to do nothing else than be our covenant partner."[3]

The goal of the divine project is to produce people who reflect the trinitarian love in all their relationships: with God, other humans and the entire creation. God's intention is that all of us come to the fullness of Jesus. Because of God's faithfulness, the goal of the project has never changed, but the means and specific paths God takes toward the achievement of the project can and do change, depending on what the divine wisdom deems best at the time. The particular path God takes to obtain his goal depends on the interaction between God and humanity in the course of the historical outworking of the project. Hence the goal of the project remains constant even as the means remain flexible.

6.3 The Nature of Divine Risk

God does not risk for risk's sake. Divine risk taking must not be divorced from the creational project, which desires a relationship of love. Furthermore, God was under no compulsion to take any risks whatsoever. God did not have to create a world at all and could have created a very different world from the one we have. God is sovereign over his sovereignty and so did not have to create a world in which humans have the freedom to enter into a personal relationship of love with himself. God sovereignly created the conditions of all creaturely working: God alone establishes the rules of the game.[4] According to Karl Barth, one of the rules that God freely makes is that God himself will be affected and conditioned by these creatures. God freely grants a degree of separateness from God so that the creature is no tool or puppet: "The activity of the creature over against that of God remains the creature's own."[5]

God solely decides whether to take any risks at all and what sorts of risks to allow. But just what do we mean by risk? Paul Helm says, "We take no risk if we knowingly set in motion events which will turn out exactly as we want them to do."[6] Though this remark might be interpreted to claim that foreknowledge rules out risk, this is not what Helm has in mind. For Helm, God foreordains everything that comes to pass. It is foreordination or exhaustive divine control over everything that rules out divine risk taking, not foreknowledge. (As I will show later in this chapter, a God with complete foreknowledge still takes risks.) William Hasker provides a more precise definition of risk when he writes, "Does God make decisions that depend for their outcomes on the responses of free creatures in which the decisions themselves are not informed by knowledge of the outcomes?"[7] Both Hasker's and Helm's definitions are formulated in terms of knowledge. However, for Hasker the crucial point is whether (1) God grants humans libertarian freedom and does not exercise exhaustive control and (2) divine planning for the future is done *on the basis of* what he knows will actually happen. Accordingly, a God with either foreknowledge or the present-knowledge model propounded here will make decisions about what to do without basing those decisions on the certainty of the outcome.

David Basinger provides a further refinement in defining risk. God is a risk taker if "God adopts certain overall strategies—for example, the granting of significant freedom—that create the potential for the occurrence of individual instances of evil which are, as such, pure loss and not a means to any greater good."[8] What Basinger means is that the central component of risk taking is not a lack of knowledge of the outcome at the time of commitment but the decision to grant creatures the freedom to be significant others from God, which entails the possibility of movement away from God's desires. For Basinger, the crucial question is not the type of knowledge God has but the specific rules of the game that God elects to establish for the creation.[9] If God adopts general strategies (for example, granting humans significant freedom) that create the possibility that at least some events may occur which God would rather not occur, then God takes risks. If God establishes a creation in which the outcome of at least some undertakings is indefinite, then God takes risks.[10] In this sense a God with simple foreknowledge or presentism takes risks, since these views of divine omniscience are usually coupled with the affirmation of libertarian freedom. The only way I know of to avoid a risk-taking God is to affirm some form of theological determinism or exhaustive sovereignty that renders it impossible for humans to thwart or hinder God's plans for each and every specific event that takes place in creation. Divine risk taking allows for some things' occurring in the creation that God does not specifically intend to occur. God does not want sin and suffering, for instance.[11]

Risk may be small or great in that (1) there may be a small or great chance (probability) of success and (2) there may be a small or great amount ventured depending on its importance (value) to the person investing. A couple of illustrations may help in grasping this distinction. Mary has a lot of money but few friends. Let us suppose that she does not care a great deal about her money but is quite sensitive and fears being hurt by others. Regarding the first sense of risk—the probability of success—Mary's investing capital in a particular company may seem to her a tremendous risk due to its poor past performance. In this case the chance for success is very poor. However, given her knowledge of Deborah's good character, Mary may believe that she takes little risk of being hurt by opening herself and becoming vulnerable to her. In this case she believes the chance for becoming close friends is very good and thus little risk is involved. Concerning the second sense of risk taking, Mary may not care a great deal about the money she has and so decides to invest it in a risky but potentially profitable company. In this case, although she ventures a large amount of money, she does not take much of a risk because it matters little to her. On the other hand, Mary, being a sensitive person, yet convinced of Deborah's trustworthiness, decides to be open with her, though only sharing a few things about her private life at first. In this case Mary risks a lot (qualitatively) even though the amount of information shared (quantity) may be small.

Mary is not obligated to invest in the company or to share herself with Deborah. But *if* she wants to help this company or develop a friendship with this person, it is incumbent on her to take some risks. Risk taking must be seen as an element in the broader structure of goals and relationships. Risk taking involves vulnerability, an openness to loss or gain, suffering or delight. Moreover, Mary can attempt to alleviate the risk by intervening in the situation if it threatens to go bad. She may withdraw what is left of her capital or break off her relationship with Deborah. The decision she makes depends on several factors. For instance, she may be patient and may accept short-term loss for long-term gain. She may have the strength of forgiveness and the depth of love to suffer the hurt in hopes of winning back the friendship. Whether she stays with the risk or withdraws depends on her overarching goals as well as her character.

God's decision to create this particular sort of world has a (1) great chance of success and little possibility of failure while concomitantly having a (2) high amount of risk in the sense that it matters deeply to God how things go. The decision to create beings who could receive and return the divine love and enter into loving personal relationships with each other was not much of a risk, given all the blessings that God provided. Although sin was possible—given this sort of world—it simply was not plausible in view of the good environment God established and the love he bestowed.[12] On the other hand, because God cared so deeply about this project—investing himself in it—God took a great risk in opening himself up to being grieved if the project went awry.

This is borne out in the biblical materials. God, because he cares, is repeatedly hurt, angered and saddened by sinful human actions. As we saw in the previous two chapters, God neither gave up on his project nor withdrew the original rules of the game. God's overarching purpose for the project, as well as his character, keeps him in the game despite the risk.

God freely chooses to act and determine some things so that not everything is at risk. God acts in order to redeem what was lost in the initial failure. Divine intervention occurs, however, within the rules God freely established because God remains faithful to the project.

6.4 The Divine Character and Providence

6.4.1 Introduction One's understanding of the nature of God is of vital importance for understanding divine providence as risk taking. A complete study of all the divine attributes is neither possible nor needed here. What is required is an examination of those attributes that have a direct bearing on our view of providence.

This book began with a consideration of the particular type of providence God chose to employ, as depicted in the biblical revelation. It did not begin with "the most perfect being" imaginable and then deduce the necessary view of providence from this model of God. For two millennia the Neoplatonic philosophical understanding of God (which begins with a particular understanding of "perfection") has been brought together with the biblical portrait of God as involved in history into one grand "biblical-classical synthesis." Philo of Alexandria, for example, defined the divine essence as "that which is" *(to ōn)*.[13] This resulted in a radical displacement of the Old Testament understanding of God as a personal being involved in a relationship of "steadfast love" *(ḥeseḏ)* with his creation. Philo dehistoricized and deeschatologized the Jewish worldview.[14] Following in the steps of Philo, the classical doctrine (both Jewish and Christian) of the divine essence was sometimes abstracted from the divine project and made a subject unto itself; thus "God" was analyzed as a nonrelational concept. That is, the nature of God was divorced from the relationship in which God created us, and God was defined in terms of utter transcendence, immutability and power apart from the project God initiated and carries on. Consequently, the attributes of omnipotence, omniscience, aseity and impassibility often acquired meanings they need not have. Such terms may be used, but they must be defined in light of the biblical understanding of the divine wisdom, love, holiness and faithfulness.

Divine immutability, omnipotence and so on could have been qualified in light of the divine project involving the sort of divine-human relationships displayed in Scripture.[15] Instead, these terms were often defined in terms of Plato's understanding of perfection—that which could never change, since any change would only be a change for the worse. A "perfect" God simply cannot change because a change would mean that

God either was not now perfect or was not perfect prior to changing.[16] This understanding of perfection has been a siren call that many have been unable to resist, and it has had a profound impact on the doctrine of providence. For instance, some argue that if a perfect being cannot change in any way, then God's thoughts and will are genuinely immutable and impassible. If so, God must decree all that comes to pass (exhaustive control). This decretal theology is then used to interpret the biblical text in such a way that a genuine give-and-take interpersonal relationship between God and humanity is denied.[17] In this model God must necessarily exercise a particular type of sovereignty (exhaustive control) in order to remain an absolutely independent being. A give-and-take relationship between God and humanity is impossible because it introduces an element of conditionality in God or in God's relations with the world.

Aristotle clearly pointed out that if God has any relationships then God is dependent on another, since any genuine relationship implies dependence. For instance, the master is dependent on the slave to be master. For God to be Lord implies "dependence" on the subjects in the sense that God cannot be Lord without them. Theologians have wrestled with whether or not we may say that God is "dependent" or related to the world. Clearly, Christians could not agree completely with Aristotle, who held that there can be no real relationship between God and others: God is unrelated, needs no friends and has no friends.[18] In my opinion, classical theism has not done a satisfactory job of integrating the notions of the philosophers with the portrait of God in the biblical witness. The impetus in the classical tradition understands the term *God* as a *category* referring to the universal principle of explanation characterized by immutability and nonrelationality.

In contrast, the gospel is not about a God abstracted from historical particularity. It is about the God who becomes human, experiences the vicissitudes of earthly existence, even to the point of death, is resurrected and seeks to work though his "body" of believers to accomplish his purposes. The biblical writers see *God* not as a category but as a person who has entered into relation with us in history. Whereas Aristotle's God had no friends, in the biblical tradition God and Abraham are friends (Jas 2:23). If we begin with the God who comes to us, especially as seen in Jesus, then it is possible to see God as interactive, parental, generous, sensitive, cooperative, wise and mighty in the working out of his project. If the divine project and the particular paths God has sovereignly elected to pursue in history are kept in mind, then it is possible to qualify the traditional list of divine attributes in light of the scriptural revelation.[19] Then it becomes clear that God has all the wisdom, knowledge and power needed to work with the sort of world he freely decided to create. If God is seen as involved in a personal way with a project in which he freely enters into give-and-take interpersonal relations, then four attributes of God come to the fore: love, wisdom, faithful freedom and almightiness.

6.4.2 Love   Western theology has had a difficult time placing "God is love" (1 Jn 4:8) at center stage when discussing the divine attributes. Instead, it emphasizes the more abstract and impersonal attributes of omnipotence and omniscience. In my opinion this results from the failure to place the discussion of the divine nature under the category of a personal God carrying out a project. Despite its claim that God is a personal being, Western thought has paid insufficient attention to the specific sort of world God decided to create—a world in which God enters into reciprocal, interpersonal relationships. Discussions of God's nature that begin with the notion of the "absolute" make it extremely difficult to speak of God's love as anything other than mere beneficence, in which case God cares for us but not about us.[20] Emil Brunner put it this way: "To think that it is correct *first of all* to deal with the metaphysical Being of God, and *then* with His Love, as His 'ethical attribute', means that the decisive element in the Biblical Idea of God has not been perceived."[21] To adapt a statement by Dietrich Bonhoeffer, only the personal God can help, for it takes a personal being to love.[22] Whereas classical theism's root metaphor is God as the pillar around which all else moves, the root metaphor for relational theism is a personal God in loving relations with creaturely persons.

A trinitarian metaphysic is illuminating in this regard. Beginning with a trinitarian God of love who enters into loving personal relations with his creatures gives some direction to the doctrine of providence. The Father, Son and Holy Spirit love one another. They are involved in a tripersonal community in which each member of the triune being gives and receives love from the others. Relationality is an *essential* aspect of God. The tripersonal God is the perfection of love and communion—the very antithesis of aloofness, isolation and domination. God is no solitary potentate forcing his will on others. The members of the Trinity mutually share and relate to one another. In this view personhood is the ultimate ontological category. Personhood, relationality and community—not power, independence and control—become the center for understanding the nature of God.[23] Whereas the main motif of the Neoplatonic God concept is that of distance and unrelatedness, the Christian doctrine of the Trinity asserts that to be God is to be related in love.[24]

Hence God did not need to create in order to love, for the Trinity experiences and manifests the fullness of love. The members of the Trinity experience the agape love of one another: an unselfish, nonmanipulative love. In loving freedom the triune God decides to create creatures with whom to share this agape love. The creation should be seen as the result of the openness of God's love to establish others who could experience this love and enter into loving relationships with God. A God who is antecedently relational and self-sufficient is free to create significant others and enter into genuine reciprocal relations with them. The triune God as both lover and beloved is free to take the gracious initiative, in both creation and incarnation, of opening the love of the Godhead to others.[25] Søren Kierkegaard understood that it was divine love that brought creation into being for the purpose of relationship:

> Everyone who assumes that a God exists naturally thinks Him as the strongest . . . but such a man hardly thinks of the possibility of a reciprocal relationship. . . . But God who creates out of nothing, who almightily takes from nothing and says, "Be," lovingly adjoins, "Be something even in apposition to me." . . . This omnipotence . . . which constrains itself and lovingly makes of the creature something in apposition to itself—oh, marvelous omnipotence of love![26]

One of the central, if not *the* central, aims of creation was to produce significant others who could experience the divine love and reciprocate that love both to God and to other creatures. God intended to create a space-time community reflective of the triune life. Love, which does not force its own way (1 Cor 13:5), allows for the creatures to be genuine others. Space is given them to freely participate in the fellowship of love. But what precisely is meant by love?

W. H. Vanstone's *The Risk of Love* and Vincent Brümmer's *The Model of Love* both provide helpful criteria for identifying love.[27] Vanstone gives a phenomenology of love in which he claims that love must be limitless, precarious and vulnerable. By *limitless* he means "unlimited concern for the other." The lover desires to give all to the beloved. In this respect love differs from kindness, for kindness is limited in the amount it gives or forgives. There are limits on the lover, but they come from without, not within. That is, the lover respects the beloved. Although love desires to expand its activity, it does not overwhelm or imprison the beloved by expressions that are untimely or excessive. In developing our relationships, we learn that an expression of love that is too sudden or overly demonstrative may backfire on us and not achieve the desired goal. Genuine love aspires to give to the beloved but respects the personhood of the other such that the lover accepts and works within the conditions of the relationship. The ultimate goal is to enlarge those conditions so that the beloved is able to experience more love.

Though love desires the highest well-being of the other, it knows that well-being must be defined in terms of the particulars of the relationship. Thus the manifestations of love vary from relationship to relationship, depending on their level of development. Applied to God, this means that God respects the rules of the game he established and so conditions his love according to the specifics of the individual or group with whom he is relating. God may want to give more to them, but they may not be ready for it. Hence, love, though limitless, is conditioned by the ability of the other to receive it.

Vanstone's second criterion is the *precarious* nature of love. Love is an activity for the sake of the other that does not control the other. It wants the other to grow in love. Consequently, love is precarious because the intentions of the lover may not be satisfied. Love may be received properly or may be rejected entirely. "Love proceeds by no assured programme. In the case of children, a parent is peculiarly aware that each step of love is a step of risk; and that each step taken generates the need for another and equally precarious step."[28] Teaching children how to ride a bicycle or how to swim and providing proper safety instructions are expressions of love that may confirm and enlarge the love in the relationship or may embitter and estrange. There is always the danger that the child may misunderstand and fail to respond properly. A love that so controlled the child that the child could not fail would be a false love. Love takes risks and is willing to wait and try again if need be. In the parable of the prodigal son God is the "waiting father" who desires the return of his children who have misunderstood his love (Lk 15). God is willing to wait if need be and to give it another try. Waiting implies a degree of passivity and dependency, whereas trying again implies that the efforts of love have failed to achieve the desired end as yet.[29]

The third criterion is that love is *vulnerable,* since lovers grant the beloved a power over themselves. The beloved can make the lover delighted or angry, joyous or grief stricken, frustrated or fulfilled because the lover cares about what transpires in the relationship. My children can affect me deeply because I care about them and our relationship. If my children wonder about whether they matter to me, they need only look at the way I respond to them. If my children have the power to make a difference in my state of being, then they have a signal that I care about my relationship with them.

Lovers reveal themselves—their names, their identities—and thus make themselves available and vulnerable to the beloved. Love reveals and communicates the person to the other. Love is vulnerable because it surrenders into other hands the final outcome of love's aspirations. Whether love results in a deep interpersonal relationship or is scorned by the beloved and results in suffering for the lover is not under the control of the lover. There is much the lover can do, but success is not guaranteed. In the case of God it may be said that God sovereignly elected to be vulnerable in creating a world of creatures with whom God could enter into loving relationships. God did not remain anonymous (in contrast to some classical theists' views) but revealed himself to us, made himself accessible for us. God is open *to* us and *for* us.[30] God makes it possible for us to cause him grief or joy, suffering or delight.

Moreover, God elects to establish a world in which the outcome of his love is not a foregone conclusion. God desires a relationship of genuine love with us and this, according to the rules of the game God established, cannot be forced or controlled and so cannot be guaranteed.[31] In the divine-human relationship God is more vulnerable than we are because God cannot count on our faithfulness in the way we may count on his steadfast love.[32] For much of the Christian tradition it was thought that God is strongly impassible and thus incapable of being open or vulnerable in any way.[33] As Creator, God is impassible in the sense that God is not forced to be open or vulnerable. However, if God freely decides to be passible and vulnerable in relation to us, who is to say that God *cannot* sovereignly do this? Has God decided to do things this way? From the survey of the biblical material it certainly appears that God has forsworn immunity from vulnerability and suffering.[34] This is especially clear from the incarnation. We see the Son of God open to others, dependent, vulnerable and victorious through suffering.[35]

A couple of qualifications are in order regarding the applicability of Vanstone's criteria to the Trinity and to our love of God. Are terms like *vulnerability* and *precarious* appropriate predications for describing the love that exists among the members of the Trinity? It hardly seems so, for we confess as part of the faith *(de dicto)* that there is harmony among the Trinity. Although the Father does not force his way on the Son or the Spirit, *precarious* may not be the best term to get at this notion. Of Vanstone's three criteria, perhaps only *limitless* legitimately applies to the intra-trinitarian life. The criteria do remain appropriate for describing the divine love toward us (limitless) and God's experience of loving free creatures (precarious and vulnerable).

The other qualification concerns whether our love for God is vulnerable. That is, how can our love for God be open to disappointment if God's love is unfailing? True, God is open to being hurt by our failure to reciprocate the divine love, but it does not seem right to say that we are open to being hurt by God's failure to love us. In other words, it seems that all risk is on God's side, since we are not concerned with God's letting us down.[36] Perhaps Vanstone's criteria of vulnerability can apply to our love for God in the following sense: Maybe the risk in our love for God is not that God will cease loving us but that we will find the divine love unfulfilling due to our sin or dysfunctional lives or simply to a lack of understanding as to how God is loving us in our present situation. When Moses complains to God that God has not done what Moses thought God ought to have done (Ex 5:22-23), the problem lies with Moses' limited understanding of what God is doing and will do in the future. In any case, this means that the problem lies with us, not God. Hence if we are going to apply vulnerability or risk to our love for God, it would be in this qualified sense in which we fail to accurately grasp the way in which God is loving us. With these modifications in mind, I think Vanstone's criteria are helpful for elucidating aspects of the love relationship between God and humans. Nonetheless, additional characteristics are needed in order to arrive at a satisfactory understanding of love.

Brümmer identifies four characteristics of love that have some differences as well as some affinities to Vanstone's. Brümmer surveys various ways in which Western thought has construed love. He concludes that traditionally it has been understood as attitudinal and as involving three aspects: intentions, evaluations and dispositions.[37] The attitude of love is *intentional* because it is something we resolve to carry out rather than something we simply experience, such as an itch. Love also involves an *evaluation* of the object loved. Love is not blind or indifferent to virtues and vices in the beloved. The lover is concerned to bring about the best for the beloved, and this cannot happen without a realistic appraisal of the beloved. In theology this idea is usually discussed under the heading of the holiness of God. The holiness of God, it is said, cannot tolerate sin and seeks to obliterate it, whereas the divine love brings forth mercy to the sinner. Emil Brunner, for instance, holds that holiness creates distance where love creates communion.[38] This sounds as though there are polarities within God, each struggling for supremacy.[39] Others have removed any form of evaluation from the notion of love, reducing love to sentimentality and permissiveness. A better approach is to speak of God's holy love, which cares deeply about the harm that the beloved does to herself.[40] The anger, wrath and judgments of God are expressions of his caring love.[41] God does not simply let us go our own way, for God desires to redeem us and so will convict and confront us, will stand in our way.

Love is not blind to the reality of what we are as sinners, nor does it dismiss us from the relationship without further ado. The divine caring is manifested in evaluating our situation and in God's concern to open it to new possibilities. These possibilities can affect both parties. They can affect us in that the God of holy love who confronts our sin is a fearsome God— a God not within our control. They also affect God, since God is open to being delighted and being grieved by his creatures, depending on our response to the new possibilities. Finally, says Brümmer, love is *dispositional*, or habitual, rather than occasional. From time to time we may feel happy, grateful or afraid, but love is not a passing state. It is more like a policy that we publicly carry out in repeated actions with the intention of achieving the goal of a mature relationship.

Brümmer adds a fourth characteristic to the three just described: the desire for *reciprocation*. This is important, he says, if we are to grasp the fact that love is more than a mere attitude; it creates a *relationship*. W. Norris Clarke, writing from the Thomistic tradition, wonderfully expresses this notion when he writes that God

> is one who enters into deep personal relations of love with His creatures. And an authentic interpersonal relation of love necessarily involves not merely purely creative or one-way love, but genuine mutuality and reciprocity of love, including not only the giving of love but the joyful acceptance of it and response to it. This means that our God is a God who really cares, is really concerned with our lives and happiness, who enters into truly reciprocal personal relations with us, who responds to our prayers—to whom, in a word, our contingent world and its history somehow make a genuine difference.[42]

Love seeks the response of the other yet respects the personhood of the other. The lover desires that the beloved reciprocate the love and so bring to fruition the goal of the relationship. In this sense, love is between persons. Persons in relation for the purpose of reciprocating love (the divine project) becomes the lens through which we view the type of providential relationship God has elected to have with the world.[43]

The nature of love, as just defined, is evident in the life of Jesus. His love was persistent, dependent on the ability of others to receive it, evaluative and vulnerable. Everything did not go precisely as Jesus intended. His concerns were rejected by many who did not desire the new possibilities he sought to bring forth. Nonetheless, he endured rejection, demonstrating the way of love as the way to a redemptive future. In this light it is possible to think of the apostle Paul's description of agape love as applicable to God:

> Love is patient; love is kind; love is not envious or boastful or arrogant or rude. It does not insist on its own way; it is not irritable or resentful; it does not rejoice in wrongdoing, but rejoices in the truth. It bears all things, believes all things, hopes all things, endures all things. (1 Cor 13:4-7)

In the Christian tradition God has been described as loving, patient and enduring, but usually not within a framework of a divine project involving vulnerability and risk. The fact that love does not selfishly insist on its own way has certainly been a neglected theme in discussions of providence and omnipotence. Instead, it has been common to insist, with Augustine, that "the will of the omnipotent is always undefeated."[44] Consequently, Paul's conception of love, which entails vulnerability, has been subjugated to absolute power. I believe this is a result of talking about these attributes in abstraction from the sort of project God has elected to set in motion. Finally, it hardly needs saying that it has not been customary to think of God as "believing" or "hoping" in anything. But if we begin with the understanding of God as bringing into being creatures with whom he desires to enter into genuine personal and loving relationships, then it is quite permissible to speak of God's believing and hoping things will go a certain way.[45] For instance, the prophets proclaim that God repeatedly hoped Israel would put away its idols and return to him, but the people seldom did. God desired the early church to be made up of Jews and Gentiles, but it did not develop exactly as God had planned. The divine love is persistent yet capable of being frustrated. Paul's characterization of love is appropriate for understanding the way of God with the world. God creates in love, elects in love, commands in love, judges in love, incarnates in love and redeems in love.[46] The triune God is the perfection of love and brings into being other creatures to share in that love.

6.4.3 Wisdom In establishing and carrying out his project, God is resourceful, proficient and innovative. In his relationships with humans God has been adept at solving problems that arose and overcoming obstacles that stood in the way of the accomplishment of the divine project. God has demonstrated in history that he has all the wisdom necessary to work with the sort of world he decided to create, despite the fact that things do not always go as God desires (for example, Israel's defection). The divine wisdom is not defined by our standard of success but by the way God works to bring about the fruition of his project. After explaining how God has decided to bring the Gentiles into the community of God by faith in Jesus, Paul declares his amazement that God would accomplish his purposes in this way: "O the depth of the riches and wisdom and knowledge of God! How unsearchable are his judgments and how inscrutable his ways!" (Rom 11:33). It was the wisdom of God to judge both Jews and Gentiles under sin so that he would show mercy to all (Rom 11:32). God did this through the reconciling ministry of Jesus, who is both the power and the wisdom of God (1 Cor 1:24).

For Paul "God's foolishness is wiser than human wisdom" (1 Cor 1:25). God's wisdom is manifested in the incarnation, death and resurrection of the Son of God. To us, death, vulnerability and risk seem utter folly, inappropriate ways of acting for a deity. Yet the way of Jesus is the way of powerful love, a love that calls us to be reconciled with God, a love that raises us in resurrection life to share in the divine love. God has not chosen immunity from the suffering involved in a relationship with sinners. Nor has God chosen to override by raw power the personhood of the creatures he made to love. Rather, it is the way of love that works to accomplish the divine project. And though in many respects history reflects a terrible mess, I believe and hope, on the basis of Jesus' resurrection, that God has made, is making and will continue to make progress toward satisfactory achievement of his goal.

Although Paul came to see the wisdom of God displayed in the foolishness of the cross, it is possible to call the divine wisdom into question. Biblical characters repeatedly called on God to explain himself (for example, Habakkuk) or failed to understand the direction God was taking the project at that particular time in history (for example, Peter in Acts 10:17). Since the Enlightenment, it has been common for people to call the entire project into question and ask whether God has bitten off more than he can chew. There is nobody who is more hated than God. Many people are dissatisfied with what they have received in life and are disappointed in God for not doing a better job of running the world. Though people are oftentimes angry at God for egocentric reasons, there is room in the model of divine risk taking to allow for questioning God's wisdom. God takes the risk that we may misunderstand his loving intentions.

Things look quite different in the no-risk model of providence, in which there is no room to question God because everything happens exactly as

God desires. There is no room for genuine lament because God is always and only to be praised.[47] Who are you to question God? Good question. You are one of the creatures he created to share a relationship of love. Because love does not overpower the other, there is the possibility that I may fail to grasp God's intentions. In the risk model everything does not happen precisely as God intends. God experiences setbacks and even defeats. Given the sort of world God created, there is opportunity to question the divine wisdom. Even if we cannot blame God for evil, we can still wonder whether it was worth the risk of embarking on the project.

But given God's track record, we have reason to trust him, confident in his wisdom. God does not hide from us but shoulders responsibility for creating this world and establishing the rules of the game under which God has chosen to operate.[48] We can hold God accountable to his purposes and intentions in the project he has undertaken. The issue, for God, is whether we will come to trust in the divine love and wisdom. The fundamental basis on which God seeks to affirm his wisdom and love is the life and work of Jesus. According to Paul, it is Jesus who justifies us and intercedes on our behalf, which is why he is convinced that nothing can separate us from the love of God in Jesus Christ (Rom 8:31-39). Jesus is the wisdom of God. If Jesus does not persuade us, who or what will? God has placed his bet that he can establish a trusting, loving relationship with us through Jesus. Will we come to faith? This is the risk that the divine wisdom takes.

The wisdom of God is displayed in biblical history as it reveals God's competency and resourcefulness in working to achieve the goal of his project.[49] Philosophers and theologians have seldom spoken of God's competence and resourcefulness. Instead, the traditional model has defined omniscience in a way that excludes any use for the concept of wisdom. Omnipotence has sometimes been explained in terms of everything's having been fixed from the beginning. But as Markus Barth remarks, "A God who has fixed every detail beforehand may retire or die."[50] However, if God gets involved in our lives and in history in genuine give-and-take relations, then the competence, resourcefulness and problem-solving abilities of God become significant. In relational theism God's creativity is highlighted. In fact, we could speculate as to which model offers a more exalted view of God. Gregory Boyd remarks that

> it takes far more self-confidence, far more wisdom, far more love and sensitivity to govern that which is personal and free than it does to govern that over which one has absolute control. . . . It reflects a far greater depth of character and confidence, requiring a more profound depth of wisdom, to

face a future with genuine openness, genuine unknowns, genuine risks, than it does to face a future with an exhaustive blueprint in hand.[51]

Moreover, in some understandings, omniscience is seen as a sort of data bank; all is simply known, with little if any role for divine wisdom. Relational theism, on the other hand, includes both the immensity of God's knowledge while allowing us to emphasize God's wisdom and problem-solving abilities. God is wise in that he is resourceful and competent in his relationship with us. Later on more will be said about the divine wisdom in relation to sovereignty, evil and planning.

6.4.4 Faithful Freedom   Divine faithfulness and freedom go together. In God's relationship with us we see the divine freedom working out the project in ways God deems best. And we see God choosing to be faithful to the project instead of giving up on it. Berkhof speaks of this as God's "changeable faithfulness": God is free to change in his relationships, yet God remains faithful in them.[52]

God possesses freedom in relation to the creation. In the triune relationship there was no need to create in order to experience love. There is no "problem of the lonely God" in the Christian Godhead. Because the tripersonal God, the one God, eternally exists in loving communion as the Father, Son and Holy Spirit, it can be said that the Godhead experienced the delight of sharing and receiving love apart from any creation.[53] God does not need the creation in order to be God. The creation is not to be explained by some necessity in the divine nature, nor by some superabundance that needs an outlet, nor by some lack in God.[54] The creation is wholly contingent; it exists out of sheer grace.[55] God is free to create or not create anything at all. God is also free, once he decided to create, to make the sort of world he desired and to establish the particular rules of the game he wanted. If God wants a world in which he tightly controls every event that happens, then God is free to do so. If God wants a world in which he sovereignly elects to establish genuine give-and-take relations such that God will, for some things, be conditioned by the decisions of the creatures, then God is free to do so. It is God's free decision whether or not to set up reciprocal relations between himself and his creatures. The divine nature does not dictate the sort of world God must make.[56]

Some understandings of the divine nature lead to the conclusion that God *must* create a world and *must* create a particular type of world. It was a proverb in Plato's day that "not even God himself can fight against necessity."[57] Some thought that the divine nature necessarily "emanated" itself into what we call reality. Such notions were unacceptable to Christianity. Nonetheless, the idea of necessity was often incorporated into the very nature of God such that the divine nature necessarily determined what God did. God is not captive to an *arche* (exterior ruler); but if libertarian freedom is not predicated of God, then God is "captive" to his own nature in that God is not free to do otherwise than what he does.[58] Though Christians claimed that God was free not to create anything at all and free not to create this particular world, the denial of libertarian freedom to God implies that God *must* create (creation is necessary) and calls into question the freedom to the creatures.[59] The divine freedom and contingency of the creatures are thus rendered suspect.

If, however, God is a personal being experiencing the fullness of love in the triune Godhead, then God is free to create a world that God does not need.[60] The world, as the product of divine personal freedom, is genuinely contingent and so does not have a sufficient rational explanation that natural theology can ferret out by logic. There is simply no way for us to get beyond our relationship with the Creator and, reaching the God beyond God, establish what the state of God's mind was at the moment of creation. Brunner observes that the "One who is Free can never be known by the way of thought—for only the Necessary can be found thus, but never the Free. . . . Never can thought of itself build up the idea of a contingent, non-necessary, freely-posited world."[61] Wolfhart Pannenberg makes the same point when he says, "If . . . an effect is not grounded in a necessity, then one cannot without further ado draw conclusions from the effect about the nature of the cause. . . . Therefore, the otherness of God in contrast to creatures is radically protected on the presupposition of the contingency of the divine operation."[62]

What we do know is that God created us and decided to enter into reciprocal relations with us as part of the way God is working to bring the divine project to fruition. Although God does not need the world in order to experience love, God is free to create beings with whom to share his love and with whom he shares their love. Brümmer holds that God has chosen to make a world in which he wants his love reciprocated. Thus in this restricted sense it can be said that God has chosen to be in "need."[63] God is free to choose to be dependent on the free response of the creatures and to *respond* to them if God so desires. Karl Barth puts it this way: "If ever there was a miserable anthropomorphism, it is the hallucination of a divine immutability which rules out the possibility that God can let himself be conditioned in this or that way by his creature."[64] The biblical materials surveyed in earlier chapters showed that Israel as well as individual humans affected what God experienced and the decisions he made. Who is to say God cannot sovereignly be this way? God is sovereign over his sovereignty. Once God freely decides to create and elects to make this particular sort of world, God is free to work out his project as he deems best. This is precisely Paul's point in Romans 9— 11. God is sovereignly free to work out his redemptive program as he sees fit. If God wants to include Gentiles by faith in Jesus, then God is free to do so, the point of the often-abused metaphor of the divine potter's having the right over the clay to work the way he desires (Rom 9:20). God has decided to get personally involved—especially in the incarnation—and to work out his project according to his loving wisdom.

The Christian faith requires a faithful God, not a risk-free God. God has repeatedly demonstrated his faithfulness to his project. Though God has been remarkably flexible, innovative and adaptable in working to achieve his goals, there is a constancy in his program. Thomas Oden asserts that God is reliable in the way he exhibits his love.[65] The author of Hebrews says that God has made promises and has given us his oath that he will fulfill them; he has a proven track record, and so we may have confidence in God's faithfulness (Heb 6:13-20). In fact, even though we have not been faithful to God, God has remained faithful to us (2 Tim 2:13). Berkhof captures this idea when he writes, "Our wavering faithfulness is upheld on all sides by God's unwavering faithfulness."[66]

The faithfulness of God has customarily been discussed as a category of divine immutability. This would not be so bad if the personal aspects of God's relationship to us had been kept in mind.[67] Too often, however, immutability has been defined apart from what we know of God in history and has been seen to imply that God is absolutely unchangeable in every respect. Plato's "argument from perfection" (any change for a perfect being is always a change for the worse) is the standard means of arriving at divine immutability.[68] This is true even of evangelicals who pride themselves on doing "biblical" rather than "natural" theology.[69] Herman Bavinck refers to Plato's dictum and then says, "He who predicates of God any change whatsoever, whether with respect to essence, knowledge, or will, belittles every one of his attributes. . . . He robs God of his divine nature."[70] If God's thoughts, will or emotions ever changed, then God could not be considered "perfect" and would in some sense be conditioned by the creatures.[71] This line of reasoning undermines the personal and living God who establishes a covenantal relationship and remains faithful to it.

It is important to remember that whereas "eternal truths are *unchangeable;* an eternal Person is *faithful.*[72] Donald Bloesch puts it well: "God's being is indestructible, his plan and purpose are unalterable. His love is unfailing and inexorable. His grace is irreversible and persevering. This is the biblical picture of God's unchangeableness."[73] The essence of God does not change, but God does change in experience, knowledge, emotions and actions.[74]

God is both faithful and free or, as Berkhof puts it, God has a "changeable faithfulness."[75] Asserting God's faithful freedom affirms the personhood of God in relation to human persons. In his sovereign love for his creatures God experiences change yet remains faithfully committed to his project. This understanding allows the biblical texts on divine repentance to be read straightforwardly. As Harry Kuitert remarks, "There is nothing—outside of theological prejudice—to prevent us from taking these words seriously."[76] From this perspective the Bible does not need to be read as a two-layered cake with the top layer representing how God appears to us *(quoad nos)* and the bottom layer representing how God really is *(in se).*[77] There is no need to dismiss as mere anthropomorphisms the texts in which God plans, repents, changes in his emotional state, anticipates or is surprised at our sinful response.[78] They are metaphors that reveal the kind of God who addresses us.

That God is personally involved in the world and is faithful to it is best exemplified in the incarnation of Jesus. God was faithful in bringing the promises to fulfillment, but he was free to fulfill them in ways that people did not anticipate. The sort of messiah Jesus chose to be was unexpected. On the basis of God's faithful freedom we may trust God to continue working toward the realization of his kingdom. Yet we must also leave God free to work things out as the divine love and wisdom deem best.

There are those who object, however, to placing their trust in a God who is free and changeable. Will such a deity be overcome by vulnerability and cease loving us? Why should we trust a God whose prophecies are mutable? Where is our security if God's future is open? The answer to such questions is found in God's work in history, especially in Jesus. He is God's definitive word that God is not overcome by vulnerability. Even though the incarnate God was vulnerable to rejection and even death, God did not turn away from us in our sin. God stood toe to toe with our sin and did not flinch. God's unfailing commitment to his project is what should persuade us that we may wholeheartedly place our trust in God.

Some, however, prefer to base their confidence in divine impassibility (strongly defined) or timelessness as metaphysical guarantees that God will not let us down.[79] This is wrongheaded, however, since it substitutes certainty in an unchanging concept for confidence in a faithful God. The reason to trust a personal God is that God has proven to be faithful. The *Christian* faith is not trust in an immutable timeless principle; it is trust in the everlasting personal and faithful God known as Father, Son and Holy Spirit. The Christian faith is about the personal address of God in Jesus Christ. The faithful concern of God witnessed in Scripture and exemplified in Jesus is the basis of our trust, not some metaphysical principle. God is not fickle; God has been faithful and loving toward his creatures. God swears by himself that he will remain faithful to his promises (Heb 6:13). God's purpose in creation has been firmly maintained even as God has freely taken various routes to accomplish it. The basis of our confidence should be in what the living God has chosen to do, not in some principle we attribute to God in order to secure our own rational certainty. We have an accumulated tradition, the "first fruits" of God's faithful love, which is our ground for trusting him. God has proven himself faithful in the past, so we have confidence that God will be faithful in the future. This is part of what it means to have a *personal* relationship with God.

6.4.5 Almightiness   Omnipotence is commonly discussed in terms of abstract power rather than in connection with God's wisdom, love and faithfulness. Almightiness should, like the attributes discussed above, be understood under the category of the divine project God has undertaken and not as a formal power. The powerful God *('el shaddai)* of the Bible is the one who is mighty to deliver and to care for his people. The almighty God is the God "for us" (Heb 9:24). God's relationship with us in history is the proper basis for understanding almightiness. Language about omnipotence, no matter how exalted or superlative, must be critiqued in light of the sort of omnipotence God has actually exercised in relation to us.[80] Just as the love, wisdom and faithful freedom of God had to be viewed in light of the gospel story, so must the almightiness of God. As A. van de Beek comments, "Christology is the great troublemaker in the domain of omnipotence beliefs."[81] The cross and resurrection of Jesus—typifying the way of God in the world—should lead us to smash our idols of the "absolute" placed above the God of salvation history.

Our general concepts of God must be critiqued by the gospel—with the historical particularity of what God actually decided to do as revelatory of the divine nature. In the gospel the lordship of God is expressed in a most unexpected and (for many in Paul's day) unsatisfactory fashion. A crucified messiah was a stumbling block for many of his fellow Jews. An incarnate and dying Son of God was foolishness to his Greek contemporaries. The gospel story made God sound weak and foolish to those who had preconceived notions of what is fitting for God to do. Paul, however, is convinced that Jesus is "the power of God and the wisdom of God. For God's foolishness is wiser than human wisdom, and God's weakness is stronger than human strength" (1 Cor 1:24-25). Elsewhere Paul says that the gospel is "the power of God for salvation" (Rom 1:16). Paul's opponents (Jews and Greeks) held views of divine power drawn from general notions of what is fitting for God to be and do. Such views are "according to the flesh" (truly anthropomorphic) and represent a worldly way of interpreting the Jesus story. For Paul, all notions of divine power and weakness must be filtered through the cross and resurrection of Jesus, since these events display the wisdom and power of God. The way in which God decided to carry out his project in Jesus was, and still is, perceived by many to be impotence instead of power.

Various distorted images of divine power have been developed.[82] In pure transcendence God is totally unrelated (the ideal of the strong male). God, as necessary being, is the transcendent Lord over us whose relational qualities of love, mercy and faithfulness are subordinated in importance to his lordship.[83] In this view divine power stands far above and apart from us. This may be legitimate in one sense, as an elaboration of the doctrine of creation out of divine freedom. God, in this sense, does not need the world to be God or to be fulfilled. God has being apart from the creation and as Creator is certainly Lord of creation. Nonetheless, the notion of divine power needs to be explicated in terms of the relationship God actually enacts with his creatures.

Another distorted image of divine power affirms a relationship between God and humans, but not a reciprocal one. Whereas Paul said that love does not force its will on the other (1 Cor 13:5), Augustine said that "the will of the omnipotent is always undefeated."[84] God is often conceived as the supreme monarch exercising the coercive power of brute force and compulsion. Many theists tend to think of God in terms of a feudal king whose person was invulnerable, whose will was irresistible and whose rule dominated everything.[85] In this line of thought God always "wins." In Western thought winning (success) is associated with power over others.[86] The more power you possess, the more you are victorious over others.[87] Unqualified power means unqualified success. And success is important, especially for God; deity is supposed to be invulnerable to any sort of failure. It seems that God must abide by the motto of legendary Green Bay Packers football coach Vince Lombardi: "Winning isn't everything; it's the only thing."

Such distorted images of omnipotence end up with a *loveless power*. God is the powerful, domineering Lord who always gets precisely what he wants. In contrast to this is process theism's God of *powerless love,* who is impotent to act unilaterally in the world in the ways depicted in Scripture.[88] The biblical portrayal depicts a God of *powerful love* who exercises his power, wisdom and love on behalf of the creatures with whom he has embarked on a project. Kierkegaard spoke of the "omnipotence of love" in which the almighty Creator lovingly established a place for us to enter into reciprocal relationships of love with himself. "If God," he says, "were only the Almighty, there would be no reciprocal relationship."[89] Love must not be construed as powerlessness, and almightiness must not be understood apart from love. Kristiaan Depoortere puts it well when he says, "God's omnipotence is the power of His love, which creates a space for human beings alongside God Himself, which endows men and women with freedom, and liberates them for its exercise. His power offers human beings opportunities for collaboration."[90]

In discussing omnipotence, philosophers have not usually defined it in terms of the actual relationship God has with us. Instead, they have focused on deriving a concept of maximal power drawn from our own experience of power. Gijsbert van den Brink's excellent study *Almighty God* examines the history of the discussion of the topic and systematically explores the similarities and differences between the concepts of almightiness and omnipotence.[91] Omnipotence, he says, is derived from our preconceived notions of God and power and refers to God's ability to do all things. Almightiness, on the other hand, is derived from God's revelatory actions in history and refers to God's ability to manage the affairs he undertakes in accordance with the character of God (which is also known only by his Word). Almightiness fits nicely with Farmer's definition of providence cited earlier: "the adequacy of God's wisdom and power to the task with which he has charged himself."

In seeking to elaborate the meaning of omnipotence, philosophers usually form themselves into two camps in regard to God's ability to do "all things." On the one hand are those such as René Descartes, who held that God can do absolutely anything, even the logically contradictory.[92] In this view God can save and damn the same individual simultaneously or make two parallel mountain ranges without an intervening valley or create a waffle so big he cannot consume it.[93] After all, is not God the Creator of all things, including logic? Does not God's logic transcend human logic? This may sound pious, but it contains a serious difficulty. Following Barth and Bloesch, it may be said that God is not bound to human logic in the sense that it stands as an independent and equal partner alongside God, limiting what God can do.[94] *We* are not in position to decree *(de re)* what God can or cannot do. But if one asserts that God can do the logically contradictory, then one has also transgressed the boundaries of what *we* can know.[95] Since God created us within certain boundaries and limits and since the principle of noncontradiction seems to be a necessary condition for coherent discourse, *we* cannot meaningfully speak *(de dicto)* of God's doing the logically contradictory.[96] It simply violates the conditions of meaningful discourse, which is one of the boundaries God has placed us in. We could not recognize a "square circle" if we saw one, nor could we comprehend two parallel mountain ranges without an intervening valley.

Problems with the first definition of omnipotence have led thinkers, following Aquinas, to qualify its meaning by asserting that God can do all that is logically possible to do. Though God's power in this sense cannot perform that which is incoherent, this has not been thought to imply any weakness on God's part. God remains able to do all things. It is just that square circles or simultaneously damning and saving a person are not "things" or meaningful states of affairs at all. God has the capacity to realize all possible states of affairs even though God does not, in fact, do so. In this regard omnipotence is virtual, not actual, power. In the Christian tradition it has been customary to distinguish God's absolute power *(potentia absoluta)* from God's actual power *(potentia ordinata)*.[97] God's absolute omnipotence concerns speculating on the kinds of things God can do but has not elected to do.[98]

God's actual power *(potentia ordinata)* is God's ability to manage all that he undertakes. God has unsurpassable power as Creator, Sustainer and Redeemer. This is the biblical understanding of God's almightiness: Divine power is disclosed for what it is from within the divine project. Almightiness is defined in the context of the relationship God has established with the creation. Almightiness is connected to God's authority, which is a relational and social category. It refers to the actual power of God, that is, what God has actually done in creating and interacting with his creatures. Barth writes that "it is not power for anything and everything, but His power with a definite direction and content."[99]

Regarding the definition of "power" there is no consensus. Van den Brink discusses four different understandings of the term.[100] There is (1) the power to do certain specific acts (for example, creation), (2) power over others, (3) power as disposition (that is, to be or to act in particular ways) and (4) power as authority. With the proper qualifications all of these senses of power may be attributed to almightiness. Yet the last one, power as authority, yields an interesting point in relation to providence. Authority may be used in both a de jure and a de facto sense. De jure authority consists of the rights to issue and carry out commands without the consent of those affected. This sort of authority may be causal or coercive in nature. De facto authority, on the other hand, consists of the right to issue commands and carry them out only with the consent of those affected. This kind of authority is not coercive, for it requires the acknowledgment of the authority's power by others in order to exist at all. In discussions of providence God's authority has often been solely construed as de jure rather than de facto. After all, is it proper to say of the omnipotent God that he needs our acknowledgment in order to be Lord?

In a sense, it is not proper, since God is the Lord, our Creator and Provider, whether we acknowledge it or not. Yet God is no Middle Eastern potentate. He is the Lord who wants to love us and establish covenantal relations with us. In this respect the biblical notion of divine authority is closer to de facto authority. The suzerain of the covenant needs the consent of the vassal for the fulfillment of the covenantal relationship. To put it differently, the lover needs the reciprocation of love by the beloved, since love cannot be forced.

The kingdom of God is inaugurated but not fully realized yet. God is *working* to bring all things to the good (Rom 8:28) and to bring it about that all may be loyal subjects and God may be all in all (1 Cor 15:27-28). It is clear that this is not a present reality but is one toward which God is working. Moreover, God enlists our collaboration toward this end, for we have been given the ministry of reconciliation (2 Cor 5:18) and are called to bring every alien worldview and evil captive to the obedience of Christ (2 Cor 10:5).[101] Finally, de facto authority is the type of authority the apostle Paul sought to achieve with the Corinthians.[102] Paul claimed that he was manifesting the same sort of authority that God demonstrated in Christ. It was embodied in the realities of earthly existence, vulnerable to rejection and distributed among God's people. The truth of it will only be fully manifested eschatologically.[103] De facto authority is the way of risk, for it is contingent on the other to accept it. The biblical understanding of almightiness does not entail that everything happens precisely as God desires because it is defined in terms of the sort of project God has decided to establish—a project in which God takes contingency seriously.

Van den Brink identifies five differences between historical philosophical definitions of omnipotence and the biblical concept of almightiness.[104] First, in the Bible God's almightiness is not divorced from God's existential relations with the creation. Second, in the Bible the nature of divine power is disclosed in God's actions, for instance, the powerful image of the Lord Jesus becoming a servant and washing the disciples' feet (Jn 13:4-17). In this passage Jesus expressly uses the action to highlight the nature of his *lordship.* Such actions are difficult to assimilate into Anselmian theology, in which omnipotence is derived from the most perfect understanding of power conceivable and lords are not expected to behave this way. Third, whereas omnipotence is usually construed in such a way that nothing can oppose God, in Scripture God's power and authority are continuously challenged and God's purposes for some things are thwarted. Fourth, the Bible does say that nothing is impossible for God (Gen 18:14; Lk 1:37) and that God's power is unlimited (Num 11:23).

Yet there are some things that God cannot do. For example, God cannot swear by someone greater (Heb 6:13) or lie (Heb 6:18) or be tempted (Jas 1:13) or deny himself (2 Tim 2:13). The biblical writers are not here thinking of "logical" impossibilities but of "factual impossibility" in that God cannot, in fact, swear by one greater than himself. The affirmations about lying or denying himself refer to the divine constancy toward his project. Although there is no attempt by biblical writers to reconcile the notion that God can do anything with the idea that God does not get everything he wants, it must be remembered that both sets of statements occur within the framework of God's relationship with the people to whom these particular statements are made. Fifth, the Bible ascribes both power and weakness to God (1 Cor 1:25), something Anselmian theology has difficulty accounting for.

In my view, the almighty God wins our hearts through the weakness of the cross and the power of the resurrection. God has made us to love, and love does not force its own way on the beloved (1 Cor 13:5). Brunner puts it well: "God so wills to be 'almighty' over us, that He wins our hearts through the condescension in His Son, in the Cross of the Son. No other Almighty Power of God could thus conquer and win our hearts. The heart is the one sphere which cannot be forced."[105] Catholic theologian William Hill argues that in the incarnation it becomes clear God is not merely lord of history but enters into history himself, revealing "his submission to that history (without any abandonment of the prerogatives of his uncreated nature). . . . His omnipotence and sovereign freedom are such that he can will to subject himself to conditions of finiteness and temporality without any sacrifice of his transcendence."[106] Dutch Reformed theologian Berkhof speaks of God's almightiness as the "defenseless superior power" in that God creates significant others and submits himself to the rules of the game he established for his relationship with them.[107]

This must not be construed as sentimentality or impotency. As Daniel Migliore states, "God is Creator, Redeemer, and Transformer of life—not mere almightiness, but creative power; not impassive but compassionate power; not immutable but steadfast, life-giving power that liberates and transforms the world."[108]

6.5 Excursus on Omniscience

6.5.1 Introduction   My preference throughout this book has been to emphasize divine wisdom, resourcefulness and competence. Because wisdom involves knowledge, it is important to discuss divine knowledge. Omniscience may be defined as knowing all there is to know such that God's knowledge is coextensive with reality. Or, following Hasker, it may be defined as "at any time God knows all propositions such that God's knowing them at that time is logically possible."[109] The advantage of these definitions is that they do not prejudice the debate regarding the content of omniscience toward any particular view. After all, there is considerable debate regarding the nature of "reality" (specifically, whether the future is real) and whether there may be propositions that God knows at one time but not another. That is, Christian philosophers disagree about the nature of omniscience, not about whether or not God is omniscient.

Similarly, in regard to omnipotence, most theists agree that God is omnipotent but disagree sharply about the nature of omnipotence. Many theists believe that omniscience includes foreknowledge: God not only knows all the past and present in exhaustive detail but also knows in complete detail everything that will ever happen in the future. However, there is considerable debate about attributing foreknowledge to God among contemporary philosophers of religion.[110] Whereas some maintain exhaustive foreknowledge (or omniprescience), others contend that God knows the past and present in exhaustive detail but does not know the future in the same way. Again, it is important to note that the debate is about the nature of God's omniscience, not whether God is omniscient.[111]

Regarding the issue of whether or not God takes risks, the debate over foreknowledge is of no consequence. The primary question is whether or not God sovereignly decides to grant creatures the freedom to do things that God does not specifically intend to happen. What sort of "control" does God decide to exercise over his creation, and what sort of freedom does God grant humans? If God creates us with libertarian freedom, then we have the possibility of doing things God does not specifically intend to happen (for example, murder). Accordingly, God does not tightly control each and every action of his creatures and thus takes risks in the sense that things may happen that God wishes would not happen. Affirming that everything creatures do is specifically controlled by God such that nothing ever happens that is contrary to the divine will is equivalent to crossing the Rubicon. A God who foreordains all things does not take risks. A God with simple foreknowledge still takes risks in deciding to embark on the sort of project of creating beings with libertarian freedom, for then God does not control the creatures in such a way that they are prohibited from doing that which God wishes they would not do (for example, murder or steal). The only way of avoiding an omniscient God who takes risks in this sense is to uphold divine foreordination of all things. Consequently, the key issue is not the type of knowledge an omniscient deity has but the type of sovereignty an omniscient God decides to exercise.

Another important dividing line that may be drawn is one between those who affirm relational theism and those who reject it. Relational theism understands that God's will is, for some things, conditioned by the creatures. The God who foreordains all things is one whose will remains completely unconditioned by the creatures. Proponents of divine determinism hold that God never responds to creatures, whereas proponents of relational theism see God entering into genuine personal relations with creatures. That God genuinely responds to what we do and that for some things the divine will is freely conditioned by the creatures is affirmed by Eastern Orthodoxy, Wesleyans, Arminianism, much mainline Protestant theology, certain strains of Reformed and Catholic thought, Pentecostalism and evangelical piety (whether each of these does so with self-consistency is another matter).[112] If God permits things to happen that he did not specifically intend to happen or if God enters into give-and-take dialogue with us or if God genuinely responds to our prayers because we ask God to do so, then God is involved in contingent relations with us. This is true, as will be shown below, whether God has simple foreknowledge or present knowledge, since both models of omniscience affirm relational theism (the fellowship model). In order to substantiate these claims I will first summarize the various positions and then focus on why even a God with foreknowledge remains a risk-taking and responding deity.

6.5.2 The Main Alternatives There are several views on the nature of omniscience as it relates to foreknowledge. One view is that God, technically speaking, does not have foreknowledge because God foreordains all things. God does not "prevision" or "look ahead" into the future to see what the creatures will do and make his decisions *on the basis* of the creature's future actions, since this would mean that God was not in tight control of the creatures—he might prevision them doing something he did not want them doing. For Calvin and, I believe, the latter Augustine, what God knows is determined solely by what God decides to do. Thus God does not take any risks.

Denying exhaustive divine sovereignty such that God grants libertarian freedom and allows for something to happen that God wishes did not happen results in a God who takes risks, whether God has simple foreknowledge, timeless knowledge, knowledge of all possibilities, middle knowledge or presentism.[113] Part of the motivation behind these theories is the development of a nondeterministic understanding of sovereignty.[114] Proponents of each of these understandings of omniscience typically affirm libertarian freedom for humans. According to simple foreknowledge, a widely held view among theists, God, prior to creation, had comprehensive direct vision of every single act that libertarian free creatures would actually do in this world. For instance, prior to creation God foresaw such things as Caesar crossing the Rubicon and the abolition of apartheid in South Africa. This view was held by several early church fathers, Arminius and John Wesley. They used it to explain how God could predestine certain individuals to salvation without overriding human freedom.[115] God simply "looked ahead" to see which people would exercise faith in God and *on that basis* God elected them. Prior to creation God *learns* what we will actually do, since prior to God's decision to create God did not know what we would actually do. Hence, a God with simple foreknowledge was open (prior to the decision to create) to being surprised, shocked and delighted, depending on what the beings whom he does not control decide to do.[116] That God takes risks in this view will be made clear below.

According to the knowledge of all possibilities view (which was called "natural knowledge" in the Middle Ages) God, prior to creation, knows all possible actions that creatures with libertarian freedom may take. In light of this knowledge God may decide what responses, if any, he will make to each action. God may eternally decide to do X if A occurs or Z if B arises. In other words, God may eternally decide to "prerespond" to each and every situation that might arise. Richard Creel says that God eternally resolved how he would deal with each possible situation. In this way there is no genuine change in God, including feelings.[117] But other proponents of this view allow for God to be temporally involved in the creation and allow for some significant change to occur in God.[118] Nevertheless, God is never caught off guard, never surprised by any event and never forced to make any ad hoc decisions.[119] Yet God remains a risk taker in the sense that God allows libertarian freedom and does not control what the creatures do with it.

A theory that shares some affinities with the foregoing view and is currently being debated by philosophers of religion is called middle knowledge, or Molinism. Luis de Molina, a sixteenth-century Jesuit theologian, developed this theory in an attempt to reconcile divine sovereignty and human indeterministic freedom.[120] According to middle knowledge, God knows not only what could possibly happen but also what *would happen if* something were different in any given situation. That is, God knows all the "counterfactuals of creaturely freedom," such as the things that would be different in the world had Moses refused to return to Egypt or had Mary rejected her role in salvation history. Proponents of middle knowledge sometimes claim that since God knows what each of us would freely decide to do in every possible set of circumstances, God simply brings about those circumstances in which we freely do precisely what he wants done and so takes no risks. "In his infinite intelligence, God is able to plan a world in which his designs are achieved by creatures acting freely."[121] According to middle knowledge God does not force the will of the creatures. God simply knows how to bring it about that the creatures freely decide to do God's will.

Perhaps an illustration will help. Suppose I want my son Caleb to wash the car. If I possess middle knowledge, then I am able to survey the various responses he will freely make in all the possible situations in which I might ask him. For instance, I may know that he will wash the car if I ask him on a warm, sunny day early in the morning and that he will refuse if I ask him in the afternoon. Similarly, God selects which situations to bring about in order to secure our freely doing his will. In fact, prior to creation God knew all the feasible worlds he could create and what would freely happen in each of these worlds. In deciding to create this world, God knows which creatures will come into being and all the circumstances these creatures will find themselves in and precisely which choices the creatures will freely make in each situation.

This does not rule out risk for God, however, since God's knowledge of the counterfactuals (what the creatures would do in any given situation) is *independent* of the divine will.[122] Prior to creation God may examine all the feasible worlds. But what the creatures would do in each of these worlds is not controlled by God. God exercises control over which of the worlds he wants to create, but there may not be any feasible world in which indeterministic freedom is present where absolutely everything goes exactly the way God would like. Like old Mother Hubbard, God may find the cupboard of creatable worlds quite bare. God may see in every world in which he grants humans freedom that he has to select from options that provide only a 60 percent (or less) divine-satisfaction rating. God may not get nearly as much as he would have liked. Similarly, there may be no possible situation in which I ask Caleb to wash the car and he will do it. If Caleb suffers from transworld anticar-washing depravity (and I believe most kids do), then there may not be any feasible world in which I am able to get him to freely wash the car.

God may, for instance, desire a world in which every single person comes into a loving relationship with God, but there may not be any such feasible world. If there is such a world, it will be due to the decisions creatures with libertarian freedom make, not to God's knowledge. God was fortunate enough that there was such a world available to create in which humans freely did what he desired. It was possible that no feasible worlds existed in which even some people came to love God. As it turns out, there was at least one such world—this one—in which some people love God. However, God could not guarantee that there would be such a world, since the creatures choose to love God or not.[123] If God does not control the free choices of individuals, then God cannot bring about in feasible world A that Alex, whom God knows will not come to love God in world A, actually comes to love God in world A. Hence, a God with middle knowledge is open to serious disappointment and even surprise in "learning" what obtains in the various feasible worlds. Such a God might be *lucky* or *unlucky* as to whether there are any feasible worlds he could create in which most of the divine desires are met. God may be fortunate to find a creatable world in which most of his desires are met, or God may be unfortunate in that the only feasible worlds available to him are ones in which he fails to obtain much of what he desires. The only degree of "control" a God with middle knowledge has over a deity with simple foreknowledge or presentism is that he selects which feasible world to actualize.[124]

The final view to be summarized is called present knowledge or presentism.[125] Like all other risk models, it affirms omniscience but denies exhaustive foreknowledge. Though God's knowledge is coextensive with reality in that God knows all that can be known, the future actions of free creatures are not yet reality, and so there is nothing to be known.[126] This does not affect the divine perfection because, as Norris Clarke comments, "it cannot be an imperfection not to know what is not in itself knowable—

i.e., the future, the not yet real, at least in its free or not yet determined aspects."[127] Richard Swinburne observes that God could know the future if he decided to enact two conditions: (1) create a fully deterministic world—one without libertarian freedom—and (2) decide at one moment all the actions God would do subsequently.[128] God could know the future if God limited his own freedom to decide in the future and did not grant humans incompatibilistic freedom.

Critics sometimes claim that presentism is an "attenuated" understanding of omniscience, branding it "limited omniscience."[129] But if omnipotence, following Aquinas, is defined as the ability to do all that is logically possible and if this is not an attenuated understanding of divine power, then why should omniscience, defined as the knowing of all that is possible to know, be an attenuated view of divine knowledge?[130] Why should Aquinas's definition of omnipotence not be labeled "limited omnipotence"? If some things are unknowable *(de dicto)*, just as contradictions are undoable *(de dicto)*, then it is no deficiency or attenuation in God's knowledge. It could be argued that the more robust and unattenuated definition of omnipotence is the one in which God can do all things, including the logically impossible. Philosophers have just grown so accustomed to the "diminished" definition of omnipotence that they have forgotten they ever reduced it in the first place.

According to presentism, the future is not fixed but is open both to what God and to what humans decide to do. God's knowledge of what creatures do is dependent on what the creatures freely decide to do. Moreover, God may genuinely dialogue with us, respond to our prayers and resourcefully adapt his plans to our actions. This model of omniscience was defended earlier (see especially 3.12 and 4.16). Presentism holds that the divine knowledge is unsurpassable in that no creature can even approximate God's exhaustive knowledge of the past and present. Due to the knowledge of all past and present, as well as God's superior abilities of analysis and inference, God is able to predict with amazing accuracy what he believes will occur. Some proponents of presentism affirm that God knows all possibilities that could ever happen, whereas other adherents affirm that God knows the general outlines of all possible futures.[131] Either way, God is still open to being surprised, shocked and delighted as God works with us in history.[132]

Clearly, the determinative issue for deciding whether God is "open" and responsive to his creatures and is a risk taker is not the kind of omniscience that is ascribed to God but is the type of sovereignty God is believed to exercise. If God foreordains all things, then God is not a risk taker. If God does not control every detail that occurs, then God takes risks—whether he has simple foreknowledge, timeless knowledge, knowledge of all possibilities, middle knowledge or present knowledge. The theory of simple foreknowledge may well be the most widely held view of omniscience among Christian theists and will be examined in some detail in order to demonstrate that this view of omniscience cannot escape divine risk taking.

6.5.3 The Uselessness of Simple Foreknowledge for Providence

6.5.3.1 Introduction   Simple foreknowledge is an ancient view whose value for divine providence is often overestimated.[133] For the past two millenia there has been an ongoing debate regarding whether foreknowledge and libertarian freedom are compatible.[134] But what is the utility of foreknowledge? Does a God with simple foreknowledge (SF hereafter) possess greater providential control than a God with present knowledge (PK hereafter)? Proponents of SF claim the answer is yes because SF allows God to predict the future through his prophets and to guarantee the end from the beginning.

David Hunt claims that "divine control will be hamstrung and God's purposes jeopardized if events can ever catch Him by *surprise,* or find Him *unprepared,* or force Him to *react* after the fact to patch things up. . . . The kind of providential control expected of a theistic God is possible only on the assumption of foreknowledge."[135] Jack Cottrell maintains that SF is a key element in God's providential control over the world

> because it is by this means that God can allow man to be truly free in his choices, even free to resist his own special influences, and at the same time work out his own purposes infallibly. For if God foreknows all the choices that every person will make, he can make his own plans accordingly, fitting his purposes around these foreknown decisions and actions. . . . Acts 2:23 is a perfect illustration of the way God works through his foreknowledge. . . . On the one hand, God had predetermined that Jesus would die as a propitiation for the sins of the world; this was his own unconditional plan for saving the world. On the other hand, the details of *how* this would be accomplished were planned in relation to God's foreknowledge of the historical situation and of the character and choices of men such as Judas.[136]

It is important to distinguish two different versions of how God's foreknowledge is accessed. SF is commonly explained as God's "seeing the whole at once" with the result that God knows all that will happen. For example, God previsioned before the creation of the world my birth, family rivalries, marriage, adoption of children and so on. What God previsioned, moreover, included all the details leading up to and surrounding all these events—right down to the number of hairs on my head at any given moment. This vision of God happens all at once. Even though he knows things will occur in sequence, God does not acquire the knowledge in sequence. I designate this version "complete simple foreknowledge" (CSF).

Unfortunately, CSF has a difficult time explaining how God can intervene in what he foresees will happen. The problem arises because of the fact that what God previsions is what will *actually* occur. Divine foreknowledge, by definition, is always correct. If what will actually happen is, for example, the Holocaust, then God knows it is going to happen and cannot prevent it from happening, since his foreknowledge is never mistaken. Furthermore, if what God has foreseen is the *entire* human history *at once*, then the difficulty is to somehow allow for God's intervention into that history. This raises a serious problem. Does simple foreknowledge imply that God previsions his own decisions and actions? If a God with CSF possesses foreknowledge of his own actions, then the problem is to explain how the foreknowledge can be the *basis* for the actions when it already *includes* the actions. Hasker explains that "it is impossible that God should use a foreknowledge derived from the actual occurrence of future events to determine his own prior actions in the providential governance of the world."[137] Such a deity would then know what he is going to do before deciding what to do. A God with CSF would be unable to plan, anticipate, or decide—he would simply know. This seems to call the divine freedom into question, making God a prisoner of his own omniprescience, lacking perfect freedom.[138]

Moreover, if God sees Abraham's birth, life and death all at once, then how does God interject the test of the binding of Isaac (Gen 22) into Abraham's life? How does God see God's own actions in Abraham's life that would alter Abraham's life and consequently change God's foreknowledge? Swinburne points out that "what God already knows is beyond his making a difference to."[139] Hunt is correct that a God "with total foreknowledge . . . is equipped to make maximally informed decisions—but there is nothing left to be decided."[140] The divine freedom is seriously curtailed.

Perhaps a different explanation of God's direct apprehension of the future can be proposed: one in which God timelessly accesses the future *in sequence* or *incrementally*.[141] This sequence is not temporal but might be called an explanatory order. Using temporal language, it might be said that God atemporally rolls the tape of the future up to a certain point and then stops it in order to interject his own actions into the tape and then rolls the tape further to see what his creatures will do in response to his actions. Then God again decides what he will do and then rolls the tape further. Hence there is a logical sequence or order of dependence in the way God comes to access his foreknowledge. In this version God still learns the future, atemporally of course, but he learns it in sequence. As a result God can weave his own actions into the flow of human history. I designate this view incremental simple foreknowledge (ISF).

6.5.3.2 Sin and Divine Risk   Could a God with SF have refrained from creating creatures with indeterministic freedom and so have prevented them from committing evil? John Hick thinks so. He says that it is "hard to clear God from ultimate responsibility for the existence of sin, in view of the fact that He chose to create a being whom He foresaw would, if He created him, freely sin."[142] Lorenzo McCabe agrees, saying that "a being who the Creator foreknew would be disobedient should not be created. . . . How easy for omnipotence to prevent the existence of those who, as his omniscience foresaw, would choose to be disobedient."[143] Cottrell explains how God could exercise such control: "It is *foreknowledge* that enables God to maintain complete control of his world despite the freedom of his creatures. God *knows* the future; it is not open or indefinite for him. This gives God the genuine option of either permitting or preventing men's planned choices, and prevention is the ultimate control."[144]

But can a God with SF prevent sinners from being born or prevent certain evil choices? No. If what God *foreknows* is the *actual* world, then God foreknows the births, lives and deaths of actual sinners. Once God has foreknowledge, he cannot change what will happen, for that would make his foreknowledge incorrect. God cannot make actual events "deoccur." If God foreknows (has knowledge of the actual occurrence) that Adam will freely choose to mistrust God, then God cannot intervene to prevent Adam's mistrust. Hence God can see the evil coming before he creates the world but is powerless to prevent it. As Hasker correctly observes,

> it is clear that God's foreknowledge cannot be used either to *bring about* the occurrence of a foreknown event or to *prevent* such an event from occurring. For what God foreknows is *not* certain antecedents which, unless interfered with in some way, will *lead to* the occurrence of the event; rather, it is *the event itself* that is foreknown as occurring, and it is contradictory to suppose that an even.⁺ is *known* to occur but then also is *prevented* from occurring. In the logical order of dependence of events, one might say, by the "time" God knows something will happen, it is "too late" either to *bring about* its happening or to *prevent* it from happening.[145]

Proponents of SF may appeal to incremental simple foreknowledge (ISF) in an attempt to rescue providential control. Thus God rolls the tape forward and learns (prior to creation) that Adam is succumbing to temptation—but does not roll the tape far enough to see whether he actually sins or not. At this point God may press the pause button on his remote and decide to intervene in order to buttress Adam's flagging trust. Will God's efforts be successful? To find out, God rolls the tape forward to see how Adam will respond.[146] If Adam chooses to continue to trust God, then the temptation is overcome. If he fails to trust God, then sin enters the world. Regardless, once God sees the actual future choice of the creature he is powerless to prevent it. Prior to the actual choice being made, God can seek to persuade Adam to trust him; but once God knows that Adam will fail to trust him, then it is too late for God to prevent the sin.

It must be remembered that a God with SF (either CSF or ISF) does not have middle knowledge and so cannot "try out" alternative scenarios in order to ascertain which one will achieve his objective in preventing Adam from sinning. A God with SF does not know before he decides to create this particular world what sorts of decisions and actions will arise in the world. Consequently, a God with SF is no less a risk taker than a God with PK. God might "luck out" in that his free creatures never, in fact, decide to sin. Even so, their decision will not be because of any advantage afforded by SF. On the other hand, a God with SF cannot (contra Hick) be blamed for not preventing sin from coming about, since this was not possible.

6.5.3.3 Damnation and Divine Risk What about those whom God foreknew would never exercise saving faith in him and thus are not part of the elect of salvation? Can God decide not to create them? James Mill, the father of John Stuart Mill, thought so. "Think of a being," he says, "who would make a hell, who would create the race with the infallible foreknowledge that the majority of them were to be consigned to horrible and everlasting torment."[147] Although this objection is appropriate to divine foreordination of all things, it is irrelevant to SF because it misunderstands the nature of foreknowledge. Though God may use foreknowledge to see which individuals will freely come to faith in Christ and so decide to elect them, he cannot guarantee that only those who exercise faith in God come into existence.

For SF, God's election is dependent on and is logically subsequent to the choice of the creatures, even though God's election of them is prior to creation. God atemporally *responds* to the free choices of his creatures. A God with SF takes risks in creating a world in which God does not foreordain all things. But this means that God cannot be held responsible for ensuring that only those people who will love God will be born. Once he decided to create, God could have learned through his foreknowledge that no humans would ever freely come into a loving relationship with him. That some people do love God is not due to the providential use of foreknowledge. Affirming that God's foreknowledge is conditioned on what creatures with libertarian freedom actually do necessitates the conclusion that God took a risk in bringing about this type of creation. The only way to avoid divine risk is to maintain some form of divine foreordination of all things. Consequently, all forms of relational theism will have divine risk taking.

6.5.3.4 Divine Guidance and Protection It is often assumed that a God with SF would be in a maximally informed position to offer guidance and protection to those who petition him in prayer. For instance, say Mandie asks God whether she should marry Matthew or Jim, believing that God knows what is best for her and will advise her accordingly. In fact, Mandie may believe, with C. S. Lewis, that a God with CSF knew of her prayer beforehand and so has prearranged things (perhaps even prior to her birth) in such a way that her request will be providentially answered.[148] Mandie believes, for instance, that God knows whether Jim will be loving or abusive toward her and would advise her appropriately. The problem is that if God *knows* that she will actually marry Jim and be quite unhappy, then it is useless for God to give her the guidance to marry Matthew. It would be incoherent to claim that God, knowing the actual future and on the basis of this knowledge, changes it so that it will *not* be the actual future. Of course, God might foreknow that Jim will be a wonderful husband for Mandie. Even so, it is not because God brought it about. A God who already knows the future cannot answer such prayers.

Appealing to ISF provides no help. If God only accesses his foreknowledge up to the point where Mandie invokes God for guidance as to whom she should marry but does not yet know whom she will actually marry nor for sure whether Jim or Matthew will be good husbands, then God's advice to her will not guarantee a good choice. God is able to advise her on the basis of his knowledge and wisdom at that point—which is no different from the knowledge and wisdom a God with PK would have.

The same is true concerning prayers for protection. If God knows that I will actually be seriously injured in an auto accident on a particular trip, then no prayer for "traveling mercies" can alter this situation. Consequently, prayers for protection would be useless and any divine interventions prohibited. Only if God does not yet know the outcome of my journey can a prayer for safe traveling be coherent within the model of SF. If God decides to act in response to my prayer, it cannot be based on his foreknowledge. Hence this situation is no different from asking a God with PK for protection.

6.5.3.5 Mistakes and Divine Predictions   Can God be mistaken about anything?[149] If God can be mistaken about what will happen in the future, then divine predictions may be in doubt. Take the case of the dialogue between God and Moses in Exodus 3—4. God explicitly says to Moses that the leaders of Israel will believe Moses. But Moses thought it was possible for God to be mistaken in this (4:1). In response God affirms that Moses could be correct and so gives him signs to perform so that *if* they do not believe him, they may believe the signs (4:5-7). Is it possible for God to have mistaken beliefs about the future? The traditional theological answer is that God cannot, but there are several biblical texts that seem to affirm that what God thought would happen did not come about (for example, Jer 3:7, 19-20). Does SF offer a way out?

It is commonly thought that one of the strongest values of a God with SF is that he can know the actual future and so is able to inform his prophets beforehand what precisely will happen. As has already been shown, CSF cannot be used as the means by which God predicts the future, for if God sees history "all at once" and, presumably, his actions were not foreseen (see 6.5.3.1), then God never foresees any prophets making predictions given by God. Moreover, it is probably clear by now why ISF cannot be used to predict the future with absolute certainty. A God with ISF does not know precisely what is going to happen after the event he is foreseeing. If God learns as he previsions the future, then it becomes impossible for God to interject something based on his knowledge of the future into the chemistry of past events that would alter his knowledge of what actually occurred in the past. For instance, if God foresees the whole of Jesus' life, he has not yet (logically speaking) foreseen the destruction of the Jerusalem temple in A.D. 70. Once God previsions the events of A.D. 70, it is "too late" for God to go back and reveal through Jesus a prediction about this event during the life of Jesus because when God previsioned Jesus' life he never foresaw Jesus uttering such a prediction. This nevertheless could be argued for by claiming that God can change the past in such a way that what God knew was going to come to pass did not come about. But then SF will have been rejected.

Consequently, a God with SF takes risks in creating the world. The God of SF is not able to prevent sin from arising, or to ensure that only those who will love God will be created, or to guide us with absolute certainty or to use the knowledge of the future to predict the future. A God with SF is not able to guarantee, from before creation, that God's plans would be successful in every detail. Hence a God with SF has no more ability to guarantee the success of his plans than does a God with PK because SF is simply useless for providential control.

Denying exhaustive divine sovereignty and asserting indeterministic freedom for humans means that God remains a risk taker and that the outcome of the world was not guaranteed prior to God's decision to create this world. The same is true for middle knowledge except that the "risk" God takes, according to this view, is whether or not God is fortunate enough that there is a feasible world God can create that satisfies God's intentions. Finally, the providential usefulness of simple foreknowledge has been vastly overstated. Proponents of this view wish to eliminate or minimize divine risk taking, but they have not been successful in showing how this can be so.

6.6 Conclusion

In the model proposed here God has the love, wisdom, perseverance and power to deal with any situation that arises in the working out of his project. When the divine nature is defined in light of the project God established and the actions God has done in history, then we have a very concrete understanding of God. God is a personal being who freely enters into loving relationships with his creatures. The nature of God is not defined in terms of the infinity of being or absolute power but rather in terms of his wise, free, faithful and powerful love manifested toward his creatures. In his relationships God is interactive, generous, sensitive and responsive. There are genuinely reciprocal relations between the God and the creatures. In establishing such relations God indeed takes risks, but this must be understood within the framework of the project God has undertaken. It is not risk for risk's sake, but the quest for loving relationships with the creatures. Moreover, two senses of risk were distinguished. In the first sense God had every reason to believe his project would work out exactly as intended (the probability of success was great). Yet God took a large risk of being hurt because God cared so deeply about the project.

Some object that this model of God is too costly; it reduces or "shrinks" God from the full majesty of what is properly divine. Several things may be said in response to this objection. To begin, what is a cost from one perspective may be a strength from another viewpoint, since all evaluations arise from within particular frameworks. The charge that relational theism is a reduction of God stems from the model of the immutable God who exhaustively controls everything. Since I do not believe such a deity exists, this model of God cannot reduce him. Moreover, since, in my mind, the openness model is a more exalted view of the wisdom, love, power and faithfulness of God, the charge of reductionism is misplaced. Although God's exhaustive control of all things has been rejected, God's genuine responsiveness has been affirmed. The notion that God remains unaffected (impassibility) by what transpires in the world has been deleted, but the rich emotional life that the Bible attributes to God has been included. Thus the openness model of God presents a fuller, richer account of the divine-human relationship than the model offered by many traditionalists.

Some may claim (process theists, for instance) that this is only a revision of the nature of God as conceived by classical theism. In a sense this is true, but so what? Aquinas revised classical theism's understanding of omnipotence (God can only do that which is logically possible). Because we now tend to take his definition for granted, we have forgotten that it was a revision. Doing theology is not merely handing on a tradition. At times the tradition needs revision—especially when, in my opinion, it has misread or ignored some of the crucial elements of the biblical portrait of God. Clearly, my contention is debatable. My point is that those who caricature the fellowship model as embracing a bumbling, ignorant, dependent deity will do so from a perspective that is itself open to serious questions. In the relational model God is wise, proficient, resourceful, loving and responsive, even though God does not get everything he desires. This, in my view, is God our Creator and Redeemer. It is not a "shrinking of God" as some allege. Rather, it is an enriching view of God, well attested in the biblical material. Such a perspective of God's nature and the risk involved in his project has profound ramifications when applied to the subjects of sovereignty, eschatology, suffering, prayer and guidance. To these subjects I now turn.

SEVEN

THE NATURE OF
DIVINE SOVEREIGNTY

· ·

7.1 Introduction

This chapter applies conclusions about risk and the divine nature to the subject of divine sovereignty. God has sovereignly decided to enter into a project in which he desires reciprocal loving relationships and so does not control everything that happens.[1] Some theologians, however, react strongly to this idea, claiming that it is not sovereignty at all. They attempt to coopt the term *sovereignty* for themselves, saying it can have only one meaning—theirs—and thus disqualifying from the discussion any position but their own. R. C. Sproul, for instance, says, "If God is not sovereign, then God is not God."[2] By *sovereign* Sproul means exercising exhaustive control over every detail that happens, and thus God by definition must exercise this sort of sovereignty. Such thinkers limit God by asserting that God cannot decide which sort of sovereignty to practice. Decretal theologians argue this way because they believe the divine nature, which allows for no conditionality, determines all of God's decisions and actions.[3] Hence God *necessarily* must determine (even if by secondary causes) all that happens in the creation.

Taking a different road, I have suggested that we begin with the actual project and the types of relations God has freely chosen to establish rather with a preconceived notion *(dignum Deo)* about what sort of world God must create. The God of the Bible is not the *Deus absolutus* but the "Lord our God," the God who enters into genuine covenantal and personal relationships with us.[4]

7.2 Types of Relationships

In his *Speaking of a Personal God,* Vincent Brümmer distinguishes between two types of "games" God could establish with human beings.[5] In game 1 God, a personal agent, creates human personal agents and establishes rules whereby both parties in the game may say yes or no to each other. In this game God makes the initial move by saying yes to us, loving us and desiring a relationship of mutual love. It is now our turn to respond to God's move, and we may respond with either a yes or a no. At this point a significant qualification needs to be added to Brümmer's explanation. God did not say that we may choose however we please—as though all that mattered to God was that we choose one way or the other (see the discussion of Gen 1—3 in chap. 3). God's initial instructions were to eat of any tree except the tree of the knowledge of good and evil. Though God did not give his permission to eat of that tree, obviously it was a possibility, since it was in fact done. Thus it can be said that humans, as personal beings, have the ability to say yes or no to God's love. Love cannot be forced. Consequently, even though God wants us to respond with a yes so that we enter into a relationship of mutual love, such a response cannot be coerced.[6] If we respond to God's yes with a yes of our own, then God achieves part of what he desired for his project. If we respond with a no, then God may either withdraw his love, saying no to us, or God may continue saying yes to us by working to redeem the situation.

In game 2 humans do exactly what God decrees they will do. God determines, directly or mediately, all that happens. In game 2 if God says yes to humanity, then humans still have to say yes or no to God, but our "response" is caused by God. Hence God may prevent us from saying no and may cause everyone to say yes (universalism), or God may predestine some to say yes and predestine others to say no.

God sovereignly chooses which game to establish: game 1 with its person-to-person relations or game 2 with its causal relations. It depends on the outcome God desires. If God wants mutual fellowship, then he will opt for game 1; but in so doing God takes the risk of our rejecting his love (the possibility of evil). If God does not want to take any risks, then he will opt for game 2. Of course, I believe God has established game 1 with its personal relations.

In his book *The Model of Love* Brümmer clarifies and enlarges his typology of relationships.[7] He classifies them as (1) manipulative relations, (2) agreements of rights and duties, and (3) mutual fellowship. Manipulative relations belong to game 2; party A is able to gain complete control over party B. The control may be for beneficent purposes, but it means that B is treated as an object or, in Martin Buber's terms, an I-It relation. Such relations are asymmetrical in the sense that only A is a personal agent. A's manipulative power means that "B loses the ability either to bring about or to prevent the relationship being established, changed or terminated. The relationship therefore becomes impersonal."[8]

In relations involving agreements of rights and duties, parties enter into contractual agreements entailing obligations. I may, for example, contract with B to supply baseball uniforms for my team. Such agreements are not strictly coercive, but they do establish obligations. If B wants my business, then she is obliged to provide the uniforms I desire. It is of no small consequence that B can earn or merit my payment by doing good work. In religious terms, it would be said that we can merit salvation by doing good works. Moreover, the relationships involved in such agreements are not like those in mutual fellowship. When looking for a supplier of uniforms for my baseball team, I am looking for someone who is *useful* to me. John Lucas explains:

> If I do business with you . . . my good will towards you is conditional and limited. I will keep my side of the bargain provided you keep yours. Your value in my eyes is contingent on your doing certain things whereby you are of use to me; and the good I am prepared to do you is proportional to your value to me. . . . Your good is not *eo ipso* my good, and your value in my eyes is simply as a person who can bring good things to me, as a furtherer of my own cause. Anybody else who could do the same would do equally well.[9]

Mutual fellowship, however, involves reciprocal relations between personal agents.[10] In this type of relation the free assent of both parties is necessary for the relationship to be established and maintained. Although one party may be the initiator and may do much more to establish the relationship, it still requires the free participation of another in order to have a personal relationship. Both parties express their wish for the relationship, and it comes about through their mutual consent. Regarding the divine-human relation it may be said that God has been the initiator in both creation and redemption and does much more than we do in establishing and maintaining the relationship. God, however, does not want to dance alone, dance with a mannequin or hire someone who is obligated to dance with him. God wants to dance with us as persons in fellowship, not with puppets or contracted performers, and thus needs our consent. Mutual fellowship requires reciprocity between two parties. Says Lucas, "The man who is wooing a woman can neither manipulate her into loving him, nor claim that she is, or would be if he performed certain feats, under an obligation to love him: but there are many things he can still do; things which are pleasing to her, things which will show her his ardent devotion."[11]

Moreover, in contrast to the two other types of relations, relations of fellowship mean that I identify with you and treat your interests as my own. It is *you* I want to collaborate with and not someone else who can do similar things. An additional difference between fellowship and the other sorts of relations is that fellowship involves a kind of risk, whereas the others do not. In reciprocal relations the two parties are dependent on each other to uphold the value of the relationship. If one party backs out and rejects the other, the one rejected bears the pain involved in the loss of love—which differs from the loss of a business transaction. Personal relations entail the risk of failure in that the relationship may be broken and love may not materialize.

God is sovereign over his sovereignty and is thus free to choose what sorts of relations he desires to create. Borrowing from Brümmer's typology, I suggest that God has sovereignly established the rules of the game for personal relations of fellowship, not manipulative or contractual relations. I reached this conclusion by tracing the establishment and outworking of the divine project in Scripture. This view has immediate implications regarding providence, human freedom and God's success.

7.3 Specific Versus General Sovereignty

7.3.1 Specific Sovereignty There are two main views regarding the nature of sovereignty in theological and philosophical discussions: specific and general. Specific sovereignty (sometimes called meticulous providence) maintains that there are absolutely no limitations, hindrances or insurmountable obstacles for God to achieve his will in every specific circumstance of the created order. God has *exhaustive* control over each situation: Only what God purposes to happen in that particular time and place to that specific creature will happen. God does not take risks in governing the world because God micromanages every detail. The popularity of this position is attested by its use by decretal theologians and some universalists and in certain atheological arguments (used by atheists). Theists and atheists generally agree that in debating the existence of "God" they have this particular conception of God in mind, but they disagree whether there is actually a deity external to the concept.

It is commonly asserted that the divine nature is omnipotent, omniscient and wholly good, which ensures that whatever happens to us was specifically chosen by God to happen and that even if we do not understand how certain events are compatible with God's goodness, we can rest assured that God has a good reason for them. If we experience something as "evil," we should view it as God's necessary means to a greater good. This is not to say that there are "possible" or "general" greater goods that "may" be achieved. Rather, God's preordained plan guarantees that *greater goods are achieved for each and every act*, including inherently morally evil acts. Hence if Susan has a job with excellent benefits, it is because God specifically wanted that to happen and it serves a specific good purpose in God's plan, even if Susan does not know it. If Susan is raped and dismembered, it is because God specifically wanted that to happen and it serves a specific good purpose in God's plan, even if Susan does not know it. For proponents of specific sovereignty there is no such thing as an accident or a genuine tragedy.[12] Alexander Pope put it thus:

> All Nature is but Art, unknown to thee;
> All Chance, Direction which thou canst not see;
> All Discord, Harmony not understood;
> All partial Evil, universal Good:
> And, spite of Pride, in erring Reason's spite,
> One truth is clear, "WHATEVER IS, IS RIGHT."[13]

John Calvin defended this position when he argued against the existence of fortune or chance. In life one person escapes shipwreck and another drowns; one is rich and another is poor; one mother has abundant breast milk and another has hardly any. Calvin says that all these circumstances are expressly arranged by God for some reason.[14] Meticulous providence asserts that nothing can stymie God's will in anything that occurs because God is in total control of every detail. Does such divine control rule out human responsibility? Proponents of specific sovereignty claim that it does not and typically appeal to compatibilistic freedom, antinomy or God's timeless foreknowledge in order to affirm meticulous providence and human responsibility. I do not find these replies successful, but since I discuss them elsewhere in this book I will say no more about them here.[15] My principle argument against exhaustive sovereignty is that it rules out certain experiences, decisions and actions that the Bible and many theists attribute to God. For instance, the biblical portrait depicts God as being grieved (Gen 6:6), changing his mind (Ex 32:14), resorting to alternative plans (Ex 4:14), being open and responsive to what the creatures do (Jer 18:6-10), being surprised at what people have done (Jer 3:7; 32:35). God sometimes makes himself dependent on our prayers (Jas 4:2).

However, these sorts of things make no sense within the framework of specific sovereignty. If God always gets precisely what he desires in each and every situation, then it is incoherent to speak of God's being grieved about or responding to the human situation. How can God be grieved if precisely what God wanted to happen did happen? If specific sovereignty is true, then it is incorrect to speak of God's getting upset with human sin because any sin is specifically what God wanted to come about. It is inconsistent to affirm exhaustive sovereignty and also claim that God wants to give us something but does not give it because we fail to ask him in prayer. Specific sovereignty claims that if God wants to give us something, then God can ensure that someone will ask for it. God's will is never thwarted in any respect. But this does not comport with my reading of Scripture or my understanding of prayer.

Finally, exhaustive divine sovereignty appears to pit Jesus against the Father. Jesus washed the disciples' feet and instructed them that Christian leaders were to emulate this style of leadership. In my opinion, the church leadership has not done a good job of fulfilling Jesus' intention. But if the Father gets exactly what he wants, then what has transpired in the history of the church is precisely what the Father intended. If Jesus desires that Christians love and forgive one another instead of domineering over one another but the Father desires that we lord our power over each other (as witnessed by what actually happens), then the desires of the Son and the Father are at odds, producing a schizophrenic Godhead. (If one posits a hidden will of God the Father behind the revealed will of God the Son, then the "revelation" of God in Jesus is undermined.)

7.3.2 General Sovereignty The other main view is called general sovereignty and maintains that God has sovereignly established a type of world in which God sets up general structures or an overall framework for meaning and allows the creatures significant input into exactly how things will turn out. God desires a relationship of love with his creation and so elects to grant it the freedom to enter into a give-and-take relationship with himself. Since God macromanages the overall project (while remaining free to micromanage some things), God takes risks in governing the world. In contrast to specific sovereignty, this model does not claim that God has a specific purpose for each and every event which happens. Instead, God has general purposes in connection with the achievement of the divine project. Within these general structures God permits things to happen, both good and bad, that he does not specifically intend. Yet God may act to bring about a specific event in order to bring the divine project to fruition. The incarnation and the exodus are examples of God's electing to bring about particular events. It is within God's ability to bring about blessing and punishment in human affairs.

But general sovereignty denies that each and every event has a specific divine intention. God may intensify his ongoing activity to bring about some particular event, but God's normal way of operating is to allow the creatures significant freedom and, consequently, not to control everything. Even when God wants humans to perform some particular task, God works to persuade free creatures to love God and serve him instead of forcing them to do so. Take Moses, for example. He was chosen by God for a specific purpose—the liberation of the Hebrews—yet God did not force his cooperation. If Moses had stubbornly refused him, God would have had to find another path toward the achievement of his goal. But most of the Israelites (and most of us) are not chosen for specific roles. Take the case of Susan. That Susan has a job with excellent benefits is part of the general structure of the world in which God gives humans the freedom to create and staff jobs. Whether her work helps fulfill God's project depends on her and her relationship with God. If she is raped and dismembered, it is not the case that God specifically chose her to experience that horror. General sovereignty allows for things to happen that are not part of God's plan for our lives; it allows for pointless evil.

Although these two views of sovereignty are clearly distinct, people tend to switch back and forth between them, depending on the situation.[16] For instance, many people would thank God for Susan's job but shy away from praising God for her rape and murder. The leadership of an organization may thank God for providing the funding for the previous year but fire the development director and embark on a new fundraising strategy the next year if funds are lacking. Many Christians vacillate from meticulous to general sovereignty. They affirm God's total control over everything that happens while also affirming that humans can bring things about that God does not intend. Some claim both that God is omnidetermining and that God genuinely responds to us. But William Alston points out that this is incoherent because an omnidetermining deity never responds to any external reality.[17] He says that if God has decided every detail of his creation (as in Augustine, Thomas Aquinas and John Calvin) then genuine divine-human dialogue is ruled out because dialogue requires two independent participants. The "conversation" an omnidetermining deity has with humans is more like that between a ventriloquist and the dummy or a computer programmer and the program or a hypnotist and the subject. Such "dialogue" is merely a sophisticated form of talking to oneself.

In terms of Brümmer's models meticulous providence goes with a manipulative view of the divine-human relationship, whereas general sovereignty connects to relations of personal fellowship. One simply cannot have it both ways: either God controls everything and the divine-human relationship is impersonal, or God does not control everything and so it is possible for the divine-human relationship to be personal. I have argued that God is wise, competent and resourceful in dealing with us instead of manipulating all that happens. This may seem to diminish sovereignty, but "the sovereignty that reigns unchallenged is not as absolute as the sovereignty that accepts risks."[18] It requires tremendous wisdom, patience, love, faithfulness and resourcefulness to work with a world of independent beings. A God of sheer omnipotence can run a world of exhaustively controlled beings. But what is magnificent about that?

In the risk model of providence God does not control everything that happens but does control many things. The word *control* has a wide range of meaning, from coercion to accountability. A ventriloquist controls her dummy in one way; a teacher controls his students in another. The ventriloquist guarantees what the dummy says, whereas the teacher does not make such guarantees. If the dummy says something indecent, the ventriloquist is responsible. If the students begin throwing things around the room, the teacher is accountable. In most of our human relationships, such as government, family and church, we use the word *control* in the sense of accountability rather than manipulation. In our impersonal relations we use the word *control* in a coercive sense. According to general sovereignty God is in control in the sense of being accountable for creating this sort of world and carrying out the project in the way God has. But God is not controlling everything that happens (as was seen in the review of the biblical "pancausality" texts). God is, however, in control in the sense that God and God alone is responsible for initiating the divine project and for establishing the rules under which the game operates.

Within the rules of the game God makes room for indeterminacy or chance.[19] Though God sustains everything in existence, he does not determine the results of all actions or events, even at the subatomic level. Peter van Inwagen's definition of a chance event is as follows: "The event or state of affairs is without purpose or significance; it is not a part of anyone's plan; it serves no one's end; and it might very well not have been."[20] In this sense chance corresponds to general sovereignty. Whatever was not specifically determined by God may not have been. That God decides to grant humans significant freedom is determined by God, but what humans do with that freedom is not always specifically part of his plan. For general sovereignty, much of what happens to us in life, even much of what seems important to us, is not specifically part of God's plan. If one of my children fell to her death as she was climbing a tree, many people would ask why that event happened. By this they would not mean to inquire about her motives for climbing the tree or about the specific reason for her fall. They would want to know why God allowed (or brought about) this particular death.

Although God may sometimes bring about, or may deliver from, a particular misfortune, there is not a divine reason for each and every misfortune. Genuine accidents or unintended events, both good and bad, do happen, for that is the sort of world God established. Does this mean that the world is out of God's control? Again, it depends on what is meant by control. God is not in control in the sense that absolutely nothing happens that God does not specifically want to happen. After all, God is fundamentally opposed to sin, yet there is sin. God is in control in the sense that he shoulders the responsibility for creating this type of world. God is the potter seeking to shape the clay into the sort of vessel he intends. However, the relation between God and humanity goes beyond the potter's relation to the clay. In the book of Hosea God is pictured as Israel's husband. In Israelite society the husband held complete authority over the wife. Yet despite such power Gomer left Hosea and prostituted herself. Yahweh's authority over Israel was absolute, but this did not prevent the people from committing apostasy.[21] Yahweh simply did not "control" his wife in a manipulative sense. Recent writings on providence develop various analogies for getting at the diversity of God's roles in a relational understanding of sovereignty.

Michael Langford suggests a climbing-party analogy.[22] The leader is responsible to plan for routes and supplies. As the party climbs, occasional ad hoc decisions will be made in light of the specifics of the terrain and the condition of the climbers. If someone injures a hand, the route may have to be modified, since the preselected path will no longer be possible. Some of these decisions may be made solely by the leader, whereas others may be made in consultation with the party. This analogy highlights the competency and resourcefulness of the leader as well as the need for ad hoc decisions on the journey. T. J. Gorringe develops the analogy of God as a theater director.[23] The director is responsible for the overall play. A good director does not manipulate the actors but seeks to bring out their own creativity. The actors play a significant part in determining how the play goes.

> To think of God in terms of the theatre director, then, is to think of one whose job it is to evoke talents, skills and capabilities the creature (who remains the "actor") did not know it had. It gives God a supremely active and creative role, leading and being alongside as Orthodoxy conceived it *(praecurrit et concurrit)*, but does not destroy the autonomy of the creature. It is creative without being manipulative.[24]

These analogies highlight God's creativity (God as potter) and ongoing involvement in the project compatible with the model of general sovereignty.[25]

7.4 Divine Permission

These analogies suggest that God is not omnidetermining but permits the actors and the climbers to be significant others in the outworking of the play or the adventure of the climb. That God permits or allows states of affairs to come about that he does not desire has long been debated.[26] Augustine held that "in a strange and ineffable fashion even that which is done against his will is not done without his will."[27] "Nothing, therefore, happens unless the Omnipotent wills it to happen. He either allows it to happen or he actually causes it to happen."[28] These remarks may sound like an affirmation of general sovereignty in which God grants permission for the creatures to do that which God specifically does not want done. However, in the same context Augustine also makes remarks that sound like an affirmation of specific sovereignty. He claims that no one resists God's will (Rom 9:19) and that neither angels nor humans, whether they do good or evil, can thwart the will of the omnipotent.[29] Calvin understood Augustine to affirm specific sovereignty. He realized more clearly than Augustine that this excluded any concept of permission. Calvin ridicules "those who, in place of God's providence, substitute bare permission—as if God sat in a watchtower awaiting chance events, and his judgment thus depended upon human will."[30] Calvin simply could not accept God's establishing genuine give-and-take relations with creatures, as this would to him imply passivity or conditionality in God.

Some in the Reformed tradition maintain that both Calvinists and Arminians affirm a notion of divine permission, or two wills in God.

Jonathan Edwards said that "all must own that God sometimes wills not to hinder the breach of his own commands. . . . But you [Arminians] will say, God wills to permit sin, as he wills the creature should be left to his own freedom. . . . I answer, this comes nevertheless to the very same thing that I say. . . . So that the scheme of the Arminians does not help the matter."[31] Reformed philosopher Paul Helm argues that even the risk view of providence entails two wills in God: "God wills (in the sense of permits) the occurrence of certain morally evil actions, which are (by definition) contrary to the command of God."[32] John Piper makes the same claim and applies it to the doctrine of election: "What are we to say of the fact that God wills something that in fact does not happen?" One could say that God wants to save everyone but cannot because other beings are more powerful than God. Or one could say "that God wills not to save all, even though he is willing to save all, because there is something else that he wills more, which would be lost if he exerted his sovereign power to save all. This is the solution that I as a Calvinist affirm along with Arminians."[33]

These writers are correct in calling attention to a similarity between the two views. Arminians and other freewill theists are committed to making some sort of distinction regarding God's desires. I will say more on this shortly. They are also correct in claiming that the concept of permission implies that God has the power to prevent sin and evil from coming about. However, there are some significant problems with the claim that the type of Calvinism represented by these three authors and various forms of freewill theism agree on the notion of two wills in God. To begin, Piper identifies a crucial problem:

> The difference between Calvinists and Arminians lies not in whether there are two wills in God, but in what they say this higher commitment is. What does God will more than saving all? The answer given by Arminians is that human self-determination and the possible resulting love relationship with God are more valuable than saving all people by sovereign, efficacious grace. The answer given by Calvinists is that the greater value is the manifestation of the full range of God's glory in wrath and mercy (Rom. 9:22-23) and the humbling of man so that he enjoys giving all the credit to God for his salvation.[34]

One side locates the concept of permission within the framework of the divine project, whereas the other locates it as a manifestation of the divine nature. This ties into the discussion in the previous chapter regarding whether the divine nature is free to create a project that involves loving relations with creatures or whether the divine nature necessarily must create a world in which God is omnidetermining. In the case of the latter, at least two questions may be asked. Can God sovereignly decide the sort of sovereignty God will exercise? Is God free to choose between specific or general sovereignty, or is God *limited* to being omnidetermining? Moreover, it may be asked, What becomes of the concept of permission if God is omnidetermining? It must disappear from the scene if there can be no question of God's will being thwarted.[35] If the divine nature requires the divine glory to be expressed in the unconditional salvation and damnation of people, then there is only one will in God.

The divine glory does not have to be conceived of as coercive power that is totally unconditioned by the creature. The debate between the Calvinists and the Arminians is, at heart, about whether God is in any sense conditioned by the creatures. If God is absolutely unconditioned in every respect, then there is no room left for the concept of permission or two wills. In this, Calvin was entirely consistent. If, as Calvin and Edwards argued, God's "foreknowledge" is determined by his foreordination and not in any way conditioned by the creature, then language about two wills in God or permission is suspect.[36]

Proponents of specific sovereignty rule out talk of chance or accident. If they are consistent, they cannot justifiably speak of divine permission. After all, if God's specific will for each and every instance always happens, then the notion of permission is nonsense, as is any talk of there being two wills in God. True, the proponent of meticulous providence may not understand how scriptural statements about God's desiring all to be saved are to be reconciled with God's not saving all. But in the final analysis, for the proponent of exhaustive sovereignty, there is only one will of God (the secret will), which is always efficacious. The integrity of the "revealed" will of God is made suspect by the "hidden" will, since the latter is never thwarted in the least detail. Thus I do not accept the claim that there is agreement on this issue between Calvinism and Arminianism.

How is the concept of divine permission to be understood? First, the doctrine of creation teaches that God permits something to be that is not God. God and the creation are distinct others in relation to each other. God does not have to create, but once God does create he grants the world to be that which is other than God. Second, God decided that this relationship would involve dialogue, not merely monologue. As a professor I can determine whether my class consists only of my lectures or includes discussion as well. If I do not allow any discussion or questions from my students, I can ensure that only what I want to be said will be said. I am free, however, to permit discussion. If I do permit it, then certain types of relationships between the students and me may develop that will not be possible if I merely lecture. But this possibility of development entails a risk, since students may say things harmful to others in the class. However, I may be confident that I have the ability to bring healing and redemption to this situation.

As the professor, I am ultimately responsible for establishing the conditions of the course and for doing my best to accomplish the course objectives. Though I can be held accountable for permitting discussion in the first place, I cannot control the speech of my students because I do not manipulate what they say. As Brümmer explains, "Although the agent does not *want* these in the strict sense of intending them, he does want them in a minimal sense of *consenting* to their occurrence."[37] It may be said that God, in permitting significant others who have in fact done evil, takes responsibility for creating a world in which such evil could obtain. But God cannot be blamed for the actual evil of the creatures, since God did not intend it. We can, if we like, hold God responsible for establishing genuine dialogue as one of the conditions of the course, but we cannot blame God for the actual dialogue that transpires. God may be said to give his "consenting ontological support" to actions that he does not support morally.[38] Moreover, God elects not to renege on the conditions he established, choosing instead to work toward redemption of the project gone awry. That is, God could simply put an end to his project and halt all sin now. However, God has decided to continue working with his project, still seeking to accomplish his goals for it.

Obviously, God is not in all respects like a professor, since God is uniquely responsible for upholding the conditions of the creational project. Although a human professor would be expected to intervene in the classroom if things were getting out of hand, the same cannot be expected of God or at least not in the same way, since God is *uniquely* responsible for preserving the conditions by which things can get out of hand. The type of human freedom required by this understanding must now be examined.

7.5 Human Freedom

Various understandings of human freedom have been propounded in the history of philosophy and theology. The compatibilist account of human freedom is very popular among those who affirm meticulous providence because it explains how God can be in complete control of every situation and yet hold humans responsible for their actions. Compatibilism maintains that freedom and determinism are compatible: "An agent is free with respect to a given action at a given time if at that time it is true that the agent can perform the action if she decides to perform and she can refrain from the action if she decides not to perform it."[39] According to this view a person is free to perform an action if she chooses. That is, a person is free as long as she desires to do it. However, her desires are determined by such things as genetics, upbringing, sinful nature or God so that she is not free to change her desires. In this schema a person is free as long as she acts on her desires, even if her desires are determined. If, for example, Susan's desires are controlled by a "sinful nature," then she will want to sin, and she is free to do so. As long as she desires to sin, she is not free not to sin. Her sinful nature functions as the remote cause producing her desires, whereas her desires function as the proximate cause for her willing. In Susan's case, her desires are in bondage to sin; only God can give her a new set of desires so that she freely chooses not to sin.

All sorts of objections have been raised against a compatibilistic conception of freedom, to which there is no ironclad refutation. Nevertheless, if compatibilism is true, then God can guarantee everything that happens by determining what the remote cause will be. At this point the charge is usually made that this would make God the author of sin. Compatibilists typically deny that this is the case. I shall return to this later. Regardless, Scripture speaks of God's grieving over sin, changing his mind, responding to what humans do and entering into genuine dialogue and reciprocal relations. If compatibilism is true, then such language is nullified. It makes no sense to speak of God's grieving over sin if God so controls things that he determines what the human desires shall be.

If the language of Scripture is taken seriously, then another view of human freedom must be affirmed. The libertarian or incompatibilist view holds that "an agent is free with respect to a given action at a given time if at that time it is within the agent's power to perform the action and also in the agent's power to refrain from the action."[40] In this sense a person does not have to act on her strongest desire. It is within the agent's self-determining ability to change her desires. Libertarians do not ignore genetics or environmental factors that influence decisions, but they maintain that a person could have done otherwise than she did in any given situation.

Various arguments are put forward in support of this view of freedom. The most common line of reasoning claims that libertarian freedom must be assumed if (1) we are to have genuine loving relationships, (2) our thought is to be rational or (3) we are to be held morally responsible for good and evil in a way that really makes a difference.[41] Alvin Plantinga argues that, furthermore, God has libertarian freedom to perform actions, which provides the grounding for human freedom.[42] In addition to these arguments I would add two more. First, if God did not intend sin but has always stood in fundamental opposition to it, then something like libertarian freedom must be affirmed. According to compatibilism God could have changed Adam's desire so that he never wanted to sin and so that he never would have sinned. But God did not do this, so God must have wanted him to sin. The libertarian, on the other hand, can maintain that God did not want Adam to sin but would not control his decision due to his faithfulness to the rules of the game God sovereignly established. Second, libertarian freedom must be presupposed in order to make sense of God's grieving over sin and entering into genuine dialogue with us. If we can truly affect the divine life, then we must be capable of doing other than what God specifically intends. Moreover, if humans have libertarian freedom, then it makes sense for the apostle James to say that we do not have because we do not ask in prayer (Jas 4:2). For these reasons I affirm libertarian freedom.

Two theological objections are often raised against the libertarian view of freedom. The first objection comes from Calvinistic compatibilists. Don Carson asks, "Must God be reduced to accommodate the freedom of human choice?"[43] For Carson, affirming that God is contingent in relation to us reduces the magnificence of God. Helm, after citing philosophers Lucas, William Hasker, Robert Adams and Richard Swinburne, says, "It will be noted from this selection of views on providence that the chief (if not the only) reason why a 'risk' view of providence is taken is a concern to preserve human freedom."[44] What may be said about Carson and Helm's claim that proponents of the risk model of providence seriously revise the doctrine of God because of their commitment to libertarian freedom?

It is correct that some proponents of the risk view begin with libertarian freedom as a control belief, using it to reshape the doctrine of God. However, that was not the method used here. I began with an examination of Scripture to see what it says about God and the nature of God's relationship with us. The biblical model of God as a personal being who enters into genuinely reciprocal relations with us fits nicely with human libertarian freedom. God is not being reduced—unless one has in mind some particular model of deity that cannot in any way be contingent on the actions of creatures. If God actually does respond, change his mind and dialogue with his creatures, then the model here explained is not a reduction of God but an affirmation of how God really operates in relation to us. If the views defended in this book on omniscience, prayer and God's love are correct, then libertarian freedom should be assumed.[45]

The second theological objection to libertarian freedom is that the Bible does not speak about freedom in this way. Adriö König raises a number of questions about this approach.[46] Why, he asks, does God get so upset with Adam and Eve (Gen 3) if they are simply exercising the "freedom of choice" God has given them? Furthermore, he argues that the biblical view of freedom is not this "formal" or libertarian freedom, but "material" freedom whereby they are free from sin and free only to obey God. After all, God does not say that they may obey or not obey as they wish (Gen 2). According to König, affirming formal freedom means that when Adam and Eve ate the forbidden fruit, they enacted their freedom but did not lose their freedom. However, according to material freedom, they did not enact their freedom but lost it. They were not free to disobey, and in doing so they lost the only freedom they had. Proponents of libertarian freedom, says König, seek to explain the inexplicable by offering an easy solution to the problem of sin. He claims that the freewill defense explains away sin as the exercise of the freedom of choice God gave humans.[47]

Though sympathetic to König's concerns, I do have a number of responses. First, I admit that some accounts of free will suggest that God gave humans the option of trusting or mistrusting; thus God has no reason to be upset with them should they sin. Richard Creel, for instance, says that God does not get upset at our lack of trust, since what God wants is not that we choose to trust God but only that we choose one way or the other.[48] But my account of Genesis 1—3 is different. In my view God gets upset with them for misusing their freedom because they do not choose what God wants for them. Although they exercise their freedom of choice, they choose against the express will of God, which is sin.

Second, regarding the distinction between formal and material freedom, I would concede that the Bible does not speak in the precise philosophical language of compatibilism or libertarianism. And it tends to speak of human freedom in relation to God. That is, apart from a loving relationship with God there is only bondage. "The Hebrew Bible," says Jon Levenson, "never regards the choice to decline covenant as legitimate."[49] However, the distinction between formal and material freedom is a common one in the history of theology, and the idea may be found expressed in various ways in Eastern Orthodoxy, Roman Catholicism and Protestantism.[50] Moreover, the Bible itself presents formal freedom as the structure in which material freedom is enacted.[51] That is, formal or libertarian freedom is understood as the infrastructure of covenantal love. It is a necessary condition for a loving relationship, since love cannot be forced: material freedom presupposes libertarian freedom. Human trust and love of God cannot be forced, which implies the possibility (as a formal structure) of mistrust and rejection of God. In sin we lose our material freedom (to be in right standing with God), yet we retain our formal freedom because we still stand, even in sin, before God.[52] Furthermore, "even the sinner is a personal being" whom God addresses.[53] When God addresses a sinful person, he addresses a who, not a what. It is the address of a holy and loving personal God to sinful human persons, and so it never becomes impersonal or manipulative.

Third, this version of the freewill defense does not explain the inexplicable. There is no good reason for sin; in fact, it is highly implausible given all that God has done. True, my account claims that God gave enough space that God's Word could be questioned, which creates the possibility (however remote) of mistrust. But this does *not* explain sin; it simply accounts for the structures of created reality. Within the structures God establishes the possibility of a loving relationship and expects this to materialize. When the divine provision is rejected, there is no explanation as to *why* humans choose to seek their well-being outside God's good provisions for them. In this way the structure whereby sin comes about is explained, but the actual breaking of the relationship is not Sin as a broken relationship remains a mystery. Perhaps, as Gorringe suggests, we should not call this the "freewill defense" but the "logic-of-love defense" because it is connected to the purpose of God in creation instead of to human autonomy.[54] In the model proposed here it is not freedom qua freedom that God values but the potential for reciprocal love. What God values is the loving relationship, and libertarian freedom is simply a means to that end.

7.6 The Concept of Divine Self-Limitation

Do the concepts of divine permission and human freedom imply that God has chosen to limit himself? The concept of divine self-limitation has become commonplace among theologians and philosophers in the twentieth century.[55] Nevertheless, the idea that God experiences certain "limits" is nothing new. Since at the time of Aquinas, at least, it has been routine to say that God cannot do the logically impossible. All sorts of things have been suggested that God cannot do, and these fall into two categories: things God cannot do in relation to himself and things God cannot do in relation to creation. Regarding the first category some claim that God cannot (1) cease to exist, (2) change his nature, (3) commit a moral evil or (4) break a promise. Any one of these would contradict the divine nature.[56] Given certain propositions about God's goodness, necessary existence, immutability and so on, it makes no sense to speak of God doing these things.

Similarly, several ideas have been put forward concerning things God cannot do in relation to creation. First, the creation of something different from God implies a limitation on God, since God is no longer the only being that exists. Says Emil Brunner, "God *limits Himself* by creating something which is not Himself."[57] One may recall Aristotle's assertions that to have friends is to be in relation and to be in relation implies dependency on the other for the relationship. Second, the concept of God's creating humans who are distinct from God implies limitation, since God is not the humans and God is dependent on them in order to be in divine-human relation. Given the tripersonal God, the godhead did not need to create in order to be in relation. But if God makes creatures, then God is dependent on them in order to be the Creator.

A third strictly logical limitation is that any decision God makes rules out other options, for God cannot do everything—selection is limitation. For instance, it is impossible for God to create and not create the same world simultaneously. Moreover, if God decides to make only certain kinds of creatures (set A instead of set B), then God limits himself to them. Furthermore, "the one kind of control God cannot logically have over free human agents is self-control."[58] A final kind of divine limitation in relation to creatures is that God cannot exercise meticulous providence and grant human beings libertarian freedom. Either God practices specific sovereignty so that his will is always and everywhere obeyed or God does not practice it. Keith Ward says that "creation is thus in one sense a self-limitation of God. His power is limited by the existence of beings, however limited, with power to oppose him. His knowledge is limited by the freedom of creatures to actualize genuinely new states of affairs, unknown by him until they happen. His beatitude is limited by the suffering involved in creaturely existence."[59]

Some object to placing any limitations on God. They attempt to gain the high ground in the discussion by claiming that all talk of divine limitation defaces the divine glory. But a moment's reflection will show that nearly everyone recognizes some sort of divine limitation.[60] If it is impossible for God to create beings over which he does not exercise specific sovereignty, then God is limited. If God must control every detail of human life in order to achieve his goals, then God is limited. If God cannot create personal agents who may act independently of the divine will, then God is limited. If it is not possible for God to create beings who can surprise and possibly disappoint him, then God is limited. If an omnipotent God cannot create a world in which the future actions of free creatures is unknown, then God is limited.[61] If it is impossible for God to make himself contingent on the decisions of creatures, then God is limited. Consequently, both sides of the sovereignty debate employ the concept of divine limitation, whether they admit it or not. Of course, it is much to the advantage of one party to maintain that it alone affirms a God without any limitations whatsoever.

Does saying that God cannot do something legitimately mean that God has limits? Most of those who define omnipotence as God's ability to do the logically possible or define omniscience as that which is knowable would deny that this is a limitation on God. Lucas, for instance, says, "We do not regard it as any limitation of God's omniscience that he cannot know that two and two make five; neither should we think it all strange that he cannot know what I am going to do in advance of my deciding what to do, since in that case there is nothing for God to know, and so no possible criticism of him for not knowing it."[62] Ward agrees with Lucas's views of omnipotence and omniscience, but he takes precisely the opposite stance regarding divine limitations: "The laws of logic are restrictions on the Divine being, but not avoidable ones; they are absolutely necessary."[63] Karl Barth objects to this line of thought, arguing that God created the laws of logic and thus God is not bound by them. Rather, God creates them and remains faithful (limits himself) to them in relating to us.[64] Barth also speaks of God's self-limitation in connection with the incarnation, in which the Son emptied himself (Phil 2:7) in love and service to the Father on our behalf. "God has limited himself to be this God and no other."[65] According to Barth, God really is the sort of God revealed in Jesus; this is a limitation because it means that God is not some other kind of God.

Though I am very sympathetic to Barth's position, I do believe that several qualifications are needed regarding the notion of divine self-limitation. First, I have argued for a conceptual limitation that renders it illegitimate for us to claim either that God is or is not bound by the laws of logic or that we can know that God created them.[66] Barth is correct that in his relationship with us God limits himself by his Word to being the sort of God revealed by Jesus. But Barth goes too far when he claims to know that God created the laws of logic, just as others go too far in claiming to know that the laws of thought are eternal verities in the divine mind. We do not know either way. What we do know is that *we (de dicto)* have to operate within the laws of thought when speaking of the divine-human relationship. There are certain conceptual limitations if we are to communicate coherently. Whether God is bound by them we cannot know. But if God is going to speak coherently to us, then he will do so within the boundaries in which he created us. The person who claims that God is the absolutely unlimited, as did the ancient Greek Anaximander, is not referring to any definite concept, for when we think of something we think of it as being in relation to something else, which implies limitation. We think within the boundaries God created us to be in, and it is useless to attempt to think the unlimited or unrelated.[67]

Second, a distinction must be drawn between a self-restricting (or self-limiting) God and a finite God. Some critics of the risk model of providence say it results in a finite God. But for one thing, anyone who says that God cannot do the logically impossible or that God limits himself to deciding one course of action or another is applying the category of limits to God and so may be open to the charge of believing in a "finite" God. But no one takes seriously the charge that Aquinas believed in a finite deity simply because he said God cannot do the logically impossible. For another thing, the accusation of finite godism fails to understand the nature of a finite God. Finite godism was defended in the school known as Boston Personalism, which was represented by the thought of Edger S. Brightman and his student Peter A. Bertocci.[68] Georgia Harkness and Nels Ferré, also students of Brightman, both call attention to the important distinction between a self-limited God on the one hand and a finite God on the other.[69] They point out that a finite God is limited by some force outside of God's power, by some rival deity or by an irrational "Given" in God's own nature. In Boston Personalism God cannot control this force even though he desires to do so. Consequently, those who speak of divine self-limitation are not advocating a finite God.

A third qualification regarding talk of divine limitation of *power* asks whether it is better to speak of God's limiting or restraining himself. Marcel Sarot argues that divine self-limitation implies that God resigns power and cannot get it back, meaning that God is no longer omnipotent.[70] According to divine self-restraint, however, God does not limit his power or abilities but does restrain the exercise of his power or the scope of his activities. Hence God gives up none of his abilities. Take the case of God's wrestling with Jacob (Gen 32:24-30). It seems better to say that God restrained his power to make it a "fair fight" than to hold that God actually gave up his power. In fact, God restrained it sufficiently that Jacob "prevailed" over God in this matter. In my view it is preferable to speak of divine restraint instead of self-limitation, but I do believe that many people who use the expression *self-limitation* actually intend what Sarot means by self-restraint. The language of self-restraint fits better with the biblical portrait of God, with the divine wisdom deciding when to act and when not to.

Nonetheless, even if we do not speak of self-limitation, it is still permissible (and necessary) for us to speak of God's working within the limits of rational discourse.

A final qualification for discussion of limits and divine power is that our discourse should be placed within the framework of God's self-giving love.[71] In light of the divine project we may speak of the limits or boundaries that God established and elects to work within. The desire to bring about a loving relationship with humans means that God does not force himself on us. He gives freely and restricts himself. It may be compared to a marriage relationship. To the outsider it may seem that self-restriction is normative whereas, in reality, it is self-giving love. The language of divine self-limitation should be qualified in this direction. Hence, the divine self-restraint should be understood as the restraint of love in concern for his creatures.

7.7 Can God's Will Be Thwarted?

Does talk of divine permission, libertarian freedom and divine restraint imply that God's will can remain unfulfilled? The psalmist writes, "Whatever the LORD pleases he does, in heaven and on earth" (Ps 135:6). Daniel says of God, "he does what he wills with the host of heaven and the inhabitants of the earth. There is no one who can stay his hand or say to him, 'What are you doing?'" (Dan 4:35). Such statements are often interpreted to mean that absolutely nothing—not the smallest detail—ever goes contrary to what God wants and that humans have no ability to stymie the will of God. Augustine, for example, says that "he is called Almighty for no other reason than that he can do whatsoever he willeth and because the efficacy of his omnipotent will is not impeded by the will of any creature."[72] Helm claims that "no course of action decided upon by a person can thwart God's purposes, even though at times God appears to change his mind."[73] This understanding of providence does not, however, fit with the biblical story as traced in earlier chapters of this book. This is especially so in light of the life of Jesus who, for instance, was prevented from doing more miracles in Nazareth due to the unbelief of the people (Mk 6:5-6). Hence, it seems some qualifications are in order.

In terms of the boundaries, structures and goals of the project that God has sovereignly established, there is no question whatsoever that God gets what he wants. God can create the world, provide for it and grant it his love without anyone or anything being able to thwart his overarching desires. If God decides to create a world with persons capable of reciprocating the divine love and if God establishes genuine give-and-take relations with them, then it is proper to say that nothing can stymie God's intentions. If God does not force the creatures to reciprocate his love, then the possibility is introduced that at least some of them may fail to enter into the divine love, and thus certain of God's specific desires might be thwarted. If God wants a world in which the possibility exists that God may not get everything he wants, then in an ultimate sense the divine will is not thwarted. It is important to note that if in some cases God does not get what he wants, it is ultimately because of the decision *God* made to create the sort of world in which God does not get everything he wants. In this sense, the responsibility falls directly on God, for nothing forced him to create such a world. Drawing on the distinction between intentions and permissions, Ward says, "Whatever God intends inevitably comes about. But even God cannot intend on behalf of another rational creature; he can hope, wish or desire. And those hopes not only can be, but are constantly thwarted; that is precisely the import of moral evil and sin."[74]

Returning to my analogy of the professor, it may be said that God intends to establish opportunity for discussion in the classroom and so permits things to be said that on a secondary level he never approved of. Not all freewill theists, however, like this conclusion. Peter Geach, for instance, affirms libertarian freedom and rejects meticulous providence along with exhaustive foreknowledge. Nevertheless, he claims that God's will is never thwarted. To lend some plausibility to this claim he proposes an analogy: God as a chess master.

> God is the supreme Grand Master who has everything under his control. Some of the players are consciously helping his plan, others are trying to hinder it; whatever the finite players do, God's plan will be executed; though various lines of God's play will answer to various moves of the finite players. God cannot be surprised or thwarted or cheated or disappointed. God, like some grand master of chess, can carry out his plan even if he has announced it beforehand. "On that square," says the Grand Master, "I will promote my pawn to Queen and deliver checkmate to my adversary": and it is even so. No line of play that finite players may think of can force God to improvise: his knowledge of the game already embraces all the possible variant lines of play, theirs does not.[75]

Geach, like William James before him, uses the grand-master analogy to assure us that, despite libertarian freedom and an indefinite future, God remains in complete control.[76] The analogy serves to highlight God's knowing in advance all possibilities and deciding beforehand how he will respond to them. But the grand-master analogy lacks the genuinely relational qualities of the other analogies suggested above: theater director, professor and climbing-expedition leader. In fact, it is doubtful that the chess-master analogy adequately handles the nature of the personal relationship between God and humans: Are things as closed as Geach suggests?[77] How can God be in total control if human beings are significantly free?[78] Does Geach mean that the grand master can guarantee victory on every move or only that he will win the game? Geach cannot say that God wins every move on account of human sin and evil. If so, we should take Geach to mean that God inevitably wins the game. But then what is meant by the "game"? Does it refer to the overall project or to each individual human (universalism)? I am not sure how to take Geach here. Furthermore, just because God knows all possibilities does not mean that God can do whatever he wills.[79] If God grants humans libertarian freedom, then they may do things that God does not want. If God is as controlling as Geach suggests, then it is difficult to see why there is sin at all.

Finally, Geach claims that God is never disappointed. The Bible, however, repeatedly says that God is disappointed with sin and human rejection of the divine love (for example, Gen 6:6). Creation has miscarried and is not what God wanted it to be. Sin and evil do thwart God's will and disappoint him. God did not want, and never has wanted, sin; he stands fundamentally opposed to it. This is seen most clearly in the life, death and resurrection of Jesus. God redeems from sin, but this was not his original plan. God is working within the rules of the game he established to overturn the results of sin, and so it is quite possible that God may not get everything he wants. Does this mean that God could fail? Again, God's overarching intentions cannot fail in that God establishes the boundaries in which the world will operate; but God's detailed or particular desires can fail in that God may not achieve all he wants for every individual. The doctrine of hell, after all, implies the failure of humans to reciprocate the divine love and the failure of God to reclaim everyone. If some people ultimately refuse to love God and God will not force their love, then what else is God to do? Unless one affirms either universalism or double predestination, it must be concluded that God's project ends in failure for some.[80]

7.8 Divine Purpose with Open Routes

In bringing about the divine project, God established a covenant with the creation. In covenanting with creation, God makes a fundamental commitment to its well-being and to seeing the project through to completion. The commitment to love his creatures and bring them into a reciprocal relationship of love is fundamental to God. Once sin enters the scene, God does not give up on his covenantal commitment but responds to this development with a strategy for redeeming the situation.[81] The flexibility of the divine strategies does not imply a change in the fundamental commitment, but it does mean that God reacts to contingencies, taking them into account in order to fulfill the goal of his project.[82] God remains faithful to his original purpose even while adjusting plans to take into account the decisions of his free creatures. God establishes general commitments and is free to decide some specific future actions that he will undertake. Hence the future is only partly open. It is not the case that anything may happen, for God has acted in history to bring about events in order to achieve his unchanging purpose.

Furthermore, the covenant or general commitment that God makes is not a detailed script but a broad intention that allows for a variety of options regarding precisely how it may be reached. "The divine plan," says Jacques Maritain, "is not a scenario prepared in advance, in which free subjects would play parts and act as performers. We must purge our thought of any idea of a play written in advance."[83] Some things are fixed whereas others are contingent. At creation God establishes a general purpose that becomes more specific as history progresses. God decides on certain routes in connection with human choices such that the specifics of the final destiny as well as the path to it take on greater definitiveness as the relationship unfolds. God's work with creation is a lot like jazz, a melody with a good deal of improvization.

In the biblical tradition it is not "what will be will be" but what will be may or may not be and what was may not have been. What God and people do in history matters. Had Jacob's family returned to Canaan after the famine was over, there would have been no bondage in Egypt and no need for an exodus. God would have continued working with them, but history would have been very different. If the midwives had feared Pharaoh rather than God and had killed all the baby boys, it would be a different story than the one we have. That God resorts to plan B in allowing Aaron to do the public speaking of Moses altered what God had in mind. Had King Josiah not been killed while attempting to prevent the Egyptian army from passing through Israel, perhaps the religious reforms he initiated would have made a significant difference for Israel's future. If the Jewish leaders had come to accept Jesus as God's way in the world, we would have had a very different book of Acts and subsequent history than we do. What people do and whether they come to trust God makes a difference concerning what God does.[84] This does not mean that God is helpless in the face of human sin. "God is not," says Brian Hebblethwaite, "stumped by men's failure to co-operate. There are things that God can do to bring good out of evil—the paradigm being the incarnation and the cross of Christ. But at every point, we realize that God does not fake the story of human action and human history."[85]

Proponents of specific sovereignty, however, object to this open-ended view of history. According to Helm, "God does not, then, exercise providential control in a way that leaves two or more possible ways of achieving some goal. Nor does he will the end but leave the means to others. . . . Rather, the providence of God is fine-grained; it extends to the occurrence of individual actions and to each aspect of each action."[86] For Helm, God has an exhaustive *blueprint* for everything: an eternal plan containing all the details that ever occur.[87] After all, is there not a single best way to achieve any goal? If so, then any change in God's plans would be a change for the worse. Yet the old Platonic assumption that any change is a change for the worse is fallacious. Behind this sentiment lies the assumption that perfection must be conceived as static. There are some kinds of change that are neither better nor worse (for example, the changes a clock makes as it keeps time). If God wants to create a world in which he takes our actions into account in formulating his own plans, this does not imply that God's plans go from best to worse, since this sort of adaptation is what God desired in the first place. Lucas suggests that God be seen as a Persian rugmaker who lets his children help in production.

> The children fail to carry out their father's instructions exactly, but so great is their father's skill, that he adapts his design at his end to take in each error at children's end, and work it into a new, constantly adapted, pattern. So too, God. He does not, cannot, have one single plan for the world, from which we, by our errors, ignorances, and sins, are even further departing."[88]

Because of the sort of rules of the game God decided to establish there is not just one great master plan or blueprint but any number of plans.

It is not possible to deduce from God's initial covenant purpose exactly how God will seek to accomplish his project. It was not possible for anyone to predict that God would elect the people of Israel for a special task. Nor was it knowable just how the people would respond and how God would react to them in the course of the covenant relationship. The studies in chapters three and four of this book considered the surprising ways in which God has worked. Nobody expected the particular kind of messiah Jesus chose to be. Who would have thought that God would "overrule" sin by the redemptive grace of the cross? Who could have known that God was going to bring the Gentiles into the people of faith as he did? The route God takes to achieve his purpose is not a direct route to a preplanned destination but, as seen in the biblical story, is an unpredictable, zigzag course. A. van de Beek puts it well: "The way of God to Christ was not an established road. It is a way which can only be read in retrospect in the light of Christ, not guaranteed in advance. It is a way on which God went past many dead ends."[89] Just as there is no way to deduce what God must do in carrying out his purpose so there is no infallible way of predicting what God will do in the future.

But God does provide us some clues about his ultimate direction based on the way God has chosen to work in history. The life, death and resurrection of Jesus are especially important in this regard. If Jesus is *the* image of God (Col 1:15), then we should look to him for the definitive statement on what God is like and for the direction in which God is working to bring his project to fruition. Wherever the Holy Spirit blows, he seeks to take people in the trajectory of Jesus. Jesus points us toward the future that the Father wants to establish. Christology informs eschatology.[90]

All things are not presently the way God wants them, for God has not yet reached his ultimate goal (1 Cor 15:25). Everything is not yet subject to God. At present God experiences both tragedy and triumph. The time until the eschaton is a time of the Holy Spirit; the Spirit tries different things in history to accomplish the divine purpose. There are signs of the Spirit's work in history (for example, Israel and the church), but the signs are ambiguous because neither Israel nor the church has lived completely as the redeemed communities God wanted. There are people who are being reclaimed and transformed by God's grace, and this gives us hope. Despite such signs it remains painfully clear that all is not right in the world.

God is Lord of history, even though not everything happens that God wants, for God has not given up on his creation. God continues to work toward the ultimate victory over sin and evil, when everything will be subject to him (1 Cor 15:28). The resurrection of Jesus points to a new order beyond death and destruction. God is still bringing about new and greater things, and we look forward in hope to a time when God's love is experienced and reciprocated in such a way that we live life in a different way than we do now. The book of Revelation speaks of this time as having no darkness (21:25), curse (22:3), sea (21:1), death (21:4) or temple (21:22). These images express the hope that there will be amazing differences between our present experience and our eschatological experience. There will be continuity, for it will still be God and us in relationship, but some things will be changed. The author of Revelation is attempting to communicate a reality that in some respects will be radically dissimilar from the one we now experience.[91] Christ has brought about our redemption, changing lives and societies, and we wait in longing expectation of the moment when we shall experience divine salvation in its fullness.

But if God cannot guarantee everything, where is our security? What guarantee is there that God will prevail, given conditions of freedom he has bestowed? Can God's purpose be ultimately thwarted? Although this issue was discussed above (7.7), a few additional comments will be helpful. The first thing to remember is that God has not given everything over to us. God is the one who established the conditions, and his overarching purposes cannot be thwarted. Whatever ability we have to thwart God's individual purposes is given us by God. Moreover, there are some things that the almighty God retains the right to enact unilaterally in the future. If the divine wisdom decides it is best to bring about some specific event in history, then God can do so. Before creation it was possible that no single human would ever come to reciprocate the divine love, but this has not happened. God has achieved his desire with a good number of people. To inquire whether God will have anyone in the future who will believe is a moot point, since God already has achieved a fair degree of victory.

Yet some proponents of the no-risk model remain troubled by this. Sproul, for instance, says, "If there is one single molecule in this universe running around loose, totally free of God's sovereignty, then we have no guarantee that a single promise of God will ever be fulfilled. . . . Maybe that one molecule will be the thing that prevents Christ from returning."[92] Will God win in the end?[93] Is it simply unwarranted posturing for proponents of relational theology to claim that God will achieve victory? The prophets envisioned a time when God would reign victorious over all and shalom (peace and well-being) would be pervasive. The most significant step in achieving this vision was taken when God, through Jesus, achieved victory over the opposing powers (Col 2:15). Yet God is still working to bring the effects of this victory to greater realization. Jesus has inaugurated the reign of the God of powerful love, but clearly it has not yet been consummated. God is still working to make his de jure rule a de facto one.

We should not underestimate God's ability or overestimate our own in this enterprise. God is omnicompetent, resourceful and wise enough to take our moves into account, mighty enough to act and faithful enough to persist. If one of God's plans fails, he has others ready at hand and finds other ways of accomplishing his objectives.[94] Are there any guarantees that

God will achieve the sort of future, in all details, that God desires? Here proponents of the risk model disagree. For Lucas the answer is yes: "We may thwart God's purposes for a season, but in the long run the pervasive pressures of rationality and love will circumvent our petty resistances."[95] In my opinion this betrays a rationalism that overlooks the irrationality of sin: the mystery of iniquity. Paul Fiddes is on track when he says that

> decisions and experiences in this life matter: they are building what we are. Since God's aim is the making of persons, he has the certain hope that we will be 'glorified,' but the *content* of that end depends upon human responses, for the content of the end is persons. . . . Thus the risk upon which God is embarked is real and serious, though not a total one. He has a certain hope of the fact of the end, but there is a genuine openness about the route and therefore the content of the end.[96]

It is our privilege to *hope* in the living God (1 Tim 4:10). We who have a taste of the victory of God look forward to our own salvation as well as the redemption of the cosmos (Rom 8:18-23; 1 Thess 5:8). We hope in the revelation of the glory of God (Rom 5:2). But it is not something we have in the bag; we must wait eagerly for it (Rom 8:24-25). God makes promises, and we may have confidence that God will keep them even though the exact way and form in which God elects to bring them about may surprise us. Though we do not know precisely what the prophets meant by the new heavens and the new earth, we long for and expect the new and greater things that he who creates ex nihilo and redeems through Jesus will bring forth. Just as we must not substitute belief in an immutable principle for trust in a personal God, so we must not exchange a demand for rational certitude for hope in the living God.

7.9 Conclusion

This chapter has explored the nature of the divine-human relationship in more philosophical and theological terms. It was an attempt to articulate what sovereignty should look like in terms of the findings of the previous chapters. The survey of the biblical materials showed that God enters into genuine give-and-take relations with humans; what God wants does not always come about. The description of the divine nature as loving, wise, faithful and almighty promotes thinking of divine sovereignty in terms of general sovereignty, in which God chooses to macromanage most things while leaving open the option of micromanaging some things. This was God's sovereign choice. In grace God grants humans a role in collaborating with him on the course that human history takes. God provides "space" for us to operate and in so doing makes it possible that some of the specific goals he would like to see fulfilled may not come about. Nonetheless, God graciously works with us, being creatively resourceful, to achieve his overall project of establishing loving relationships with significant others. God is yet working with us to open up new possibilities for the future. God faithfully works toward his overarching goals while remaining flexible as to how he brings these about. Relational theology, which involves a risk model of providence, will now be examined to see how it explains some important areas of the Christian life.

EIGHT

APPLICATIONS TO THE CHRISTIAN LIFE

. . . .

8.1 Introduction

Whereas previous chapters drew on the disciplines of biblical, philosophical and systematic theology, this chapter delves into practical theology. Previous chapters examined the biblical materials to see God's working in human history and looked at the divine nature and the particular type of sovereignty God has chosen to enact. This chapter explores the risk and no-risk, or relational and nonrelational, models of providence in light of various aspects of the Christian life. This chapter focuses on the third criterion for evaluating a theological proposal—adequacy to the demands of life. What do these two models of providence have to say about sin, grace and salvation? What insight do they give us into the problem of human suffering and into our experience of evil? Are Christians justified in believing that prayers of petition make a difference to God? Can we ever fail to understand God's guidance? The risk and no-risk models of providence give quite different answers to these questions.

8.2 Salvation and Grace

8.2.1 Introduction "For by grace you have been saved through faith, and this is not your own doing; it is the gift of God—not the result of works, so that no one may boast" (Eph 2:8-9). These words of Paul have traditionally specified who gets the credit for our salvation. Any view suggesting that humans, not God, should receive praise for our redemption is out of bounds. The doctrine of sin asserts that we are in bondage to sin and cannot free ourselves from it (Eph 2:1-3). God, in grace, liberates us from this bondage, reclaiming us as his own. In Christ Jesus God has elected a people for himself. Few would object to the preceding remarks. However, probing more deeply into the bondage to sin, the effect of grace and the nature of election reveals divergent viewpoints. In this section two models—the no-risk and risk views of providence—are examined in terms of grace and salvation.

8.2.2 The No-Risk Model of Salvation   The no-risk position understands sin as a condition that must be changed. Sin is a state of corruption in which humans find themselves, and this condition manifests itself in sinful behavior. Typically this is explained as a result of inheriting a sinful nature. In compatibilistic terms this sinful (Adamic) nature is the remote cause that produces sinful desires. As long as we do what we desire, we are free. Due to our sinful nature we are only free to sin. We can never desire God because our sinful nature excludes such "good" desires. In order to confess Jesus as Lord, we need to have the remote cause of our desires replaced by a new entity or condition that produces a desire to confess Jesus. Obviously, we are in no position to bring this about. God is the sole and complete cause that replaces our sinful nature with a regenerate nature. There is nothing we do to initiate this change or aid in bringing it about for, so to speak, there is no one home for God to address.

This is so because of our inability and also because of the nature of God. If God is totally unconditioned by the creature in such a way that God's will is never affected by or dependent on the creature, then God must be the one to bring about salvation in the life of an individual. The decision God makes to release a person from the bondage of sin is never in response to anything the human sinner may do. The election of God must be totally unconditioned by anything external to God. John Calvin, for instance, is very clear that God ordained some for eternal salvation and others for eternal damnation simply because God decreed it, not because God had foreknowledge of their faith or wickedness.[1]

God's knowledge of the future is not dependent on the creature. God knows the future because he decrees or foreordains the future. The divine decree of election is atemporal, unconditional and ahistorical. But if God is totally unconditioned by the creature such that God *never responds* to us, then what about sin? Did God decree that humans should sin? Calvin, as is well known, admitted that this was the case. This admission became the basis for what was later called supralapsarianism. According to this view God decreed salvation and damnation prior to decreeing the Fall into sin. As Louis Berkhof points out, early supporters of infralapsarianism maintained that God foreknew the Fall but did not decree it.[2] The problem with this, he says, is that it introduces conditionality in God because it means that something happened that God did not want to happen; it was something to which God had to atemporally *respond*. This would make God dependent on the creatures, forcing God to react to them. For this reason, says Berkhof, infralapsarians need to affirm that the Fall was included in the decree (and so become supralapsarians).

When the notion of sin as a condition is joined with the rejection of any conditionality in God, then the grace God gives to sinners must be understood as irresistible grace. Affirming specific sovereignty means that God gets precisely what he wants in every situation. If God wants Bob converted, then Bob will be converted. There is no way Bob can thwart God's specific decision to convert him. It is like a game of billiards. God pushes the cue stick of power, which strikes the cue ball of irresistible grace, which in turn implants faith in the eight ball (the sinner), which rolls into the specific pocket that God had eternally decreed for it. God, who never misses a shot, puts all the balls into the pockets of salvation and damnation as he pleases.[3] The balls cannot resist his shooting expertise. God never takes any sort of risks that those he elects will fail to inherit salvation. Everything works out with absolute precision, guaranteeing exactly what God desires for every single individual.

There are several problems with this model. First, even allowing for the notion of secondary causes, it must be maintained that every sin is specifically intended by God. If so, then why is God not rightfully held responsible for sin? Second, in this view there can be no reciprocity or conditionality regarding salvation because it is necessarily monergistic: Faith is solely a divine work in us. In terms of Vincent Brümmer's three models of relationships, this view is the manipulative model in which God is fully personal but human beings are not.[4] It is an I-It relation. Salvation is not the restoration of a broken relationship but consists in being freed from the condition of corruption. In view of compatibilism, it can be said that when Bob confesses Jesus, it is Bob's confession. But it cannot be said that the desire to confess came from Bob because he cannot determine his own desires. The desire for faith must be implanted in the sinner. Once it is, the result is guaranteed, for Bob must act on this desire. Irresistible grace may be thought of positively as divine liberation from an invincible prison. But it may also be seen negatively as divine rape because it involves nonconsensual control; the will of one is forced on the will of the other. Of course, the desire God forces on the elect is a beneficent one—for their own good—but it is rape nonetheless. Love cannot be forced because it involves the consent of persons.

Another interesting issue emerges in regard to sanctification. According to specific sovereignty *nothing* happens that God does not want to happen. Every state of affairs, including my personal holiness, is precisely what God desires. If I do not desire a greater degree of holiness, my lack of desire and degree of holiness is precisely what God wants for me at that moment. It cannot be said that I am frustrating any desire of God for me to be more sanctified at this point in my life. If God wants me to exhibit greater personal holiness, then God can unconditionally guarantee that I will manifest it. Compatibilism affords no escape from this problem. According to compatibilism I can be held responsible for my actions but not my desires. Hence I cannot be blamed for not desiring a greater degree of holiness because such a desire is not under my control. But without a desire for greater holiness I will never act in a more holy manner. Unless the Holy Spirit gives me the desire, it will not come about. For example, Ananias may be blamed for lying to the Holy Spirit, but his lying was specifically intended by God. Thus in this model the degree of sanctification in Christians at any particular moment is exactly what God wants; if God wanted them more holy, they would be. It makes no sense for proponents of exhaustive sovereignty to affirm that the Holy Spirit may be grieved (Eph 4:30).

Third, a typical complaint raised against specific sovereignty is, Why does God not save everyone? It certainly seems to be within his power to do so. Proponents of the no-risk model typically make a threefold response to this question. First, although it is within the divine power to save all, God, for inscrutable reasons, is not willing to save all. Scriptures asserting that God desires everyone to be saved (1 Tim 2:4) and does not want any to perish, but all to come to repentance (2 Pet 3:9) are interpreted by proponents of the manipulative model to mean that God wants all the *elect* saved and does not want any of them to perish. The "any" and "all" refer to those whom God has chosen for salvation, not to every single human being. The logic behind this interpretation is simple. God gets precisely what he wants for each individual human life. Scripture says that not all humans will be saved. Thus the "all" cannot mean all people generally but only "all the elect" or "all kinds of people."[5] After all, if the God of specific sovereignty actually did want absolutely everyone saved, then God could guarantee universal salvation because God's will is never thwarted in any respect. This necessitates the doctrine of "limited atonement" (Jesus died only for the elect).[6] Hence, this reading of Scripture is done through the theological lens of specific sovereignty. Anyone who does not agree with specific sovereignty is not likely to buy into this handling of Scripture.

The second response to the suggestion that God should save all is to deny that saving all is within the divine power. This notion, made popular by Augustine, holds that God *cannot* save or damn all people because such an action would leave part of the divine nature unfulfilled. If God damns everyone, then the divine mercy would fail to be manifested. If God saves everyone, then the divine justice would remain unexpressed.[7] Either way the universe would not reflect the complete harmony of God. God is not in control of his nature, and his nature dictates that it is necessary for some to be saved and others to be damned. Hence it simply is not possible for God to redeem all people. John Piper appears to follow Augustine when he claims that the essential nature of God is to dispense mercy and wrath on whomever he pleases apart from anything originating outside his own will.[8] Of course, in one sense this is correct, for God is free and is not constrained to love us. But I think Piper has Augustine's notion in mind, according to which the divine nature must damn some people in order for it to find expression.

There are several implications of this teaching that trouble me. God *cannot* save all and *cannot* even desire to save all because the divine nature forbids it. God is not free even to want the salvation of all but is bound by the righteous element of his nature that requires manifesting itself in the damnation of some. Is this the proper way to think of the divine nature? Even if it were granted that the divine nature dictates what the divine will shall be, there are at least two possible escapes from the conclusion that God cannot desire the salvation of all. First, even if God must manifest his justice, it could be manifested in the cross rather than in some necessity requiring a large population of the damned *(massa damnata)*. In this way God would manifest his justice, but it would be on himself rather than on his creatures.[9] Second, it could be affirmed that love is an essential attribute of God (which must be manifested) while denying that justice (so construed) or wrath is an essential attribute of God.

Another troubling aspect of the teaching advocated by Augustine and Piper is, Why God does not intend to save all? If God must express his justice in the damnation of certain people, then God is *dependent* on the damned (as well as the saved) for the fulfillment of his nature.[10] It would seem that God *needs* the damned in order to be who God wants to be. This would appear to call into question God's self-sufficiency *(aseity)*, that God was free to create or not create, and sounds in certain respects like panentheism, wherein God needs the world in order to be God. In my opinion, the idea that the divine nature requires the damnation of some arises from a consideration of the divine nature abstracted from Jesus Christ. In fact, I suspect that the ancient "principle of plenitude" has influenced this strand of theology. Since plenitude necessarily diffuses itself into the full range of being, the divine nature must create those who are saved and those who are damned in order to manifest the full range of plenitude: God's mercy and wrath. Thus the divine glory requires God to create beings intended for damnation because without them the glory of God would be deficient.

The third response to the suggestion that God should save all centers around the notion of divine freedom: Divine grace is freely bestowed or withheld at will. "The very inequality [distribution] of his grace," says Calvin, "proves that it is free."[11] But to say that God gives his love freely does not require that God withhold it from some. God's loving all people does not make his love any less free. Moreover, as Jerry Walls observes, the "idea that grace is freely bestowed is easily run together with the idea that it is undeserved. That is to say, it is easy to think that because none of us deserves grace, God can give it to whomever he will, overlooking the rest."[12] Suppose a father has two sons who flaunt his wishes and live recklessly, eventually becoming drug addicts. After a time they request help from their father. Neither of them deserves the father's aid, but the father gladly helps them anyway and pays for their rehabilitation. When they both relapse into drugs, the father rehabilitates them again. This scenario repeats itself several times. Suppose that the father knows that rehabilitating them one more time will permanently transform both of them. But suppose the father decides to rehabilitate only one of the sons and leave the other in lifelong addiction. The father does not owe help to either son. Yet if he knows that both sons would get straight from one last rehabilitation but denies rehabilitation to one of them, then we have reason to doubt that the father loves both sons.

The issue is not whether God owes sinners anything but whether he loves sinners and even all sinners (see chap. 4). According to the model of specific sovereignty God does not love all sinners. R. C. Sproul says that God does not owe love to anyone, since it is of grace. Hence people who hate God get what they deserve.[13] It is true that God does not owe us his love, but Sproul overlooks an important point. Strange as it may seem, according to exhaustive sovereignty God specifically intends that certain people hate him. If God specifically did not want anyone to hate him, then God would ensure that no one did. But if God desires that some people hate him, what has become of the divine love we read about in the Gospels? In the parables of the vineyard (Mt 20:1-16) and the talents (Mt 25:14-30) divine generosity is lavished on all. Judgment comes only after all had been shown divine favor and had been given an opportunity to respond. Such parables bring out the distributive justice of God, whereas proponents of specific sovereignty typically emphasize only the retributive justice of God.[14] Things are quite different, however, in the model of general sovereignty.

8.2.3 The Relational Model of Salvation

8.2.3.1 Sin According to general sovereignty God does not control every single detail that occurs. Some things happen that God does not want to happen but permits to occur. God takes a risk in creating the sort of world in which he desires a relationship of love but love cannot be forced. This relational, or fellowship, model produces an understanding of sin, election, grace and salvation that is quite different from the manipulative model.

According to the relational model sin is a broken relationship with God. When we fail to trust in God's good provision for us and reject the boundaries in which he placed us, we are refusing to respond in love to the divine love. This is irrational because there is no good reason not to trust God (see discussion in chap. 3).[15] In this sense sin has no cause. If it did, then it would not be blameworthy and it could be readily prevented or corrected. God took a risk in creating the type of world in which it was possible (though not plausible) that humans would fail to reciprocate the divine love. God grants enough space that sin may come about but does a great deal to ensure it will not. Sin did occur, however, and God is genuinely grieved because it is not what he wanted. Since its arrival on the scene, sin has become a universal human experience. Each of us grows up in relation to other sinners and sinful institutions and organizations. Socially, we are born into sin.[16] Individually, we follow our forbears in sin. All of us are in bondage to sin; each of us becomes a slave to sin (Rom 6:17). We serve a master other than God.

In the discussion of libertarian freedom (7.5) it was said that we are formally free and materially unfree. Yet we remain persons even in sin. The address of a holy God to sinners is still personal address.[17] There is no need to resort to the impersonal language of causes or the manipulative model. Karl Barth puts it thus: "Though Adam is fallen and disgraced, he is not too low for God to make Himself his Brother, and to be for him a God who must strangely contend for his status, honour and right."[18]

8.2.3.2 Contingency in God Barth's remark that God must contend for our love raises the most important issue in the discussion: Is God in any way dependent on us for the relationship of love? Does God make himself at all contingent on our response? Does God ever respond to us? Our answers to these questions shape the way we understand election, grace and salvation. The debate surrounding Arminius, John Wesley and their Calvinistic counterparts was not primarily about salvation but about the nature of God.[19] Whether God ever *responds* to us and does things *because* of us (not merely through us) is the crux of the debate. Whether God is completely unconditioned by anything external to himself or whether God, for some things, allows himself to be conditioned by others takes us to the taproot of the issues surrounding providence.[20]

Obviously, I am defending the view that God does make certain of his decisions and actions contingent on what we do. If we had done otherwise, then God may have done otherwise also. Interestingly, a fair number of Reformed theologians reject Berkhof's claim that Reformed theology denies any conditionality in God. James Daane says that "classical, creedal Reformed theology is not an unconditional theology. . . . Election in Reformed thought is God's gracious *response* to a sinful world."[21] Brümmer and David Fergusson argue that the Reformed confessions were attempting to be both theocentric and personal (in the sense of the fellowship model) but at times fell into the language of the manipulative model.[22] These writers claim that the Reformed tradition wants to affirm that salvation is God's unmerited gift, which excludes human boasting. But this does not rule out all conditionality in God.

Other traditions also allow for divine conditionality in election. The early fathers used simple foreknowledge to explain how God is responsive to the human act of faith. God "previsions" human faith and responds by electing them to salvation.[23] God's election (in part) is *based on* what *humans* decide to do. Eastern Orthodoxy, Arminius, Wesley and Pentecostals follow this move in allowing for conditional election.[24] In all these traditions God allows himself to be conditioned, for some things, on human actions. God is responsive to his creatures in bringing about salvation. In all these traditions God does not coerce the act of faith, for salvation involves a relationship between persons.

Affirming that God allows himself to be conditioned by his creatures amounts to crossing the Rubicon on this issue. The essential dividing line is between those who maintain relational theism in which God is, for some things, dependent on us and those who believe that God never responds to us and so deny genuine relationality in God, not between those who affirm foreknowledge and those who do not. Upholding the fellowship model in which God enters into genuine give-and-take relations with us is rejecting divine determinism, or the no-risk model of providence. This is true whether or not one affirms presentism or foreknowledge. Those who uphold foreknowledge, such as the Eastern Orthodox or the Arminians, believe that God's foreknowledge is dependent on or conditioned by what creatures actually decide to do.[25] Thus the key issue is not the type of knowledge an omniscient deity has but the type of sovereignty an omniscient God decides to exercise.[26]

8.2.3.3 Grace for Fellowship In a previous chapter (6.4.2) divine personal love was described as (1) limitless but conditioned by the ability of the other to receive it, (2) precarious because it does not control the other, (3) vulnerable because it may not get its way and (4) desiring reciprocation. If salvation is seen as a personal relationship of mutual love, then, says Brümmer, there are three conditions for salvation.[27] First, God must be personal, and we must be persons. Second, we cannot compel God to love us. We are solely dependent on his grace to initiate and enter into relation with us. God does not have to enter into this relationship with us; he does so in divine freedom. Third, we have to choose to enter it; our choice cannot be manipulated if it is to remain a personal relationship. God may enable us to enter the relationship and provide demonstrations of his love for us, but God cannot make us respond as he desires without its ceasing to be a personal choice. If the relationship is unavoidable for the human partner, then it has ceased to be a *personal* relationship.

But if humans are in bondage to sin, how can they respond to God and enter into a personal relationship of mutual love? The answer is enabling grace. Sinners do not trust or love God; they have turned away from God's love and are not inclined to accept his love. Libertarian freedom *(liberum arbitrium)* is to be distinguished from the ability to respond favorably to God *(liberum consilium)*.[28] We are formally free while being materially unfree: unable to be reconciled to God unless the Holy Spirit enables us. God can provide enabling or prevenient grace by which we are enabled but not coerced to give our consent to God. Enabling grace is a necessary, though not sufficient, condition for our redemption. This grace is the revelation of God's mercy and love, which opens up new options in the lives of sinners (1 Pet 1:3). The gospel story enlightens, convicts and enlivens us to a future that was closed to us before. The foolishness of the cross is God's wisdom and power to save (Rom 1:16). In hearing the gospel, we come to a realization of God's stance toward us, which provides a way out of our darkness. The love of Jesus elicits our loving response and motivates our imitation of his love.

Enabling grace is invincible, but it is not factually irresistible.[29] God wants a relationship with persons, so his grace cannot then be factually unavoidable for humans. A person who is enabled by the Spirit may nevertheless reject the divine love. A person who is made willing has no such option. God can enable all and give everyone an opportunity to experience salvation.[30] Yet some reject his grace; God cannot save them without destroying the rules of the game he has established for his project of having a reciprocal relationship of love with us. God does not rape us, even for our own good.

God takes risks with enabling grace in that people are not forced to believe. God does not believe in himself through us. The love of Christ and the prompting of the Spirit create the context in which we may respond in penitence and faith to God's gracious gift. God is the initiator and provider of salvation, yet he does not want a relationship without our consent. Our penitence and faith are necessary (though not sufficient) conditions for divine forgiveness. God is willing to forgive, and he has suffered the breech in our relationship for it. Yet our acknowledgment of the harm we have caused God and our willingness to desire restoration are necessary if reconciliation is to be personal in nature.[31] All of these conditions are required for the break in the personal relationship to be sufficiently healed. Faith is coming into a trusting relationship with God. God provides the light by which we are enabled to see his love. This light does not break our will or force our desires in a certain direction. Faith, then, is altogether the work of God and altogether the work of human persons.[32] This statement makes sense in the fellowship model but not in the manipulative model, for in the latter faith is solely of God. Paul says that we are saved by grace (Eph 2:8-9) that comes from God and that we enter into a relationship of love with God by faith. The process of salvation in the divine-human encounter is personal in nature. Because of this, divine risk is not eliminated, since it is possible for us (however unreasonably) to refuse the gift. Even those enabled by God's grace may refuse salvific love; there are no guarantees here.[33] The divine love is patient and enduring, bears with our sinful obduracy and hopes for our return but does not force itself on us (1 Cor 13:4-7).

The nature of the divine-human relationship in the fellowship model may be likened to a dance of personal partners. In salvation humans are receptive of grace but are not merely passive because grace is not overpowering. It is truly an I-Thou relationship in which God desires to be the Lord *our* God, the Lord "of" (de facto) and not merely "over" (de jure) humanity. It is a fellowship of love wherein God not only gives love but also receives love from the redeemed. This is quite different from the no-risk model, in which God is incapable of receiving our love because God is impassible and wholly unconditioned by us. God is then beneficent rather than loving toward us, caring for us rather than about us.[34] In relational theism, however, God actually enters into reciprocal loving relationships with us.

8.2.3.4 Some Objections Several objections are raised against the fellowship model of salvation. Paul Helm inquires whether this model would allow human pride to take credit for our salvation. "Given that there is more than one contributory causal factor how does one ascribe to one of them more importance than the others? . . . No arithmetical measure of the size of the various causal factors is available."[35] He then claims that if a person's relation to God is based on an act of free will, then the person might take pride in this because every result brought about by the person's free will allows for pride. Several responses may be made to these charges.[36] Helm is correct to call our attention to a sinful tendency—taking credit away from God. But if a person responds to God's gracious love with thanksgiving and love, then pride is excluded. Using the language of causes, it is possible, with J. R. Lucas, to distinguish between the complete cause and the most significant cause. For instance, if an arsonist uses gasoline in setting fire to a building, then gasoline and combustible material are certainly causal factors in the fire. In the moral realm, however, we would look for the most significant cause and that would be the arsonist. God is clearly the most significant cause, but not the complete or sole cause, of the personal relationship.[37] An alcoholic cannot cure himself. He must admit his need and then undergo a thorough program to escape his bondage to drink. But does this allow the alcoholic to take credit for his cure? Hardly.

Imagine that a beggar[38] living in terrible misery is approached by a rich man and is offered a gift that can lift the beggar out of poverty. Suppose that the beggar accepts the gift. In accepting the gift, the beggar is actively involved—the act of acceptance is his, not the benefactor's. Yet boasting on the part of the beggar is ruled out by the fact that we do not consider acceptance of a gift a meritorious act. It would be ludicrous for the beggar to take credit for his newfound wealth. The credit goes to the benefactor. There remains an asymmetrical aspect to the relationship between the benefactor and the beggar. Although there must be another for the benefactor to show grace to, the benefactor does not have to give; if he does, then he is the initiator and sole source of the gift. In such cases we readily acknowledge the benefactor as the most significant cause. No precise arithmetical measurement is possible here, but so what? Arithmetical measurements are appropriate to impersonal relations but not to personal ones (except for hard rationalists). Divine grace functions in ways appropriate to persons, not billiard balls.[39]

A. A. Hodge asks why humans should not get the glory if they are the ultimate cause of their own salvation? Should we pray for humans to convert themselves?[40] Such questions betray a seriously deficient understanding of the Eastern Orthodox, Wesleyan and certain Reformed views of salvation, which are in general agreement with the view articulated here.[41] These questions arise from the mentality behind the manipulative model, which uses the language of causal forces, not interpersonal relations. Humans are neither the initiators nor the givers of salvation, so in what sense can they be said to achieve their own salvation? We love God because God first loved us (1 Jn 4:19). We cannot compel God to love us nor can we oblige God to save us. Love or fellowship simply cannot be spoken of in such terms. And if salvation is understood in a relational sense, then we cannot earn eternal life. Our response of trust to God's enabling grace is not meritorious. Neither does it bring about salvation, for God is the one who establishes the conditions by which salvation is possible. If God does not initiate the process of reconciliation and seek to heal the break in our relationship, then it will not happen. We can only respond in trust or hatred to the divine gift; we cannot initiate it.

Why then do some not exercise faith in God after receiving the gospel? As mentioned above, the proponent of specific sovereignty will claim they do not believe because God has chosen not to make them believers. Thus the answer lies with God. If it is asked why God decides this way, the answer is that it is a mystery belonging to the unsearchable counsel of God's will. Hence the proponent of specific sovereignty arrives at a point where further explanations are impossible. The proponent of the fellowship model also arrives at a point where further explanations are impossible, but for a different reason.[42] According to Lucas,

> two people may have the gospel preached to them in the same way, and have the same opportunities of hearing God's call for each, and one may harken and the other harden his heart. We ask "Why?" No answer can be given except that the one decided to, and the other not to.[43]

The model of personal relations simply comes to a point where there is mystery, but it is the mystery of iniquity in the human heart rather than any sort of mystery in the heart of God. God's stance toward sinners is not mysterious; the cross of Christ demonstrates his love for them.

Regarding the issue of personal holiness, specific sovereignty holds that an individual at any point in time is exactly what God desires her to be, no more and no less. If I ask why God does not want her to be more sanctified at this time, the answer is that God, for some secret reason, has not willed it so. Things are different, however, in the relational model. God has given everything necessary for a life of holiness, but we need to make use of God's gifts (2 Pet 1:3-11). In the fellowship model God may want us to exhibit a greater degree of holiness and may be frustrated with us because we do not follow the leading of the Spirit. It is possible for us to thwart God's will for our sanctification. It is possible for us to lie to the Holy Spirit and bring the Spirit to grief (Eph 4:30) even though God does not intend such to happen. We cannot achieve personal holiness without the Holy Spirit, but the Holy Spirit will not do it without us. God has supplied all we need for holiness, but the complete set of sufficient conditions requires our consent and active participation.

What about assurance of salvation? Final perseverance? Does the relational model imply that God takes the risk that those who respond in faith to his salvific love may later on reject it and apostatize? In the parable of the sower (Lk 8:9-15) some people initially believe but are later overcome with the cares of the world. Paul says that Christians will be presented holy and blameless before God *if* they continue in faith, not moving away from the hope of the gospel (Col 1:22-23). The book of Hebrews warns its audience not to fall away from the living God (3:12; 6:4-6). Of course, all of these texts receive different interpretations, depending to a large extent on the interpreter's views of sovereignty. The proponent of specific sovereignty will say that God does not take any risk that those he has eternally elected to salvation will apostatize. If God wants them to persevere in faith, then they will. The biblical texts warning of apostasy are then usually understood as either hypothetical warnings (since it cannot actually occur) or as warnings that apply to those who resemble genuine Christians but, in fact, are not.[44] Christians can be assured that they are saved because there is no risk that they will fail to persevere.

Proponents of general sovereignty usually affirm that God does take the risk that believers may apostatize. God may want them to persevere in faith and seek to uplift them when they are tempted to apostatize, thus making falling away extremely difficult. But in the final analysis, apostasy is not rendered impossible.[45] Proponents of specific sovereignty commonly claim that this view produces insecurity in believers because there is a risk that they will not persevere. At this juncture some clarifications are needed. It is correct that the God of specific sovereignty takes no risk that genuine believers will apostatize *if* God decides that this will be the case. If, however, God decides that some genuine believers will apostatize, then they will do so. But even this entails no risk on God's part, since it is precisely what he wants to happen. Furthermore, it is correct that the God of general sovereignty does take the risk of genuine believers' committing apostasy *unless* God takes steps to ensure that this will not happen.[46] Hence, God may or may not take risks concerning human apostasy, depending on what he has decided to do.

Whether or not God takes the risk of genuine believers' committing apostasy has no bearing on *our* assurance or security unless we are able to know that we are genuine believers. Even if God always prevents genuine Christians from committing apostasy, that does not imply that there is no risk for *us*. The no-risk model of sovereignty does not imply assurance for the believer, since the "believer" may be deceived that she is genuinely regenerated. After all, God may have sovereignly decided to have certain individuals erroneously believe they are genuine Christians. In this case they would be convinced of their salvation when in fact they would be damned.

It is commonly agreed that some (even clergy, according to Calvin) who look like Christians are not. If so, how can anyone know that he or she is a genuine believer? Wesley and Jonathan Edwards explained that people can recognize their regenerate condition by the fruit of the Spirit in their lives and, for Wesley, the internal witness of the Holy Spirit.[47] The confirmation of past conversion is present convertedness, not some religious ceremony performed in the past.[48] Whether general or specific sovereignty is affirmed, the same problem remains: There is no absolute security *for us* of being believers because we do not possess infallible certainty that we are genuinely redeemed.

This leaves some people feeling insecure in their relationship with God. But Eberhard Jüngel points out that the desire for security is an attempt to gain control over the other, a lack of trust.[49] Trust in the relationship renders the need for control superfluous. When the divine-human relationship is understood in the model of mutual fellowship, the basic issue becomes, Are the two partners faithful to each other? Our end of the relationship may ebb and flow, but we can be assured that God will be faithful. Because of the divine faithfulness we do not take any risks. We may count on God's faithfulness in a way that he cannot count on ours. Hendrikus Berkhof says, "Our wavering faithfulness is upheld on all sides by God's unwavering faithfulness. That faithfulness is not dependent on our faith."[50] The seminal question in the apostasy issue is what it means to be a Christian. In the fellowship model it means being in a relationship of reciprocal love with God, for this is life truly lived.

8.2.4 Conclusion to Salvation   The fellowship model understands sin as the breaking of a relationship rather than as some sort of entity or condition. God takes it on himself to overcome this breech and restore the relationship through the cross and resurrection of Christ and by giving us the grace that enables us to see the injury we have done, thus making reconciliation possible. God does not manipulate our love but makes himself contingent on our response. Thus it is God who takes the risks involved with our responding to enabling grace with trust and love and continuing to mature in the relationship. This does not mean that we merit God's love; we are the recipients of grace. Grace opens up possibilities for us that otherwise would not be open. We can only thank God for such opportunities. Yet grace does not fix the outcome. God neither forces our response to his love nor guarantees that we shall develop the degree of personal holiness he desires. God takes the risk that we may not enter and may not grow in the divine love.

8.3 Evil

8.3.1 Introduction   There is no *single* problem of evil. Different models of God and different views of providence generate different problems of evil.[51] Can God create a world in which free creatures never commit a moral evil? Surprisingly, the answer does not depend on whether compatibilistic or libertarian freedom is affirmed. The compatibilist could answer yes if God always provided creatures with desires that produce righteousness and never allowed sinful desires to arise. Of course, this raises the question of why God has not done so. The libertarian can also say yes *if* the creatures never in fact decide to sin, for then it will be true that God created free beings who never committed a moral evil. Can God create a world in which God can *guarantee* that free creatures will never sin? In this case the compatibilist can rightfully claim that God is able to make such guarantees and take no risks. The libertarian, on the other hand, is committed to saying that God takes a risk in creating beings with morally significant freedom. Thus these two views of human freedom engender different sets of questions or problems regarding evil.

Can an omnipotent God ensure that creatures with libertarian freedom never sin? If an omnipotent God can do the logically contradictory, then God can give such assurances. But if we *(de dicto)* cannot meaningfully speak of omnipotence as doing the logically contradictory, then the answer is no. As proponents of the freewill defense have shown, it is contradictory to assert that an omnipotent God totally controls libertarian free creatures.[52] Clearly, different views of sovereignty give rise to different answers to this question. Someone who affirms specific sovereignty may claim that God can guarantee a sinless world. Someone who affirms general sovereignty cannot make this claim. It may come about that sin never occurs, but this is not because God can guarantee it. Because these two models produce different sets of questions regarding evil, it is incorrect to speak of "the" problem of evil.

Different understandings of the nature of God, human freedom and providence have given rise to quite a number of standard responses to suffering and evil. These may be summarized as follows.[53] (1) Evil is a punishment for sin. Though there are biblical references supporting the idea that some suffering is divine punishment for sin, this is not the whole picture. The Bible rejects the notion that all suffering is due to divine punishment (see 4.11). (2) It is sometimes claimed that evil is necessary, since we are able to understand the good only by contrasting it to evil. However, this hardly explains the degree and amount of evil in the world. (3) Perhaps God is the great educator who brings about evil so that our souls may mature and develop as persons.[54] Yet many people do not experience such growth. They become embittered or overwhelmed, thus casting doubt on God's ability to teach. Must my children suffer debilitating illnesses in order for me to grow? Furthermore, the inequitable distribution of suffering is disproportionate to the needs of the learners. How can it be shown that no one suffers more than is necessary for maximum spiritual benefit?[55]

(4) Some have claimed that this is the best of all possible worlds. Personally, I doubt that this claim is coherent. Even so, it is hard to reconcile this claim with the depth and amount of evil actually present in the world. (5) Others hold that if we could only see things from God's perspective, we would see that all is well with the world. Some suggest that God's morality is not the same as our morality. Who are we to blame God? One problem with this approach is that it leads to a vacuous understanding of morality, since we no longer know what divine morality actually is. God becomes inscrutable, which leads to a denial of evil and resignation.[56] The Bible clearly says that things are a mess—even from God's perspective (for example, Gen 6:6). (6) Finally, some claim that all evil will result in higher goods in the future, either in this life or the next. However, it is open to

serious question whether each and every evil or each and every experience of suffering will produce some greater good. And it is not at all clear that future goods justify the present evil.

8.3.2 Evil and the No-Risk Model   According to the no-risk model of providence there is a specific divine reason for ordaining each and every particular occurrence of evil and suffering.[57] According to Helm, since "God works everything for good" (Rom 8:28), there are no such things as accidents and there are no real tragedies in life.[58] If Jones is afflicted with a debilitating mental illness in which he loses touch with reality, or if a three-year-old child contracts an incurable and intractably painful bone cancer, or if a number of kindergartners are murdered in a school gymnasium in Scotland, or if Christian woman and children are raped and sold into slavery in Sudan, such experiences were specifically selected by God to happen to these individuals. In the no-risk view all the poverty, genocide, ethnic conflicts, debilitating illnesses, rapes, birth defects, blindness, destructive government policies and so on are all specifically ordained by God, who applies them to the particular individuals involved. *We* may not know the divine reasons, but, we are told, we can be sure they are good ones because God is good. Jerry Bridges writes that "God's sovereignty over people . . . means that God is in control of our pain and suffering, and that he has in mind a beneficial purpose for it. There is no such thing as pain without a purpose."[59]

For instance, God may desire to teach someone a lesson. God as educator selects and sends these painful lessons into our lives. Because God is perfect, he never fails (according to specific sovereignty) to get the pupil to learn the intended lesson. In this model it cannot be claimed that God wanted Jones to learn a particular lesson (for example, humility) and that Jones in fact failed to learn it. If those who suffer become embittered toward God, then that is precisely what God intended to come about, since the divine educator perfectly achieves the result he wants from each and every lesson. Saying that God wanted Jones to learn humility but failed to achieve that intention would mean that God's will was thwarted—which is impossible, given the no-risk model. Moreover, whatever view we take toward social responsibility, for example, in matters of racism and economic inequality, is also ordained by God. If we take the stand that these are wrong and we work to overcome them, then that is what God intended for us to do. If we do not work to overcome them, then this also is what God intended for us to do. If we choose to feed people starving in Ethiopia or Somalia and God wants them fed, then this will happen. If we choose to feed them but God wants them to starve (for some good reason, of course), then God will ensure that the food we send will never reach the people who need it. Those working for racism and those working against racism are doing exactly what God intends them to do at that particular time, for God's perfect plan is never thwarted in any detail.

Does this make God the author of sin and moral evil? Proponents of the no-risk model vigorously attempt to deflect this charge. Calvin, for instance, says that God is the "remote cause" and we are the "proximate cause," so God is not the author of sin.[60] Since God accomplishes his purposes through his chosen instruments, it is the fault of the instruments! Calvin admits that God wanted Adam to fall into sin, and so he had to fall, since God's will is never thwarted. Nevertheless, God is not blameworthy as long as God does not directly determine such events but only establishes the causes by which they come about. Calvin, moreover, says that God is perfectly good, so whatever God does is right and we have no justification to question God concerning this.[61]

Why then did God not ensure that humans would have a nature of compatibilistic freedom whereby they always and only desire the good and so would be incapable of sin? Calvin admits that this was possible for God to accomplish and that "such a nature would, indeed, have been more excellent."[62] The reason, he says, lies hidden in the divine plan that "from man's Fall he might gather occasion for his own glory." The glory of God will be more manifest if sin occurs than if it does not. Helm, articulating the no-risk view of evil, follows Calvin by suggesting that the fall was not actually bad, since good came from it. He takes the *O felix culpa!* (happy fault) approach to theodicy. The fall of Adam

> is happy because it, and it alone, makes possible the divine redemption from which the blessings of pardon and renewal follow. . . . The states of forgiveness and of renewal and all that these imply are of greater overall good than a state of primitive innocence. . . . Finally, without the permission of moral evil, and the atonement of Christ, God's own character would not be fully manifest.[63]

God could have guaranteed a world without evil but did not want this because it would have meant that part of the divine nature—God's mercy—would not have been displayed. The revelation of the full divine nature is the "greater good," which makes the divine desire for sin and evil justifiable. On this account evil is necessary for God to accomplish his own self-manifestation.

This view is beset with difficulties. As was shown above (7.4), the use of the term *permission* is problematic in the no-risk model. According to specific sovereignty, everything that occurs is precisely what God intended to occur. We do not use the term *permit* to mean intend. At best, the term *permission* could be used in the following sense. Suppose God had a rat that he wanted to run through a maze. Suppose further that every time the rat began to go down a path that God did not intend it to go, God placed a gate in its way that did not "permit" him to go that way. Eventually, the rat goes in the direction in which God "permits," since other paths are closed. This, however, would be a tendentious use of the word *permission*.

Second, as was argued above (8.2.2), it seems that the philosophical background for saying that evil is necessary for the divine nature to be fully manifested is the principle of plenitude. Does God really need sinners in order to display his justice and mercy?[64] Does God need the creation in order to be fulfilled? Does God have a deficiency that would be left unfilled without the occurrence of evil? If so, then what has happened to God's absolute independence, which the no-risk model supposedly affirms?

Moreover, saying that the fall was necessary so that some might experience Christ's redemption *(O felix culpa)* means that Jesus comes to clean up the mess the Father caused. In my view, Father, Son and Holy Spirit stand fundamentally opposed to sin and evil. It may be claimed that God is only the remote cause of moral evil, but for the no-risk model, every specific act of moral evil arises from God's specific intention for that individual. Hence it cannot be claimed that God is *fundamentally* opposed to sin. If God finds our sin "happy" because it allows God to achieve a greater good which would not have otherwise been achievable, then how can the biblical writers portray God as implacably opposed to sin and as never being "happy" about it? God laments the wickedness of creatures (for example, Gen 6:6; Mt 23:37), and the divine love does not rejoice in unrighteousness (1 Cor 13:6). How would one come to the conclusion that God was ever delighted in our moral evil? As A. van de Beek comments, "Sin does not proceed from his divine will. The predominant classic Reformed idea was that all things came from the hand of God. This view is not based on the knowledge of Jesus Christ, however, but on the idea that God is the cause of all things. It is based on our idea of God, not on God as he really is."[65]

The proponent of specific sovereignty may object that God is only the remote cause of sin, which gets God off the hook. But does it? If a child is raped and dismembered, there is a human agent who is the proximate cause, but God is the remote cause. The rapist is doing specifically what

God ordained him to do. Hence the human agent is the immediate rapist and God is the mediate rapist. George Mavrodes wonders who is ultimately responsible in such cases. He gives the following illustration:

> If a woman pushes a child down a stairway, and the child is thereby injured, we may be inclined to blame the woman, to hold her morally responsible. But if we bring in a more remote cause of the incident—if, for example, we come to believe that the woman herself was pushed so that she fell . . . then the moral responsibility of the woman seems to disappear. The child's injury remains, but the woman is not to blame for it, although she is the proximate cause of it.[66]

David Hume, brought up amid proponents of the no-risk model, said that it was impossible in such a system of thought to reconcile God as the mediate "cause of all the actions of men without being the author of sin and moral turpitude."[67] Human reason must, he said, be discarded here and appeal made to unfathomable mystery. Some adherents of the no-risk model do, in fact, appeal to antinomy at this point, claiming that God's ways are not our ways so that an omnipotent God can guarantee that morally responsible creatures never sin.[68]

Third, there is no room for the biblical lament tradition in the specific sovereignty model. If everything happens for the greater good, then complaint is out of the question because it reveals an immature faith. According to specific sovereignty the complaints and laments of Moses (Ex 5:22-23), David (Ps 13) and Habakkuk show that they did not see things from God's perspective. If only they had allowed for the "big picture," they would not have spoken to God in such accusatory fashion. But then again, according to specific sovereignty, God specifically ordained their laments for some reason—perhaps so we would see their folly, if God also ordains that he wants us to see the folly of lament.

A fourth problem with this explanation of sin and evil is that it implies that God causes (remotely, of course) only those evils that serve his specific purposes for a greater good. This puts human morality in a bind, however, since either (1) God will prevent me from doing harm to another if doing harm is not for a greater good or (2) God will not prevent me from doing harm to another if the harm will produce a greater good.[69] Therefore, I can only serve as God's instrument for good and cannot bring it about that I cause anyone an ultimate harm. It is all for the best. If each specific sin happens by divine decree, then whatever is, is right for that particular time and place. Helm denies that exhaustive sovereignty implies that what is coincides with what ought to be.[70] Helm is correct that what is does not imply that it ought to be for all time. But he fails to recognize that whatever is, is specifically intended by God to be for that particular time and so it ought to be for that particular time and place. God may, of course, decide to change things tomorrow, in which case whatever will be, tomorrow, will be right. Moreover, even if the proponent of specific sovereignty claims that it is wrong for *us* to commit morally evil acts, it is, nonetheless, "right" in the sense of being precisely what God intended to happen.

Finally, it does not make sense in the no-risk model for the biblical writers to say that God was genuinely grieved (Gen 6:6) or angered (Is 1:10-15) by sin. These must be reinterpreted as mere anthropopathisms. If God gets precisely what he intends in each and every specific situation (since his secret will is never thwarted), then it is incoherent to also claim that God gets upset at certain of these situations. Does God get upset with himself? Moreover, it may be asked whether this view entails a serious split between the purposes of Jesus and the purposes of the Father. For instance, Jesus instructs his disciples to be servant leaders and models this by washing their feet. The church, however, has often operated on the basis of power relations. But if the Father gets precisely what he wants in each and every situation, then power-loving people in the church have done specifically what the Father wanted them to do. Since the followers of Jesus have not always done things the way he wants them done but have always done things the way the Father wants them done, there seems to be a serious problem within the Godhead regarding divine intentions. The Son and the Father seem to be at odds with each other.

8.3.3 Evil and the Risk Model

8.3.3.1 The Divine Project Throughout this study the problem of evil has been discussed in light of the divine project in which God desired to create beings capable of entering into genuine give-and-take relationships of love with him and with one another. Unfortunately, the problem of evil, like the divine attributes, is often discussed without concern for the type of relationship God desires. Bearing in mind the divine project, however, it becomes possible to place the issue within the context of divine wisdom and love in pursuing such relationships. This enables us to see the difficulties raised by evil and suffering within the context of personal relationships and trust rather than simply attempting to reconcile evil with the abstract concepts of omnipotence, omniscience and omnibenevolence.

God has established the structures within which the divine project is possible. God made human beings capable of responding to the divine love with love of their own. God is solely responsible for bringing this possibility about, yet what God desires is a reciprocal relationship of love. Love is vulnerable and does not force itself on the beloved. Thus there is the risk that the beloved may not want to reciprocate love. In creating such conditions God takes the implausible yet possible risk that his creatures may reject him. This view may be called the "logic-of-love defense" instead of the "freewill defense." Instead of beginning with human freedom, it starts with the nature of the divine project of producing significant others who are able to enter into reciprocal fellowship with God.

The freewill defense is grounded in God's taking the risk of creating people with libertarian freedom and refusing to exercise specific sovereignty. Proponents of the freewill defense, however, tend to affirm the intrinsic (as opposed to instrumental) value of libertarian freedom. At times it is freedom for freedom's sake or, at best, freedom as requisite for morality that is trumpeted. However, as was argued above (7.5), God does not desire that we have the liberty of choice without concern for what we choose. Rather, God wants a relationship of personal love and grants freedom to that end. God is not satisfied until we reciprocate the divine love. Thus the freewill defense needs to be grounded in the love of God, God's desire for give-and-take relationships and the conditions necessary for this to come about. The logic-of-love defense connects the discussion to God's purposes in creation rather than to the supposed intrinsic worth of human freedom.[71]

In order for the conditions of love to be met, God must exercise general rather than specific sovereignty, which explains why God does not prevent all evil. God has sovereignly established the structures whereby he does not always get what he desires in each and every specific situation. If God habitually prevented moral evil, then God would overturn the very project he initiated.[72] Peter van Iwagen observes that if God either immediately cancels all memory of our experienced suffering or habitually prevents us from experiencing the effects of the pain and suffering that the separation of ourselves from God has led to, then God would be a deceiver and we would be living in a world of illusion.[73] He adds that in order for God to redeem us, it is important for us to become dissatisfied with our state of separation from him. If, however, we cannot recall our sins or they never lead us into difficulties, we would not become dissatisfied with our plight (we would not even be aware of our plight) and would not desire God's redemption.

Some object that if God is like a human parent, then God ought to act more often to prevent harm and suffering. After all, what parent would simply stand by and allow her child to be assaulted? In some respects God is like a human parent, but God is also unlike a human parent. God is uniquely responsible for upholding the ontological, moral and relational structures of the universe. God has a role that is unlike any human being's role.[74] Most people play different roles in life. As a parent I have responsibility for the health of my children. But this does not obligate me to prescribe medical drugs for them or perform surgery on them. In his role as the one who establishes and sustains the project, God cannot also bring it about that he abandons the very conditions for the project.

Take morality, for example. What if God prevents us from intentionally harming another? W. S. Anglin provides a number of illustrations that render this supposition problematic.[75] Suppose I accidentally discharged a gun while it was pointed at someone's heart. In this case God would not prevent it and the person would be killed. But if I fired it intentionally, then God would prevent it and the person would remain unharmed. A scientist seeking to discover truth would get the correct results of an experiment, whereas if a scientist sought to demonstrate superiority to a hated rival God would ensure that the experiment failed. If God practiced such a policy, then our intending harm to someone would be a sure way to avoid hurting them accidentally. God simply cannot operate this way without undermining the very project he has established.[76] In this respect, God's role is fundamentally different from the role of, for example, a teacher whose responsibility is to put a halt to any trouble in the classroom, by physical force if necessary. Only God occupies such a unique role. The almighty God could veto any specific act, but if he made a habit of it then he would turn the beloved into an automaton and thus find himself alone, which is not the sort of relationship he wants. God *cannot* prevent all the evil in the world and still maintain the conditions of fellowship intended by his overarching purpose in creation.

Yet several objections may be raised against the view just described. First, it may be asked why God did not create only people he knew would love and trust him. Why did God create those who would do evil and those who would be damned? The risk or personal fellowship model claims that this was not possible for God to do. It does not matter whether the proponent of the risk model affirms present knowledge or simple foreknowledge, since divine risk is not eliminated by knowledge but only by foreordination. If present knowledge is affirmed, then God did not know, for a fact, when he decided to create that we would commit moral evils. God did not foreknow that we would actually sin, only that it was possible; thus he cannot be held morally culpable.[77]

But even if God has simple foreknowledge or timeless knowledge of what creatures with libertarian freedom will do, divine risk is not eliminated. John Hick says that foreknowledge makes God ultimately responsible for sin because God chose to create a being whom he foreknew would freely sin.[78] This position, however, displays a misunderstanding of foreknowledge. According to simple foreknowledge (or timeless knowledge) God decides to create this particular type of world and then atemporally *learns* what will happen in this world. God did not know prior to his decision to create what would happen in this world. Once God becomes aware of what will *actually happen* in this world, he cannot make events "deoccur" such that what does actually happen does not actually happen, for that would falsify God's foreknowledge. As long as the fellowship model is affirmed, divine risk remains, regardless of the view of omniscience that is taken. According to both simple foreknowledge and presentism the present world is something of a divine adventure or experiment, the results of which were not foreknown when God decided to create. This allows the risk model to say that this world could have been better than it is and that God is not responsible for failing to create only those beings he knew would ever love him.

Second, it may be objected that God should at least act to remove moral monsters such as Adolf Hitler. But this assumes a rather individualistic understanding of human life. The Adolf Hitlers, Joseph Stalins and Idi Amins of the world do not act alone and they do not develop alone. Their personal development and their horrendous actions arise out of complex social frameworks. Hence it is not simply a matter of God's removing a single individual and thereby correcting the problem.[79] If God is going to act to prevent such terrible evils, then God is going to have to radically alter the conditions of the project. It is not self-evident that the elimination of such tyrants would prevent someone else's taking their place. Given the web of social relationships, God cannot prevent such moral monsters from arising without abandoning the type of project he established.

Finally, Gordon Kaufman criticizes the idea that God does *any* sort of special acts in human history. Such intervention, he believes, would imply that (1) God was incompetent in creating the world if he has to intervene in it and (2) God plays favorites because he does not do the same for everyone.[80] Kaufman and others label such a God a "magician" or a "spook." Several responses are in order. Does performing special acts in history make God an incompetent Creator? Not if the sort of world that God desired was one of divine interaction with the creatures. That is, it depends on the type of project God wishes to embark. If God desires interpersonal relationships with the creatures, then Kaufman's objection has no validity. Moreover, a God who answers prayer is a God who acts in history.[81] Since Kaufman is willing to sacrifice belief in a deity who enters into personal relationships with us, it is not surprising that he jettisons the idea of a God who answers prayer.

Concerning Kaufman's other objection, that such a deity would be playing favorites, a couple of points may be made. What Kaufman and others really want is a uniform code of egalitarian relations that God must follow.[82] Some people would rather have an impersonal principle, manageable by human ideals, than a personal God who gets involved with us. But we have no grounds for believing that a personal God is under some obligation to ensure total equality for us regarding life's circumstances. Moreover, no human has any sort of claim or right to a special act of God. Nevertheless, in my opinion, God is much more active than we can ever identify. But most of his work—like most of an iceberg—goes largely unseen. Theists simply do not know all the reasons behind God's actions, such as why God may act in one situation for one person but not, insofar as we know, in another situation for someone else.[83] Does this imply God's acts are arbitrary? In order to establish arbitrariness we would have to have access to all of God's knowledge and intentions. Critics such as Kaufman utilize the principle of egalitarianism in order to rule out any possibility of divine action and so opt for some form of deism. Those who affirm a personal God who interacts with us will prefer to live with the uncertainty of knowing why God does some things and not others. Admittedly, that God does some things and not others means that providence is not run on a purely egalitarian basis.

However, we can only hold God accountable for what he does intentionally. We may hold God responsible for creating the sort of world in which such evils are possible—even though it seemed unlikely from the outset. But we cannot hold God responsible for the particular acts of moral evil, since God does not specifically intend them. Though God permits them under the conditions of the project, he does not intend them. But if God is love and does not want us to commit moral evils and has no purpose for them, is there pointless evil?

8.3.3.2 Gratuitous Evil The distinction between permission and intention (7.4) and the discussion of the ways in which God's will may be thwarted (7.7) laid the framework for claiming that at least some evil is pointless.[84] Saying that some evil is gratuitous does not mean that it fails to fit into any purpose of God whatsoever. Rather, God adopts certain overall strategies and policies by which he seeks to accomplish his project. The overarching structures of creation are purposed by God, but not every single detail that occurs within them. Within general providence it makes sense to say that God intends an overall purpose for the creation and that God does not specifically intend each and every action within the creation. Thus God does not have a specific divine purpose for each and every occurrence of evil. Some evil is simply pointless because it does not serve to achieve any greater good. The "greater good" of establishing the conditions of fellowship between God and creatures does not mean that gratuitous evil has a point. Rather, the possibility of gratuitous evil has a point but its actuality does not.[85] That is, God has a reason for not preventing gratuitous evil—the nature of the divine project—but there is no point for the specific occurrence of gratuitous evil.

It is generally agreed that some evils are justified for some greater good. Furthermore, it is usually recognized that for certain goods to be possible it must also be possible that certain evils could obtain. How can one be brave, for example, if cowardice is not possible? Moreover, it is also generally admitted that theodicists have not shown that each and every evil serves a greater good or that the possibility of each and every evil is logically necessary. When a two-month-old child contracts a painful, incurable bone cancer that means suffering and death, it is pointless evil. The Holocaust is pointless evil. The rape and dismemberment of a young girl is pointless evil. The accident that caused the death of my brother was a tragedy. God does not have a specific purpose in mind for these occurrences. Some may wish to claim that God intends such suffering in order to teach the parents something or the Jews something or the young girl something. Indeed, numerous well-meaning believers attempt to comfort the suffering with standard responses regarding God's intentions for the sufferer.[86]

But is such pedagogy justifiable? Does it even work? After my conversion some Christians informed me that my brother's death was ordained for the purpose of bringing me to faith in Christ. What? God killed my non-Christian brother so that I would become a Christian? But without middle knowledge God could not have known that this would happen. This would mean that God kills people and causes disasters in the hope that some may then repent and confess Christ. However, the model of general sovereignty does not allow for each and every such evil to be explained this way, since God is only responsible for the structures within which we operate and for those specific acts in history God elects to do.

Some may wish to make the more modest claim that God uses these evils to stimulate people to repentance and love. But does God always succeed in this? Even in the church I see a fair number of people who have become embittered toward God—though they seldom say so publicly. They typically lead lives of quiet resignation while secretly hating God. In my view, God does seek to bring good even out of tragedy, but there are no guarantees. God is working in the lives of those who love God to redeem even evil situations and bring forth something good (Rom 8:28). But contrary to specific sovereignty, the God of general sovereignty cannot ensure that people who are suffering will respond positively to his redemptive love. Given the fellowship model of providence wherein God does not force his will on us, it is possible that we thwart God's attempts to redeem suffering in our lives. Considering the personal aspects of the divine-human relationship, though God works to bring good out of evil, God cannot *guarantee* that a greater good will arise out of each and every occurrence of evil.[87]

8.3.3.3 Natural Evil What relationship exists between the risk model of providence and natural evil? If it is believed that God created a world in which air currents and water vapor bring needed rain but God cannot prevent these elements from sometimes forming hurricanes, then God takes the risk that people will suffer from them and may turn away from his love.[88] Water sustains us but we can also drown in it. Lightning brings essential nitrogen to the soil, but it may also strike us dead. Certain genetic traits make us resistant to malaria, but the same genes make us susceptible to other diseases.[89] The risk of human suffering simply is not avoidable in the world as we know it. If it is believed that all natural evils represent either God's punishment on human sin or demonic forces, then God takes the risk that in creating such a world these evils may eventuate.[90] Attributing natural evils to human or demonic sin implies that God took the risk of creating the context in which such evil and the suffering it brings could arise.

My intention here is to highlight the risks God takes in light of natural evils, not to provide a theodicy. If God creates a world in which humans have a great deal of say regarding government policies, food distribution, agricultural practices and so on, then possibilities arise for human suffering that God did not intend. For instance, the policies of the Ethiopian government were largely to blame for the famine of the 1980s. Many thousands of people suffered and died because of human decisions. The same sort of thing has recurred countless times throughout history. The earth produces enough food to feed everyone, but it is not well distributed. In this God depends on us to care for one another. If we do not care for others, then suffering that God did not intend may come about. We make choices, individually and corporately, about how to spend our resources. A good deal of relief from diseases and even natural disasters could be accomplished if we chose to spend them on such enterprises. That we often do not do what we can do and then blame God when we suffer is the risk God takes in establishing this sort of world. If we cut down the rain forests, build cities on fault lines or spray pesticides on our food, we may bring on ourselves devastation and disease that God never wanted us to experience.

Does the Holy Spirit get us to respond favorably to natural evils? Anglin thinks so: "For every one person who chooses to respond to the evil by rejecting God, there are a hundred who choose to respond by leading better lives."[91] Though I often observe people sending aid in response to a natural disaster, I am not at all sure that Anglin's claim is correct (especially when diseases are involved). Regardless, it still implies risk for God, since people do not have to respond positively to these situations.

8.3.3.4 Jesus Is God's Answer to Evil   God's policy decision to permit gratuitous moral and natural evil means that God takes the risk that his project may not go exactly as he would like in every detail. The biblical narratives amply demonstrate that things did not always go the way God desired and that those experiencing suffering did not always respond with confidence in God. God is not in exhaustive control of the world, but neither does God stand impotent before it.[92] God seeks to convey his powerful love to us in various ways and faithfully works with us, soliciting our trusting response. God's definitive way of addressing evil is the cross of Christ. We know where God stands in relation to sin and suffering on the basis of the cross and resurrection of Jesus. God fights against them, not by playing their game but by opening up new possibilities for life. This may seem weak and foolish to those who want a display of brute force against evil. But God chooses to bear the full force of evil. God brought redemption (good) out of a most horrendous evil. God himself became involved in our struggle and suffering in order to overcome suffering and evil. Jesus, human and divine, experienced our troubles and mortality yet remained powerful in love. Through the resurrection he completed the victory over suffering and evil. The resurrection is our sign of hope that the future will bring a transformation of our present situation. The resurrection is a promise that suffering and death do not have the last word—they cannot ultimately separate us from the love of God in Christ (Rom 8:35-39). God is victorious over evil but not in the way we sometimes want. We want God to change the natural order and remove the possibility of moral evil, freeing our lives from suffering. We do not really want God to transform our hearts to share his values and love. We would prefer that God remove the possibility of suffering, not work through it with us.

This must not be construed to mean that God never heals, liberates or establishes justice. He does, but not as often as we would wish him to. And so we look forward to a time when God's sovereignty will be more fully manifested de facto against the forces of evil and suffering. In this respect we are like the biblical characters. Israel *remembered* God's mighty hand that delivered them from bondage and *hoped* for a future in which they would again experience such liberation (for example, Judg 6:13).[93] So too the church *remembers* the power of the resurrection and *hopes* for the time when all will be renewed in glory. Obeying the command to remember helps us cope with suffering for several reasons. First, we may count on and experience the comforting presence of a God who was unafraid of sharing our plight in Jesus. Second, we do see in the world from time to time signs of God's provisional liberating power. These give us, third, both the confidence that God will continue his work and the courage to persist in our efforts to be God's fellow laborers in the struggle for shalom. The witness of God as both suffering and powerful love gives us hope for a future wherein God is victorious over all evil.

That God has not given up on us is clearly manifested in the cross. Despite our sin God perseveres. Barth writes that

> God's mercy does not act in such a way as to overpower and blot out its object. God does not take the place of the creature in such a way as to annihilate it. . . . [God' mercy] is so powerful that it can wait, allowing us to continue. The abyss in the heart of God is so deep that in it the other, the reality distinct from God, can be contained in all its wretchedness.[94]

God does not destroy us but seeks to transform us through redemptive love. The Spirit continues working to bring good out of evil. God is not causing the evil, for Jesus stands against it. In the light of Jesus and the ministry of the Spirit we have no doubt that God intends our well-being. God is not causing our suffering but is seeking to bring something redemptive even out of terrible suffering. But God's efforts do not meet with success apart from us, since God has sovereignly chosen not to do it without us. Repeatedly in the biblical narrative God called on people to trust him in the face of suffering (for example, Hab 2:4). God desires to be known as a God of goodness, wisdom and justice who is ever present with us. Yet we might misread God's actions, thinking him a bumbling, absent deity who is silent before his suffering creatures. Will anyone have confidence that God is wise and loving in working this way? And the answer, as far as I can tell, is yes; some people do enter into loving fellowship with God.

8.3.3.5 Questioning God's Wisdom   Despite God's faithful track record, biblical characters such as Moses (Ex 5:22-23) and Habakkuk (Hab 1:2-4, 12-17) confronted God with their anger and disappointment. Moses blamed God for worsening oppression, and Habakkuk railed against God for not doing anything about the terrible injustices in the land. God took these complaints seriously, but God did not always answer questions in the way they were asked. People of faith may, at times, find themselves calling divine wisdom into question. In the church, however, we are usually taught not to question God but to acquiesce to the divine will. The biblical witness is that we may question God and may, at times, even prevail such that God alters his plans to take our concerns into account. The lament tradition should be part of our worship. Lament does not demonstrate immature faith. God's redemptive love does not exclude all questions about how the world manifests divine wisdom.

Some (for example, Hume) have suggested that the world must be the product either of an infant deity who knows no better or an decrepit deity who simply cannot do what needs to be done.[95] Fyodor Dostoyevsky's Ivan Karamazov asks whether this world—this project in which God takes risks—is worth the price. He tells of a little girl who is horribly abused by her parents and cries to "dear, kind God to protect her. . . . Do you understand why this infamy must be and is permitted? Without it, I am told, man could not have known good and evil. Why should he know that diabolical good and evil when it costs so much?"[96] Ivan sees too much injustice in the world to affirm God's wisdom. Consequently, he claims that God's experiment is too costly. It is not worth the price of all the suffering, and so he desires to return his ticket for admission to God. Ivan's brother, the monk Alyosha, does not find faith in God easy in light of Ivan's descriptions of human evil, but he sees in Jesus reason to trust God. We may know that God loves us, but we may nevertheless question God's wisdom in creating this sort of world. The Creator cannot be absolved of this responsibility.[97]

The skeptic may be confident that God was wrong to establish this type of project but still faces some serious questions. As Stephen Davis writes, "Of course it is possible that if I knew all relevant facts I would create a world very different to this one. But it is also possible that I would create a world as much like this one as I could. I just don't know enough to say, and neither does anyone else, in my opinion."[98] We may evaluate God's policy decisions, but we do not know all the relevant facts. So how can we justifiably claim that any decision God made was a bad one? God is still striving to achieve his purposes, which means that the project is not yet complete—the results are not yet in. A complete evaluation of the cost-effectiveness of the policy awaits the eschaton.

Although these points deflect the critic's charge we do not arrive at indubitable certainty. Instead, we are faced wtih the decision whether or not to trust in the God of Jesus Christ. God has demonstrated his love toward us in Jesus (Rom 5:8). If Jesus does not convince us of God's concern for us, what can? According to Paul, not even suffering and death can separate us from God's love in Christ Jesus (Rom 8:35-39). What then are we to do with our questions and periods of uncertainty? In our church life we often get the impression that we must simply hide them from others. Concealment, however, leads to denial and acts as a cancer that slowly destroys one's faith.

Instead, we should follow the example of those in Scripture who let their troubles be made known to God. We may pray to God the way Moses, Habakkuk and even Jesus did. Such prayers were not always calm and submissive. At times they were emotional outbursts. They took God seriously and occasionally even contended with God against God. God took them seriously even if he did not always do precisely what they requested. Contending wtih God is a sign that we still trust in God and that we have not given up. Even in lament we are still talking to God. If God can handle being nailed to a cross, then God can handle our cries of lament, our outbursts of anger and the voicing of our confusions. Despite our trials and tribulations, faith in God has a solid basis in Jesus, and we have good reason to be confident that the redemptive work God has begun will be completed. Paul could view his present tribulations as worthwhile because through the work of the Holy Spirit they can produce good qualities in us that serve as indicators of the divine love in our lives (Rom 5:3-5). We hope for what God will accomplish in the future in bringing about new and greater things that are incomparable to our present reality (Rom 8:18).[99] In love we seek to follow the path Jesus has blazed. It is God's desire that we will respond to his love in faith, hope and love despite our experience of suffering and evil.

8.3.4 Conclusion to Evil The logic-of-love defense provides a way of understanding the structures in which suffering and evil could come about in God's creational project even though he never intended them. The structure of love coupled with general sovereignty yields the conclusion that there is gratuitous evil. Horrible events happen that God does not specifically want to occur. This was a risk God took in establishing these structures. Natural evil poses a risk for God in that it may hamper love as well as human trust in the divine-human relationship. In the face of both moral and natural evil Jesus stands fundamentally opposed to them and seeks to overcome them by suffering and resurrection. Moreover, God continues to work to redeem the evil situation. God is not yet finished, and as long as God is working, there is hope that the future will be different from what we presently experience. Although this approach does not eliminate all ambiguity in regard to suffering and evil, there is, in light of the cross and resurrection, reason to trust God, hope for the future and respond in love to God.

8.4 Prayer

8.4.1 Introduction   Prayer has many forms, including praise, confession, intercession and contemplation. Though all forms of prayer bear some relation to the doctrine of providence, it is petitionary prayer—prayer that requests something of God—that is of interest here. The following discussion focuses on a particular aspect of petitionary prayer that is especially relevant to our inquiry: "impetratory" prayer. By impetratory I mean receiving something *because* one requests it. Does God ever respond to us and do something God would not otherwise do because we ask for it? Does God ever not do something he would otherwise do because we do not ask for it? How should we understand James's assertion that "you have not because you ask not" (4:2)? Predictably, different understandings of providence give rise to different views regarding impetratory prayers. The specific and general sovereignty models generate different understandings of prayer.

The problem of reconciling petitionary prayer with the attributes of God is quite old. In A.D. 233 Ambrose referred to Origen some issues that a woman named Tatiana had brought to his attention:

> First, if God foreknows what will come to be and if it must happen, then prayer is in vain. Second, if everything happens according to God's will and if what He wills is fixed and no one of the things He wills can be changed, then prayer is in vain.[100]

In short, does foreknowledge or foreordination render prayer useless? In his reply Origen says that God's foreknowledge does not rule out God's responding to our prayers, and so this doctrine may be accepted. However, since divine foreordination of all things would rule out any divine response to our prayers, it must be rejected. Having already dealt with the subject of foreknowledge and prayer (6.5.3.4), I will concentrate on the relationship between the two types of divine sovereignty and prayer.

8.4.2 The No-Risk Model and Prayer Proponents of specific sovereignty may rightly claim that prayers of praise, confession and petition play a significant role in our lives. God has ordained that we should, at a particular time and place, praise God, confess our sins or make a request. Each and every such prayer is precisely what God intended it to be. Regarding prayers of petition it may be said that God not only decrees what will happen after the prayer but also the very prayers themselves as the means by which God will bring the results about. Calvin says that petitionary prayer is not superfluous even though God is asked to provide things that he has decreed from all eternity to provide because God ordains not only goals but also the means to accomplish these goals.[101] Proponents of the no-risk model think it is presumptuous for humans to believe that their prayers may actually change God's mind. All change, rather, is in us. Helm agrees, saying that for the no-risk model "intercessory prayer is not one means of settling God's mind on a course of action, but one of the ways in which the already settled mind of God effects what he has decreed."[102]

Suppose, for example, that God has eternally decreed for Mary to be converted on July 28, 1999. Suppose further that God desires to regenerate her only after my prayer for her salvation on July 27. Can I place her salvation in jeopardy if I decide not to pray for her on July 27? Not at all, since according to specific sovereignty God's will cannot be thwarted in the least detail. Consequently, God can guarantee that I will pray on July 27 and that he will on July 28 give Mary the grace by which she will inevitably believe. God not only decrees her salvation but also my praying for her the day before. Thus petitionary prayers are meaningful in the sense that God wills them as the means through which he brings about what he desires.

But what about impetratory prayers? Does it make sense for proponents of specific sovereignty to claim that God grants something *because* of or in *response* to the request made? Helm says that even if the impetratory prayer is divinely decreed, it may be said that "God answers because men pray."[103] C. Samuel Storms agrees: "Divine sovereignty does not preempt prayer, nor does prayer render God's choice contingent. The God who is pleased to ordain the salvation of sinners, based solely on his good pleasure, is no less pleased to ordain that he will save them in response to the prayers of others."[104]

But what does it mean for the God of specific sovereignty to "respond," or to do something "because" he was so requested? It cannot mean that because of the request God did something that God was not otherwise going to do. Both Storms and Helm are clear that there is no contingency in God. But if there is no divine contingency, then how are their remarks to be understood? I suggest that what they mean (or should mean) is something like the following: to say that God "responds" to the petitioner means that God, who ordained the specific request by that particular petitioner, ordained to fulfill that request *after* it was requested. That is, for a God of specific sovereignty to "respond" means simply that God decided first to have someone pray for a particular request after which God would do what was requested. "Response" simply means to do one thing after another, but not because of or in reaction to someone else. Obviously, this is not normally what we mean by the word *response,* since God is "responding" in terms of his own decrees. The "God who hears" prayers is the God who hears himself speaking through second causes.

Furthermore, to say that God does something "because" of what the creature requests sounds as though God is in this respect dependent on the petitioner. According to Storms, "From the human perspective, it may rightly be said that God's will . . . is dependent upon me and my prayers, as long as it is understood that God, by an infallible decree, has secured and guaranteed my prayers as an instrument."[105] Hence it is only from a "human perspective" or anthropomorphism that God may be thought to be dependent. In actuality, however, God is not dependent on our prayers; rather, our prayers are dependent on God's decreeing them. Thus God may be said to do X "because" we prayed only in the sense that God had always decreed that God was going to do X after we prayed the prayer he also decreed. In this respect Edwards put it correctly: "Speaking after the manner of men, God is sometimes represented *as if* he were moved and persuaded by the prayers of his people; yet it is not to be thought that God is properly moved or made willing by our prayers. . . . He is self-moved. . . . God has been pleased to constitute prayer to be antecedent to the bestowment of mercy; and he is pleased to bestow mercy in consequence of prayer, *as though* he were prevailed upon by prayer."[106]

Hence, the God of specific sovereignty is not actually prevailed on by prayer. God never responds to us or does anything because of our prayers because this would imply contingency in God. In this model it is difficult to make sense of James's statement that "you have not because you ask not" (Jas 4:2) because if the God of specific sovereignty wanted you to have it, then he would ensure that you asked for it. If God's will is never thwarted in any detail, then we can never fail to receive something from God *because* we failed to ask for it. Moreover, James says that we sometimes petition God from wrong motives and so we do not receive (4:3). But if the God of specific sovereignty desires to give us something, we can rest assured that he will get us to ask properly because there is no risk that God's desires will be frustrated in any way. Consequently, proponents of specific sovereignty may rightfully claim that petitionary prayer is justified because God has decreed that he would perform a certain action after the request is made. Moreover, in this model it makes sense to say that God has ordained such prayers for therapeutic benefit to those who pray as well as to those who are aware that others are praying for them. But proponents of the no-risk model of sovereignty cannot legitimately claim that God responds to our prayers or does something because we prayed. There is no place for impetratory prayer in this model.

8.4.3 The Risk Model and Prayer   The situation regarding impetratory prayer is quite different in the risk model, which asserts that God enters into genuine personal relations with us. According to the fellowship model God is genuinely responsive to us. For instance, God removed certain plagues at the request of Moses (Ex 8:13, 31). When God told Moses that he was going to destroy the people and start over again with Moses, Moses cited reasons why God should not follow through with this plan. God changed his mind to accommodate Moses' desires (Ex 32:10-14). When God announced to King Hezekiah through the prophet Isaiah that he would die very soon, Hezekiah prayed and gave God reasons why he should let him live longer. Because of his prayer God sent Isaiah back to Hezekiah to inform him that God had changed his mind and would grant his request (2 Kings 20:1-6). If Moses and Hezekiah had not prayed to God about these matters, biblical history would have been different. To modify James's statement: They received because they asked. In the risk model it is quite possible for us to miss a blessing that God desires to give because we fail to ask for it (Jas 4:2-3).

Our prayers make a difference to God because of the personal relationship God enters into with us. God chooses to make himself dependent on us for certain things. It is God's sovereign choice to establish this sort of relationship; it is not forced on God by us. God once asked Moses to leave him alone so that the divine anger might grow against the people (Ex 32:10). God repeatedly instructed Jeremiah to stop praying for the people (Jer 7:16; 11:14; 14:11; 15:1). Why would God say such things if Moses and Jeremiah had no impact on the divine life? James says that the prayers of righteous people make a difference (Jas 5:16). The prayers of God's people make a difference not only in the lives of the people but also in God's life. For Abraham Heschel, God is not at home where his will is defied. Thus "to pray means to bring God back into the world . . . to expand his presence . . . His being immanent in the world depends on us."[107] Allowing for overstatement, Heschel is correct that God takes our prayers seriously and weaves them into purposes and actions for the world. God desires a deep personal relationship with us, and this requires genuine dialogue rather than monologue. The fellowship of love God desires entails a give-and-take relationship wherein God gives and receives from us.

Some object to this, claiming that we have no business advising God, who possesses vastly superior wisdom. Is it not the epitome of hubris to think that we can counsel an omniscient God who already knows all the data?[108] Such remarks may arise out of a sense of humility and a desire to be still before God. But the biblical record is more than a call to silence. It also calls us to make our requests known to God (Phil 4:6; 1 Jn 5:14-15) and to ask what we will in Jesus' name (Jn 14:13-14). Abraham, Moses, Elijah and Jesus reasoned with God and did not always acquiesce in God's presence.[109] They dialogued with God in order to determine together what the future would be. God wants this sort of conversation not because we have anything stupendous about which to advise him but simply because God decides to make our concerns his concerns. God wants us to be his partners not because he needs our wisdom but because he wants *our* fellowship. It is the *person* making the request that makes the difference to God. The request is important because God is interested in us. God loves us and takes our concerns to heart just because they are our concerns. This is the nature of a personal, loving relationship.[110] The relationship is not one of domination or manipulation but of participation and cooperation wherein we become colaborers with God (1 Cor 3:9). It did not have to be this way. It is so only because God wanted a reciprocal relationship of love and elected to make dialogical prayer an important element in such a relationship.

The discussion in chapter three (3.7, 11) identified several biblical texts showing that God may be prevailed on. God makes himself open to us, and in some respects the future is open because God elects not to decide everything apart from our input.[111] Biblical characters prayed boldly because they believed their prayers could change things—even God's mind. They understood that they were working with God to determine the future.

In impetratory prayer we show that we believe things can be different. God has open routes into the future, and he desires that we participate with him in determining which ones to take. This should not be construed, however, to mean that we get whatever we want. We may prevail with God because God genuinely takes our desires into account. Yet God may also prevail with us, getting us to change our minds and pursue a course of action that we did not initially think best. In this regard prayer provides a dialogical resource for God to work in the world.[112] When we turn to God in prayer, we open a window of opportunity for the Spirit's work in our lives, creating new possibilities for God to carry out his project. Dialogical prayer affects both parties and changes the situation, making it different from what it was prior to the prayer.

Our failure to practice impetratory prayer means that certain things that God wishes to do for us may not be possible because we do not ask. In the words of Peter Baelz, "Our asking in faith may make it possible for God to do something which he could not have done without our asking."[113] Consequently, if God's bringing about a certain state of affairs is contingent and our requesting God for it is contingent, then God is taking a risk that some particular good may not come about. It might be objected that God, being omnibenevolent, must always act to bring about the most valuable state of affairs, whether he is asked to do so or not.[114] God must, it is claimed, always act to help without being asked in order to maximize goodness. Two points may be made in response. First, it is not clear whether it is coherent to claim that there is a most valuable state of affairs.[115] God has multiple options for action, depending on what those in fellowship with him decide to do. Second, if what God holds as "most valuable" is the personal relationship with us, then God will not want to do everything for us without our asking because this would lead to a breakdown of the type of relationship God desires to have with us.

Another problem might be raised at this juncture. What if we prayed for something that God did not believe was in our best interest? Would God grant it anyway? Would God open himself up to the requests of finite and even sinful creatures? In my opinion, God has at times done so. God allowed Aaron to do the public speaking for Moses even though God wanted Moses to do it (Ex 4:14). God gave the people of Israel a king even though he questioned the advisability of their request (1 Sam 8). God fulfilled these requests, I believe, in the hope that people would mature in their relationship with him. Parents often face the same sort of problem. A child may want something that the parent believes unwise. The parent may go ahead and give the child what she wants in the hope that the child will learn from the experience. In this sense, of course, the parent (or God) has the long-term best interest of the child in mind.

Impetratory prayer is significant not only for our own individual lives but also for the lives of other people who make up the community of faith. There are numerous biblical references to Christians' praying for one another and injunctions for us to pray for one another (for example, 2 Cor 9:14; 13:7; 2 Thess 1:11; 3:1; Heb 13:18; Jas 5:14). Impetratory prayer matters: Jesus wanted his disciples to pray with him and for him in Gethsemane. The body of believers, by praying for one another, helps to shape the future of the community.[116] What God decides to do for others sometimes seems to depend on my prayers. That is, God might sometimes refrain from acting beneficially in one person's life because others have failed to pray.[117] This may not sound fair to those of us in the West with our high value on individualism, but God values community and desires that it be fostered, in part, by our concern for one other and by our manifesting this concern in intercessory prayer for others. This is one means that God uses to build a community of fellowship and mutual concern. Keith Ward argues, moreover, that

> our actions usually involve others, so that our good acts help others and our evil acts harm them. It is not sensible to complain, that, if I fail to pull my neighbor out of a ditch when I could easily do so, God is responsible for leaving him there. It is no more sensible to complain that, if I fail to pray for my neighbor when I could easily do so, God is responsible for not doing what my prayer might have effected. . . . Our request may make it possible for him to help them in ways which otherwise would have been constrained by the structures of the natural order.[118]

Thus God takes the risk that at times he may want to do something for us or for someone else but may not do it because we fail to ask for ourselves or for others. In the fellowship model it is not possible to say that God gets precisely what he desires in each and every situation. Yet God is responsible overall for establishing the conditions for this sort of relationship. God took the risk that we might not ask for ourselves or intercede on behalf of others and so things might not go exactly the way God desired. This does not mean, however, that God cannot act unilaterally in earthly affairs. God can and does. Yet God has decided to seek a personal relationship with us and works to build a community of believers who love one another. In this sort of project it becomes possible to affirm that we have not because we ask not. God genuinely responds to our petitions and sometimes acts *because* of our impetratory prayers.

8.5 Divine Guidance

8.5.1 The No-Risk View of Divine Guidance

Although the ways in which God guides his people is an important topic, it will not be addressed here.[119] Following the pattern established so far, the no-risk view of guidance will be examined first and the risk model, second.

According to the no-risk view of providence God always has something specific he intends for us to accomplish. In each and every situation God has a definite act in mind that fulfills part of his exhaustive plan. God has a master blueprint that he ensures is carried out in exacting detail. For instance, if God wants Bob and Susan to marry, then God brings it about (through secondary causes of course) that they are married. God has a specific will for whether I should be married and, if so, God also has a particular person selected for me to marry. God has a specific will for our lives concerning issues of vocation, where to live, how many children to have, what sort of education to pursue, where to go on vacation, what clothes to purchase, and so on. God's exhaustive sovereignty is comprehensive, overlooking nothing. There is no decision too insignificant for God's concern and sovereign control. Similarly, there is no circumstance so unimportant that God does not have it planned. Every specific thing that happens to us is part of the blueprint. For specific sovereignty, it will be remembered, there are no such things as chance events or accidents. So each and every circumstance serves as God's mouthpiece identifying part of the divine plan.[120]

Moreover, according to the no-risk model we can never fail to be led by the Spirit. Whatever guidance God wishes to bestow on us at any particular time is infallibly given to us and understood by us in precisely the way God intends us to understand it.[121] Our interpretation of divine providence in our lives at any moment is precisely the interpretation God intends us to have. This does not mean, however, that *we* are never confused about the leading of the Spirit. It only means that if we are confused, it is because God intends for us to be confused at that particular time in our lives. If we do not clearly perceive where God is guiding us, we may rest assured that God does not intend for us to grasp his direction at that particular moment. We may hope that God will see fit to remove the confusion in the future, but there are no guarantees that he will.

We can never fail to align ourselves with the divine plan, since God's blueprint is infallibly carried out in every detail. This does not, however, inform us what we ought to do. Helm correctly observes that "the fact that everything that happens is subject to divine providence . . . in and of itself offers no guidance as to what you or I ought to do."[122] Although the no-risk model affirms that what is implies that it ought to be for that moment, it does not imply that it ought to be so in the future, for God may have imminent changes planned. Nevertheless, it remains inappropriate for proponents of the no-risk model to ask whether we are following God's guidance, for we cannot but follow it. It is never a question of whether or not we submit to God's leading, for God's leading is never thwarted or frustrated in the least detail. Otherwise, God would in some sense be dependent or contingent on us to follow his guidance.[123] Clearly, the no-risk model cannot allow that God's exhaustive plan would fail to be fulfilled in the least detail, for God is in no way dependent on us for our following his direction. For instance, if Susan wonders whether God wants her to write a novel, she cannot fail to receive and follow the precise guidance God intends for her at that particular time. If God wants her to write it, then God ensures that she is so guided and that she, in fact, does it. If God desires that she remain uncertain for a period of years as to whether or not to write the novel, then that is what she will do. Although no risk is involved for God, there is plenty of room for uncertainty on our part as to what God wants us to do.

8.5.2 The Risk View of Divine Guidance   According to the fellowship model of sovereignty God does not have a blueprint that we are to follow. God has a goal for our lives, but there are numerous open routes to its achievement. This is not to say, however, that God never desires a specific individual to do some particular act. After all, God requested certain people in the Bible to perform specific acts (for example, God asked Gideon to tear down the alter of Baal, Judg 6:25). Yet for most of us there is no such specific guidance. The will of God for our lives is not a list of activities regarding vocation, marriage and the like. Rather, it is God's desire that we become a lover of God and others as was exemplified in God's way in Jesus. "When people talk about God's leading," says van de Beek, "it is usually not rooted in the way of Christ, but in a general concept of omnipotence and protection."[124] The way of Jesus is a way of life not concerned about blueprints but about being the kind of person God desires. God's major goal is to renew us in the likeness of Jesus (with all the attending individual and social implications). In this sense it could be said that God has a specific will for each and every situation: to live as Jesus would. This is not, however, what people usually have in mind when they seek specific divine guidance.

It is God's desire that we enter into a give-and-take relationship of love, and this is not accomplished by God's forcing his blueprint on us. Rather, God wants us to go through life together with him, making decisions together. Together we decide the actual course of my life. God's will for my life does not reside in a list of specific activities but in a personal relationship. As lover and friend, God works with us wherever we go and whatever we do. To a large extent our future is open and we are to determine what it will be in dialogue with God. God does not simply turn us loose to do whatever we please. Rather, we are to seek God's wisdom for our lives (Jas 1:5). For example, there may be a variety of vocations available to me with which God is pleased, not just one that is "best" or "perfect" in comparison to the others. I am free to make my choice in consultation with God and others in whom I detect godly wisdom. In my opinion, God is concerned about which vocation I select but is much more concerned about how I live my life in that vocation. Whatever vocation I choose God wants me to do it Christianly.

Furthermore, according to the relational model explored in this book there are "chance" happenings and genuine accidents that God did not specifically intend. God has granted humans significant freedom such that we may do things to others that God does not intend us to do. An employer, for instance, may harass and fire Jane without good reason. Jane should not view this circumstance as a "sign" that God's will for her life has changed. She may, however, be confident that no matter what others do to her God is working in her life to redeem the situation. Since the broad range of circumstances that we experience in life, from being in a train accident to meeting an old friend on the street corner, are brought about by human freedom, we should not typically think of them as divine pointers for guidance. God resourcefully works with us in any and every situation, but God is not causing all our circumstances because this would imply a great deal of manipulation of humans. God has sovereignly chosen not to practice that sort of providence as his normal way of dealing with us. Though God can (even unilaterally) bring certain circumstances about, God normally works with us in whatever circumstances we experience. Hence, according to the risk model of providence Christians should not attempt to read all circumstances as signs of God's will for their lives.[125]

King Saul, for example, made this mistake when he had David trapped, exclaiming that "God has given him into my hand" (1 Sam 23:7). Of course, God had done no such thing. When those who murdered Saul's son told David that *God* had avenged David of Saul, David rejected their interpretation of providence and had them killed (2 Sam 4:8-12). In the no-risk model of providence, texts such as these are problematic because misinterpretation of what God is doing is not meaningful for specific sovereignty, since everything that happens is specifically decreed by God, as well as its interpretation or misinterpretation. In the risk model, however, it is possible to mistake a divine action and misconstrue circumstances.

Regarding the leading of the Spirit, the risk model implies that we may or may not fail to understand the Spirit's direction. We may not understand what God expects of us in a particular instance. We may not accurately grasp the divine wisdom God attempts to give us for some problem. God will do all he can to help us, but since God is dependent on us for some things there is no guarantee that we will properly appropriate the divine wisdom. Moreover, even though we might correctly understand the Spirit's leading, we might fail to carry it out. Suppose that God is guiding me to spend more time with my children. I may or may not get God's leading straight, and even if I understand it I may or may not do it. The deeper our personal relationship with God develops, however, the better we experience his love, which enables us to better understand how we should live and better give ourselves in loving service to God. In so doing we follow his leading.

8.6 Conclusion

This chapter has developed the theme of divine sovereignty in light of the particular sort of project God freely chose to establish. It was God's sovereign grace that brought about a creation in which it was possible for creatures to enter into personal relations of fellowship with God. In the fellowship model God does not exhaustively control every event that happens. God grants humans "space" in order that we may freely respond to the divine love with our own love. God desires genuine give-and-take relations with us. Consequently, God restrains the use of his power so as not to overwhelm us. In such a relationship God has established the conditions within which certain of God's desires may be thwarted. Yet even in the face of some defeats God does not give up on us but works in various ways to achieve the fulfillment of the divine project. All this is in contrast to the no-risk model of sovereignty in which absolutely everything happens according to what God specifically intends to happen.

The risk and no-risk models were compared and contrasted to see how each model would explicate the doctrines of salvation, suffering and evil, impetratory prayer and divine guidance. It was seen that certain claims could be made within one model that were incompatible with the other model. Overall, a key issue that arose in the course of the discussion was whether or not God ever makes himself conditioned by us in any respect. That is, is there any contingency in God? Does God ever respond or react to us *because* of what we do? Relational theism gives an affirmative answer to these questions, whereas the specific sovereignty model does not. Although the manipulative view of sovereignty provides God with great security in that God takes no risks, it denies certain understandings of our fellowship with God that most Christians assume as an integral part of their piety. I have sought to defend these common practices as well as provide a theological framework for understanding what a personal relationship with God involves.

NINE

CONCLUSION

· ·

This study has examined the biblical, historical, theological, philosophical and practical issues surrounding two basic models of providence: the risk view and the no-risk view. Although the models have been compared and contrasted, the main purpose has been to develop a constructive proposal for a risk-taking God within relational theism. It has been argued that the risk model meets the three criteria outlined in chapter two: consonance with the tradition (especially the Bible), conceptual intelligibility and adequacy to the demands of life. Chapters three and four discussed several texts that are commonly overlooked or are given a different interpretation by the no-risk model of providence. It was observed that the Scriptures depict God in dynamic give-and-take relationships with his creatures. God has sovereignly decided not to control everything that happens. Rather, God is sensitive to us and has decided to be responsive to us. In some things, God has decided to be conditioned by us. Divine conditionality is the watershed issue between the risk and no-risk views of providence. According to relational theism, which entails the risk view of providence, God adapts his strategies to take account of our decisions. There is no eternal blueprint by which all things happen exactly as God desires.

Chapter five examined these issues in light of the theological tradition. It was found that the risk model of providence is consonant with major themes of the Christian tradition in both Eastern and Western forms. The relational model of providence finds agreement with the intentions, though not always the material content, of many theologians in the church. The tradition has continually affirmed God's personhood and God's personal relationships with humans. Moreover, there is a strong element in the tradition which asserts that God is, for some things, conditioned by the creatures. The tradition has not always sufficiently articulated providence in light of what is entailed in reciprocal personal relationships. Hence the model of a God who, in some respects, is conditioned by his creatures is a God who takes risks in working out the divine project. The tradition has sometimes rejected the notion of divine conditionality while simultaneously affirming the personal, responsive and loving nature of God's relationship to us. The relational theism (fellowship model) defended in this book addresses this problem. Thus it may be claimed that the risk model does greater justice to the heart of the tradition: God in personal relationship with us.

Chapters six and seven discussed the conceptual intelligibility of the proposed model. It was claimed that the risk model better articulates the type of sovereignty God has actually decided to exercise in history—a sovereignty connected to the nature of God as loving, wise, free, faithful and almighty. This is the God who takes the risk that we might not respond to his love yet who is extremely resourceful and proficient in working with us. This demonstrates to us the wisdom and the powerful love of God. God does not give up on us, even in our sin, but comes to us in the person of Jesus to win back our trust and love. Since Jesus manifests the real nature of God, there is no conflict between the type of providence he displayed and that of the Godhead. The God who comes to us in history is a God who relates, adapts, responds and loves. This is what God is actually like.

This is a wise God who is able to meet the challenges we face in life and work to bring good out of our evil. Chapter eight examined how the risk model of providence is adequate to the demands of life. God is working to bring about a future that redeems us from sin and suffering. The God who takes the risk of love provides a coherent model of God in relation to human suffering: God is opposed to it. Since God stands against suffering and sin, there is no need to posit a "secret" intention in God that takes precedence over his revealed intentions. There is no question about God's intentions toward us, for he loves us and desires our best. Thus when things do not go as God desires, we may share God's sense of outrage—there is a place for lament in the Christian life. But there is more than lament in the Christian life; there is also hope because God is working to redeem his entire creation. God has the wisdom, power, love and perseverance necessary to meet the challenges ahead. God is competent and resourceful in working with us. We are called to have confidence in the way God seeks to carry out his project.

The core of relational theism includes four major points. First, God loves us and desires for us to enter into reciprocal relations of love with him and with our fellow creatures. The divine intention in creating us was for us to experience the triune love and respond to it with love of our own. In this we would freely come to collaborate with God toward the achievement of God's goals. Second, God has sovereignly decided to make some of his actions contingent on our requests and actions. God establishes a project and elicits our free collaboration in it. Hence there is conditionality in God, for God truly responds to what we do. Third, God chooses to exercise general rather than meticulous providence, allowing space for us to operate and for God to be creative and resourceful in working with us. Fourth, God has granted us the libertarian freedom necessary for a truly personal relationship of love to develop. In summary, God freely enters into genuine give-and-take relations with us. This entails risk taking on his part because we are capable of letting God down. This understanding of divine providence deeply affects our views concerning salvation, suffering and evil, prayer and divine guidance.

Although the risk model of providence meets the three criteria for evaluating a theological model, it has not been "proved" in any hard sense of the term. Nor is it the only possible version that could be developed within relational theism.[1] Nonetheless, what I have sketched out is what I see being taught in the biblical narrative and having good theological, philosophical and practical support. A cumulative case involving biblical, theological-philosophical and practical arguments has been set forth such that the model has plausibility. But there is much more that needs to be said in order to respond to all the questions it poses for the various doctrines and life applications of the Christian faith. Doctrines, as well as our applications of them, are interconnected. A change in a key model means more changes elsewhere, and these must be examined. There is more to be written about the God who takes risks, and I invite others to join in the development of this model.

Notes

Chapter 1: Introduction

[1]This can be seen in the Nicene Creed in two respects. First, the Father eternally begets the Son, and since the Son is fully divine, it can be said that God receives. Thus there is an internal receptivity in God. Second, it says that the three persons of the Trinity are worshiped by us. I take this to mean that God receives our worship; our worship makes a difference to God. Thus God is receptive to beings external to himself. This could supply the basis for revising strong notions of impassibility and immutability.

[2]See the discussions in 6.5 and 8.2.3.2.

[3]In Clark Pinnock et al., *The Openness of God: A Biblical Challenge to the Traditional Understanding of God* (Downers Grove, Ill.: InterVarsity Press, 1994), my coauthors and I sought to lay out in programmatic fashion major issues and areas for further research. The present work represents another segment in the continuing development of this theological model. Several important questions and criticisms that were raised in response to *Openness* are addressed here. This is especially the case with the biblical material, which represents a much fuller account of how proponents of this model read Scripture. Nonetheless, this book covers the subject of providence, an important (but by no means the only) topic that this "research project" needs to address. It is only one more work in that growing body of literature that I call relational theism. I am glad to see several other authors now joining in its development (see 5.6.2).

Chapter 2: The Nature of the Task

[1]Helpful on the application of metaphors to God is Terence E. Fretheim, *The Suffering of God: An Old Testament Perspective,* Overtures to Biblical Theology (Philadelphia: Fortress, 1984), pp. 1-12.

[2]See George Lakoff and Mark Johnson, *Metaphors We Live By* (Chicago: University of Chicago Press, 1980); and Janet M. Soskice, *Metaphor and Religious Language* (New York: Oxford University Press, 1985). On the primacy of metaphor for developing a postcritical philosophy, see Jerry H. Gill, *On Knowing God: New Directions for the Future of Theology* (Philadelphia: Westminster, 1981).

[3]See Sallie McFague, *Metaphorical Theology: Models of God in Religious Language* (Philadelphia: Fortress, 1982); McFague, *Models of God: Theology for an Ecological, Nuclear Age* (Philadelphia: Fortress, 1987).

[4]The term is borrowed from Vincent Brümmer's *The Model of Love: A Study in Philosophical Theology* (New York: Cambridge University Press, 1993), p. 20. The following discussion is indebted to him.

[5]Helpful on models in theology are Hans Küng, *Theology for the Third Millennium: An Ecumenical View,* trans. Peter Heinegg (New York: Doubleday, 1988); Brümmer, *Model of Love;* and John Goldingay, *Models for the Interpretation of Scripture* (Grand Rapids, Mich.: Eerdmans, 1995). See also my "God as Personal," in *The Grace of God, the Will of Man,* ed. Clark Pinnock (Grand Rapids, Mich.: Zondervan, 1989), pp. 165-80.

[6]For more on this, see 3.12.

[7]Excellent discussions of these and additional criteria are found in Christoph Schwöbel, *God: Action and Revelation* (Kampen, Netherlands: Kok Pharos, 1992), pp. 132-52; Brümmer, *Model of Love*, pp. 22-29; and David L. Wolfe, *Epistemology: The Justification of Belief,* Contours of Christian Philosophy (Downers Grove, Ill.: InterVarsity Press, 1982), pp. 43-69. Schwöbel and Wolfe are particularly helpful in situating the criteria into the larger "practical" project of making sense of life. Overall, my general epistemological approach is known as "critical realism." On this, see Wentzel van Huuyssteen, *Theology and the Justification of Faith: Constructing Theories in Systematic Theology* (Grand Rapids, Mich.: Eerdmans, 1989); and Trevor Hart, *Faith Thinking: The Dynamics of Christian Theology* (Downers Grove, Ill.: InterVarsity Press, 1995). Critical realism seeks to overcome the dual myths of pure objectivity and pure subjectivity by noting that all understanding involves both elements. On this, see Lakoff and Johnson, *Metaphors We Live By*, pp. 185-226; and Arthur F. Holmes, *Contours of a World View* (Grand Rapids, Mich.: Eerdmans, 1983), pp. 145-52.

[8]See the stimulating work by David S. Cunningham, *Faithful Persuasion: In Aid of a Rhetoric of Christian Theology* (Notre Dame, Ind.: University of Notre Dame Press, 1991).

[9]Even the Bible displays this dynamism wherein canonical texts are modified by later biblical authors in order to remain faithful to the tradition. See John Goldingay, *Models for Interpretation of Scripture* (Grand Rapids, Mich.: Eerdmans, 1995), pp. 121-27.

[10]Van Huuyssteen, *Theology and the Justification of Faith*, pp. 180-86, discusses how healthy traditions are open to change. He criticizes fundamentalism for equating its own theological formulations with Scripture and for killing off most of the essential biblical metaphors.

[11]For a detailed examination of the "coherence" condition, see Richard Swinburne, *The Coherence of Theism*, rev. ed. (New York: Oxford University Press, 1993), pp. 11-50.

[12]Brümmer, *Model of Love*, p. 25.

[13]I am not alone in this undertaking. Something that surprised me as the study unfolded was the number of Reformed (Dutch Reformed in particular) thinkers who support the risk model (e.g., Adriö König, Vincent Brümmer, Nicholas Wolterstorff, James Daane and Harry Boer). Things are certainly changing in Reformed theology!

[14]Any new proposal will be viewed with skepticism by some: Could so many theologians and philosophers have been wrong? Whether they were wrong on this issue remains to be seen. That they have been wrong on many other issues is historically apparent. After all, certain "clear" passages of Scripture were used in the past to justify a geocentric solar system, deny women any relief from the pain of childbirth, justify persecution of the Jews and legitimize slavery of blacks. It is fascinating that until the late 1800s most Christian theologians used the Bible to sanction slavery and that, in America, many southern clergy took up arms against the "infidel" northern clergy because they believed the Yankee Christians were rejecting the clear truth of the Bible! In this case the southern Christians were the biblical conservatives and their northern counterparts were the liberals. See Kevin Giles, "The Biblical Argument for Slavery: Can the Bible Mislead? A Case Study in Hermeneutics," *Evangelical Quarterly* 66, no. 1 (1994): 3-17.

[15]Adriö König, *Here Am I: A Believer's Reflection on God* (Grand Rapids, Mich.: Eerdmans, 1982), pp. 60-72, discusses the history of this move in Western theology.

[16]Cited in W. T. Jones, *A History of Western Philosophy: The Classical Mind*, 2nd ed. (New York: Harcourt Brace Jovanovich, 1970), p. 19.

[17]David Hume, *Dialogues Concerning Natural Religion*, ed. Nelson Pike (Indianapolis, Ind.: Bobbs-Merrill, 1970), p. 156. Whether or not this is Hume's position is not my concern here.

[18]Ludwig Feuerbach, *The Essence of Christianity*, trans. George Eliot (New York: Harper/Torchbooks, 1957), p. 33.

[19]Karl Barth, *Church Dogmatics* 2/1, trans. Geoffrey W. Bromiley and T. F. Torrance (Edinburgh: T & T Clark, 1957), pp. 179-254.

[20]See Catherine Mowry LaCugna, *God for Us: The Trinity and Christian Life* (New York: HarperCollins, 1991), p. 302.

[21]Fretheim, *Suffering of God*, p. 6.

[22]See the studies by Abraham J. Heschel, *The Prophets* (New York: Harper & Row, 1962), 2:48-58; and König, *Here Am I*, pp. 59-109.

[23]Dietrich Bonhoeffer, *Creation and Fall: A Theological Interpretation of Genesis 1—3* (London: SCM Press, 1959), p. 43.

[24]See Heschel, *Prophets*, 2:51-52; and Fretheim, *Suffering of God*, p. 11.

[25]See Gordon Kaufman, *Systematic Theology: A Historicist Perspective* (New York: Scribner's, 1968), pp. 120 n. 4, 302; John Macquarrie, *God-Talk: An Examination of the Language and Logic of Theology* (New York: Harper & Row, 1967), p. 213; J. I. Packer, *Evangelism and the Sovereignty of God* (Chicago: InterVarsity Press, 1967), p. 24; and Geoffrey W. Bromiley, "Providence," in *International Standard Bible Encyclopedia*, ed. Geoffrey W. Bromiley, rev. ed. (Grand Rapids, Mich.: Eerdmans, 1986), 3:1021.

[26]See Barth, *Church Dogmatics*, 2/1, pp. 286-87; and G. C. Berkouwer, *The Providence of God*, trans. Lewis Smedes (Grand Rapids, Mich.: Eerdmans, 1952), p. 209.

[27]More on this in 3.12.

[28]Herman Bavinck, *The Doctrine of God*, trans. William Hendriksen (Grand Rapids, Mich.: Baker, 1951), pp. 85-98, has a very helpful discussion of this point. See also Barth, *Church Dogmatics* 2/1, pp. 222, 265; Eberhard Jüngel, *God as the Mystery of the World*, trans. Darrell L. Gruder (Grand Rapids, Mich.: Eerdmans, 1983), pp. 258-60; Berkouwer, *Providence of God*, p. 73; and G. Ernest Wright, *The Challenge of Israel's Faith* (Chicago: University of Chicago Press, 1944), pp. 66-67.

[29]Bavinck, *Doctrine of God*, pp. 86, 92. Unfortunately, he also claims that Scripture, though giving us a true knowledge of God, does not reveal who God is in himself since God is "anonymous"—a claim Bavinck cannot possibly know.

[30]Helpful here is König, *Here Am I*, pp. 72-84.

[31]For more on these, see Gary Alan Long, "Dead or Alive? Literality and God-Metaphors in the Hebrew Bible," *Journal of the American Academy of Religion* 62, no. 2 (1994): 521-23; and Geoffrey W. Bromiley, "Anthropomorphism," in *International Standard Bible Encyclopedia*, 1:136-37. Nelly Stienstra, *YHWH Is the Husband of His People: Analysis of a Biblical Metaphor with Special Reference to Translation* (Kampen, Netherlands: Kok Pharos, 1993), pp. 55-59, distinguishes between literal and metaphorical anthropomorphisms. Metaphorical anthropomorphisms depict God in roles that he obviously cannot perform literally, such as being the husband or father of Israel. The biblical writers understood that they were speaking metaphorically in such cases about the kind of relationship that existed between God and Israel. Literal anthropomorphisms occur primarily in Genesis and Exodus. God is depicted as walking and calling out to Adam (Gen 3), visiting Abraham as one of three men and declaring that he has come down to investigate the outcry from Sodom to see just what is the case (Gen 18), wrestling with Jacob (Gen 32) and standing in front of Moses, Aaron and the elders, who actually "see God" (Ex 24:9-11).

[32]See Charles Hartshorne and William Reese, eds., *Philosophers Speak of God* (Chicago: University of Chicago Press, 1953), p. 416.

[33]König, *Here Am I*, p. 111.

[34]Thomas Aquinas, *Summa Theologica*, ed. Anton C. Pegis, 2 vols. (New York: Random House, 1945), 1. Q13. A1.

[35]Hillary of Poitiers *On the Trinity* 4.14, in *Nicene and Post-Nicene Fathers*, ed. Philip Schaff, 2nd series (Grand Rapids, Mich.: Eerdmans, 1983), 9:75.

[36]Language serves as an intermediary for God, and if it represents God then we must think *(de dicto)* of God sharing some of the same characteristics of reference that we experience. When I say the words of the Bible depict what God is really like, I do not mean that my knowledge of God is direct or complete. But I do want to say that we have no basis for claiming that the true being of God *(theologia)* is any different from the revealed God *(oikonomia)*.

[37]John Calvin is here discussing Isaiah 40:18. See *The Commentaries of John Calvin on the Old Testament* (Edinburgh: Calvin Translation Society, 1843-1848), 15:223, and Calvin, *Institutes of the Christian Religion*, ed. John T. McNeill (Philadelphia: Westminster, 1960), 1.13.21.

[38]The notion of a shared context is insightfully discussed by Frank G. Kirkpatrick, *Together Bound: God, History and the Religious Community* (New York: Oxford University Press, 1994).

[39]I owe this insight to my colleague Dean Fredrikson.

[40]Fretheim, *Suffering of God*, p. 40.

[41]Brian Hebblethwaite, "Some Reflections on Predestination, Providence and Divine Foreknowledge," *Religious Studies* 15, no. 4 (1979): 436 (italics mine).

[42]Macquarrie, *God-Talk*, pp. 220-21.

[43]If one suggests that there is an infinite difference between the analogates when speaking of God and humanity, then the doctrine of analogy fails to give us any knowledge of God. See Kirkpatrick, *Together Bound*, pp. 40-41. Jüngel, *God as the Mystery*, pp. 260-61, claims that the doctrine of analogy was developed to abrogate the scandal of anthropomorphism. Vincent Brümmer, *Speaking of a Personal God: An Essay in Philosophical Theology* (New York: Cambridge University Press, 1992), pp. 43-51, provides some further substantive criticisms of the doctrine of analogy.

[44]Douglas Kelly chides me for taking some of the biblical descriptions of God univocally. What an irony that a conservative evangelical theologian criticizes me for taking Scripture in its evident sense! Kelly, however, seems to believe that terms such as "infinite" and "uncreated being" are used univocally of God. Kelly sounds just like Gordon Kaufman when he says theologians should not "limit the infinite God by what they are able to understand." See his "Afraid of Infinitude," *Christianity Today* 39, no. 1 (1995): 32-33.

[45]Aquinas *Summa Theologica* 1. Q13. A3.

[46]Even the Christian Platonist Origen argued against the claim put forth by Celsus that "God" must be a totally ineffable deity. Origen admits that we do not know God exhaustively but points out that we do not even know how to express "the sweetness of a date" exhaustively. Moreover, he claims we know positive things about God because God gives us the grace to do so. See his *Contra Celsus* 6.65, in *The Ante-Nicene Fathers*, trans. Alexander Roberts and James Donaldson (New York: Scribner's, 1913).

[47]Stephen Davis, for example, uses it in this way. He states explicitly that he is not claiming God to be "unlimited" in an absolute sense, since that would be incoherent. See his "Why God Must Be Unlimited," in *Concepts of the Ultimate: Philosophical Perspectives on the Nature of the Divine*, ed. Linda J. Tessier (New York: St. Martin's, 1989), pp. 3-22.

[48]See Swinburne, *Coherence of Theism*, pp. 51-87; Swinburne cites Scotus and Ockham on pages 74-76; George Berkeley, *Alciphron* 4.21, in *Berkeley: Essay, Principles, Dialogues*, ed. Mary Calkins (New York: Charles Scribner's Sons, 1929); William Alston, "Can We Speak Literally of God?" in *Divine Nature and Human Language* (Ithaca, N.Y.: Cornell University Press, 1989), pp. 39-63; Thomas Tracy, *God, Action and Embodiment* (Grand Rapids, Mich.: Eerdmans, 1984), p. 152; and Paul Helm, "The Role of Logic in Biblical Interpretation," in *Hermeneutics, Inerrancy and the Bible*, ed. Earl Radmacher and Robert Preus (Grand Rapids, Mich.: Zondervan, 1984), p. 853.

[49]Moreover, there is something that is literally true of God's relationship with us communicated by the richness of the metaphors. Metaphors embrace and do not rule out literalness in the sense that they do tell us something about their subject. However, affirming univocity does not commit us to the "picture theory" of meaning according to which one word refers to one empirical referent.

[50]See Frederick Ferré, "In Praise of Anthropomorphism," in *God in Language*, ed. Robert Scharlemann and Gilbert Ogutu (New York: Paragon House, 1987), pp. 182-93.

[51]The history of this quest for a priori knowledge (the *dignum Deo*) by which humans determine what the divine nature must be like is documented in my "Historical

Considerations," in *The Openness of God: A Biblical Challenge to the Traditional Understanding of God,* by Clark Pinnock et al. (Downers Grove, Ill.: InterVarsity Press, 1994).

[52]Whether Plato believed we could know the essence of the Forms is a matter of debate. Middle Platonism held that this was impossible by reason but was possible by mystical encounter.

[53]Immanuel Kant, "Critique of All Theology Based upon Speculative Principles of Reason," in *Critique of Pure Reason,* trans. Norman Kemp Smith (London: Macmillan, 1933), p. A640.

[54]See Gordon Kaufman's *In the Face of Mystery: A Constructive Theology* (Cambridge: Harvard University Press, 1993); *Theological Imagination: Constructing the Concept of God* (Philadelphia: Westminster, 1981); and *God the Problem* (Cambridge: Harvard University Press, 1972).

[55]John Hick, *An Interpretation of Religion: Human Responses to the Transcendent* (New Haven: Yale University Press, 1989). Curiously, for Hick the various deities of the religions (Yahweh, Allah, heavenly Father, etc.) are "finite" manifestations of the infinite Real. If so, those who actually participate in worshiping these deities are worshiping finite beings. The only beings "available" for worship are, according to Hick, finite.

[56]Cited in Kirkpatrick, *Together Bound,* p. 46.

[57]Paul Knitter accuses anyone who worships Jesus as the unsurpassable revelation of God of being an idolater, since Jesus is "finite." Given his definition of idolatry, I concede that I commit idolatry. See my "Idolater Indeed!" in *The Uniqueness of Jesus: A Dialogue with Paul F. Knitter,* ed. Leonard Swidler and Paul Mojzes (Maryknoll, N.Y.: Orbis, 1997). See also Jüngel, *God as the Mystery,* pp. 232-45; and John B. Carman, *Majesty and Meekness: A Comparative Study of Contrast and Harmony in the Concept of God* (Grand Rapids, Mich.: Eerdmans, 1994), p. 256.

[58]See Thomas Morris, *Our Idea of God: An Introduction to Philosophical Theology* (Notre Dame, Ind.: University of Notre Dame Press, 1991), p. 20.

[59]Søren Kierkegaard, *Philosophical Fragments,* trans. Howard Hong and Edna Hong (Princeton: Princeton University Press, 1985), p. 45.

[60]See Brümmer, *Speaking of a Personal God,* p. 41; and Stephen Davis, *Logic and the Nature of God* (Grand Rapids, Mich.: Eerdmans, 1983), p. 142.

[61]Hume, *Dialogues Concerning Natural Religion,* p. 158, asserts that religious believers who maintain the absolute incomprehensibility of God do not differ from skeptics or atheists.

[62]Donald G. Bloesch, *God the Almighty: Power, Wisdom, Holiness, Love,* Christian Foundations (Downers Grove, Ill.: InterVarsity Press, 1995), p. 53.

[63]Feuerbach, *Essence of Christianity,* p. 16.

[64]McFague, *Models of God,* p. 39.

[65]Kierkegaard, *Philosophical Fragments,* p. 37. For Kierkegaard the "absolute paradox" of the incarnation is not a logical contradiction, though it does go against our preconceived notions of what it means to be God. He is often misunderstood on this point and is thought to be an irrationalist instead of simply one who claimed that we cannot escape our conditionedness to know God. See C. Stephen Evans, *Passionate Reason: Making Sense of Kierkegaard's Philosophical Fragments* (Bloomington: Indiana University Press, 1992), pp. 96-107.

[66]Kirkpatrick, *Together Bound,* p. 23. He adds that our speculation about the ontologically transcendent tells us more about ourselves than about whether it really exists (p. 47). Mathematicians have attempted to arrive at the set of all sets. See Timothy J. Pennings, "Infinity and the Absolute: Insights into Our World, Our Faith and Ourselves," *Christian Scholar's Review* 23, no. 2 (1993): 159-80.

[67]Brümmer, *Speaking of a Personal God,* p. 38.

[68]On the subjectivism of Hick, see Paul R. Eddy, "Religious Pluralism and the Divine: Another Look at John Hick's Neo-Kantian Proposal," *Religious Studies* 30 (1994): 467-78.

[69]Kirkpatrick, *Together Bound,* p. 31, argues that the "principle of sufficient reason" is the

motive behind this move.

[70]Feuerbach, *Essence of Christianity,* pp. 14-15.

[71]Concepts such as omniscience and omnipotence are not then wholly unqualified concepts of infinity, since to affirm unlimited knowledge is to claim that God has the property of having knowledge. For more on the concept of divine limitation, see 6.6.

[72]Again, this does not mean that we could not use the terms *infinite* or *unlimited* with respect to God, but we would do so in a qualified sense in keeping with the Christian tradition rather than in the absolute sense of Hick and Kaufman.

[73]See the excellent essay by Michael Williams, "Crossing Lessing's Ditch," in *God and Man: Perspectives on Christianity in the Twentieth Century,* ed. Michael Bauman (Hillsdale, Mich.: Hillsdale College Press, 1995), pp. 103-26; and David Clines, "Yahweh and the God of Christian Theology," *Theology* 83 (1980): 323-30.

[74]In the debate over religious pluralism, the universal and the particular can be held together. See Clark Pinnock, *A Wideness in God's Mercy: The Finality of Jesus Christ in a World of Religions* (Grand Rapids, Mich.: Zondervan, 1992). The "wider hope" asserts that Jesus is both the final (particular) and universal Savior. For the various expressions of the wider hope, see part three of my *No Other Name: An Investigation into the Destiny of the Unevangelized* (Grand Rapids, Mich.: Eerdmans, 1992).

[75]See the discussion in 3.12.

[76]Though I do not rule out natural theology per se, I believe it has often been misused in reading the biblical narrative in order to strain out certain understandings of God thought to be inappropriate by the one using the strainer. In my opinion, many of these elements should not have been filtered out because they are, in fact, true of the nature of God. At times, the concept of Absolute Being has usurped the God of Jesus Christ, constraining in negative ways what the gospel was allowed to say. I acknowledge that our background beliefs (including natural theology) come into play when we read the biblical text. For instance, we no longer take the biblical references to a geocentric solar system in a straightforward way. Nonetheless, I think that those working from the concept of the Most Perfect Being have often been too quick to believe that they are correct in their intuitions regarding perfection and so too ready to interpret the biblical text in light of them. Since I see the biblical narrative as entailing a personal God entering into give-and-take relations with human persons, any natural theology that contradicts this must be judged faulty. A more careful dialogical relationship between the biblical text and our background beliefs is needed lest we throw the baby out with the bath water. Helpful here is Nicholas Wolterstorff's *Divine Discourse: Philosophical Reflections on the Claim That God Speaks* (New York: Cambridge University Press, 1995), pp. 206-18.

[77]Calvin *Institutes* 1.13.1.

[78]Robert Sokolowski, *The God of Faith and Reason: Foundations of Christian Theology* (Notre Dame, Ind.: University of Notre Dame Press, 1982). This is a fine book on the importance of the distinction between Creator and creature. Also helpful is David B. Burrell's *Freedom and Creation in Three Traditions* (Notre Dame, Ind.: University of Notre Dame Press, 1993), which discusses this distinction in Judaism, Christianity and Islam. Burrell and Sokolowski defend the notions of God's uniqueness and free creation and are particularly helpful in criticizing the Greek philosophical conceptions of the divine, according to which God is incapable of being without the world. God is then simply the highest being among other beings. Though I agree, I add that *we* cannot but think of God as a being.

[79]See Keith Ward, *Rational Theology and the Creativity of God* (New York: Pilgrim, 1982), p. 62.

[80]See Pennings, "Infinity and the Absolute," pp. 178-79.

[81]Here I am making a *de dicto* (what can be said on the basis of the Christian faith) rather than a *de re* (what can be said apart from the faith) claim. This distinction is more fully developed in 6.4.5.

[82]J. I. Packer, "Paradox in Theology," in *New Dictionary of Theology*, ed. Sinclair Ferguson, David Wright and J. I. Packer (Downers Grove, Ill.: InterVarsity Press, 1988), p. 491. Perhaps another example occurs in 1 Samuel 15. Samuel declares that Yahweh changed his mind about Saul's being king (15:11, 35) and also says that God will not change his mind (15:29). But this is only an antinomy for those who believe it impossible for God to change his mind. For those who believe God can and does change his mind, verse 29 means that God is not going to change his mind in this particular situation regarding Saul.

[83]Packer, *Evangelism and the Sovereignty of God*, p. 24.

[84]Donald Carson, *Divine Sovereignty and Human Responsibility: Biblical Perspectives in Tension*, 2nd ed. (Grand Rapids, Mich.: Baker, 1994), p. 218. Carson goes on to say that he does not believe the two are actually self-contradictory. If not, where is the problem?

[85]Packer, *Evangelism and the Sovereignty of God*, p. 24. One wonders why we shall be able to understand them in heaven. Will we then escape the boundaries? Will God grant us a different logic? These are possibilities, but what reason do we have to expect them?

[86]For further discussion, see David Basinger, "Biblical Paradox: Does Revelation Challenge Logic?" *Journal of the Evangelical Theological Society* 30, no. 2 (1987): 205-13; and Paul Helm, *The Providence of God*, Contours of Christian Theology (Downers Grove, Ill.: InterVarsity Press, 1994), pp. 61-66.

[87]Thomas Morris argues that the doctrines of the Trinity and the Incarnation are not, in fact, contradictory. See his *The Logic of God Incarnate* (Ithaca, N.Y.: Cornell University Press, 1986).

[88]See G. R. Evans, *The Language and Logic of the Bible: The Earlier Middle Ages* (New York: Cambridge University Press, 1984), p. 126.

[89]David Ciocchi's "Reconciling Divine Sovereignty and Human Freedom," *Journal of the Evangelical Theological Society* 37, no. 3 (1994): 395-412, correctly points out another problem with the appeal to antinomy: if the antinomy is "intelligible," then there can be no reason to affirm that a logical reconciliation is impossible. In this regard I find Donald Bloesch's discussion of the divine sovereignty/human freedom issue extremely frustrating: (1) he asserts that they are only apparently contradictory but fails to show that they are not —he refuses to carefully define his terms; (2) he claims that God's logic is not the same as our logic without demonstrating how *he* knows this to be the case; and (3) he says that no final rational solution of this issue is possible. See Bloesch's *God the Almighty*.

[90]Helm, "The Role of Logic in Biblical Interpretation," p. 843.

[91]Davis, *Logic and the Nature of God*, p. 16.

[92]Some evangelicals reject the use of antinomies. See, for example, Carl F. H. Henry, *God, Revelation and Authority* (Waco, Tex.: Word, 1976): 4:225-44; and Arthur Holmes, *All Truth Is God's Truth* (Grand Rapids, Mich.: Eerdmans, 1977), pp. 87-90.

Chapter 3: Old Testament Materials for a Relational View of Providence Involving Risk

[1]See Anna Case-Winters, *God's Power: Traditional Understandings and Contemporary Challenges* (Louisville, Ky.: Westminster/John Knox, 1990); and my "God as Personal," in *The Grace of God, the Will of Man*, ed. Clark Pinnock (Grand Rapids, Mich.: Zondervan, 1989), pp. 167-78.

[2]Vincent Brümmer, *The Model of Love: A Study in Philosophical Theology* (Cambridge: Cambridge University Press, 1993), p. 33. This idea is eloquently discussed by Colin Gunton, *The One, the Three and the Many: God, Creation and the Culture of Modernity*, 1992 Bampton Lectures (New York: Cambridge University Press, 1993).

[3]This is the thesis of Robert W. Jenson's *The Triune Identity* (Philadelphia: Fortress, 1982).

[4]For discussion, see Samuel E. Balentine, *Prayer in the Hebrew Bible: The Drama of Divine-Human Dialogue*, Overtures to Biblical Theology (Minneapolis: Augsburg Fortress, 1993), pp. 225-59.

[5]Douglas A. Knight identifies six different cosmogonies in the Hebrew Bible and compares

them with others in the ancient Near East in his "Cosmogony and Order in the Hebrew Tradition," in *Cosmogony and Ethical Order: New Studies in Comparative Ethics*, ed. Robin Lovin and Frank Reynolds (Chicago: University of Chicago Press, 1985), pp. 133-57.
[6]On the variety of interpretations and the validity of this understanding, see Victor P. Hamilton, *The Book of Genesis: Chapters 1—17*, New International Commentary on the Old Testament (Grand Rapids, Mich.: Eerdmans, 1990), pp. 103-17; Gordon J. Wenham, *Genesis 1-15*, Word Biblical Commentary (Waco, Tex.: Word, 1987), pp. 11-17, 36-38; and Bruce Waltke, "The Creation Account in Gen. 1:1-3," *Bibliotheca Sacra* 132 (1975): 25-36, 136-44, 216-28, 327-42.
[7]See Wolfhart Pannenberg, *Basic Questions in Theology*, trans. George H. Kehm (Philadelphia: Westminster, 1983), 2:138, 171.
[8]A danger of equating the omnipotent power of God's creative act with an omnipotent rule of providence is that it may mislead us into concluding that omnipotence must always get its way, never encountering any serious opposition to the divine rule. This results in a reading of the Old Testament that downplays the fragility of creation and its vulnerability to what we experience as chaos. One might come away with the impression from Genesis 1 that, because of God's almightiness, everything works out exactly as God desires, which is why one must read "the rest of the story."
[9]See Jon D. Levenson, *Creation and the Persistence of Evil: The Jewish Drama of Divine Omnipotence*, updated ed. (Princeton: Princeton University Press, 1994); and Adriö König, *New and Greater Things: Re-evaluating the Biblical Message on Creation*, trans. D. Roy Briggs (Pretoria: University of South Africa, 1988). Both authors say that the Hebrew Bible affirms both views, but König does more with ex nihilo. Both writers agree that there is no such thing as an absolute nothing in Hebrew thought.
[10]Even the evangelical Waltke, in "The Creation Account" (p. 338), admits that Genesis 1 does not teach ex nihilo nor that God created these forces.
[11]Levenson, *Creation and the Persistence of Evil*, p. 17.
[12]See Bernhard W. Anderson, "The Kingdom, the Power and the Glory," *Theology Today* 53, no. 1 (1966): 6-8.
[13]Both Levenson, *Creation and the Persistence of Evil*, and König, *New and Greater Things*, maintain that it was not the concern of biblical writers to discuss the abstract issue of origins. Rather, says König, conflict texts provide comfort and hope for Israelites who are suffering (p. 77). If God overcame chaos in the past, then God can do it again. He rejects as "contrived" (without any stated reasons) the view that God created the chaotic forces that subsequently disobeyed him (p. 120). Yet König seems to allow for this very reading when he says that certain biblical writers would naturally have assumed that God created these forces, which, after creation, became inimical toward God (pp. 72, 77). König fears, rightfully, that important insights are lost when the conflict texts are ignored and ex nihilo is made *the* biblical view. I believe, however, that ex nihilo may be affirmed regarding the question of origins without discarding the significance of the conflict-and-victory motif.
[14]Levenson believes that the priestly sources sanitized the myth of the *Chaoskampf* but could not completely rid the Hebrew Bible of "snippets" that refer to it.
[15]Levenson, *Creation and the Persistence of Evil*, p. 24.
[16]König's *New and Greater Things* is very helpful in connecting the doctrines of creation and redemption. For a study of how the concept of order in the creation and the threat of disorder was expressed in Israel's faith, see Rolf Knierim, "Cosmos and History in Israel's Theology," *Horizons in Biblical Theology* 3 (1981): 59-123.
[17]Levenson, *Creation and the Persistence of Evil*, p. xvi.
[18]For an instructive comparison of these stories, see Nahum Sarna, *Understanding Genesis* (New York: Schocken, 1970), pp. 1-18.
[19]For this interesting comparison, see Levenson, *Creation and the Persistence of Evil*, pp. 140-48; and König, *New and Greater Things*, pp. 31, 76.

[20]One may say that God creates order out of chaos, although not all chaos is removed. On how God both brings order out of chaos and chaos out of order, see D. J. Bartholomew, *God of Chance* (London: SCM Press, 1984).

[21]Emil Brunner, *Christian Doctrine of God*, trans. Olive Wyon (Philadelphia: Westminster, 1949), p. 147.

[22]Thomas Morris, *Our Idea of God: An Introduction to Philosophical Theology* (Notre Dame, Ind.: University of Notre Dame Press, 1991), pp. 28-45, believes that Perfect Being theology, when buttressed by creational theology and biblical theology, can arrive at the best concept of God. He acknowledges that "the method of perfect being theology needs a revelational control. But it's also true that perfect being theology itself can act as an interpretive constraint on how we read the Bible" (p. 43). We should not, he says, ascribe to God "any limitations *which imply imperfection*" (p. 85, emphasis his). In my opinion, the classical philosophical conception of God has far too often been allowed to overturn the biblical text in favor of what we deem it fitting for God to be *(dignum Deo)*. See my "Historical Considerations," in *The Openness of God: A Biblical Challenge to the Traditional Understanding of God*, by Clark Pinnock et al. (Downers Grove, Ill.: InterVarsity Press, 1994), pp. 59-100.

[23]The notions of static perfection and uniformity of divine action have wreaked havoc on the doctrine of providence.

[24]On the variety of interpretations of this phrase, see Hamilton, *Book of Genesis*, pp. 132-34. Levenson, *Creation and the Persistence of Evil*, p. 5, believes it refers to the divine assembly mentioned elsewhere in the Hebrew Bible where it "played an active role and made fresh proposals to God, who nonetheless retained the final say."

[25]Terence Fretheim, *The Book of Genesis*, The New Interpreter's Bible (Nashville: Abingdon, 1994), 1:335.

[26]Terence Fretheim, "Creator, Creature and Co-creation in Genesis 1—2," *Word and World*, supp. 1 (1992): 13. This is a very helpful study on God's entering into responsive relationships with his creatures.

[27]On the interpretation of the image of God, see Hamilton, *Book of Genesis*, pp. 134-40, 145-47.

[28]Jean-Jacques Suurmond, *Word and Spirit at Play: Towards a Charismatic Theology* (Grand Rapids, Mich.: Eerdmans, 1994), maintains that both humans and God are at "play" within the boundaries God has created.

[29]Levenson, *Creation and the Persistence of Evil*, p. 141. He argues that the common notion that the covenant was between two parties who are equally free to assent and dissent is the product of Western political thought, for both Adam and Israel already owe their freedom to God (pp. 146-47).

[30]A meticulous providence where everything proceeds just as God wants has a very difficult time accounting for this (without impugning God's goodness).

[31]John Sailhamer emphasizes that these verses are about trusting God and suggests that in verse 15 God placed humans in the garden to "worship and obey" rather than to till the garden. See his *Genesis*, Expositor's Bible Commentary 2, ed. Frank Gaebelein (Grand Rapids, Mich.: Zondervan, 1990), p. 45.

[32]For an interesting discussion that utilizes testing to argue for a theodicy without blame, see Mark S. McLeod, "Religious Plurality and Realist Christianity: Idolatry and the Testing of One's Faith," *Faith and Philosophy* 11, no. 2 (1994): 224-41. McLeod follows Marilyn McCord Adams in arguing that Genesis 3 involves the sin of the failure to live within our boundaries (an ontological concept) rather than a sin committed in full knowledge of good and evil (a moral concept).

[33]Wenham, *Genesis 1—15*, p. 73.

[34]Douglas John Hall, *God and Human Suffering: An Exercise in the Theology of the Cross* (Minneapolis: Augsburg, 1986), p. 71.

[35]I prefer this to Barth's "impossible possibility," as I do not find such language illuminating.
[36]Paul S. Fiddes, *The Creative Suffering of God* (New York: Oxford University Press, 1988), p. 220. Fiddes is responding to those who claim that God could not be "taken by surprise" or have to adjust his plans in any way. If human sin was planned by God, then it must somehow be a necessity in life (perhaps as an instrument for moral growth).
[37]It does not mean "you shall become mortal," for they were already mortal. Nor does it mean they were "doomed" to die. For discussion of the meaning of death in this passage, see Fretheim, *Book of Genesis*, p. 352; Hamilton, *Book of Genesis*, pp. 172-74; and Wenham, *Genesis 1—17*, pp. 67-18, 73-75, 88-89.
[38]See Hamilton, *Book of Genesis*, p. 173.
[39]This interpretation fits with the context, since the next two speeches to the woman and the man contain both judgment and promised blessings. Eve will have pain but will be blessed with children. Adam will suffer toil but will be blessed with food. Hence, the speech to the serpent probably does also. On this, see Hamilton, *Book of Genesis*, pp. 198-200. On the issue of a *protoevangelium*, see the discussion and bibliography in Wenham, *Genesis 1—15*, pp. 79-81.
[40]Irenaeus said that God did this so that they would not exist forever in sin and so that they might be redeemed. See his *Against Heresies* 3.23.6, in *The Ante-Nicene Fathers*, translated by Alexander Roberts and James Donaldson (New York: Christian Literature Company, 1896).
[41]König, *New and Greater Things*, p. 77.
[42]In fundamental opposition to this interpretation is Richard Creel, *Divine Impassibility: An Essay in Philosophical Theology* (Cambridge: Cambridge University Press, 1986), pp. 141-46, who holds that a mature lover does not grieve if he is rejected by the free choice of another. For him, God is emotionally impassible and remains perfectly happy whether we choose for or against his kingdom.
[43]Philip Yancey, *Disappointment with God: Three Questions No One Asks Aloud* (Grand Rapids, Mich.: Zondervan, 1988), pp. 63-64. It should be noted that Yancey qualifies the divine learning to mean the taking on of new experiences, since he affirms divine timelessness.
[44]Fretheim, *Book of Genesis*, p. 389.
[45]It has been suggested that the sign of the rainbow symbolizes an archery bow pointing toward God. If so, then this is self-imprecatory on God's part. See J. Richard Middleton and Brian J. Walsh, *Truth Is Stranger Than It Used to Be: Biblical Faith in a Postmodern Age* (Downers Grove, Ill.: InterVarsity Press, 1995), p. 148.
[46]YHWH actually changes his mind twice in this story, once to destroy and then to never again destroy (6:5-7; 8:21). Both reversals are based on the *same* data: humans are sinful.
[47]See Hamilton, *Book of Genesis*, p. 429.
[48]See Fretheim, *Book of Genesis*, pp. 446-47, 449.
[49]Ibid., pp. 451-52.
[50]See Walter Brueggemann, *Genesis*, Interpretation (Atlanta: John Knox, 1982), p. 159.
[51]For a thorough and enlightening discussion of this chapter, see Fretheim, *Book of Genesis*, pp. 494-501.
[52]Brueggemann, *Genesis*, p. 187.
[53]On the Talmudic and medieval discussion of this verse, see Seymour Feldman, "The Binding of Isaac: A Test-Case of Divine Foreknowledge," in *Divine Omniscience and Omnipotence in Medieval Philosophy: Islamic, Jewish and Christian Perspectives*, ed. Tamar Rudavsky (Boston: Reidel, 1985), pp. 105-33.
[54]In chapter six I will seek to demonstrate that one view of divine foreknowledge—incrementally obtained—would interpret the text in the same way I have here (see 6.5).
[55]R. W. L. Moberly, "The Earliest Commentary on the Akedah," *Vetus Testamentum* 38, no. 3 (1988): 320.
[56]Balentine, *Prayer in the Hebrew Bible*, p. 38.

[57]Terence Fretheim, "Prayer in the Old Testament: Creating Space in the World for God," in *A Primer on Prayer,* ed. Paul Sponheim (Philadelphia: Fortress, 1988), p. 57.

[58]See Fretheim, *Book of Genesis,* pp. 565-70; and Balentine, *Prayer in the Hebrew Bible,* pp. 64-71. Some scholars see in this story (and others) a "demonic" side of God. See, for instance, Jack Miles, *God: A Biography* (New York: Knopf, 1995). For a careful refutation of this theory regarding Genesis 32 and other texts, see Fredrik Lindström, *God and the Origin of Evil: A Contextual Analysis of Alleged Monistic Evidence in the Old Testament,* trans. Frederick H. Cryer (Lund: CWK Gleerup, 1983). See also p. 298, n. 170, and p. 317, n. 58, in this book.

[59]Yet even the risk model affirms that God can unilaterally intervene in human affairs if he so decides.

[60]Fretheim, *Book of Genesis,* p. 646.

[61]A risk-free reading would say that God works through secondary causes and so is not directly responsible for evil. More on this in 6.4.

[62]For a helpful discussion of God's being "with" the biblical characters, see Donald E. Gowan, *Theology in Exodus: Biblical Theology in the Form of a Commentary* (Louisville, Ky.: Westminster John Knox, 1994), pp. 54-75. He points out that this expression usually occurs in times of danger.

[63]See Roy L. Honeycutt, *Exodus,* Broadman Bible Commentary 1 (Nashville: Broadman, 1969), p. 325.

[64]See H. L. Ellison, *Exodus,* Daily Study Bible (Philadelphia: Westminster, 1982), p. 20.

[65]See Terence Fretheim, *Exodus,* Interpretation (Louisville, Ky.: John Knox, 1991), p. 65.

[66]Brevard Childs, *The Book of Exodus,* Old Testament Library (Philadelphia: Westminster, 1974), p. 77.

[67]Walter Brueggemann, *The Book of Exodus,* New Interpreter's Bible 1 (Nashville: Abingdon, 1994), p. 716.

[68]See Terence Fretheim, *The Suffering of God: An Old Testament Perspective,* Overtures to Biblical Theology (Philadelphia: Fortress, 1984), pp. 47-49.

[69]On the nature of divine sovereignty in Exodus, see Terence Fretheim, "Suffering God and Sovereign God in Exodus: A Collision of Images," *Horizons in Biblical Theology* 11, no. 2 (1989): 31-56.

[70]For bibliography on hardening, see Walter Kaiser Jr., *Towards an Old Testament Ethics* (Grand Rapids, Mich.: Zondervan, 1983), p. 253. Robert B. Chisholm Jr., "Divine Hardening in the Old Testament," *Bibliotheca Sacra* 153 (October 1996): 410-34, provides an overview of the positions as well as a helpful structural analysis of the hardening narratives.

[71]The word *hazaq* is usually translated by the words *encourage* or *strengthen* in the rest of the Old Testament. If that were done with the Pharaoh text, it is doubtful that a deterministic reading would prevail. See Roger T. Forster and V. Paul Marston, *God's Strategy in Human History* (Minneapolis: Bethany House, 1983), pp. 155-77.

[72]Fretheim, *Exodus,* p. 97. The following discussion is indebted to Fretheim's excellent study (pp. 96-103).

[73]Chisholm, "Divine Hardening," p. 420 n. 31, agrees with Fretheim that a negative decision is not the only one available to Pharaoh. However, he maintains that Yahweh had complete foreknowledge of which decision Pharaoh would make and that this does not render God's offer ingenuine. Chisholm's position, however, is incoherent unless he assumes something like molinism or "incremental simple foreknowledge," which I explain in 6.5.

[74]Gowan, *Theology in Exodus,* p. 137.

[75]On the divine hardening of people for redemptive purposes, see Abraham J. Heschel, *The Prophets* (New York: Harper & Row, 1962), 1:191-2.

[76]On Exodus 12:12, see Nahum Sarna, *Exploring Exodus* (New York: Schocken, 1987), pp. 78-80; and John J. Davis, *Moses and the Gods of Egypt* (Winona Lake, Ind.: BMH Books, 1971), pp. 86-129.

[77]Even when Yahweh gives up on Pharaoh and brings about the destruction of his army,

God is still attempting to get the Egyptian people to know that he is Yahweh (Ex 14:4).
[78]Gowan, *Theology in Exodus,* p. 139.
[79]See Fretheim, "Suffering God and Sovereign God in Exodus," pp. 35-37.
[80]Sarna, *Exploring Exodus,* p. 134.
[81]On the eagle metaphor, see Walter Kaiser Jr., *Exodus,* Expositor's Bible Commentary, vol. 2, ed. Frank Gaebelein (Grand Rapids, Mich.: Zondervan, 1990), p. 415.
[82]Brueggemann, *Book of Exodus,* p. 834.
[83]See Walter Kaiser Jr., *Towards an Old Testament Theology* (Grand Rapids: Zondervan, 1978), pp. 93-94, 111, 130, 156-57.
[84]Walter Eichrodt, *Theology of the Old Testament,* trans. J. A. Baker, Old Testament Library (London: SCM Press, 1961), p. 37. Balentine claims that the majority of Old Testament theologies, including those of Eichrodt and Gerhard von Rad, are deficient on divine-human relationality. The relationship has been described in one-sided terms where divine solicitation of human input was regarded as unworthy of deity. See his *Prayer in the Hebrew Bible,* pp. 229-49.
[85]Adrio König, *Here Am I: A Believer's Reflection on God* (Grand Rapids, Mich.: Eerdmans, 1982), pp. 128-29.
[86]Levenson, *Creation and the Persistence of Evil,* p. xxx, says the aspect of divine dependence on the people has generally been missed.
[87]Jürgen Moltmann, *The Crucified God,* trans. R. A. Wilson and John Bowden (New York: Harper & Row, 1974), p. 271.
[88]More will be said on God's successes and failures in working with humans in the section on Acts 10—15 and Romans 9—11 in the next chapter.
[89]See Gowan, *Theology in Exodus,* pp. 217-43.
[90]Brueggemann, *The Book of Exodus,* p. 931.
[91]On these intercessory prayers of Moses, see Balentine, *Prayer in the Hebrew Bible,* pp. 135-39; and Patrick D. Miller, *They Cried to the Lord: The Form and Theology of Biblical Prayer* (Minneapolis: Fortress, 1994), pp. 270-74.
[92]Some conservative evangelicals reject this interpretation, claiming that Moses' prayer is simply the means by which God has foreordained to enact what God had already decided to do. According to this view, the change is entirely on the human side.
[93]On the ascription of evil to God in such prayers, see Balentine, *Prayer in the Hebrew Bible,* pp. 127-29.
[94]See Fretheim, "Prayer in the Old Testament," p. 60.
[95]Fretheim, *Exodus,* p. 287.
[96]U. Cassuto, *A Commentary on the Book of Exodus,* trans. Israel Abrahams (Jerusalem: Magnes, 1967), p. 433.
[97]On the significant changes between these verses and the earlier statement in 20:5, see Fretheim, *Exodus,* p. 302. Mercy and grace are clearly extended here!
[98]Patrick D. Miller, "Prayer as Persuasion: The Rhetoric and Intention of Prayer," in Miller's *They Cried to the Lord.* First published in *Word and World* 13, no. 4 (1993): 361-62.
[99]Gowan, *Theology in Exodus,* pp. 231-32.
[100]Balentine, *Prayer in the Hebrew Bible,* pp. 268-69. Another interesting instance of this is the case of Hannah and her prayer for a son in 1 Samuel 1. It does not seem that God was going to act on her behalf. But once she enters into an intense time of prayer with God, making a vow where *she* predestines her son to be a champion for Yahweh, Yahweh responds to her request. I believe her vow opened up new possibilities for God in his relationship to Israel.
[101]See Lester J. Kuyper, "The Suffering and the Repentance of God," *Scottish Journal of Theology* 22 (1969): 257-77.
[102]W. Bingham Hunter holds that the destruction of all Israelites except Moses would involve breaking a divine promise. He understands Genesis 49:10, "the scepter shall not depart

from Judah," to be a messianic prediction. Since Moses is from the tribe of Levi, the Messiah could not have come from Judah had God destroyed that tribe. Hence, God did not change his mind. See Hunter's *The God Who Hears* (Downers Grove, Ill.: InterVarsity Press, 1986), p. 53. These remarks reflect a common evangelical understanding of prophecy whereby the future is set in concrete and all conditionality is ruled out. Regarding Genesis 49:10, see Fretheim, *Book of Genesis*, pp. 665 and 668, where he observes that this text is not a full-blown messianism. Evangelicals tend to read more into prophecy than is actually there. This is especially true concerning messianic prophecy, which is a late development in the Old Testament.

[103]See John Calvin, *Commentaries on the First Book of Moses*, trans. John King (Grand Rapids, Mich.: Eerdmans, 1948), pp. 1:248-49; and Calvin *Institutes of the Christian Religion* 1.17.12-14.

[104]Calvin *Institutes* 1.17.12.

[105]See ibid., 1.13.1. Reformed theologian James Daane, *The Freedom of God* (Grand Rapids, Mich.: Eerdmans, 1973), pp. 90-91, observes that decretal theologians have been interested only in those anthropomorphisms that imply an internal divine response to creatures. He claims that for decretal theology God is not personally affected by creatures and so God is not in a *personal* relationship with the world.

[106]Paul Helm, *The Providence of God*, Contours of Christian Theology (Downers Grove, Ill.: InterVarsity Press, 1994), pp. 54, 52.

[107]Norman L. Geisler, *Creating God in the Image of Man? The New Open View of God—Neotheism's Dangerous Drift* (Minneapolis: Bethany House, 1997), pp. 78, 89.

[108]Geisler, *Creating God in the Image of Man?*, pp. 90, 108.

[109]Bruce Ware, "An Evangelical Reformulation of the Doctrine of the Immutability of God," *Journal of the Evangelical Theological Society* 29, no. 4 (1986): 442.

[110]See 2.5.1.

[111]Evangelicals commonly assert that only "liberals" revise the Word of God in light of what is "acceptable" to human reason. But clearly evangelicals are not immune from this practice.

[112]For more on this "two-layered" approach to interpreting Scripture, see my "Historical Considerations," pp. 94-95.

[113]Calvin *Institutes* 1.17.12-13.

[114]Ibid., 1.13.21.

[115]I believe that Calvin is here following the long tradition of ruling out certain Scripture texts because they do not fit with a preconceived notion of what is fitting for God to be *(dignum Deo)*. See my "Historical Considerations." For a discussion of Calvin and some of the church fathers on divine accommodation, see Ford Lewis Battles, "God Was Accommodating Himself to Human Capacity," *Interpretation* 31, no. 1 (1977): 19-38. Unfortunately, Battles never inquires as to either *how* Calvin knows God has to accommodate himself or what criterion Calvin uses to elevate one biblical truth above another.

[116]I am not protesting the use of control beliefs but only want us to acknowledge, as Geisler does, which ones we are using. Regarding how to distinguish metaphorical from "literal" language about God in the Bible, Nicholas Wolterstorff makes some helpful suggestions in his *Divine Discourse: Philosophical Reflections on the Claim That God Speaks* (New York: Cambridge University Press, 1995), pp. 183-222. In brief, everything hinges on whether or not we come to the conviction that regarding an assertion of a particular biblical text God would not have intended to communicate this in a literal way. Such convictions will depend on the background beliefs of the interpreter and the particular tradition within which the interpreter operates. He acknowledges the problem that Scripture may become a "wax nose" that we shape to fit our own theological preunderstandings. Given our preunderstandings, there will be no easy way to settle all interpretive disputes—such as

the one highlighted here—but, says Wolterstorff, we can contend that not anything goes in the interpretation of Scripture (pp. 223-39).

[117]On this text, see Terence Fretheim, "Divine Foreknowledge, Divine Constancy and the Rejection of Saul's Kingship," *Catholic Biblical Quarterly* 47, no. 4 (1985): 595-602. Gowan, *Theology in Exodus*, p. 226, disagrees with Fretheim's explanation. Gowan claims that the texts on divine repentance (especially 1 Sam 15) are in tension with one another and cannot be reconciled.

[118]In all three instances the same Hebrew word *(nāham)* is used.

[119]Francis Beckwith seems to interpret Deuteronomy 18:21-22 in this way. Unfortunately, he does not address the case of Jonah or the case of Isaiah with Hezekiah. See his "Limited Omniscience and the Test for a Prophet: A Brief Philosophical Analysis," *Journal of the Evangelical Theological Society* 36, no. 3 (1993): 357-62.

[120]Many evangelicals believe that this expression connotes a definitive and unalterable divine utterance. The thinking behind this is the belief that if God says something but fails to do it, then God's word cannot be trusted.

[121]Fretheim, *Suffering of God*, p. 42. That past, present and future are real for God, see pages 40-44.

[122]For biblical documentation on change in God, see Richard Rice, "Biblical Support," in *The Openness of God: A Biblical Challenge to the Traditional Understanding of God*, by Clark Pinnock et al. (Downers Grove, Ill.: InterVarsity Press, 1994), pp. 22-50.

[123]See Fretheim, *Suffering of God*, pp. 1-12.

[124]See Terence Fretheim, "The Repentance of God: A Key to Evaluating Old Testament God-Talk," *Horizons in Biblical Theology* 10, no. 1 (1988): 47-70; Fretheim, "Divine Foreknowledge," pp. 595-602; and Fretheim, "The Repentance of God: A Study of Jeremiah 18:7-10," *Hebrew Annual Review* 11 (1987): 81-92. Also helpful is the study of *nhm* with God as subject in Francis I. Andersen and David Noel Freedman, *Amos: A New Translation with Introduction and Commentary*, The Anchor Bible 24a (New York: Doubleday, 1989): 638-79.

[125]On *niham* see H. Van Paunak, "A Semantic Survey of *NHM*," *Biblica* 56 (1975): 512-32.

[126]See also J. P. Hyatt, *Exodus*, New Century Bible Commentary (Grand Rapids, Mich.: Eerdmans, 1971), p. 307; Kaiser, *Exodus*, p. 479; and Anderson and Freedman, *Amos*, pp. 644-45.

[127]Heschel, *The Prophets*, 2:66.

[128]Fretheim, "The Repentance of God: A Key to Evaluating Old Testament God-Talk," p. 54.

[129]David Allen Hubbard, *Joel and Amos*, Tyndale Old Testament Commentaries (Downers Grove, Ill.: InterVarsity Press, 1989), pp. 35, 58.

[130]Fretheim, *Suffering of God*, pp. 45-59.

[131]R. K. McGregor Wright, *No Place for Sovereignty: What's Wrong with Freewill Theism* (Downers Grove, Ill.: InterVarsity Press, 1996), pp. 162-63, suggests three reasons why God would command sinners to do something he knows they cannot do: (1) to show them their spiritual incompetence; (2) to prompt them so that they "might" seek God's mercy; or (3) to bring judgment on them. Given Wright's theological determinism, the first two reasons make no sense because people cannot see their own spiritual incompetence unless God causes them to do so. Furthermore, what sense does it make to say they "might" seek God's mercy? This sounds as if the future is open, but it is not for Wright—given his no-risk model of divine sovereignty. If not, then it is difficult to see how he can escape the charge of conditional language being ingenuine. Brümmer points out that the Synod of Dort drew back from the sort of conclusions Wright makes that grace is conceptually or factually irresistible. See his *Speaking of a Personal God*, pp. 71-73.

[132]See Fretheim, *Book of Genesis*, pp. 521, 523, 538.

[133]Ibid., p. 601.

[134]Actually, the Roman authorities rescued Paul from the mob and they, not the Jewish authorities, bound him. Of course, one could argue that the prediction did come true in a

"general" sense. I agree, but those who affirm divine foreknowledge are the ones using such prophecies to claim God knows the future in detail. If so, then either God or the prophet cannot get the details straight.

[135]Personally, I believe the prophet in Acts was speaking in figures of speech and so was correct. The problem is for those who emphasize the "apologetic value of fulfilled prophecy" by claiming that the predictions in Scripture are all fulfilled with exacting detail. In my view some are and some are not. The openness model of divine omniscience can accommodate this by saying that some predictions are foreordained by God to come to pass (e.g., the destruction of Tyre, Ezek 28), whereas others are conditional or are simply what God thinks will happen based on his present knowledge (see 4.16 for more discussion). Proponents of exhaustive foreknowledge typically ignore such "problem" texts.

[136]I owe this insight to Greg Boyd.

[137]See Heschel, *The Prophets*, 2:58-59, 79-86; and my "Historical Considerations," pp. 69-80. For a survey of contemporary approaches to the relationship between divine love and wrath, see Fiddes, *The Creative Suffering of God*, pp. 21-25; and Donald G. Bloesch, *God the Almighty: Power, Wisdom, Holiness, Love*, Christian Foundations (Downers Grove, Ill.: InterVarsity Press, 1995), pp. 139-45.

[138]Heschel, *The Prophets*, 1:201.

[139]Ibid., 2:72.

[140]On divine grief, see Fretheim, *Suffering of God*, pp. 109-13.

[141]Heschel, *The Prophets*, 2:66.

[142]Ibid., 2:65.

[143]See Fretheim, *Exodus*, pp. 227, 302.

[144]On the development of this formula in the Old Testament and for further bibliography, see Gowan, *Theology in Exodus*, pp. 241-43, 283 n. 25.

[145]Fretheim, *Suffering of God*, pp. 61-65.

[146]See ibid., pp. 70-71.

[147]See Fredrik Lindström, *Suffering and Sin: Interpretations of Illness in the Individual Complaint Psalms*, trans. Michael McLamb (Stockholm: Almqvist & Wiksell, 1994); and Samuel E. Balentine, *The Hidden God: The Hiding Face of God in the Old Testament* (Oxford: Oxford University Press, 1983), pp. 45-79.

[148]See J. L. Crenshaw, "The Birth of Skepticism in Ancient Israel," in *The Divine Helmsman: Studies on God's Control of Human Events*, ed. J. L. Crenshaw and S. Sandmel (New York: KTAV, 1980), pp. 1-19. That questioning of God is early in the Old Testament is attested in Judges 6:13.

[149]Walter Brueggemann, "The Costly Loss of Lament," *Journal for the Study of the Old Testament* 36 (1986): 59.

[150]See Balentine, "The Lament Tradition: Holding to God Against God," in *Prayer in the Hebrew Bible*, pp. 146-98.

[151]For the placement of Habakkuk's prayers in the lament tradition, see Balentine, *Prayer in the Hebrew Bible*, pp. 183-89; and Miller, *They Cried to the Lord*, pp. 70-79. Balentine asserts that such questioning of God is risky because it destroys old worlds and builds new ones (pp. 292-95).

[152]The metaphor of potter and clay has, according to Louis Berkhof, played a dominant role in Calvinism. See his *Systematic Theology*, 3rd ed. (Grand Rapids, Mich.: Eerdmans, 1946), p. 120. Examples of those who cite these pancausality texts in order to claim that God's control of the details in history is total include Wright, *No Place for Sovereignty*, pp. 181-96; John Piper, "Are There Two Wills in God?" in *The Grace of God, the Bondage of the Will*, ed. Thomas Schreiner and Bruce Ware (Grand Rapids, Mich.: Baker, 1995), 1:119-23; and Jerry Bridges, "Does Divine Sovereignty Make a Difference in Everyday Life?" in *The Grace of God*, 1:209-13.

[153]Calvin *Institutes* 1.16.7.

[154]Ibid., 1.16.5.

[155]Lindström, *God and the Origin of Evil*, pp. 208-9, issues a scathing attack on biblical scholarship for its general failure in this regard. My own suspicion is that the pancausality of the Stoics had a tremendous influence on the classical concept of God. Add to this the influence of German idealism on modern biblical scholarship, and you have a recipe for overlooking the particulars of historical life for the universal truths of reason.

[156]König, *New and Greater Things*, pp. 61-62.

[157]Lindström, *God and the Origin of Evil*, p. 198.

[158]On Amos, see Hubbard, *Joel and Amos*, p. 149; and Douglas Stuart, *Hosea—Jonah*, Word Biblical Commentary (Waco, Tex.: Word, 1987), p. 325.

[159]Lindström, *God and the Origin of Evil*, p. 118. Lindström observes that the majority of scholars seek to deflect this criticism by claiming that YHWH does not cause sinful human behaviors, only natural disasters. I would add that many theologians attempt to duck the criticism by invoking the concept of secondary causes or compatibilistic freedom.

[160]Bridges, "Does Divine Sovereignty Make a Difference?" p. 211.

[161]Fretheim, *Exodus*, p. 72.

[162]Kaiser, *Exodus*, 2:328.

[163]See Fretheim, *Suffering of God*, 73-74.

[164]G. C. Berkouwer, *The Providence of God*, trans. Lewis Smedes (Grand Rapids, Mich.: Eerdmans, 1952), p. 127.

[165]Here again I wish to acknowledge my indebtedness to one of Fretheim's excellent studies: "The Repentance of God."

[166]A. van de Beek, *Why? On Suffering, Guilt and God*, trans. John Vriend (Grand Rapids, Mich.: Eerdmans, 1990), pp. 105-7, reads these texts as supporting divine arbitrariness. I wish to affirm the divine freedom in these passages, but God's actions here are not arbitrary because they pertain to the divine project.

[167]Walter Brueggemann, *To Pluck Up, to Tear Down: Jeremiah 1—25*, International Theological Commentary (Grand Rapids, Mich.: Eerdmans, 1988), p. 161. Brueggemann makes some very helpful observations on this passage.

[168]See John Boykin, *The Gospel of Coincidence: Is God in Control?* (Grand Rapids, Mich.: Zondervan, 1986), pp. 66-68.

[169]For a study of this metaphor, see Nelly Stienstra, *YHWH Is the Husband of His People: An Analysis of a Biblical Metaphor with Special Reference to Translation* (Kampen, Netherlands: Kok Pharos, 1993).

[170]I acknowledge that there are some texts in which God is described as sending an evil spirit against Saul (1 Sam 16:14) or inciting David to the census so he can punish Israel (2 Sam 24:1). Such texts are in tension with the divine love, but even in the most problematic text, in which God incites David and then gets angry with him, Yahweh's fundamental concern for the covenant people is not doubted (2 Sam 24:14, 16). David does not understand all that God is doing, but he knows that God is merciful. Moreover, there are "texts of terror" such as the banishment of Hagar (Gen 21), the rape of Tamar (2 Sam 13) and the gang rape and dismemberment of a concubine (Judg 19). Such texts are preserved in the canon as dissenting voices; there is more going on than simply the mighty deeds of God. But there is no "dark side" to God. For a refutation of the identification of God with "demonic" elements in the Old Testament, see Lindström, *God and the Origin of Evil*. I have not addressed the development of the demonic or the Satan figure, even though they are significant in showing that there is a definite war going on between God and other powers. On this, see Gregory Boyd's *God at War: The Bible and Spiritual Conflict* (Downers Grove, Ill.: InterVarsity Press, 1997).

Jon D. Levenson rejects the position taken here. He discusses a number of these texts and concludes that there is an "uncanny, ghastly, ferocious, hostile, and nearly Satanic" side to God. Yahweh may be vengeful beyond what is just, may be the cause of evil or may renege on his covenant promises. Levenson finds unacceptable the attempt to elevate the divine goodness above the, at times, capricious omnipotence. Moreover, he rejects what I call "external dualisms" in which God is not in exhaustive control of all beings. Instead, he prefers an "internal dualism," or what he calls the "coincidence of opposites," in the deity. As he reads the Hebrew Bible, Yahweh struggles within himself and does not always act in good and loving ways. See Levenson, "Cataclysm, Survival and Regeneration," in *Confronting Omnicide: Jewish Reflections on Weapons of Mass Destruction,* ed. Daniel Landes (Northvale, N.J.: Jason Aronson, 1991), pp. 39-68.

Positing a "dark side" in God surfaces in various writers. It is found in the Boston Personalism of Peter Bertocci and E. S. Brightman, which posits an irrational surd of evil in the divine nature. It also bears affinities to Calvin's thought (though Calvin would claim that certain deeds of God in the Bible are only apparently evil). Jack Miles's *God: A Biography* takes a similar stance in seeing a dark side in God. Moreover, the same notion arises in various strands of the world religions. See John B. Carman, *Majesty and Meekness: A Comparative Study of Contrast and Harmony in the Concept of God* (Grand Rapids, Mich.: Eerdmans, 1994). See also p. 292, n. 58, and p. 317, n. 58, in this book.

[171]For other texts on divine humiliation, see Fretheim, *Suffering of God,* pp. 144-48.

[172]John Rogerson argues that the belief in an unfolding divine plan is read into the Old Testament from nineteenth-century meliorism. See his "Can a Doctrine of Providence Be Based on the Old Testament?" in *Ascribe to the Lord: Biblical and Other Studies in Memory of Peter C. Craigie,* ed. Lyle Eslinger and Glen Taylor, JSOT Supplement 67 (Sheffield: JSOT Press, 1988), pp. 529-43. Bertil Albrektson, *History of the Gods: An Essay on the Idea of Historical Events as Divine Manifestations in the Ancient Near East and in Israel* (Lund: Gleerup, 1967), p. 81, says the Old Testament does not affirm a divine plan that embraces all of history.

Chapter 4: New Testament Materials for a Relational View of Providence Involving Risk

[1]Gregory of Nyssa *The Great Catechism* 24.

[2]Karl Barth, *Church Dogmatics* 3/3, trans. Geoffrey W. Bromiley and T. F. Torrance (Edinburgh: T & T Clark, 1960), pp. 30-33.

[3]T. J. Gorringe, *God's Theatre: A Theology of Providence* (London: SCM Press, 1991), p. 58.

[4]E. Frank Tupper, *A Scandalous Providence: The Jesus Story of the Compassion of God* (Macon, Ga.: Mercer University Press, 1995). His book is an enlargement of his earlier article, "The Providence of God in Christological Perspective," *Review and Expositor* 82, no. 4 (1995): 579-95.

[5]Tupper, *Scandalous Providence,* chap. 1.

[6]John Calvin spoke of God's fatherly relation to us (*Institutes of the Christian Religion,* ed. John T. McNeill [Philadelphia: Westminster, 1960], 3.20.36-40), but A. van de Beek is correct when he inquires what sort of father Calvin's God is when he pushes the baby carriage over exploding land mines or beneath moving trucks. See A. van de Beek, *Why? On Suffering, Guilt and God,* trans. John Vriend (Grand Rapids, Mich.: Eerdmans, 1990), p. 102.

[7]E. Frank Tupper, "The Bethlehem Massacre—Christology Against Providence?" *Review and Expositor* 88, no. 4 (1991): 417-18, ascribes this to a Christology "from above" without reference to the historical events in which Jesus is situated.

[8]In contrast to Zacharias's question, Mary's did not contain an element of unbelief (compare Lk 1:18).

[9]Tupper, *Scandalous Providence,* pp. 95-97. For other reasons for the inclusion of these women, see D. S. Huffman, "Genealogy," in *Dictionary of Jesus and the Gospels,* ed. Joel B. Green, Scot McKnight, I. Howard Marshall (Downers Grove, Ill.: InterVarsity Press, 1992), pp. 255-56; and D. A. Carson, *Matthew,* Expositor's Bible Commentary, ed. Frank Gaebelein (Grand Rapids, Mich.: Zondervan, 1984), 8:66.

[10]M. Eugene Boring, *Matthew*, The New Interpreter's Bible, vol. 8 (Nashville: Abingdon, 1995), pp. 148-49, believes that such questions only arise if we take this story as historical instead of as "confessional language." He thinks Matthew's point is only to affirm divine preservation in the life of the infant Jesus. However, even if it is confessional language, Boring cannot escape the fact that Matthew tells a story that potentially calls the divine wisdom and goodness into question.

[11]Tupper, *Scandalous Providence*, pp. 101-2, 113.

[12]Ibid., p. 106.

[13]Also, it is interesting that later in Matthew Jesus calls a child to him and says, "It is not the will of your Father in heaven that one of these little ones should be lost" (18:14). In these words, which occur only in Matthew, Jesus speaks of God's compassion for children.

[14]On these parallels, see Carson, *Matthew*, Expositor's Bible Commentary, vol. 8 (Grand Rapids, Mich.: Zondervan, 1984), p. 112.

[15]Some people believe that Jesus could not have failed this test because he is *God*. This claim, however, is based on preconceived notions of what it means to be divine instead of paying attention to the actual way of God in the world. How does anyone know that it is impossible for the divine son to fail a test? Why is it that the incarnation cannot involve the genuine experience of vulnerability and testing? After all, Jesus' experience in Gethsemane seems to be just that.

[16]For various interpretations of the temptation, see Boring, *Matthew*, p. 165.

[17]Tupper, *Scandalous Providence*, p. 133.

[18]See N. T. Wright, *The New Testament and the People of God*, Christian Origins and the Question of God (Minneapolis: Fortress, 1992), pp. 473-74. On the connection between the Messiah and dominating power, see William Placher, *Narratives of a Vulnerable God: Christ, Theology and Scripture* (Louisville, Ky.: Westminster John Knox, 1994), pp. 9-17.

[19]For discussion, see Walter Liefeld, "Transfiguration," in *Dictionary of Jesus and the Gospels*, ed. Joel Green et al. (Downers Grove, Ill.: InterVarsity Press, 1992), pp. 839-40.

[20]With van de Beek, *Why?* Indeed, the reading of the Old Testament legitimately provides for a world-ruling messiah, but God simply chose differently in Jesus.

[21]Jürgen Moltmann, *Jesus Christ for Today's World*, trans. Margaret Kohl (Minneapolis: Fortress, 1994), p. 15.

[22]See Larry W. Hurtado, *Mark*, New International Biblical Commentary (Peabody, Mass.: Hendrickson, 1989), p. 90.

[23]William L. Lane, *Commentary on the Gospel of Mark*, New International Commentary on the New Testament (Grand Rapids, Mich.: Eerdmans, 1974), p. 204.

[24]I recognize that the no-risk view of providence will interpret all of these stories differently. For the no-risk view, nothing in the stories occurs for Jesus' benefit but only for the benefit of others (that is, Jesus wanted to reveal to the people the state of their faith—after all Jesus was not testing to see if they had faith, since the no-risk view affirms that Jesus already knew that).

[25]See William Klassen, *Judas: Betrayer or Friend of Jesus?* (Minneapolis: Augsburg Fortress, 1996).

[26]Ibid., p. 69.

[27]Ibid., p. 107. Klassen discusses all the New Testament texts about Judas and how he came to be villainized in spite of the ambiguous biblical information about his actions.

[28]See D. J. Williams, "Judas Iscariot," in *Dictionary of Jesus and the Gospels*, pp. 407-8.

[29]See George R. Beasley-Murray, *John*, Word Biblical Commentary (Waco, Tex.: Word, 1987), p. 238.

[30]Much is read into Luke 22:22 and John 17:12 that this was all predetermined. I understand the verse to mean that Jesus and the father have agreed or determined which path they will take. That these narratives need not imply divine foreknowledge, see Lorenzo McCabe, *The Foreknowledge of God* (Cincinnati: Cranston & Stowe, 1887), pp. 99-139; and Richard Rice,

God's Foreknowledge and Man's Free Will (Minneapolis: Bethany House, 1985), pp. 95-97. That the "woe" Jesus pronounces is not a curse on Judas, see Klassen, *Judas*, p. 84.
[31]On the agony Jesus experienced, see John R. W. Stott, *The Cross of Christ* (Downers Grove, Ill.: InterVarsity Press, 1986), pp. 73-77.
[32]See Stott, *Cross of Christ*, pp. 76-77.
[33]Tupper, *Scandalous Providence*, p. 324.
[34]Ibid., p. 325.
[35]See James L. Mays, *Psalms*, Interpretation (Louisville, Ky.: John Knox, 1994), pp. 105-6, 109-11; and John Goldingay, *Models for Interpretation of Scripture* (Grand Rapids, Mich.: Eerdmans, 1995), pp. 153-54. Goldingay asserts that our interpretations of Scripture are influenced by our theologies, as is, at times, the wording of the biblical text that we choose to preserve.
[36]Those who believe that everything that happens in the world was fixed (or at least foreknown) prior to the creation need to explain how this comports with names being blotted out of the book of life (Rev 3:5). It would seem that either total foreordination or foreknowledge would exclude the possibility of revising the book.
[37]On corporate election, see William W. Klein, *The New Chosen People: A Corporate View of Election* (Grand Rapids, Mich.: Zondervan, 1990).
[38]See George Eldon Ladd, *A Commentary on the Revelation of John* (Grand Rapids, Mich.: Eerdmans, 1972), p. 181.
[39]See, for instance, Norman L. Geisler, *Creating God in the Image of Man? The New Open View of God—Neotheism's Dangerous Drift* (Minneapolis: Bethany House, 1997), p. 143.
[40]Another possibility would be to affirm a cosmic fall prior to the creation of humans, leading God to think it likely that humans will succumb to sin, in which case the death of the Son is incorporated into the divine plan for creation.
[41]Paul Helm, *The Providence of God*, Contours of Christian Theology (Downers Grove, Ill.: InterVarsity Press, 1994), pp. 100, 215. Is Helm suggesting that God "needs" the Fall?
[42]Colin E. Gunton, *Christ and Creation* (Grand Rapids, Mich.: Eerdmans, 1992), p. 96. On the history of this view, see Eugene TeSelle, *Christ in Context: Divine Purpose and Human Responsibility* (Philadelphia: Fortress, 1975), pp. 35-45; and Robert North, *Teilhard and the Creation of the Soul* (Milwaukee: Bruce, 1967), pp. 120-62.
[43]See Jürgen Moltmann, *The Trinity and the Kingdom*, trans. Margaret Kohl (New York: Harper & Row, 1981), p. 46. Herbert W. Richardson, *Toward an American Theology* (New York: Harper & Row, 1967), p. 126, suggests a similar idea when he says, "Since, therefore, God created the world for Sabbath holiness, He must personally enter the world and dwell therein." Paul R. Sponheim, *Faith and the Other: A Relational Theology* (Minneapolis: Fortress, 1993), pp. 93-96, utilizes Richardson in holding that the incarnation was more than restorative, since it was intended from the beginning in order to establish a special sort of relationship between God and his creatures.
[44]See TeSelle, *Christ in Context*, p. 45.
[45]The idea behind this overworked expression is so taken for granted in the commentaries that the commentators no longer wrestle with the text.
[46]McCabe, *Foreknowledge of God*, pp. 104-5, claims that the atonement only required the suffering and death (being mortal) of Jesus, not the crucifixion specifically. Jesus was handed over to die, but "the instruments by whom he finally was put to death were by no means predestined" (p. 105).
[47]For instance, if a first-year member of Congress were to attempt to discontinue the social-security system of the United States, there is little doubt about the sort of reception he or she would receive.
[48]Jürgen Moltmann, *The Crucified God*, trans. R. A. Wilson and John Bowden (New York: Harper & Row, 1974), p. 201.
[49]On God's defining himself through the cross, see Paul S. Fiddes, *The Creative Suffering of*

God (Oxford: Clarendon, 1992), p. 265; and Eberhard Jüngel, *God as the Mystery of the World: On the Foundation of the Theology of the Crucified One in the Dispute Between Theism and Atheism,* trans. Darrell L. Gruder (Grand Rapids, Mich.: Eerdmans, 1983), pp. 363-64. Fiddes correctly observes that the doctrine of God should not be built entirely out of the crucifixion, for the suffering of God is not limited to the suffering that Jesus experienced. I have sought to show this in my survey of the Old Testament material. Furthermore, I would add that the resurrection must also be taken into account in defining God.

[50]See Moltmann, *Crucified God,* pp. 214-16.

[51]Vincent Brümmer's *The Model of Love: A Study in Philosophical Theology* (New York: Cambridge University Press, 1993) is especially helpful on understanding the atonement in relational terms. See also Colin Gunton, *The Actuality of Atonement: A Study of Metaphor, Rationality and the Christian Tradition* (Grand Rapids, Mich.: Eerdmans, 1989); Stott, *Cross of Christ;* Leon Morris, *The Apostolic Preaching of the Cross* (Grand Rapids, Mich.: Eerdmans, 1956); and for a historical survey, H. D. McDonald, *The Atonement of the Death of Christ: In Faith, Revelation and History* (Grand Rapids, Mich.: Baker, 1985).

[52]Brümmer, *Model of Love,* p. 197. The following discussion is indebted to his eighth chapter.

[53]See ibid., pp. 185, 201-3.

[54]The person forgiven by God experiences unconditional forgiveness in that there are no conditions this person must fulfill in order to obtain divine forgiveness. Yet, there is a condition that the forgiven must meet in order to heal the relationship: accept the forgiveness of the one forgiving and desire that the relationship be restored. See ibid., p. 185.

[55]Ibid., p. 202.

[56]Clark H. Pinnock and Robert C. Brow, *Unbounded Love: A Good News Theology for the 21st Century* (Downers Grove, Ill.: InterVarsity Press, 1994), pp. 99-110; and Paul Fiddes, *Creative Suffering of God,* p. 162, emphasize that the cross is more personal forgiveness than punishment, more a filial relationship than a legal one. Stott, *Cross of Christ,* pp. 141-49, however, claims that the forensic element cannot be dismissed.

[57]Some believe that Jesus, in quoting the first part of Psalm 22, has the entire psalm in mind and so this should actually be understood as including victory. "In first-century Judaism, was the citation of the opening of a psalm designed to recall the psalm in its entirety? Evidence for this phenomenon is very late" (Joel B. Green, "Death of Jesus," in *Dictionary of Jesus and the Gospels,* p. 151). Moreover, Moltmann thinks such a view far-fetched because the psalm ends with thanksgiving for deliverance from death, "and there was no deliverance on the cross" (*Jesus Christ for Today's World,* p. 35). For discussion of the interpretation of this cry, see William L. Lane, *Commentary on the Gospel of Mark,* New International Commentary on the New Testament (Grand Rapids, Mich.: Eerdmans, 1974), pp. 572-73; Boring, *Matthew,* p. 492; Carson, *Matthew,* p. 782; and James L. Mays, "Prayer and Christology: Psalm 22 as Perspective on the Passion," *Theology Today* 42 (October 1985): 322-31. Fredrik Lindström, *Suffering and Sin: Interpretations of Illness in the Individual Complaint Psalms,* trans. Michael McLamb (Stockholm: Almqvist & Wiksell, 1994), p. 463, argues that the note of praise at the end of Psalm 22 does not come about until after the resurrection when Jesus says, "Go and tell my brothers" (Mt 28:10), which he takes as an allusion to "I will tell of your name to my brothers" (Ps 22:23).

[58]On the nature of the lament tradition and its importance for our relationship with God today, see Walter Brueggemann, "The Costly Loss of Lament," *Journal for the Study of the Old Testament* 36 (1986): 57-71. Also helpful is Lindström, *Suffering and Sin.*

[59]Fiddes, *Creative Suffering,* p. 32, makes the important observation that God is victorious through suffering and is not rendered impotent by it.

[60]Dietrich Bonhoeffer, *Letters and Papers from Prison* (New York: Macmillan, 1972), pp. 360-61.

[61]Moltmann, *Crucified God,* p. 249.

[62]Wright, *The New Testament and the People of God,* p. 399.

[63]See Barth, *Church Dogmatics* 3/3, p. 56.

[64]The following account is greatly indebted to the cultural and literary analysis of Kenneth E. Bailey's *Poet and Peasant and Through Peasant Eyes: A Literary-Cultural Approach to the Parables in Luke,* combined ed. (Grand Rapids, Mich.: Eerdmans, 1990), pp. 158-206.

[65]This section is indebted to Robert Capon's *The Parables of Judgment* (Grand Rapids, Mich.: Eerdmans, 1989).

[66]For more on this and a discussion of the similar parable in Luke, see Bailey, *Poet and Peasant,* 88-113.

[67]There will be an eschatological judgment (for example, Mt 25:46; 2 Thess 1:6-9). For discussion of the purpose of eschatological judgment and the nature of hell, see Jerry L. Walls, *Hell: The Logic of Damnation* (Notre Dame, Ind.: University of Notre Dame Press, 1992); and William Sigountos, ed., *Four Views on Hell* (Grand Rapids, Mich.: Zondervan, 1992). For a nonretributionist account of hell, see Jonathan Kvanvig, *The Problem of Hell* (New York: Oxford University Press, 1993).

[68]See Charles E. Carlston, "Matthew 6:24-34," *Interpretation* 41 (April 1987): 179-83.

[69]See Carson, *Matthew,* pp. 179-80.

[70]See Richard J. Dillon, "Ravens, Lilies and the Kingdom of God: Matthew 6:25-33/Luke 12:22-31," *Catholic Biblical Quarterly* 53, no. 4 (1991): 614, 621.

[71]Jesus' own ministry depended on the gifts of people (especially women) who worked to earn enough to support themselves and give to others.

[72]See, for instance, John G. Cook, "The Sparrow's Fall in Mt 10:29b," *Zeitschrift für die Neutestamentliche Wissenschaft und die Kunde der Alteren Kirche* 79, no. 1-2 (1988): 138-44.

[73]See Dale C. Allison Jr. "Matthew 10:26-31 and the Problem of Evil," *St. Vladimir's Theological Quarterly* 32, no. 4 (1988): 293-308.

[74]See Lindström, *Suffering and Sin.* He argues that Old Testament scholarship erroneously assumes that all suffering is caused by God as retribution for sin. But this assumption is patently false, owing to the realm of death in which disorder and disease may arise if the divine presence does not subdue them. Hence, some suffering is simply irrational. For a study of the development in Scripture rejecting the idea that material well-being is directly proportional to one's character, see David L. Thompson, "The Godly and the Good Life in Biblical Thought," *Christian Scholar's Review* 22, no. 3 (1993): 248-66.

[75]See Walter Liefeld, *Luke,* Expositor's Bible Commentary, vol. 8 (Grand Rapids, Mich.: Zondervan, 1984), p. 970.

[76]See C. K. Barrett, *The Gospel According to St. John,* 2nd. ed. (Philadelphia: Westminster, 1978), p. 356; and Leon Morris, *The Gospel According to John,* rev. ed., New International Commentary on the New Testament (Grand Rapids, Mich.: Eerdmans, 1995), pp. 424-26.

[77]See van de Beek, *Why?* pp. 282-94. For van de Beek, God has been moving increasingly toward grace and compassion and away from domination and punishment. In Jesus, he sees God as saying he will never again order the extermination of any people or send suffering and so on. There is much in his book with which I agree. In the Old Testament section I sought to show, however, that the changes God makes are not those van de Beek affirms.

[78]G. C. Berkouwer, *The Providence of God,* trans. Lewis Smedes (Grand Rapids, Mich.: Eerdmans, 1952), p. 127.

[79]Reformed theologian James Daane says that decretal theology does not allow these biblical texts to have their force. Instead, appeal is made to seeing things from the "eternal" or divine point of view in which case all works out justly, as God desires. See his *The Freedom of God: A Study of Election and Pulpit* (Grand Rapids, Mich.: Eerdmans, 1973), pp. 83-84.

[80]Adriö König, *Here Am I: A Believer's Reflection on God* (Grand Rapids, Mich.: Eerdmans, 1982), p. 40.

[81]Van de Beek, *Why?* p. 164.

[82]Philip Yancey, "Cosmic Combat," *Christianity Today* 38, no. 14 (1994): 21.

[83]See James Dunn, *Jesus, Paul and the Law* (Philadelphia: Westminster, 1990), especially chap. 7.

[84]See James Dunn, *The Partings of the Ways Between Christianity and Judaism and Their Significance for the Character of Christianity* (London: SCM Press, 1991), pp. 130-55; and *Jesus, Paul and the Law*, pp. 118-21, 160-63.

[85]Tragically, the Antioch church seems to have turned against Paul, forcing him to seek a support base elsewhere. See Dunn, *Jesus, Paul and the Law*, p. 161.

[86]Robert C. Tannehill's "Israel in Luke-Acts: A Tragic Story," *Journal of Biblical Literature* 104, no. 1 (1985): 69-85, provides a great deal of evidence from Luke-Acts that God's intentions for Israel were not realized and describes the resultant tragedy.

[87]Tannehill, "Israel in Luke-Acts," p. 82.

[88]See Dunn, *Partings of the Ways*. This decision had huge consequences for the future of the church, at least after A.D. 130, when the church became essentially Gentile in its identity. The parting of the ways took a long time, and it was never a foregone conclusion that Christianity would become a Gentile body. Nevertheless, there are relatively few Jews after this date who believe that Jesus is the focal point of God's providence. •

[89]See Derek Tidball, *The Social Context of the New Testament: A Sociological Analysis* (Grand Rapids, Mich.: Zondervan, 1984), pp. 51-64.

[90]See, for instance, John Piper, *The Justification of God: An Exegetical and Theological Study of Romans 9:1-23* (Grand Rapids, Mich.: Baker, 1983); and Thomas R. Schreiner, "Does Romans 9 Teach Individual Election unto Salvation?" *Journal of the Evangelical Theological Society* 36, no. 1 (1993): 25-40.

[91]See James Dunn, *Romans*, Word Biblical Commentary 38 (Waco, Tex.: Word, 1988), p. 520.

[92]This section is greatly indebted to N. T. Wright, *The Climax of the Covenant: Christ and the Law in Pauline Theology* (Philadelphia: Fortress, 1992) especially pp. 231-57; and Dunn's *Romans*.

[93]C. E. B. Cranfield, *Romans: A Shorter Commentary* (Grand Rapids, Mich.: Eerdmans, 1985), p. 234.

[94]Ibid., pp. 234-35.

[95]Dunn, *Romans*, p. 566.

[96]Helpful on Paul's use of the Old Testament texts in this chapter is James D. Strauss's "God's Promise and Universal History: The Theology of Romans 9," in *Grace Unlimited*, ed. Clark Pinnock (Minneapolis: Bethany House, 1975), pp. 190-208.

[97]Louis Berkhof takes an ahistorical reading of the potter and claims that Romans 9 actually "speaks from a pre-creation standpoint." See his *Systematic Theology*, 3rd ed. (Grand Rapids, Mich.: Eerdmans, 1946), p. 120.

[98]See Dunn, *Romans*, pp. 568-69.

[99]Here I disagree with Dunn (*Romans*, pp. 671, 690-91) and Wright (*Climax of the Covenant*, pp. 239-41), who seem to suggest that God specifically brought about Israel's rejection of Jesus in order to direct the gospel to the Gentiles. In Romans I do not think Paul is saying that God caused Israel's unbelief but that God made use of it. Wright does not seem consistent in his claim, however, for he says both that God had always intended Israel's rejection (this was the divine plan) and that Israel "did not submit to God's own covenant plan" (p. 241). If God's plan was for Israel to rebel, then it cannot also be claimed that God planned for Israel to submit. Dunn has a similar problem in holding that God purposed Israel's unbelief as a means of starting the mission to the Gentiles. He also believes that Israel was to blame for its own unbelief. From Acts 10—15 I sought to show how God first began the Gentile mission from among Jewish Christians. It was only subsequent development that forced God to modify his plans.

[100]See Dunn, *Romans*, p. 689.

[101]See Jan Bonda, *The One Purpose of God* (Grand Rapids, Mich.: Eerdmans, 1997), chap. 6.

Also see Wright, *Climax of the Covenant,* pp. 249-51; and Dunn, *Romans,* pp. 681-83, 691-93.

[102]See van de Beek, *Why?* p. 279.

[103]Adriö König, *The Eclipse of Christ in Eschatology: Toward a Christ-Centered Approach* (Grand Rapids, Mich.: Eerdmans, 1989), pp. 183-89.

[104]Ibid., p. 183.

[105]Ibid., p. 184.

[106]Some people believe the cosmic signs were fulfilled in detail at the time of Jesus' crucifixion; others believe they are yet to come. See I. Howard Marshall, *Acts,* Tyndale New Testament Commentaries (Grand Rapids, Mich.: Eerdmans, 1988), pp. 73-74; and F. F. Bruce, *The Book of Acts,* rev. ed., New International Commentary on the New Testament (Grand Rapids, Mich.: Eerdmans, 1988), p. 62.

[107]See Marshall, *Acts,* pp. 252-53; and Bruce, *Book of Acts,* pp. 293-94.

[108]Van de Beek, *Why?* p. 300.

[109]König, *Here Am I,* pp. 198-99.

[110]Tupper, *Scandalous Providence,* pp. 68-70.

[111]On the difficulty of translating this verse and for discussion regarding whether all things are, in fact, advantageous for Christians, see Tupper, *Scandalous Providence,* p. 338; Cranfield, *Romans,* pp. 202-5; John R. W. Stott, *Romans* (Downers Grove, Ill.: InterVarsity Press, 1994), pp. 246-48; and Dunn, *Romans,* pp. 480-82.

[112]Stott, *Romans,* p. 247.

[113]James H. Evans Jr., *We Have Been Believers: An African-American Systematic Theology* (Minneapolis: Fortress, 1992), p. 75.

[114]This is opposed to Paul Helm, *Providence of God,* p. 116, who claims that God sends trouble into our lives in order to transform character. Given his risk-free view of providence, that God accomplishes whatever God wants, one wonders why God wants some Christians to lose their faith, since some do lose confidence in God amid trials. One would think a risk-free God could do a better job.

[115]Gabriel Fackre believes that God continues to work toward salvation of people even after death. See his "Divine Perseverance," in *What About Those Who Have Never Heard?* ed. John Sanders (Downers Grove, Ill.: InterVarsity Press, 1995), pp. 71-95. Donald G. Bloesch, *God the Almighty: Power, Wisdom, Holiness, Love,* Christian Foundations (Downers Grove, Ill.: InterVarsity Press, 1995), pp. 143-44, believes that divine grace pursues sinners even in hell.

[116]Van de Beek, *Why?* p. 297.

[117]Ibid., pp. 305-16.

[118]Gorringe, *God's Theatre,* pp. 50-55, is helpful here.

[119]Augustine, for instance, says a God without foreknowledge is not God (*City of God* 5.9, as translated by Marcus Dods [New York: Random House, 1950]).

[120]Gorringe, *God's Theatre,* p. 63.

[121]According to presentism, God's knowledge is coextensive with reality. In other words, God knows all there is to know. Since, it is claimed, the future actions of free beings are unknowable, God does not know them. This does not count against divine omniscience, since there is nothing there to know. Admittedly, this is a highly contested point.

[122]See Colin Brown, ed., *The New International Dictionary of New Testament Theology* (Grand Rapids, Mich.: Zondervan, 1975), 1:692-93.

[123]I find it interesting that translators (who typically hold to exhaustive divine foreknowledge) do not translate the two references to human foreknowledge as "foreknowledge." Perhaps they do this because they cannot bring themselves to believe that humans could have the same sort of foreknowledge (though not to the same degree) God has.

[124]See Klein, *New Chosen People,* pp. 277-78.

[125]McCabe, *Foreknowledge of God,* pp. 102-10, claims that the death of Jesus as a human was foreordained, but the precise means of death was not foreknown. He says that Jesus' death

itself, not how he died, is the important point in atonement.

[126]See, for instance, Geisler, *Creating God in the Image of Man?* pp. 137-38. For a brief discussion of this sort of interpretation of prophecy in Judaism, Islam and Christianity, see John F. A. Sawyer, *Prophecy and Biblical Prophets,* rev. ed., Oxford Bible Series (New York: Oxford University Press, 1993), pp. 153-59.

[127]R. K. McGregor Wright, *No Place for Sovereignty: What's Wrong with Freewill Theism* (Downers Grove, Ill.: InterVarsity Press, 1996), pp. 59-61, 94-95.

[128]William Lane Craig, *The Only Wise God: The Compatibility of Divine Foreknowledge and Human Freedom* (Grand Rapids, Mich.: Baker, 1987), pp. 25-37. Some texts usually cited are 1 Samuel 23:10-12; 1 Kings 13:2; Psalm 139:4, 16; Isaiah 44:7; Daniel 2:28-29; and Luke 22:34. See also Geisler, *Creating God in the Image of Man?* pp. 129-38, 147-52.

[129]Richard Rice, *God's Foreknowledge,* pp. 75-81; and his "Biblical Support," in *The Openness of God,* pp. 50-53. Craig, *Only Wise God,* pp. 42-43, 36, believes these explanations a failure. He thinks that conditional prophecies require middle knowledge. Moreover, he claims that the openness model denudes the biblical passages of any theological significance. It may denude them of the particular theological significance that Craig affirms, but it hardly evacuates all theological meaning.

[130]McCabe, *Foreknowledge,* agrees and adds the observation that God can also overrule human freedom if necessary to accomplish a divine purpose. McCabe points out that if God does this, then the human agents whom God overrules are not held responsible for these particular actions. Though correct, McCabe appeals more than is needed to divine overruling in order to explain predictions and does not adequately consider other explanations available to presentism.

[131]Proponents of exhaustive foreknowledge need to explain how a conditional prediction by God can be genuine when God already knows the future result. How is it truly a conditional?

[132]See the discussion of this text in 3.8.

[133]See the discussion in 6.5.3.5.

[134]G. C. Berkouwer, *The Person of Christ,* trans. John Vriend (Grand Rapids, Mich.: Eerdmans, 1954), pp. 113-54.

[135]Evangelicals tend to understand "fulfilled" to mean only the exact instantiation of some specific Old Testament prediction.

[136]The same is true in John's gospel (13:18). Jesus says this Scripture (that one who eats with him betrays him) is fulfilled. Jesus here applies to Judas what David had applied to Absalom. It was not a prediction but a similar event. For other examples of this practice, see Sawyer, *Prophecy and Biblical Prophets,* pp. 142-46.

[137]Boring, *Matthew,* p. 154. Boring also makes the insightful observation that Matthew is not writing to non-Christian Jews in an attempt to convince them by these "proofs" that Jesus is the Messiah, for Matthew's procedure would be unconvincing. Rather, he writes to believers seeking to build their faith.

[138]See Goldingay, *Models for Interpretation,* pp. 122-27, 146-48. He observes that there is both an absoluteness and a flexibility in the way later biblical writers handle earlier material.

[139]Boring, *Matthew,* p. 477.

[140]Raymond E. Brown, "How Much Did Jesus Know?" *Catholic Biblical Quarterly* 29, no. 1 (1967): 9-39, discusses the various texts and concludes that Jesus did not have foreknowledge.

[141]For an overview of the issues, see H. F. Bayer, "Predictions of Jesus' Passion and Resurrection," in *Dictionary of Jesus and the Gospels,* pp. 630-33.

[142]Ibid., p. 632.

[143]Brown, "How Much Did Jesus Know?" p. 14. Also see McCabe, *Foreknowledge,* pp. 106-11.

[144]Brown, "How Much Did Jesus Know?" p. 19. I discussed predictions that were not fulfilled or were not fulfilled in the precise way predicted (for example, Acts 21:11) in the excursus

on divine repentance in the previous chapter.

[145]See William L. Lane, *Commentary on the Gospel of Mark,* New International Commentary on the New Testament (Grand Rapids, Mich.: Eerdmans, 1974), pp. 451-53.

[146]McCabe, *Foreknowledge,* pp. 86-94.

[147]Craig, *Only Wise God,* p. 36, claims that the denial of foreknowledge to Jesus evacuates such events of all theological significance. He seems to suggest that if Jesus lacks foreknowledge, then he cannot be considered a prophet. If so, then it appears that Craig is assuming the truth of foreknowledge and reading the texts from that perspective. But, as I pointed out in the previous chapter, one can be accounted a prophet without exhaustive foreknowledge. Craig correctly observes that the New Testament writers ascribe to Jesus the same sort of predictive ability given to God in the Old Testament. But this ability does not necessitate exhaustive foreknowledge.

[148]In which case it is doubtful that it would ever have been recorded.

[149]Rice, *God's Foreknowledge,* pp. 95-97, understands Jesus' predictions about his disciples' actions, including those of Judas, to be conditional as well.

[150]David Basinger, "Can an Evangelical Christian Justifiably Deny God's Exhaustive Knowledge of the Future?" *Christian Scholar's Review* 25, no. 2 (1995): 142. And, it should be noted, there is no simple way to establish one view or the other, since proponents of each view disagree as to how certain passages of Scripture should be interpreted. In similar fashion there is no simple way of settling from Scripture the age-old Calvinist-Arminian debate.

Chapter 5: Divine Relationality in the Christian Tradition

[1]For surveys of the doctrine of providence in Christian theology, see Benjamin Wirt Farley, *The Providence of God* (Grand Rapids, Mich.: Baker, 1988); Horton Davies, *The Vigilant God: Providence in the Thought of Augustine, Aquinas, Calvin and Barth* (New York: Peter Lang, 1992); and Langdon Gilkey, *Reaping the Whirlwind: A Christian Interpretation of History* (New York: Seabury, 1976), pp. 159-238.

[2]H. P. Owen, *Concepts of Deity* (New York: Herder & Herder, 1971), p. 1. Both Owen and G. L. Prestige, *God in Patristic Thought* (London: SPCK, 1975), defend this synthesis.

[3]On this history, see my "Historical Considerations," in *The Openness of God: A Biblical Challenge to the Traditional Understanding of God,* by Clark Pinnock et al. (Downers Grove, Ill.: InterVarsity Press, 1994). On the effect this synthesis has had on various doctrines, practices and spirituality, see the excellent study by Donald G. Bloesch, *God the Almighty: Power, Wisdom, Holiness, Love,* Christian Foundations (Downers Grove, Ill.: InterVarsity Press, 1995), pp. 205-40. Regarding the early history of the synthesis, see Joseph C. McLelland, *God the Anonymous: A Study in Alexandrian Philosophical Theology,* Patristic Monograph Series (Cambridge, Mass.: Philadelphia Patristic Foundation, 1976); Richard A. Norris, *God and the World in Early Christian Thought: A Study in Justin Martyr, Irenaeus, Tertullian and Origen* (New York: Seabury, 1965); Henry Chadwick, *Early Christian Thought and the Classical Tradition: Studies in Justin, Clement and Origen* (New York: Oxford University Press, 1966).

[4]Justin Martyr *First Apology* 13, 61; and *Second Apology* 6.

[5]Justin Martyr *First Apology* 28.

[6]Ibid., 28, 43.

[7]Ibid., 43-45. On the history of providence, foreknowledge and freewill, see Farley, *Providence of God*; and Roger Forster and V. Paul Marston, *God's Strategy in Human History* (Minneapolis: Bethany House, 1983), pp. 243-95.

[8]Irenaeus *Against Heresies* 1.12.2; 2.12.1; 2.13.3-4; 2.28.4; 3.8.3; 3.16.6; 4.11.2; 4.21.2. It is interesting that, for the most part, the Gnostics and fathers agreed on these points. The Gnostics failed, however, to connect God with creation.

[9]Ibid., 2.1-2; 2.6. As opposed to Eusebius, who said that God cannot be involved in time, and thus the need for a middle being.

[10]Tertullian *Against Marcion* 2.24.

[11]See Joseph M. Hallman, *The Descent of God: Divine Suffering in History and Theology* (Minneapolis: Fortress, 1991), pp. 51-66; and Robert W. Jenson, *The Triune Identity* (Philadelphia: Fortress, 1982), pp. 70-74.

[12]Tertullian *Against Marcion* 2.16.

[13]Tertullian *On the Flesh of Christ* 5.

[14]Tertullian *Against Marcion* 2.5-6, 23-24. See Farley, *Providence of God*, pp. 95-97.

[15]For references and discussion, see McLelland, *God the Anonymous*, pp. 50-125; Farley, *Providence of God*, pp. 87-90; Hallman, *Descent of God*, pp. 36-46; and J. K. Mozley, *The Impassibility of God: A Survey of Christian Thought* (New York: Cambridge University Press, 1926), pp. 59-63.

[16]See Origen, *On Prayer*, in *Origen*, trans. Rowan Greer, Classics of Western Spirituality (New York: Paulist, 1979), pp. 90-97.

[17]See Origen *De Principles* 2.4.4; Origen *Contra Celsus* 4.37, 72; 6.53.

[18]See Origen *Contra Celsus* 4.14-15; and McLelland, *God the Anonymous*, pp. 108-22. McLelland points out that history is not significant for Origen, since history and incarnation are but temporary accommodations until the final cure of humanity is complete and Christians ascend to full participation in divine being.

[19]The text is known as *Ad Theopompum*. See Mozley, *Impassibility of God*, pp. 63-72; and Hallman, *Descent of God*, pp. 46-49.

[20]See Mozley, *Impassibility of God*, pp. 48-52; and Hallman, *Descent of God*, pp. 66-70.

[21]See Lacantius *Against the Heathen* 1.27.

[22]See Lacantius *On the Divine Anger* 4.

[23]Ibid., 17.

[24]See Catherine Mowry LaCugna, *God for Us: The Trinity and Christian Life* (New York: HarperCollins, 1991), pp. 37-39; and Hallman, *Descent of God*, pp. 78, 83-85.

[25]Jenson, *The Triune Identity* (Philadelphia: Fortress, 1982), p. 85.

[26]LaCugna, *God for Us*, pp. 14, 63-66.

[27]See Jenson, *Triune Identity*, pp. 106-7, 111-14.

[28]Gregory of Nyssa *Against Eunomius* 1.42.

[29]Yet even here there was no consensus. See Chadwick, *Early Christian Thought*, pp. 46-47, 85. Moreover, some fathers speculated that God created out of his goodness (nature), which necessarily diffuses itself. See Wolfhart Pannenberg, *Basic Questions in Theology*, trans. George H. Kehm (Philadelphia: Westminster, 1983), 2:175. On the history of the idea that God necessarily creates, see Arthur Lovejoy, *The Great Chain of Being* (Cambridge: Harvard University Press, 1964).

[30]Augustine *City of God* 8.6; Augustine *Confessions* 7.11, in *Augustine: Confessions and Enchiridion*, trans. Albert C. Outler, Library of Christian Classics, vol. 7 (Philadelphia: Westminster, 1955); and Augustine *Studies in John* 1.8.

[31]Augustine *Confessions* 11.12.

[32]Ibid., 11.12-13. See also Augustine *City of God* 11.14, 21 (here he explicitly refers to Plato's *Timaeus*); 12.15, 17; and *The Trinity* 1.1.3. It is interesting to compare this answer with that of Irenaeus, who said that we do not know what God was doing before the creation since Scripture is silent on the subject (*Against Heresies* 2.28.3).

[33]Augustine *Confessions* 12.15; 13.16.

[34]Augustine *City of God* 11.21.

[35]See ibid., 5.9-10.

[36]See Augustine *Confessions* 11.18; *City of God* 11.21; 5.10; *Psalms* 106.31; and *Gift of Perseverance* 15.

[37]See Augustine *Predestination of the Saints; Gift of Perseverance;* and *Enchiridion* 24-28.

[38]Augustine acknowledged that God works through secondary causes but failed to see that this did not settle the problem of determinism. What he did was to argue that fate and human

responsibility were incompatible and that fate and divine causality are different. Thus, he thought, divine causality and human responsibility are compatible. But this is no solution because arguing that *A* is incompatible with *B* and that *A* is different from *C* does not yield the conclusion that *B* is compatible with *C*. See W. T. Jones, *A History of Western Philosophy: The Classical Mind*, 2nd ed. (New York: Harcourt Brace Jovanovich, 1970), 99-100.

[39]Augustine *Enchiridion* 26. See also 24.

[40]Ibid., 27.

[41]See Augustine *Gift of Perseverance* and *Rebuke and Grace*, 10-21.

[42]Augustine *On Free Will* 3.68. See also *Enchiridion* 24.

[43]Augustine *The Trinity* 1.1.2.

[44]Augustine *Psalms* 106.31; *City of God* 11.18, 21; 14.9, 11.

[45]Augustine *Psalms* 132.11.

[46]Augustine *City of God* 9.5.

[47]See Hallman, *Descent of God*, p. 112.

[48]Augustine *City of God* 22.2.

[49]See Hallman, *Descent of God*, pp. 120-21.

[50]Augustine *On the Trinity* 5.16.17. See also Christopher Kaiser, *The Doctrine of God: An Historical Survey* (Westchester, Ill.: Crossway, 1982), p. 80.

[51]See LaCugna, *God for Us*, pp. 86-87.

[52]Jaroslav Pelikan, *The Christian Tradition: A History of the Development of Doctrine* (Chicago: University of Chicago Press, 1971), 2:296.

[53]See LaCugna, *God for Us*, p. 101; Kaiser, *Doctrine of God*, p. 81; and Emil Brunner, *Christian Doctrine of God*, trans. Olive Wyon (Philadelphia: Westminster, 1949), p. 239.

[54]See Joseph Stephen O'Leary, *Questioning Back: The Overcoming of Metaphysics in Christian Tradition* (Minneapolis: Winston, 1985), chap. 4.

[55]LaCugna, *God for Us*, p. 87.

[56]See Justo González, *A History of Christian Thought* (Nashville: Abingdon, 1987), 2:128-35; Jones, *History of Western Philosophy*, 172-84; Hallman, *Descent of God*, pp. 125-26; and Mozley, *Impassibility of God*, pp. 109-11.

[57]John Scotus Erigena *The Division of Nature*, quoted in Mozley, *Impassibility of God*, p. 110.

[58]The following discussion is based on his *Summa Theologica* 1.1-26.

[59]See Farley, *Providence of God*, pp. 127-30.

[60]See Norman Kretzmann, "Goodness, Knowledge and Indeterminacy in the Philosophy of Thomas Aquinas," *Journal of Philosophy* (supplement to vol. 80) no. 10 (1983): 631-49. The problem here is how a non-Calvinist can explain divine knowledge of *evil*—free actions—if God is the cause of his own knowledge. This consideration may have led Aquinas to back away from the notion of causal knowledge in his later work. See R. T. Wallis, "Divine Omniscience in Plotinus, Proclus and Aquinas," in *Neoplatonism and Early Christian Thought*, ed. H. J. Blumenthal and R. A. Markus (London: Variorum, 1981), p. 231.

[61]See Paul Althaus, *The Theology of Martin Luther*, trans. Robert Schultz (Philadelphia: Fortress, 1963), p. 31.

[62]See B. A. Gerish, "'To the Unknown God': Luther and Calvin on the Hiddenness of God," *The Journal of Religion* 53, no. 3 (1973): 263-92; and Alister McGrath, *Luther's Theology of the Cross: Martin Luther's Theological Breakthrough* (New York: Basil Blackwell, 1985), pp. 148-75.

[63]Martin Luther, *The Bondage of the Will*, trans. J. I. Packer and O. R. Johnston (Old Tappan, N.J.: Revell, 1957), p. 170.

[64]Ibid., p. 80.

[65]See Farley, *Providence of God*, pp. 139-41.

[66]Gerish, "'To the Unknown God,'" p. 274.

[67]McGrath, *Luther's Theology of the Cross*, p. 167.

[68]John Calvin *Institutes of the Christian Religion* 1.10.2.

[69]Ibid., 1.16.3. See also 1.17.1; 1.18.3. On Calvin's definition of power, see Anna Case-Winters, *God's Power: Traditional Understandings and Contemporary Challenges* (Louisville, Ky.: Westminster John Knox, 1990), pp. 44, 50, 89.

[70]Calvin *Institutes* 3.23.6. See also 3.23.7; 3.21.5. Calvin's teaching on predestination is quite similar to that of Aquinas.

[71]In his theodicy Calvin uses circular reasoning and equivocation, resorts to name calling and, when he gives up on rational argument, appeals to mystery. See Case-Winters, *God's Power*, pp. 73-80.

[72]Calvin *Institutes* 1.16.3; 1.17.1.

[73]See the discussion in Gerish, "'To the Unknown God,'" p. 285 n. 84.

[74]Calvin *Institutes* 1.17.2. Calvin locates our assurance of salvation solely in Christ, but it hardly affords *us* assurance since the hidden will of God may have decreed that we only "look like" genuine believers, when, in fact, we are reprobate. Only God knows for sure!

[75]See Case-Winters, *God's Power*, pp. 45, 84-85.

[76]Calvin *Institutes* 1.13.1.

[77]Ibid., 1.17.12-14.

[78]See the discussion in 3.12 of this book.

[79]Calvin *Institutes* 3.20.11-16. Furthermore, in his commentary on Jeremiah (18:7-10) he vacillates back and forth between the "theologically correct" speech of absolute omnipotence, which does not respond to anything, and the "preaching voice" of divine responsiveness, which does not control everything. He even says that the Israelites' sin was the "cause" of the divine judgment. (Was this a slip of the pen?)

[80]On this, see Walker Butin, *Revelation, Redemption and Response: Calvin's Trinitarian Understanding of the Divine-Human Relationship* (New York: Oxford University Press, 1995), pp. 125-26, 168 n. 7, 189 n. 81. For Calvin, the will of God is prior to and more essential than the revealed Trinity.

[81]Brunner, *Christian Doctrine of God*, p. 315.

[82]Richard A. Muller's *God, Creation and Providence in the Thought of Jacob Arminius* (Grand Rapids, Mich.: Baker, 1991) makes it quite clear that the real debate was over the doctrine of God.

[83]On the influence of Eastern Orthodoxy on John Wesley's thought see Randy L. Maddox, *Responsible Grace: John Wesley's Practical Theology* (Nashville: Abingdon, 1994), pp. 23, 28. I am indebted to Maddox's fine study for my views on Wesley.

[84]See ibid., p. 56.

[85]On the relational themes in Wesley, see Mildred Bangs Wynkoop, *A Theology of Love: The Dynamic of Wesleyanism* (Kansas City, Mo.: Beacon Hill, 1972), pp. 87-91, 209-13.

[86]Sermon 67, "On Divine Providence," in John Wesley, *The Works of John Wesley*, ed. Albert C. Outler (Nashville: Abingdon, 1985), 2:541.

[87]See Sermon 58, "On Predestination," in *Works of John Wesley*, 2:417.

[88]Paul Tillich, *Systematic Theology*, 3 vols. (Chicago: University of Chicago Press, 1951-1963).

[89]Tillich, *Systematic Theology*, 1:271-72.

[90]Ibid., 1:223.

[91]Ibid., 3:120. See also 3:192. In this way Tillich attempts to overcome the "subject-object" schema.

[92]A. W. Tozer, *The Knowledge of the Holy: The Attributes of God, Their Meaning in the Christian Life* (San Francisco: Harper & Row, 1978), p. 60.

[93]W. Bingham Hunter, *The God Who Hears* (Downers Grove, Ill.: InterVarsity Press, 1986), pp. 52-53.

[94]Paul Helm, *The Providence of God*, Contours of Christian Theology (Downers Grove, Ill.: InterVarsity Press, 1994), p. 141.

[95]See my discussion of this simile in 3.15.

[96]Carl F. H. Henry, *God, Revelation and Authority* (Waco, Tex.: Word, 1982), 5:304. The

relevant sections are volume 5, chapters 6, 12, 14-16, and volume 6, pages 84-85. At one point Henry says that at every moment in history God has alternatives open to him (5:304). This seems inconsistent, however, given what he says immediately following.

[97]See David Basinger, *Divine Power in Process Theism* (Albany: State University of New York Press, 1988).

[98]See the excellent critique by Gregory Boyd, *Trinity and Process: A Critical Evaluation and Reconstruction of Hartshorne's Di-Polar Theism Towards a Trinitarian Metaphysics* (New York: Peter Lang, 1992).

[99]James Oliver Buswell Jr., *A Systematic Theology of the Christian Religion* (Grand Rapids, Mich.: Zondervan, 1962), 1:56.

[100]Nicholas Wolterstorff, "God Everlasting," in *God and the Good*, ed. Clifton Orlebeke and Lewis Smedes (Grand Rapids, Mich.: Eerdmans, 1975), pp. 181-203; Stephen Davis, *Logic and the Nature of God* (Grand Rapids, Mich.: Eerdmans, 1983).

[101]Jack Cottrell, *What the Bible Says About God the Ruler* (Joplin, Mo.: College Press, 1984), p. 217. For Cottrell, God's foreknowledge is conditioned by what his creatures decide.

[102]Richard Foster, *Prayer: Finding the Heart's True Home* (New York: HarperCollins, 1992), pp. 181, 225, 247, 249; and Foster, *Celebration of Discipline: The Path to Spiritual Growth*, rev. ed. (New York: HarperCollins, 1988), pp. 35, 40.

[103]Foster, *Celebration of Discipline*, p. 35.

[104]Donald Bloesch, *Essentials of Evangelical Theology* (New York: Harper & Row, 1982), 1:31. See also 1:27-31; 2:57-58.

[105]Gabriel Fackre, *The Christian Story*, rev. ed. (Grand Rapids, Mich.: Eerdmans, 1984), 1:250-65.

[106]Among those who affirm the risk model of providence are the following: David Basinger, "Practical Implications," in *The Openness of God: A Biblical Challenge to the Traditional Understanding of God* (Downers Grove, Ill.: InterVarsity Press, 1994); Richard Rice, *God's Foreknowledge and Man's Free Will* (Minneapolis: Bethany House, 1985); Clark Pinnock, "Between Classical and Process Theism," in *Process Theology*, ed. Ronald Nash (Grand Rapids, Mich.: Baker, 1987); Pinnock, "God Limits His Knowledge," in *Predestination and Free Will*, ed. David Basinger and Randall Basinger (Downers Grove, Ill.: InterVarsity Press, 1986); John Sanders, "God as Personal," in *The Grace of God, the Will of Man*, ed. Clark Pinnock (Grand Rapids, Mich.: Zondervan, 1989); Gregory Boyd, *Trinity and Process* and *God at War: The Bible and Spiritual Conflict* (Downers Grove, Ill.: InterVarsity Press, 1997); and Henry H. Knight III, *A Future for Truth: Evangelical Theology in a Postmodern World* (Nashville: Abingdon, 1997). From the Reformed side see Harry Boer, *An Ember Still Glowing* (Grand Rapids, Mich.: Eerdmans, 1990). It has also been held by numerous Arminian theologians, among whom the work of Lorenzo D. McCabe stands out as he discusses virtually every biblical text relating to foreknowledge. See his *Divine Nescience of Future Contingencies a Necessity* (New York: Phillips & Hunt, 1882) and *The Foreknowledge of God* (Cincinnati: Cranston & Stowe, 1887). Gordon Olson, *The Foreknowledge of God* and *The Omniscience of the Godhead* (Arlington Heights, Ill.: Bible Research Corporation) closely follows McCabe. See also chapter five, n. 125, in this book.

Other theologians affirming relational theism include the following: Jack Cottrell, *What the Bible Says About God;* William Pratney, *The Nature and Character of God* (Minneapolis: Bethany House, 1988); James Daane, "Can a Man Bless God?" in *God and the Good*, ed. Clifton Orlebeke and Lewis Smedes (Grand Rapids, Mich.: Eerdmans, 1975), pp. 165-73. Philip Yancey, *Disappointment with God: Three Questions No One Asks Aloud* (Grand Rapids, Mich.: Zondervan, 1988), speaks of God's taking risks and limiting himself (pp. 59-61, 140) and of God's having a give-and-take relationship with us (p. 149). God suffers with us (p. 91) and even though God has foreknowledge and is timeless, yet God "learns" in the sense of taking on new experiences (pp. 63, 197-99). Gilbert Bilezikian, *Christianity 101* (Grand Rapids, Mich.: Zondervan, 1993), says that God freely chooses not to know the future. John Boykin, *The Gospel of Coincidence: Is God in Control?* (Grand Rapids, Mich.: Zondervan, 1986), argues for a nondetermining God and seems to suggest (p. 80 n. 2) that even though God has foreknowledge, we can prevent what God knows will happen.

[107]See Stephen J. Land, *Pentecostal Spirituality* (Sheffield: Sheffield Academic Press, 1993).

[108]Major Jones, *The Color of God: The Concept of God in Afro-American Thought* (Macon, Ga.: Mercer University Press, 1987), p. 95.

[109]See especially Terence Fretheim's *The Suffering of God*, Overtures to Biblical Theology (Philadelphia: Fortress, 1984); and *Exodus*, Interpretation (Louisville, Ky.: John Knox, 1991).

[110]Thomas Torrance, *Space, Time and Incarnation* (New York: Oxford University Press, 1969), pp. 74-75.

[111]Thomas C. Oden, *The Living God* (San Francisco: Harper & Row, 1987), pp. 53-130.

[112]Paul Fiddes, *The Creative Suffering of God* (New York: Oxford University Press, 1988).

[113]Jürgen Moltmann, *Theology of Hope* (London: SCM Press, 1967); Moltmann, *The Crucified God,* trans. R. A. Wilson and John Bowden (New York: Harper & Row, 1974); Wolfhart Pannenberg, *Systematic Theology,* trans. Geoffrey W. Bromiley (Grand Rapids, Mich.: Eerdmans, 1991). It should be noted that these two theologians are heavily influenced by Georg Hegel and that they use the dialectic. Hence, certain passages suggest the open God whereas others seem to take it back, intimating that God is not genuinely involved in the temporal process, only in the dialectical (logical) process.

[114]See Jenson's *Triune Identity.*

[115]Emil Brunner, *Christian Doctrine of God;* Karl Barth, *Church Dogmatics* 3/3, trans. Geoffrey W. Bromiley and T. F. Torrance (Edinburgh: T & T Clark, 1960), p. 149; Eberhard Jüngel, *God as the Mystery of the World,* trans. Darrell L. Guder (Grand Rapids, Mich.: Eerdmans, 1983); Colin Gunton, *The Promise of Trinitarian Theology* (Edinburgh: T & T Clark, 1991); Thomas Finger, *Christian Theology: An Eschatological Approach* (Scottsdale, Penn.: Herald, 1989), 2:481-508. C. S. Lewis, *God in the Dock: Essays on Theology and Ethics,* ed. Walter Hooper (Grand Rapids, Mich.: Eerdmans, 1970), p. 106, says that God grants significant freedom to his creatures and allows a certain amount of free play to his own plans, which can be modified in response to our prayers.

[116]Particularly helpful is Vincent Brümmer's *Speaking of a Personal God* (New York: Cambridge University Press, 1992). This, along with his other works, will be much used in the next three chapters of this book. See also Hendrikus Berkhof, *Christian Faith,* trans. Sierd Woudstra (Grand Rapids, Mich.: Eerdmans, 1979); and Adriö König, *Here Am I* (Grand Rapids, Mich.: Eerdmans, 1982).

[117]LaCugna, *God For Us;* and Elizabeth A. Johnson, *She Who Is: The Mystery of God in Feminist Theological Discourse* (New York: Crossroad, 1992).

[118]W. Norris Clarke, *God, Knowable and Unknowable,* ed. Robert J. Roth (New York: Fordham University Press, 1973); Clarke, *The Philosophical Approach to God* (Winston-Salem, N.C.: Wake Forest University Press, 1979); William J. Hill, *Search for the Absent God: Tradition and Modernity in Religious Understanding,* ed. Mary Catherine Hilkert (New York: Crossroad, 1992); John H. Wright, "The Eternal Plan of Divine Providence," *Theological Studies* 27 (1966): 27-57; Wright, "Divine Knowledge and Human Freedom: The God Who Dialogues," *Theological Studies* 38 (1977): 450-77. I am appreciative of the moves these "Thomists" are making, though not all Thomists are pleased with including receptivity in God. See the debate between Steven A. Long, "Personal Receptivity and Act," *The Thomist* 61, no. 1 (1997): 1-32; and Kenneth L. Schmitz, "Created Receptivity," *The Thomist* 61, no. 3 (1997): 339-72. It is wonderful that some Thomists see the need to include receptivity and responsiveness in God.

[119]Clarke, *God, Knowable and Unknowable,* p. 44.

[120]See Bishop Maximos Aghiorgoussis, "Orthodox Soteriology," and John Breck, "Divine Initiative: Salvation in Orthodox Theology," in *Salvation in Christ: A Lutheran-Orthodox Dialogue,* ed. John Meyendorff and Robert Tobias (Minneapolis: Augsburg, 1992); and

Kallistos (Timothy) Ware, *The Orthodox Church* (London: Penguin, 1987), pp. 223-30.
[121]Ware, *Orthodox Church*, p. 227.
[122]See William Hasker, *God, Time and Knowledge,* Cornell Studies in the Philosophy of Religion (Ithaca, N.Y.: Cornell University Press, 1989); Hasker and Basinger have chapters in *Openness of God*; A. N. Prior, "The Formalities of Omniscience," *Philosophy* 32 (1962): 119-29; J. R. Lucas, *The Freedom of the Will* (Oxford: Oxford University Press, 1970); Lucas, *The Future: An Essay on God, Temporality and Truth* (Cambridge, Mass.: Basil Blackwell, 1989); Peter Geach, *Providence and Evil* (Cambridge: Cambridge University Press, 1977); Richard Swinburne, *The Coherence of Theism,* rev. ed. (New York: Oxford University Press, 1977); Richard Purtill, "Fatalism and the Omnitemporality of Truth," *Faith and Philosophy* 5 (1988): 185-92; and Keith Ward, *Holding Fast to God: A Reply to Don Cupitt* (London: SPCK, 1982); Ward, *Divine Action* (San Francisco: Torch, 1991).

Chapter 6: Risk and the Divine Character
[1]H. H. Farmer, *The World and God: A Study of Prayer, Providence and Miracle in Christian Experience,* rev. ed. (London: Nisbet, 1955), p. 236.
[2]On a relationship of love, see Vincent Brümmer, *The Model of Love* (New York: Cambridge University Press, 1993). On friendship, see Sallie McFague, *Models of God: Theology for an Ecological, Nuclear Age* (Philadelphia: Fortress, 1987), pp. 157-80.
[3]Hendrikus Berkhof, *Christian Faith: An Introduction to the Study of the Faith,* trans. Sierd Woudstra (Grand Rapids, Mich.: Eerdmans, 1979), pp. 106, 222.
[4]See Karl Barth, *Church Dogmatics* 3/3, trans. Geoffrey W. Bromiley and T. F. Torrance (Edinburgh: T & T Clark, 1960), pp. 45, 119, 285.
[5]Barth, *Church Dogmatics* 3/3, p. 149. Also see pp. 92-93.
[6]Paul Helm, *The Providence of God,* Contours of Christian Theology (Downers Grove, Ill.: InterVarsity Press, 1994), p. 40.
[7]William Hasker, *God, Time and Knowledge,* Cornell Studies in the Philosophy of Religion (Ithaca, N.Y.: Cornell University Press, 1989), p. 197.
[8]David Basinger, "Middle Knowledge and Divine Control: Some Clarifications," *International Journal for Philosophy of Religion* 30 (1991): 135.
[9]David Basinger, *The Case for Freewill Theism: A Philosophical Assessment* (Downers Grove, Ill.: InterVarsity Press, 1996), p. 48.
[10]Richard Rice uses this definition of risk in his *God's Foreknowledge and Man's Free Will* (Minneapolis: Bethany House, 1985), p. 42.
[11]At this point the concept of permission is usually introduced (see 7.4).
[12]Admittedly, it is somewhat speculative to say that prior to his decision to create, God thought sin to be improbable. But I think a case can be made for it in light of God's repeated expression of surprise at sin despite all the steps he takes to eradicate it in the Old Testament.
[13]See Joseph C. McLelland, *God the Anonymous: A Study in Alexandrian Philosophical Theology,* Patristic Monograph Series (Cambridge, Mass.: Philadelphia Patristic Foundation, 1976), pp. 25-44; and Samuel Sandmel, *Philo of Alexandria* (New York: Oxford University Press, 1979).
[14]N. T. Wright, *The New Testament and the People of God,* Christian Origins and the Question of God (Minneapolis: Fortress, 1992), p. 248 n. 15.
[15]Elizabeth A. Johnson attempts to remain faithful to the intentions of classical theism while reforming it in light of a relational God. See her wonderful book *She Who Is: The Mystery of God in Feminist Theological Discourse* (New York: Crossroad, 1993). Other Catholics of interest in this regard are W. Norris Clarke, *God, Knowable and Unknowable,* ed. Robert J. Roth (New York: Fordham University Press, 1973); Clarke, *The Philosophical Approach to God* (Winston-Salem, N.C.: Wake Forest University Press, 1979); William J. Hill, *Search for the Absent God: Tradition and Modernity in Religious Understanding,* ed. Mary Catherine

Hilkert (New York: Crossroad, 1992).

[16]J. R. Lucas, *The Future: An Essay on God, Temporality and Truth* (Cambridge, Mass.: Basil Blackwell, 1989), p. 216, and William Hasker, "A Philosophical Perspective," in *The Openness of God: A Biblical Challenge to the Traditional Understanding of God*, by Clark Pinnock et al. (Downers Grove, Ill.: InterVarsity Press, 1994), pp. 132-33, point out that this argument is fallacious because it assumes a linear scale of excellence for everything. But such is not the case with our experiences in life.

[17]See James Daane, *The Freedom of God: A Study of Election and Pulpit* (Grand Rapids, Mich.: Eerdmans, 1973), pp. 81-90.

[18]Aristotle *Eudemian Ethics* 1244b can be found in *The Basic Works of Aristotle*, ed. Richard McKeon (New York: Random House, 1941). For Aristotle, God can neither be an efficient cause nor be aware of the existence of others, since this would imply a change, as well as dependence, in the being of God.

[19]Helpful in this regard are Clark Pinnock's "Systematic Theology," in *Openness of God*, William Hasker's "Philosophical Perspective" and his *God, Time and Knowledge*. Frank G. Kirkpatrick's *Together Bound: God, History and the Religious Community* (New York: Oxford University Press, 1994) is especially helpful in tracing out the implications of God as personal agent in relation to us.

[20]Feuerbach, Freud and other atheist critics are correct in some of their criticisms concerning the Christian doctrine of God. In many respects this God is secular, constructed without careful attention to salvation history. For helpful discussions of the atheistic philosophers and their conceptions of God, see Eberhard Jüngel, *God as the Mystery of the World: On the Foundation of the Theology of the Crucified One in the Dispute Between Theism and Atheism*, trans. Darrell L. Guder (Grand Rapids, Mich.: Eerdmans, 1983); and Hans Küng, *Does God Exist?* trans. Edward Quinn (New York: Vintage, 1981). Unfortunately, Küng seems to end up with the absolutistic God beyond God concept.

[21]Emil Brunner, *Christian Doctrine of God*, trans. Olive Wyon (Philadelphia: Westminster, 1949), p. 192.

[22]On the historical debate over God as a "person," see Berkhof, *Christian Faith*, pp. 130-33; and Brunner, *Christian Doctrine of God*, pp. 121-27, 139-41. It is common for people to say that "religiously" we need a personal God who enters into relationships with us but then go on to reject this either as being infantile or as not being the true nature of God—back to the "God beyond God." In this vein are the works of Gordon Kaufman, *God the Problem* (Cambridge: Harvard University Press, 1972); and Kaufman, *In Face of Mystery: A Constructive Theology* (Cambridge: Harvard University Press, 1993). For a solid defense of God as personal agent, see Kirkpatrick, *Together Bound*, pp. 54-102.

[23]Extremely helpful here are Catherine Mowry LaCugna's *God for Us: The Trinity and Christian Life* (New York: HarperCollins, 1991), pp. 14-15, 243-317; and Robert W. Jenson's *The Triune Identity* (Philadelphia: Fortress, 1982). See also Ted Peters, *God as Trinity: Relationality and Temporality in Divine Life* (Louisville, Ky.: Westminster John Knox, 1993). Colin E. Gunton provides an illuminating study of the disastrous impact wrought on Western culture by the lack of trinitarian relationality in Christian theology in *The One, The Three and the Many: God, Creation and the Culture of Modernity*, The 1992 Bampton Lectures (New York: Cambridge University Press, 1993). Interestingly, both John Calvin and Jonathan Edwards seemed to affirm a dynamic conception of the Trinity, even though they failed to consistently apply this to the divine-human relationship. For Edwards, God enlarges himself as he relates to more and more souls. On Calvin, see Walker Butin, *Revelation, Redemption and Response: Calvin's Trinitarian Understanding of the Divine-Human Relationship* (New York: Oxford University Press, 1995); for Edwards, see Sang Hyun Lee, *The Philosophical Theology of Jonathan Edwards* (Princeton: Princeton University Press, 1988), chaps. 7-8.

[24]Jenson, *Triune Identity*, p. 85, observes that if the Father begets the Son, then to be God is not only to give but to receive.

[25]See Gregory A. Boyd, *Trinity and Process: A Critical Evaluation and Reconstruction of Hartshorne's Di-Polar Theism Towards a Trinitarian Metaphysics* (New York: Peter Lang, 1992).

[26]Søren Kierkegaard, *Christian Discourses*, trans. Walter Lowrie (New York: Oxford University Press, 1939), p. 132.

[27]W. H. Vanstone, *The Risk of Love* (New York: Oxford University Press, 1978); Brümmer, *Model of Love*.

[28]Vanstone, *Risk of Love*, p. 46.

[29]Classical theism has resisted attributing to God the notions of waiting and trying. Barth, *Church Dogmatics* 2/1, pp. 409-11, says that God is patient, giving the other space and time to develop.

[30]Helpful here is Paul R. Sponheim, *Faith and the Other: A Relational Theology* (Minneapolis: Fortress, 1993), pp. 84-98.

[31]The appeal to antinomy (God can force our love) was determined to be an illegitimate theological move in 2.5.2.

[32]See Brümmer, *Model of Love*, pp. 163, 172.

[33]On the history of the discussion, see J. K. Mozley, *The Impassibility of God: A Survey of Christian Thought* (New York: Cambridge University Press, 1926); Joseph M. Hallman, *The Descent of God: Divine Suffering in History and Theology* (Minneapolis: Fortress, 1991); Richard Bauckham, "Only the Suffering God can Help: Divine Passibility in Modern Theology," *Themelios* 9, no. 3 (1984): 6-12; and Paul S. Fiddes, *The Creative Suffering of God* (New York: Oxford University Press, 1988).

[34]Berkhof, *Christian Faith*, pp. 133-40, sees God as the "defenseless superior power."

[35]LaCugna, *God for Us*, p. 301, is correct when she asserts that the traditional denial of any real suffering to the godhead was a defeat for trinitarian theology because it allowed the attributes of God from Neoplatonism to remain intact, controlling the reading of the Bible.

[36]Concerning whether God could ever act in unloving ways towards us see note 61 below.

[37]Brümmer, *Model of Love*, pp. 150-56.

[38]Brunner, *Christian Doctrine of God*, p. 188.

[39]On the notion of polarities or tensions in the godhead in Judaism, Christianity, Hinduism and Buddhism, see the insightful study by John B. Carman, *Majesty and Meekness: A Comparative Study of Contrast and Harmony in the Concept of God* (Grand Rapids, Mich.: Eerdmans, 1994).

[40]See Donald G. Bloesch, *God the Almighty: Power, Wisdom, Holiness, Love*, Christian Foundations (Downers Grove, Ill.: InterVarsity Press, 1995), pp. 141-43. The sermons and fiction of George MacDonald bring out this idea better than any other writings I know.

[41]See Clark H. Pinnock and Robert C. Brow, *Unbounded Love: A Good News Theology for the 21st Century* (Downers Grove, Ill.: InterVarsity Press, 1994), pp. 67-77; and Karl Barth, *Church Dogmatics* 2/1, pp. 376, 418-19. G. C. Berkouwer says the basic problem with Barth's theology of God is that "the love of God dominates over His righteousness, His grace over His wrath." See his *The Providence of God*, trans. Lewis Smedes (Grand Rapids, Mich.: Eerdmans, 1952), p. 264.

[42]Clarke, *God, Knowable and Unknowable*, p. 44.

[43]I would add that the "goodness" of God is not to be thought of in the abstract but, rather, defined in terms of the divine project. This will keep us from defining divine love and goodness in egocentric ways.

[44]Augustine *Enchiridion* 26, in *Augustine: Confessions and Enchiridion*, trans. Albert Outler, Library of Christian Classics Vol. 7 (Philadelphia: Westminster, 1955), p. 400.

[45]For a philosophical defense of this idea, see William Hasker, "Yes, God Has Beliefs," *Religious Studies* 24, no. 3 (1988): 385-94.

[46]An introduction to the Christian faith oriented around the theme of divine love is Pinnock and Brow's *Unbounded Love*. The classic work on divine love is by Anders Nygren, *Agape*

and Eros, trans. Philip S. Watson (Philadelphia: Westminster, 1953).

[47]The church loses a significant aspect of life if it does not permit lament. See Walter Brueggemann, "The Costly Loss of Lament," *Journal for the Study of the Old Testament* 36 (1986): 57-71.

[48]See Barth, *Church Dogmatics* 2/2, p. 165.

[49]Someone with a penchant for "omni" may say that God is omnicompetent.

[50]Markus Barth, *Ephesians: Introduction, Translation and Commentary on Chapters 1—3* (Garden City, N.Y.: Doubleday, 1974), p. 106.

[51]Boyd, *Trinity and Process,* p. 336.

[52]Berkhof, *Christian Faith,* pp. 140-47.

[53]See Cornelius Plantinga Jr., "Social Trinity and Tritheism," in *Trinity, Incarnation and Atonement,* ed. Ronald J. Feenstra and C. Plantinga (Notre Dame, Ind.: University of Notre Dame Press, 1989); Clark H. Pinnock, *Flame of Love: A Theology of the Holy Spirit* (Downers Grove, Ill.: InterVarsity Press, 1996), pp. 21-48; Robert L. Wilkin, "Not a Solitary God: The Triune God of the Bible," *Pro Ecclesia* 3 (1994): 36-55; John L. Gresham, "The Social Model of the Trinity and Its Critics," *Scottish Journal of Theology* 46 (1993): 325-43; and Bloesch, *God the Almighty,* pp. 185-91.

[54]See Barth, *Church Dogmatics* 2/1, p. 499; and David B. Burrell, *Freedom and Creation in Three Traditions* (Notre Dame, Ind.: University of Notre Dame Press, 1993).

[55]Jean-Jacques Suurmond says the creation is "useless," since it exists for no reason at all. God just takes pleasure in it because God is a "playful God." See his *Word and Spirit at Play: Towards a Charismatic Theology* (Grand Rapids, Mich.: Eerdmans, 1994).

[56]I do not know this *de re* (as if I know God in himself apart from revelation). Rather, I affirm God's freedom in creation *de dicto,* as part of the faith—that is, in its relation to other beliefs. The statements that God did not have to create and did not have to create this sort of world are, in some respects, speculative. But they are legitimate as long as they are seen as explications of the doctrine of creation.

[57]Plato *Laws* 818, as found in *The Dialogues of Plato,* trans. B. Jowett (New York: Random House, 1937), 2:571. See also *Laws* 741 and *Timaeus* 30.48.

[58]Alvin Plantinga studies this most thoroughly in *Does God Have a Nature?* (Milwaukee: Marquette University Press, 1980). See also James F. Sennett, "Is God Essentially God?" *Religious Studies* 30, no. 3 (1994): 295-303; Wesley Morrison, "Is God 'Significantly Free?'" *Faith and Philosophy* 2, no. 3 (1985): 257-64; and Thomas Flint, "The Problem of Divine Freedom," *American Philosophical Quarterly* 20 (1983): 255-64.

There are some key questions. Must God have the properties that he has essentially? Are only some of the divine properties essential? Is God sovereign over his nature, or must God do what the divine nature determines? Does God have libertarian freedom (to do otherwise)? Does God have morally significant freedom in the sense that God could do a moral evil, or is God essentially good? If God lacks morally significant freedom then, though God may be perfectly good, can it be held that God is "morally" good and praiseworthy? Though the Christian tradition has held that it is "impossible" for God to sin, there has not been agreement on the sense in which it is impossible. Impossible may be understood as ontological (the divine nature prevents it) or volitional (God never chooses to sin).

If God lacks libertarian freedom, then it would seem that creation and redemption were necessary and God could not have done otherwise. A more traditional approach is to say that God is essentially good and could not sin because his nature constrains him. God has perfect goodness but not moral goodness. If God has libertarian freedom but lacks morally significant freedom, one may ask whether divine grace, love and salvation are necessary expressions of God's essential goodness. *Must* God manifest these properties? Can God do otherwise? *Must* God love us? Or does his "love" consist of acts of supererogation? Thomas V. Morris, *Our Idea of God* (Notre Dame, Ind.: University of Notre Dame Press, 1991), pp.

54-64, 77-80, suggests that though God is necessarily good, God does not have to perform *all* the good actions he does; some are supererogatory. But how does Morris know which acts are supererogatory and which ones are necessary? Does God love us freely? Since God, according to this perspective, is not morally praiseworthy, is such a being a proper object of worship? Also, if God has libertarian but not significant freedom and so is unable to sin, then why did not God create humans with libertarian but not significant freedom? Does this not raise problems for the freewill defense? Is significant freedom or is only libertarian freedom necessary for loving relationships? If libertarian freedom is all that is required, then one might suggest that God could have created libertarianly free beings who would freely love him and one another. But since these beings would lack (as God lacks) morally significant freedom, there would be no moral evil. If so, then why did God not do so?

On the other hand, ascribing to God both libertarian freedom as well as morally significant freedom leads to the question, Could God commit a moral evil? Does God have freedom from sin contingently or volitionally? Is it possible for God to sin? If so, could we place ultimate trust in a being for whom this was an option? Is God simply consistently good? Proponents of this approach often say that God could do evil but never does, and so God is morally praiseworthy. God is then perfectly and consistently good though not essentially good. See Stephen T. Davis, *Logic and the Nature of God* (Grand Rapids, Mich.: Eerdmans, 1983), pp. 86-96; Richard R. La Croix, "Omniprescience and Divine Determinism," *Religious Studies* 12 (September 1976): 375-76. Robert F. Brown, "God's Ability to Will Moral Evil," *Faith and Philosophy* 8, no. 1 (1991): 3-20, believes that God "may" sin from time to time but would nevertheless remain a vastly morally superior being. A. van de Beek, *Why? On Suffering, Guilt and God*, trans. John Vriend (Grand Rapids, Mich.: Eerdmans, 1990), pp. 261-76, thinks that God actually has committed moral evils on occasion, but in Jesus we now know that God will never take such paths again.

Some authors posit a "dark side" in the divine nature. Jon D. Levenson, "Cataclysm, Survival and Regeneration," in *Confronting Omnicide: Jewish Reflections on Weapons of Mass Destruction*, ed. Daniel Landes (Northvale, N.J.: Jason Aronson, 1991), pp. 39-68, discusses various texts in the Hebrew Bible that he claims depict God as doing evil and possessing a "nearly Satanic" side. He maintains that in some texts Yahweh is vengeful beyond reason or is the source of evil. (For a response to such claims, see p. 292, n. 58, and p. 298, n. 170, of this book.) The notion of a dark side in God is also found in the philosophical school known as Boston Personalism (Brightman and Bertocci) in Jack Miles's *God: A Biography* (New York: Knopf, 1995) and in various world religions. See Carman, *Majesty and Meekness*.

If God has morally significant freedom, are we justified in trusting God? Vincent Brümmer, *Speaking of a Personal God* (New York: Cambridge University Press, 1992), pp. 90-107; and Brümmer, "Paul Helm on God and the Approval of Sin," *Religious Studies* 20 (June 1994): 223-26, replies that God, being omniscient and perfectly free from constraint, would never be "disposed" to act out of character, which is all Christians need to affirm *(de dicto)* as part of the faith. In *Model of Love*, p. 178, he says that God loves us because he wants to, not because he lacks the ability to reject us.

In my opinion, the Christian faith does not stand or fall on God's having essential goodness; it stands or falls on Jesus Christ. Regardless of the outcome of this debate, we may still say, following the biblical material, that God has repeatedly demonstrated his love, wisdom and faithfulness to us—despite the fact that there have been some rough spots in the divine-human relationship from our perspective. We have solid reasons to trust God because of the kind of character God has manifested toward us in the outworking of his project. Paul says that God has *demonstrated* his love toward us in Jesus (Rom 5:8) and that nothing can separate us from the love of God in Christ Jesus (Rom 8:35-39). If we believe that God could do evil, but never does, then do we have ground for not trusting God? Must we affirm God's essential goodness in order to trust God? If the work of Christ does not convince you that God loves you, what will? What is the ultimate basis for distinctively *Christian* trust in God? Is it the work of Christ? Or is it some philosophical understanding of the divine nature? Is Jesus not enough?

[59]See Norman Kretzman, "Goodness, Knowledge and Indeterminacy in the Philosophy of Thomas Aquinas," *The Journal of Philosophy* (supplement to vol. 80), no. 10 (1983): 631-49; and Keith Ward, *Rational Theology and the Creativity of God* (New York: Pilgrim, 1982), pp. 74-80, 171. Also see Robert Merrihew Adams, "Must God Create the Best?" *Philosophical Review* 81 (1972): 312-32. Paul Helm believes that creation is contingent and that God had to create this particular world, since God did not select from "options." That is, God had no choices as to what sort of world to create given his nature. See his *Eternal God: A Study of God Without Time* (New York: Oxford University Press, 1988), pp. 186-87.

[60]Unfortunately, Ward, *Rational Theology,* pp. 81, 86, 141, caricatures social trinitarians as polytheists. After properly criticizing the doctrine of divine necessity, Ward falls prey to saying that God is not self-sufficient and so *must* create other beings for relationship. He goes on to qualify the way God "needs" the world by saying God does not need anything outside himself but that God "would not be completely what he is without it; though he need not have been just what he is in every respect" (p. 144).

[61]Brunner, *Christian Doctrine of God,* pp. 144, 147. Burrell, *Freedom and Creation,* pp. 8-26, points out that the notion of a freely created world could only arise in Judaism, Christianity and Islam as an explication of religious faith.

[62]Wolfhart Pannenberg, *Basic Questions in Theology,* trans. George H. Kehm (Philadelphia: Westminster, 1983), 2:171. (See also p. 138.)

[63]Brümmer, *Model of Love,* p. 237. Disappointingly, he goes on to reject the social Trinity. He erroneously believes that it negates the unity of the Godhead and rules out the need of God to love us. But a social Trinity could still freely choose to "need" our love in the sense described by Brümmer. There is nothing to prevent the social Trinity from deciding to be conditioned by our love. In my opinion both Ward and Brümmer fail to grasp what contemporary social trinitarians are saying. See the references in note 53 above.

[64]Barth, *Church Dogmatics* 3/4, pp. 108-9. Fiddes, *Creative Suffering of God,* p. 67, observes that this does not rule out divine self-sufficiency regarding God's self-existence.

[65]Thomas C. Oden, *The Living God* (San Francisco: Harper & Row, 1987), pp. 110-14.

[66]Berkhof, *Christian Faith,* p. 476.

[67]See Isaak August Dorner, *Divine Immutability: A Critical Reconsideration,* trans. Robert R. Williams and Claude Welch, Fortress Texts in Modern Theology (Minneapolis: Fortress, 1994); and Rem B. Edwards, "The Pagan Dogma of the Absolute Unchangeableness of God," *Religious Studies* 14 (1978): 305-13.

[68]This argument is fallacious because there are changes that are required in order to remain in a constant state of excellence. See Hasker, "Philosophical Perspective," pp. 132-33.

[69]See, for instance, Carl F. H. Henry, *God, Revelation and Authority* (Waco, Tex.: Word, 1982), 5:304; and J. I. Packer, *Knowing God,* 20th anniversary ed. (Downers Grove, Ill.: InterVarsity Press, 1993), p. 77.

[70]Herman Bavinck, *The Doctrine of God,* trans. William Hendriksen (Grand Rapids, Mich.: Baker, 1977), p. 151.

[71]It was difficult not to conclude that God was perfectly immobile. But the purely immobile is death. See Barth, *Church Dogmatics* 2/1, p. 494.

[72]T. E. Pollard, "The Impassibility of God," *Scottish Journal of Theology* 8 (1955): 360.

[73]Bloesch, *God the Almighty,* p. 94.

[74]A. van de Beek holds that the very being of God changes and so one cannot speak of *the* omnipotence or *the* goodness of God but only of the sort of divine omnipotence or goodness manifested in a particular historical situation. It is through changes in God's goodness that he attempts to deal with the problem of evil. See his *Why?* pp. 261-74. Opposed to this are Bloesch, *God the Almighty,* p. 262; Pinnock, "Systematic Theology," pp.

117-18; and Berkhof, *Christian Faith,* p. 141. All maintain that the being of God does not change. I agree that the essence of God does not change, but I think we can only affirm this as a consequence of the faith *(de dicto),* not demonstrate it in itself *(de re).* On the Catholic side W. Norris Clarke and William Hill affirm that though God changes in his relationships, there is no change in the divine nature or perfection. See Clarke's *God, Knowable and Unknowable,* pp. 48-49, and Hill's *Search for the Absent God,* p. 64.

[75]Berkhof, *Christian Faith,* pp. 140-47.

[76]Harry M. Kuitert, *Signals from the Bible,* trans. Lewis B. Smedes (Grand Rapids, Mich.: Eerdmans, 1972), p. 54.

[77]See Lester J. Kuyper, "The Suffering and the Repentance of God," *Scottish Journal of Theology* 22 (1969): 257-77; and Daane, *Freedom of God,* pp. 90-91.

[78]Things that a timeless deity cannot do! Though I believe that God is everlasting and so experiences temporal duration, it is not absolutely essential to my argument. Certain Catholic writers, in the Thomistic tradition, attempt to reconcile divine simultaneity with God's personal give-and-take relations with us. See Clarke, *God, Knowable and Unknowable*; Clarke, *Philosophical Approach to God*; Hill, *Search for the Absent God*; John H. Wright, "The Eternal Plan of Divine Providence," *Theological Studies* 27 (1966): 27-57; Wright, "Divine Knowledge and Human Freedom: The God Who Dialogues," *Theological Studies* 38 (1977): 450-77. I am appreciative of the moves these "Thomists" are making, though not all Thomists are pleased with including receptivity in God—see the debate in *The Thomist* between Steven A. Long, "Personal Receptivity and Act," (61, no. 1 [1997]: 1-32) and Kenneth L. Schmitz, "Created Receptivity," (61, no. 3 [1997]: 339-72). I find it terrific that some Thomists see the need to move in this direction, even though I do not find the general framework of Thomism satisfactory.

In my view, the Bible depicts God as experiencing duration rather than timelessness or simultaneity. For a survey of the biblical evidence for everlastingness with attention to the philosophical issues, see Allen G. Padgett, *God, Eternity and the Nature of Time* (New York: St. Martin's, 1992), pp. 23-37. Roderick M. Chisholm and Dean W. Zimmerman, "Theology and Tense," *Noûs* 31, no. 2 (1997): 262-65, argue that theology does not require tenseless propositions for God or for "eternal verities." On the biblical words for *time,* see James Barr, *Biblical Words for Time,* 2nd ed. (London: SCM Press, 1969); and Oscar Cullman, *Christ and Time,* rev. ed., trans. F. V. Filson (London: SCM Press, 1962). In my opinion, God is everlasting through time rather than timeless or having simultaneity (all of time at once). "Time" in the sense of the measurement between objects was indeed created. "Time" in the sense of consciousness, duration and relations between persons is uncreated, since the Trinity is everlasting. See Nicholas Wolterstorff, "God Everlasting," in *God and the Good,* ed. Clifton Orlebeke and Lewis Smedes (Grand Rapids, Mich.: Eerdmans, 1975), pp. 181-203; Hasker, *God, Time and Knowledge,* pp. 144-85; and Davis, *Logic and the Nature of God,* pp. 8-24. For a helpful discussion of the impact Greek philosophical notions of time and eternity had on Christian thought, see W. Kneale, "Time and Eternity in Theology," *Proceedings of the Aristotelian Society* 61 (1960-1961): 87-108. For a defense of the compatibility of temporalism and *creatio ex nihilo,* see Thomas Senor, "Divine Temporality and Creation *ex Nihilo,*" *Faith and Philosophy* 10, no. 1 (1993): 86-92.

Interestingly, William Alston, "Divine and Human Action," in *Divine and Human Action: Essays in the Metaphysics of Theism,* ed. Thomas V. Morris (Ithaca, N.Y.: Cornell University Press, 1988), p. 279, acknowledges that the religious life seems to require a divine temporal agent but says "this more concrete picture cannot literally apply to God." Neither a timeless being nor one having simultaneity can genuinely respond, deliberate and do many of the things the Bible ascribes to God. On this see Helm, *Eternal God*; Eleonore Stump and Norman Kretzman, "Eternity," *Journal of Philosophy* 78 (1981): 429-58; and William Alston, "Functionalism and Theological Language," in *The Concept of God,* ed. Thomas Morris (New York: Oxford University Press, 1987), p. 37.

[79]Richard Creel, *Divine Impassibility: An Essay in Philosophical Theology* (Cambridge: Cambridge University Press, 1986), founds his trust on this principle. William Placher, *Narratives of a Vulnerable God: Christ, Theology and Scripture* (Louisville, Ky.: Westminster John Knox, 1994), pp. 27-52, claims that a God possessing simultaneity is necessary to ensure that God will continue to love his creatures. It is particularly disappointing that Placher, so sensitive to the gospel, would turn to an abstract principle instead of the personal God as the source of his confidence.

[80]See Barth, *Church Dogmatics* 2/1, pp. 536-38.

[81]Van de Beek, *Why?* p. 103. A good many theologians take the gospel into account when discussing omnipotence, but philosophers of religion and conservative evangelical theologians tend to ignore it.

[82]See Daniel L. Migliore, *The Power of God* (Philadelphia: Westminster, 1983), pp. 34-40.

[83]See Jüngel, *God as the Mystery of the World*, pp. 21, 48, 213, who says that metaphysics assigns God a place over us in absolute superiority. Death works under us, so whoever dies cannot be the absolutely superior. The death of Jesus is then understood to reflect a deficient God—a God who is not necessary.

[84]Augustine *Enchiridion* 26.102. It might be objected that Augustine sought to qualify this with a notion of "permission" where God "allows" some things to happen (24.95-96). But it is clear even in this context that Augustine affirms "specific sovereignty" in the sense that no detail in history is other than what God specifically wills it to be.

[85]See Anna Case-Winters, *God's Power: Traditional Understandings and Contemporary Challenges* (Louisville, Ky.: Westminster John Knox, 1990), pp. 39-93.

[86]See Paul. G. Hiebert, *Anthropological Reflections on Missiological Issues* (Grand Rapids, Mich.: Baker, 1994), pp. 204-8.

[87]Migliore, *Power of God,* p. 68, asks whether our evangelism or church government, for example, reflect a gospel understanding of power or our secret craving for invulnerability and control.

[88]See David Basinger, *Divine Power in Process Theism: A Philosophical Critique* (Albany, N.Y.: State University of New York Press, 1988).

[89]Kierkegaard, *Christian Discourses*, p. 132.

[90]Kristiaan Depoortere, *A Different God: A Christian View of Suffering*, Louvain Theological and Pastoral Monographs (Grand Rapids, Mich.: Eerdmans, 1995), p. 84.

[91]In what follows I will freely draw on his work, though making some important modifications. This is the best philosophical study of the subject I have read. On the theological side, the discussions by Barth, Brunner and Berkhof most closely approximate my own. It should be noted that Peter Geach had earlier made the distinction between omnipotence and almightiness. Though they are helpful, I do not agree with all of Geach's points or arguments and find van den Brink a more careful guide here. See Geach's "Omnipotence," in *Providence and Evil* (Cambridge: Cambridge University Press, 1977), pp. 3-28. Thomas P. Flint and Alfred J. Freddoso argue against Geach that God is omnipotent and not merely almighty. See their "Maximal Power," in *The Concept of God*, ed. Thomas Morris (New York: Oxford University Press, 1987), pp. 134-67.

[92]For a contemporary defense of this position, see D. Goldstick, "Could God Make a Contradiction True?" *Religious Studies* 26 (1990): 377-87.

[93]The "paradox of the stone" is not nearly so delectable as the "paradox of the waffle."

[94]Barth, *Church Dogmatics* 2/1, pp. 532-38; and Bloesch, *God the Almighty*, pp. 34-35.

[95]Regarding the status of the laws of thought and mathematics, along with other "abstract objects," there are several views. One may say that they are created by God and that God was free to determine their modal status at creation or that God had to create them the way they are or that they are uncreated and have eternally existed in the mind of God as necessary thoughts. For a review of the positions, see Gijsbert van den Brink, *Almighty God: A Study of the Doctrine of Divine Omnipotence* (Kampen, Netherlands: Kok Pharos, 1992),

pp. 184-203. Van den Brink agrees with Philo, Augustine and Plantinga that they are uncreated necessary objects in the mind of God. Hence, God *cannot (de re)* do the logically contradictory or make 2 + 2 = 5. For Plantinga, if 2 + 2 = 4 is a necessary truth, then it is necessary for God as well as for us. The issue is then whether it is a necessary truth, not whether it is necessary for God.

Barth takes an entirely different approach (*Church Dogmatics* 2/1, pp. 533-38), claiming that the laws of thought are not eternal verities but created laws that God could have made otherwise. Hence, God could have made the "necessary" truths different from what we actually have; they are not necessary for God. My position is distinct from both Barth's and Plantinga's. What *we* know is that God works with us within the rules of the game he established for us at creation. These rules include the laws of thought and mathematics. Whether God created them or whether God could have made them otherwise or could break them, we cannot *(de re)* say. But we have to *(de dicto)* think this due to the conditions of the created order. They are necessary for us, but whether they are necessary for God is beyond our ken. This does not mean, however, that we can then claim that God's logic *is*, in fact, different from ours, for we cannot know that either. As creatures we have to operate within the conditions God made us to be in. If God is going to relate to us meaningfully, then God must do so within the boundaries (the rules) in which he created us. Whether God can or cannot do the logically impossible is more than I can know. But if God is going to relate to us in meaningful ways, then doing the logically impossible will not be one of them. Consequently, we can say that God has established necessary truths for us and God abides by them in relating to us. Whether they are necessary for God or not is more than we can say.

[96]Some philosophers, such as Paul Helm, *Providence of God,* p. 215, claim that God cannot do the logically contradictory. Others, however, such as Morris, *Our Idea of God,* p. 67, and Davis, *Logic and the Nature of God,* p. 78, argue only for *de dicto* knowledge on this point. On this issue of antinomies, see 2.5.2.

[97]Van den Brink, *Almighty God,* pp. 43-115, traces the historical shift of emphasis in the Christian tradition from the *potentia ordinata* to *potentia absoluta.* One very important purpose of this distinction is to rebut the principle of plenitude, whereby God's nature is so full that it must diffuse itself (p. 73). On the havoc the principle of plenitude has wreaked in Western history see Arthur O. Lovejoy, *The Great Chain of Being* (Cambridge, Mass.: Harvard University Press, 1964). Barth, *Church Dogmatics* 2/1, pp. 539-42, says the distinction has been abused in the tradition to support a *Deus absconditus* behind the *Deus revelatus.*

[98]As long as the speculation and hypothesizing is kept within the framework of what we know about the divine project, I have no objection to this. But when the *potentia absoluta* takes precedence over the *potentia ordinata,* then we again encounter the danger of defining God apart from what he has revealed to us, which will give rise to important side effects on the doctrine of providence. Brunner, *Christian Doctrine of God,* pp. 248-49, is very critical of this.

[99]Barth, *Church Dogmatics* 2/1, p. 544.

[100]Van den Brink, *Almighty God,* pp. 119-34. See also Morris, *Our Idea of God,* pp. 69-73.

[101]That Paul (in 2 Cor 10:5) is speaking about worldviews (that is, Hellenism and the Judaizers) and not the psychological control of my own inner thoughts is defended by Murray J. Harris, *2 Corinthians,* Expositor's Bible Commentary, vol. 10, ed. Frank Gaebelein (Grand Rapids, Mich.: Zondervan, 1976), pp. 380-81; and Philip E. Hughes, *Paul's Second Epistle to the Corinthians,* New International Commentary on the New Testament (Grand Rapids, Mich.: Eerdmans, 1962), pp. 352-53.

[102]See the cogent study "The Authority of Paul," in Francis Young and David F. Ford, *Meaning and Truth in 2 Corinthians* (Grand Rapids, Mich.: Eerdmans, 1988), especially pp. 215-17.

[103]Needless to say, the church has not always embodied this sort of authority but has, instead,

resorted to worldly forms where authority is not shared, but is coercive and is thought to have the final word already.

[104]Van den Brink, *Almighty God,* pp. 178-83.

[105]Brunner, *Christian Doctrine of God,* p. 254.

[106]Hill, *Search for the Absent God,* pp. 118-19.

[107]Berkhof, *Christian Faith,* pp. 133-40.

[108]Migliore, *Power of God,* p. 71.

[109]Hasker, "A Philosophical Perspective," p. 136.

[110]For a helpful survey of the debate, see Nelson Pike, "A Latter-Day Look at the Foreknowledge Problem," *International Journal for the Philosophy of Religion* 33 (June 1993): 129-64.

[111]Basinger, *The Case for Freewill Theism,* pp. 39-56, does an excellent job of demonstrating why this is so.

[112]See 8.2.3. Some conservative evangelicals believe the most important dividing line is between those who affirm foreknowledge and those who do not. Norman Geisler and Robert Strimple, for instance, claim that proponents of the openness model cannot be considered "Arminian" because Arminians affirm foreknowledge. Though this is a difference between the views, it is not the crucial difference. There are two watershed differences between the family of views I refer to as relational theism and the no-risk model. The first difference is the point made above regarding the type of sovereignty God exercises and whether God grants libertarian freedom. The second difference is that according to relational theism, God's will is, for some things, conditioned by the creatures. Geisler and Strimple affirm that God is completely unconditioned by the creatures. There is an important division between proponents of divine determinism, where God never responds to creatures, and proponents of relational theism, where God enters into genuine personal relations with creatures. Arminians and proponents of openness are relational theists, whereas Geisler and Strimple are not. See Geisler, *Creating God in the Image of Man? The New Open View of God—Neotheism's Dangerous Drift* (Minneapolis: Bethany House, 1997), pp. 131, 141; and Strimple, "What Does God Know?" in *The Coming Evangelical Crisis,* ed. John H. Armstrong (Chicago: Moody Press, 1996), p. 140. For further discussion, see also 8.2.3.2.

[113]I have not included process theology in this list because it is *not* a risk model of providence. The God of process theology does not create the world and so cannot be held accountable for what transpires in it. A process God was not faced either with a decision to create or with a decision of what sort of sovereignty to exercise. The God of process thought is impotent to act unilaterally in human affairs. See Basinger's *Divine Power in Process Theism.*

[114]David Basinger's "Middle Knowledge and Classical Christian Thought," *Religious Studies* 22, no. 3 (1986): 407-22; and *Case for Freewill Theism,* pp. 43-48, explore the elements of divine control and risk in middle knowledge, simple foreknowledge and presentism.

[115]On the fathers, see James Jorgenson, "Predestination According to Divine Foreknowledge in Patristic Tradition," in *Salvation in Christ: A Lutheran-Orthodox Dialogue,* ed. John Meyendorff and Robert Tobias (Minneapolis: Augsburg, 1992), pp. 159-69.

[116]Timeless knowledge works out in essentially the same way as simple foreknowledge, but it is not "fore" knowledge at all. God atemporally knows all of history at once. There is no before or after in the divine knowledge. A timeless deity *knows* the future but does not "think" or "plan" about it, since drawing inferences or deliberating implies moving from premises to conclusion—from ignorance to knowledge. Nevertheless, proponents of this theory attempt to explain how a timeless deity may relate and even respond to us. See, for example, William Alston, "Divine-Human Dialogue and the Nature of God," *Faith and Philosophy* 2, no. 1 (1985): 5-20. Several Catholic writers have sought to reconcile, using the vocabulary of Thomism, a strongly immutable God with divine conditionality, adaptability and even frustration. See Clarke, *Philosophical Approach to God;* Hill, *Search*

for the Absent God; Wright, "Eternal Plan of Divine Providence" and "Divine Knowledge and Human Freedom." See also note 78 above.

Objections may be raised against this theory. (1) It seems to exclude divine deliberation and planning. On this criticism, see Tomis Kapitan, "Can God Make Up His Mind?" *International Journal for the Philosophy of Religion* 15 (1984): 37-47; Kapitan, "Deliberation and the Presumption of Open Alternatives," *Philosophical Quarterly* 36, no. 143 (1986): 230-51; Kapitan, "Providence, Foreknowledge, and Decision Procedures," *Faith and Philosophy* 10, no. 3 (1993): 415-20. (2) If God cannot deliberate, then questions arise about the divine freedom. Does God freely choose which creative option to actualize? Does God freely choose to become incarnate? On this problem, see La Croix, "Omniprescience and Divine Determinism," and David Basinger, "Omniscience and Deliberation: A Response to Reichenbach," *International Journal for the Philosophy of Religion* 20 (1986): 169-72. See also note 138 below.

[117]Creel, *Divine Impassibility,* pp. 17-34. Though Creel does an admirable job of defending classical theism, I do not believe his defense resonates well with the biblical picture of God. Moreover, it seriously alters the understanding of the personal relationship between God and humanity. How can God be said to be in a relationship of love with us? See Fiddes, *Creative Suffering of God,* pp. 58-59.

[118]See Thomas V. Morris, "Properties, Modalities and God," *The Philosophical Review* 93, no. 1 (1984): 35-55; and Rice, *God's Foreknowledge,* pp. 56-59. Moreover, according to this view, though God does not learn what *can* possibly happen, God learns what *does,* in fact, happen. God learns what does occur in the actual world either prior to creation (as in simple foreknowledge or timeless knowledge) or as history unfolds (as in presentism). Thus, for the knowledge of all possibilities view, God may or may not have foreknowledge. Regardless, God still takes risks in creating a world in which he does not exercise exhaustive sovereignty. Furthermore, there may still be room for an element of divine shock or joy in this theory if we distinguish between possibility and probability. In this case, though God knows it is possible, for example, that Israel could defect from his love, God may not consider it likely and so may be shocked at Israel's unfaithfulness.

[119]There are several issues that this model of divine omniscience must resolve. Is it actually possible for God to eternally know all possibilities in an indeterministic creation—both on the physical and human levels? Do we want to say that God cannot generate new ideas and possibilities? (If I am correct, John Duns Scotus believed that the divine will could establish new orders and was not bound by the eternal archetypes in the divine mind.) Ward, *Rational Theology,* pp. 154, 165, and Fiddes, *Creative Suffering,* p. 97, both affirm that God knows the general outlines of all possible events but that there is no fixed sum of eternal ideas. Rather, there is a changing supply of imaginatively created possibilities as God works with us in history. Also, Richard Swinburne, *The Existence of God* (New York: Oxford University Press, 1979), pp. 238-39, questions whether a God who "preresponds" to everything renders the divine-human relationship impersonal.

[120]See Luis de Molina, *On Divine Foreknowledge,* trans. with an introduction by Alfred J. Freddoso (Ithaca, N.Y.: Cornell University Press, 1988). For a popular introduction to middle knowledge, see William Lane Craig, *The Only Wise God: The Compatibility of Divine Foreknowledge and Human Freedom* (Grand Rapids, Mich.: Baker, 1987). Thomas Flint, "Two Accounts of Providence," in *Divine and Human Action: Essays in the Metaphysics of Theism,* ed. Thomas V. Morris (Ithaca, N.Y.: Cornell University Press, 1988), compares Molinism with Thomism.

[121]Craig, *Only Wise God,* p. 135.

[122]There is considerable debate whether Molinism entails divine risk taking. Here I am following the lead of David Basinger, "Divine Control and Human Freedom: Is Middle Knowledge the Answer? *Journal of the Evangelical Theological Society* 36, no. 1 (1993): 55-64; Basinger, "Middle Knowledge and Divine Control"; W. S. Anglin, *Free Will and the*

Christian Faith (New York: Oxford University Press, 1990), chap. 4; and Peter Y. Windt, "Plantinga's Unfortunate God," *Philosophical Studies* 24 (1973): 335-42. Some critics of Molinism and Molinists themselves do not agree that Molinism entails divine risk taking. A proponent of Molinism, Thomas Flint, "Two Accounts of Providence," pp. 157-60, admits that what creatures do in the feasible worlds is not under God's control and that God "permits" some events to happen that God does not intend. Nevertheless, Flint attempts to play down the providential risk factor for a deity with middle knowledge by claiming that God's plan will be achieved with certainty. It is correct that once God decided which feasible world to create, then God knew with certainty all that would transpire in that world. But this does not negate the fact that God may not get much of what he wanted in that world. Again, the central issue here is not the type of knowledge God possesses but the kind of sovereignty he freely chooses to exercise. However, even if Molinism does entail divine risk taking, I am not sure whether it should be classified as a member of relational theism.

[123]Strong Calvinists reject middle knowledge because it makes some of God's knowledge contingent. See, for example, Richard A. Muller, "Grace, Election and Contingent Choice: Arminius's Gambit and the Reformed Response," pp. 265-69; and J. A. Crabtree, "Does Middle Knowledge Solve the Problem of Divine Sovereignty? pp. 429-58, both in *The Grace of God, the Bondage of the Will*, ed. Thomas Schreiner and Bruce Ware (Grand Rapids, Mich.: Baker, 1995). It should be noted that some proponents of middle knowledge are determinists, however, and thus affirm foreordination of all things.

[124]In his latest work, *Divine Providence: The Molinist Account* (Ithaca, N.Y.: Cornell University Press, 1998), Thomas Flint thinks that this gives God significantly greater control than a God with only simple foreknowledge or present knowledge would have. I do not agree.

[125]For a list of proponents of presentism, see the discussion in 5.6.2 (especially notes 106, 122). Even some defenders of classical theism hold that Perfect Being theology is quite compatible with presentism. See H. P. Owen, *Concepts of Deity* (New York: Herder & Herder, 1971), pp. 32-33, and Morris, *Our Idea of God*, p. 102. In the ancient world presentism was defended by Cicero and Alexander of Aprodisias (second century A.D.; see Sanders, "Historical Considerations," in *The Openness of God: A Biblical Challenge to the Traditional Understanding of God*, by Clark Pinnock et al. [Downers Grove, Ill.: InterVarsity Press, 1994], p. 183 n. 30). In the sixteenth century Fausto Socinus propounded it. Unfortunately, he also rejected the Trinity and the deity of Christ and is thus heretical. On Socinus, see Charles Hartshorne and William Reese, eds., *Philosophers Speak of God* (Chicago: University of Chicago Press, 1953), pp. 225-27. In the nineteenth century the French Roman Catholic Jules Lequyer argued for it. See Donald Wayne Viney, "Jules Lequyer and the Openness of God," *Faith and Philosophy* 14, no. 2 (1997): 212-35. Several American Methodists of the last century affirmed it. To mention but a few: Billy Hibbard, *Memoirs of the Life and Travels of B. Hibbard*, 2nd ed. (New York: self-published, 1843); Lorenzo McCabe, *The Foreknowledge of God* (Cincinnati: Cranston & Stowe, 1887); McCabe, *Divine Nescience of Future Contingencies a Necessity* (New York: Phillips and Hunt, 1862). See the debates that this sparked in the *Methodist Review* in 1899. I would like to thank Randy Maddox for calling my attention to Hibbard and the debate in the journal.

[126]Hasker, *God, Time and Knowledge*, pp. 64-74, and "A Philosophical Perspective," pp. 147-48, provides a carefully constructed argument that exhaustive foreknowledge is incompatible with libertarian freedom. However, it should be noted that I rejected exhaustive foreknowledge on the grounds of the construal of the divine-human relationship in the biblical record. In my opinion, presentism best handles the give-and-take relationship with God, though I admit more work needs to be done to fully develop this understanding of omniscience. Though God's openness to life far transcends ours, it could be argued that God is our model for openness and learning. On this, see John M. Hull, *What Prevents Christian Adults from Learning?* (Philadelphia: Trinity Press International, 1991), pp. 219-38.

[127]Clarke, *God, Knowable and Unknowable*, p. 65.
[128]Swinburne, *Coherence of Theism*, pp. 181-83.
[129]For example, Helm, *Eternal God*, pp. 125, 195.
[130]Swinburne, *Coherence of Theism*, p. 180, makes this same point with Aquinas, but unfortunately (in my opinion) describes this as an "attenuated" understanding of omniscience.
[131]See note 112 above.
[132]The degree of surprise a God with present knowledge experiences is often exaggerated by critics. See, for instance, Craig, *Only Wise God*, pp. 134-35, and Hasker's reply, *God, Time and Knowledge*, p. 197 n. 13. Some critics charge that such a deity is a bumbling, unfulfilled God who makes mistakes and cannot accomplish all he desires. It is true that God does not get everything he wants, but this is *not* due to the type of knowledge God has! Rather, it is due to the type of sovereignty God elects to practice. Indeed, proponents of exhaustive divine sovereignty argue that all the risk views of omniscience share this problem. David Basinger's "Can an Evangelical Christian Justifiably Deny God's Exhaustive Knowledge of the Future?" *Christian Scholar's Review* 25, no. 2 (1995): 133-45, handles many of these criticisms.
[133]Much of the material in this section is from my more complete discussion, "Why Simple Foreknowledge Offers No More Providential Control Than the Openness of God," *Faith and Philosophy* 14, no. 1 (1997): 26-40.
[134]For some of the problems in affirming both divine foreknowledge and incompatibilistic human freedom, see William Hasker, "Philosophical Perspective," pp. 147-49; and Hasker, *God, Time and Knowledge*, chaps. 4-7.
[135]David P. Hunt, "Divine Providence and Simple Foreknowledge," *Faith and Philosophy* 10, no. 3 (1993): 394-59.
[136]Jack Cottrell, *What the Bible Says About God the Ruler* (Joplin, Mo.: College Press, 1984), pp. 208-9. It seems that what Cottrell is actually describing is closer to middle knowledge than SF, but he describes himself as a traditional Arminian theologian. Traditional Arminians are not always clear where they want to come down on this issue. They affirm libertarian freedom and contingency in God, yet sometimes they suggest that God does not take risks. Critics of Arminianism (and SF) claim that exhaustive foreknowledge entails determinism that would rule out divine risk. But Arminians reject determinism. In my way of thinking Arminianism (and SF) is a risk model of providence in spite of itself.
[137]Hasker, *God, Time, and Knowledge*, p. 63. See also the following note.
[138]This problem holds unless, of course, one wishes to say that God sees his own actions in his foreknowledge (which, it seems, SF needs to affirm). Unfortunately, this seriously challenges the divine freedom. See Richard Swinburne, *The Coherence of Theism*, rev. ed. (New York: Oxford University Press, 1993), p. 181; J. R. Lucas, "Foreknowledge and the Vulnerability of God," in *The Philosophy in Christianity*, ed. Godfrey Vesey (New York: Cambridge University Press, 1989), p. 126; and Basinger, "Middle Knowledge and Classical Christian Thought," p. 416. (See also note 116 above.)
[139]Swinburne, *Coherence of Theism*, p. 181.
[140]Hunt, "Divine Providence," p. 408.
[141]See Hasker, *God, Time, and Knowledge*, pp. 57-59.
[142]John Hick, *Evil and the God of Love*, rev. ed. (New York: Harper & Row, 1978), p. 69.
[143]McCabe, *Foreknowledge of God*, p. 364.
[144]Cottrell, *What the Bible Says About God*, p. 214. I do not understand how Cottrell can consistently maintain both that the future is closed for God and that God is able to alter that same future.
[145]Hasker, *God, Time and Knowledge*, pp. 57-58. This same point was made in 1843 by Hibbard, *Memoirs*, p. 387, and is also discussed by Ward, *Rational Theology*, p. 152.
[146]The tape analogy may itself be deceiving because it assumes the future is available to be

known. Is the rest of the actual future already on the tape? If so, then ISF may be incoherent.

[147]Quoted in McCabe, *Foreknowledge of God,* p. 25.

[148]C. S. Lewis, "On Special Providences," in *Miracles* (New York: Macmillan, 1974), pp. 180-87.

[149]See the discussion in 4.16.

Chapter 7: The Nature of Divine Sovereignty

[1]For similar views of sovereignty, see Clark Pinnock et al., *The Openness of God* (Downers Grove, Ill.: InterVarsity Press, 1994); Pinnock, "God's Sovereignty in Today's World," *Theology Today* 53, no. 1 (1996): 15-21; Pinnock, "God Limits His Knowledge," and Bruce Reichenbach, "God Limits His Power," both in *Predestination and Free Will: Four Views of Divine Sovereignty and Human Freedom,* ed. David Basinger and Randall Basinger (Downers Grove, Ill.: InterVarsity Press, 1986); Jack Cottrell, *What the Bible Says About God the Ruler* (Joplin, Mo.: College Press, 1984); Michael J. Langford, *Providence* (London: SCM Press, 1981); Shirley C. Guthrie, "Human Suffering, Human Liberation and the Sovereignty of God," *Theology Today* 53, no. 1 (1996): 22-34; and Cynthia L. Rigby, "Free to Be Human: Limits, Possibilities and the Sovereignty of God," *Theology Today* 53, no. 1 (1996): 47-62.

[2]R. C. Sproul, *Chosen by God* (Wheaton, Ill.: Tyndale, 1986), p. 26.

[3]See James Daane, *The Freedom of God: A Study of Election and Pulpit* (Grand Rapids, Mich.: Eerdmans, 1973), pp. 81-90.

[4]See Emil Brunner, *The Divine-Human Encounter,* trans. Amandus W. Loos (Philadelphia: Westminster, 1943), pp. 55-59, 66, 123-28. In his various writings Brunner is very critical of the tendency in the Reformed tradition to speak of the divine-human relationship in causal-mechanistic rather than covenantal-personal terms.

[5]Vincent Brümmer, *Speaking of a Personal God* (New York: Cambridge University Press, 1992), pp. 61-65.

[6]This is how we have to think *(de dicto)* about love. I do not say *de re* that God could not force love, but I have no understanding what that would mean. Those theologians who appeal to antinomy at this point in order to claim that God forces our love are, in my view, speaking incoherently.

[7]Vincent Brümmer, *The Model of Love* (New York: Cambridge University Press, 1993), pp. 149-205.

[8]Ibid., p. 158. George Mavrodes reviews various philosophical models of divine causation in reference to the hardening of Pharaoh's heart. All of them, he says, are beset with serious problems. See his "Is There Anything Which God Does Not Do?" *Christian Scholar's Review* 16, no. 4 (1987): 384-91. Paul Helm rejects Brümmer's definition of personal relations. See Helm, *The Providence of God,* Contours of Christian Theology (Downers Grove, Ill.: InterVarsity Press, 1994), pp. 149-53; Helm, "Prayer and Providence," in *Christian Faith and Philosophical Theology,* ed. Gijsbert van den Brink et al. (Kampen, Netherlands: Kok Pharos, 1992), pp. 103-9. Helm conflates influence with coercion and then claims that all personal relations involve coercion. He provides two criteria, stated in compatibilist terms, for defining personal relations. Though Helm is correct that even personal relations involve influence, he fails to answer how God can practice the sort of exhaustive control required of specific sovereignty without this dissolving the personal relationship into manipulation. In my opinion, Helm's understanding of personhood is deficient.

[9]J. R. Lucas, *Freedom and Grace* (Grand Rapids, Mich.: Eerdmans, 1976), p. 57.

[10]Regarding personal relations, the Gifford lectures of John MacMurray are outstanding: MacMurray, *Persons in Relation* (London: Faber & Faber, 1961); and MacMurray, *The Self as Agent* (Atlantic Highlands, N.J.: Humanities, 1969). Also of benefit is Peter A. Bertocci's *The Person God Is* (New York: Humanities, 1970). I also find the personalist theology of Emil

Brunner rewarding.

[11]Lucas, *Freedom and Grace,* p. 19.

[12]See Helm, *Providence of God,* pp. 141-42.

[13]Alexander Pope *An Essay on Man* 1.289-94, in Martin Price, *The Selected Poetry of Pope* (New York: Meridian, 1980), pp. 132-33. When Pope says, "Whatever is, is right," I take him to mean that every single event is the right one, but he could mean only that the system as a whole is the best.

[14]John Calvin *Institutes of the Christian Religion* 1.16.2-3.

[15]Regarding the appeal to antinomy, see 2.5.2; on compatibilism, see 7.5; on foreknowledge, see 6.5.

[16]For more on this, see David Basinger and Randall Basinger, "In the Image of Man Create They God: A Challenge," *Scottish Journal of Theology* 34 (1981): 97-107; Basinger and Basinger, *Predestination and Free Will: Four Views of Divine Sovereignty and Human Freedom* (Downers Grove, Ill.: InterVarsity Press, 1986), pp. 9-10.

[17]William P. Alston, "Divine-Human Dialogue and the Nature of God," *Faith and Philosophy* 2, no. 1 (1985): 5-20.

[18]Albert C. Outler, *Who Trusts in God: Musings on the Meaning of Providence* (New York: Oxford University Press, 1968), p. 96.

[19]Some Christians are quite put off by this because they think it leaves too much to chance. But chance never causes anything to happen. The concept of chance must not be reified or personified into the goddess Fortuna or Lady Luck. Chance is merely the name we use to describe the indeterminate or unplanned relation between things. A very helpful study of how chance functioned in the Bible, how God makes use of chance and how we utilize it so often in our lives to make things fair or predict patterns is D. J. Bartholomew's *God of Chance* (London: SCM Press, 1984).

[20]Peter van Inwagen, "The Place of Chance in a World Sustained by God," in *Divine and Human Action: Essays in the Metaphysics of Theism,* ed. Thomas Morris (Ithaca, N.Y.: Cornell University Press, 1988), p. 220.

[21]See Nelly Stienstra, *YHWH Is the Husband of His People: An Analysis of a Biblical Metaphor with Special Reference to Translation* (Kampen, Netherlands: Kok Pharos, 1993), pp. 116-17.

[22]Langford, *Providence,* p. 5. I will modify his discussion slightly.

[23]T. J. Gorringe, *God's Theatre: A Theology of Providence* (London: SCM Press, 1991).

[24]Ibid., p. 82.

[25]For other analogies of divine action in connection to theological and scientific theories, see Langford, *Providence,* pp. 56-95; Gorringe, *God's Theatre,* pp. 68-87; and Bartholomew, *God of Chance.*

[26]See John Gill, *The Cause of God and Truth* (London: W. H. Collingridge, 1855).

[27]Augustine *Enchiridion* 26.100.

[28]Ibid., 24.95.

[29]Ibid., 25.99; 26.102.

[30]Calvin *Institutes* 1.18.1. Calvin's analogy of God in the watchtower does bring out the aspect of God's conditionedness. But it fails to see that for the model of general sovereignty God is not always or only in the watchtower. After all, God is seeking out the lost: Hosea actively sought out Gomer, and the woman in Jesus' parable diligently looked for her lost coin (Lk 15:8). G. C. Berkouwer, *The Providence of God,* trans. Lewis B. Smedes (Grand Rapids, Mich.: Eerdmans, 1952), pp. 137-41, follows Calvin in rejecting "permission," since it makes God a balcony observer, a mere reactor. For Berkouwer, any explanation or logical synthesis is impossible.

[31]Jonathan Edwards, "Concerning the Decrees in General, and Election in Particular," in *The Works of Jonathan Edwards* (Edinburgh: The Banner of Truth Trust, 1974), 2:528.

[32]Helm, *Providence of God,* p. 132.

[33]John Piper, "Are There Two Wills in God? Divine Election and God's Desire for All to be

Saved," in *The Grace of God, the Bondage of the Will,* ed. Thomas Schreiner and Bruce Ware (Grand Rapids, Mich.: Baker, 1995), 1:123-24.

[34]Piper, "Are There Two Wills in God?" p. 124.

[35]George Mavrodes shows the incoherence of Louis Berkhof's views in this regard in his "Adopting a Different Model of Sovereignty," *Perspectives* 12, no. 3 (1997): 12-15.

[36]Edwards, "Concerning the Decrees," 2:532. He goes on to say (2:535) that God cannot be dependent on human choices because God is timeless and humans are in time. A temporal being cannot be the cause of something eternal! Hence, all of God's decisions are timeless and unconditioned. If so, then the Arminians cannot, as Edwards claimed, be saying the same thing he is.

[37]Vincent Brümmer, "On Thanking God Whatever Happens," *Journal of Theology for Southern Africa* 48 (September 1984): 9.

[38]See Stephen T. Davis, *Logic and the Nature of God* (Grand Rapids, Mich.: Eerdmans, 1983), p. 70.

[39]William Hasker, "A Philosophical Perspective," in *The Openness of God: A Biblical Challenge to the Traditional Understanding of God,* by Clark Pinnock et al. (Downers Grove, Ill.: 1994), p. 137.

[40]Hasker, "Philosophical Perspective," pp. 136-37.

[41]On these and more arguments, see W. S. Anglin, *Free Will and the Christian Faith* (New York: Oxford University Press, 1990), pp. 1-28. C. Stephen Evans, *Preserving the Person: A Look at the Human Sciences* (Downers Grove, Ill.: InterVarsity Press, 1977), explores the loss of the personal in the natural and behavioral sciences if significant freedom is not assumed.

[42]See, for example, Alvin Plantinga, "Prologue: Advice to Christian Philosophers," *Faith and Philosophy* 1, no. 3 (1984): 31-32.

[43]D. A. Carson, *Divine Sovereignty and Human Responsibility: Biblical Perspectives in Tension* (Grand Rapids, Mich.: Baker, 1994), p. 1. R. K. McGregor Wright, *No Place for Sovereignty: What's Wrong with Freewill Theism* (Downers Grove, Ill.: InterVarsity Press, 1996), p. 12, makes the same accusation.

[44]Helm, *Providence of God,* p. 42.

[45]Moreover, it could be argued that Calvinists usually affirm compatibilism due to their control belief of exhaustive divine sovereignty, whereas Wesleyans affirm libertarian freedom due to their control belief of God's goodness to all. See Jerry L. Walls, "The Free Will Defense, Calvinism, Wesley and the Goodness of God," *Christian Scholar's Review* 13, no. 1 (1983): 19-33.

[46]Adrió König, "Providence, Sin and Human Freedom: On Different Concepts of Human Freedom" (unpublished paper).

[47]König also asks why God would grant humans libertarian freedom when God himself does not have such freedom. After all, God's freedom does not include the possibility to sin. Two responses are in order. To begin, König argues that God cannot sin and that this is the sort of material freedom God gave humanity. Thus human sin is totally inexplicable. But if humans were not given the possibility to sin and they did sin, then what is to prevent one from saying the same about God? God does not have the possibility of sinning, but may, inexplicably, sin. How can König be so sure that God cannot sin, given the total mystery of sin? The second response is to point out that Christians are divided on the question of divine impeccability. Throughout history numerous theologians have held that the divine nature is such that it is impossible for God to commit a moral evil. What prevents it is God's goodness, omnipotence, omniscience and the fact that God lacks morally significant freedom. See Thomas V. Morris, *Our Idea of God: An Introduction to Philosophical Theology* (Notre Dame, Ind.: University of Notre Dame Press, 1991), pp. 56-64, 77-80. Why did God not create us with the same sort of nature? Because those attributes are "incommunicable" (not possible to be shared). The other alternative is to hold that it is possible for God to commit a moral evil, since God does have morally significant freedom. God does not, in

fact, do evil but remains faithful in his love toward his creation. (See Davis, *Logic and the Nature of God*, pp. 86-96; Brümmer, *Speaking of a Personal God*, pp. 90-107; and p. 316, n. 58 of this book.)

[48]Richard Creel, *Divine Impassibility* (Cambridge: Cambridge University Press, 1986), pp. 141-46.

[49]Jon D. Levenson, *Creation and the Persistence of Evil: The Jewish Drama of Divine Omnipotence* (Princeton: Princeton University Press, 1988), p. 141.

[50]See the discussion in G. C. Berkouwer, *Man: The Image of God,* trans. Dirk Jellema (Grand Rapids, Mich.: Eerdmans, 1962), pp. 37-66, 310-48.

[51]See Emil Brunner, *The Christian Doctrine of Creation and Redemption,* trans. Olive Wyon (Philadelphia: Westminster, 1952), pp. 55-61.

[52]See C. Stephen Evans, "Salvation, Sin and Human Freedom in Kierkegaard," in *The Grace of God, the Will of Man,* ed. Clark Pinnock (Grand Rapids, Mich.: Zondervan, 1989), pp. 181-89.

[53]Brunner, *Christian Doctrine of Creation and Redemption,* p. 123. This is the thesis of Reformed theologian Harry Boer in his *An Ember Still Glowing* (Grand Rapids, Mich.: Eerdmans, 1990).

[54]Gorringe, *God's Theatre,* pp. 45-46.

[55]See Karl Barth, *Church Dogmatics* 2/1, trans. Geoffrey W. Bromiley and T. F. Torrance (Edinburgh: T & T Clark, 1957), p. 518; Barth, *Church Dogmatics* 2/2, p. 50; Jürgen Moltmann, *The Trinity and the Kingdom,* trans. Margaret Kohl (New York: Harper & Row, 1981), pp. 108-11; Reichenbach, "God Limits His Power"; Pinnock, "God Limits His Knowledge"; and Helm, *Providence of God,* p. 103.

[56]I discussed this in 6.4.4.

[57]Emil Brunner, *Christian Doctrine of God,* trans. Olive Wyon (Philadelphia: Westminster, 1949), p. 251. See also his *Christian Doctrine of Creation and Redemption,* p. 175.

[58]Axel D. Steuer, "The Freedom of God and Human Freedom," *Scottish Journal of Theology* 36, no. 2 (1983): 173.

[59]Keith Ward, *Rational Theology and the Creativity of God* (New York: Pilgrim, 1982), p. 84.

[60]I say nearly everyone, since there are those who appeal to antinomy. I argued that this approach fails in 2.5.2.

[61]See J. R. Lucas, *The Future: An Essay on God, Temporality and Truth* (Cambridge, Mass.: Basil Blackwell, 1989), p. 227.

[62]Lucas, *Freedom and Grace,* p. 36.

[63]Ward, *Rational Theology,* p. 122.

[64]Barth, *Church Dogmatics* 2/1, pp. 537-38.

[65]Ibid., p. 518.

[66]See 2.4, 2.5 and 6.4.5 (especially note 95).

[67]This is the thesis of the fine book by Frank G. Kirkpatrick, *Together Bound: God, History and the Religious Community* (New York: Oxford University Press, 1994).

[68]Edgar S. Brightman, *The Problem of God* (New York: Abingdon, 1930); and Bertocci, *The Person God Is.*

[69]Georgia Harkness, *The Providence of God* (New York: Abingdon, 1960), p. 105; and Nels Ferré, *The Christian Understanding of God* (New York: Harper, 1951), pp. 104-6.

[70]Marcel Sarot, "Omnipotence and Self-Limitation," in *Christian Faith and Philosophical Theology: Essays in Honour of Vincent Brümmer,* ed. Gijsbert van den Brink et al. (Kampen, Netherlands: Kok Pharos, 1992), pp. 172-85. In my opinion there is an unstated assumption in the debate over whether God is essentially omnipotent: meticulous providence. That is, it is often assumed that omnipotence must mean exhaustive divine control over everything.

[71]E. Frank Tupper provides an excellent discussion on the limits of God in relation to the gospel story of Jesus and the life of prayer in his *A Scandalous Providence: The Jesus Story of the Compassion of God* (Macon, Ga.: Mercer University Press, 1995), pp. 326-35.

[72]Augustine *Enchiridion* 24.96.

[73]Helm, *Providence of God,* p. 103.

[74]Ward, *Rational Theology,* p. 83.

[75]Peter Geach, *Providence and Evil* (Cambridge: Cambridge University Press, 1977), p. 58.

[76]William James, *The Will to Believe and Other Essays in Popular Philosophy* (New York: Dover, 1956), pp. 181-82.

[77]Vincent Brümmer, *What Are We Doing When We Pray? A Philosophical Inquiry* (London: SCM Press, 1984), pp. 44-45, 68, uses Geach's analogy but fails to see its inadequacies in light of the fellowship model of the divine-human relationship.

[78]David Basinger criticizes Geach for this in his "Human Freedom and Divine Providence: Some New Thoughts on an Old Problem," *Religious Studies* 15 (1979): 491-510.

[79]Paul Helm makes this point against Geach. However, since Helm affirms compatibilism and specific sovereignty, he only criticizes Geach for affirming an indefinite future, which is incompatible with exhaustive divine control. See his *Eternal God: A Study of God Without Time* (New York: Oxford University Press, 1988), pp. 122-25.

[80]Universalists, however, claim that God never forecloses on anyone. For an explanation and evaluation of the arguments for universalism, see my *No Other Name: An Investigation into the Destiny of the Unevangelized* (Grand Rapids, Mich.: Eerdmans, 1992), pp. 81-128. Concerning the issue of whether hell is justifiable, see Jerry L. Walls, *Hell: The Logic of Damnation* (Notre Dame, Ind.: University of Notre Dame Press, 1992); and Jonathan Kvanvig, *The Problem of Hell* (New York: Oxford University Press, 1993). On whether hell should be understood as eternal conscious punishment or as annihilation of the finally impenitent, see William Crockett, ed., *Four Views on Hell* (Grand Rapids, Mich.: Zondervan, 1992).

[81]Even those who affirm timeless knowledge or simple foreknowledge have to say that God atemporally either planned ahead for this contingency or responded to it in this way once God in foreknowledge "saw" sin would obtain.

[82]For a helpful discussion of this notion, see Eugene TeSelle, *Christ in Context: Divine Purpose and Human Responsibility* (Philadelphia: Fortress, 1975), pp. 148-55. Wolfhart Pannenberg, *Systematic Theology,* trans. Geoffrey W. Bromiley (Grand Rapids, Mich.: Eerdmans, 1991), 1:380, 388, disagrees with this approach, saying that the concept of a goal implies a difference between the goal and its fulfillment. God, according to Pannenberg, can have no goals because a God with goals left to fulfill is a finite God. This point was made earlier by Plato, who claimed that God could not love or desire something because that would indicate a lack in God (an imperfection), and Spinoza, who held that God could not pursue purposes because this would imply that God lacks (a deficiency) what he purposes to achieve. For Pannenberg, God does not have unfinished goals because God experiences all time at once (simultaneity). Consequently, God does not have an open future at all! This is quite contrary to what many have thought Pannenberg was saying regarding God's actual experience in history. His use of simultaneity (following Boethius and Plotinus) and his disavowal of talk of God as an agent leads me to suspect that Pannenberg is uneasy, at best, with the notion of a personal God working with us in history toward an open future.

[83]Jacques Maritain, *Existence and the Existent,* trans. Lewis Galantiere and Gerald Phelan (New York: Random House, 1966), p. 116. Unfortunately, Maritain inconsistently attempts to reconcile this idea with God's timeless knowledge's being totally unconditioned by the creature. He believes simultaneity rescues him from this contradiction.

[84]Proponents of specific sovereignty can say that what people do matters in the sense that God is using people as secondary causes. But they cannot say that it makes a difference for God, since every single detail God wants to happen does happen according to specific sovereignty.

[85]Brian Hebblethwaite, "Some Reflections on Predestination, Providence and Divine Foreknowledge," *Religious Studies* 15, no. 4 (1979): 437.

[86]Helm, *Providence of God,* p. 104.

[87]It seems to me that this reifies all historical action into ideas resembling some sort of Platonic archetype.

[88]Lucas, *Freedom and Grace*, pp. 39-40.

[89]A. van de Beek, *Why? On Suffering, Guilt and God*, trans. John Vriend (Grand Rapids, Mich.: Eerdmans, 1990), p. 300.

[90]A point badly neglected in many discussions of eschatology. See Adriö König, *The Eclipse of Christ in Eschatology: Toward a Christ-Centered Approach* (Grand Rapids, Mich.: Eerdmans, 1989).

[91]Precisely what the eschaton will be like I do not know. Regarding the issue of free will and the afterlife, see note 94 of chapter 7.

[92]Sproul, *Chosen by God*, pp. 26-27.

[93]That foreknowledge is of no value to God in guaranteeing the success of his plans before he enacts them was discussed in 6.5.3.3.

[94]See Lucas, *Freedom and Grace*, pp. 29-30.

[95]Lucas, *Future*, p. 231.

[96]Paul S. Fiddes, *The Creative Suffering of God* (New York: Oxford University Press, 1988), p. 105.

Chapter 8: Applications to the Christian Life

[1]See John Calvin's *Institutes of the Christian Religion* 3.23.6. It is quite unfortunate that Calvin failed to integrate his doctrine of election with his relational understanding of the Trinity. For Calvin, the will of God is prior to and is more essential than the economic Trinity. On this see Walker Butin, *Revelation, Redemption and Response: Calvin's Trinitarian Understanding of the Divine-Human Relationship* (New York: Oxford University Press, 1995), pp. 125-26, 168 n. 7, 189 n. 81.

[2]Louis Berkhof, *Systematic Theology*, 3rd ed. (Grand Rapids, Mich.: Eerdmans, 1946), pp. 118-25. He claims that if infralapsarians affirm conditionality in God, then they are Arminians and no longer Calvinists.

[3]Some would deny that God shoots balls into the pocket of damnation and would say, rather, that all the balls are rolling toward the pocket of damnation but God shoots some of them into the pocket of salvation.

[4]A problem in the Reformed tradition is that it has used both the language of personal relationships and also the causal language of impersonal relationships. See Vincent Brümmer's comments on the Synod of Dordt in *Speaking of a Personal God* (New York: Cambridge University Press, 1992), pp. 83-89. Ben Carter, *The Depersonalization of God* (Lanham, Md.: University Press of America, 1989), discusses how decretal theology ends up with an impersonal divine-human relationship.

[5]This is the view of R. K. McGreggor Wright, *No Place for Sovereignty: What's Wrong with Freewill Theism* (Downers Grove, Ill.: InterVarsity Press, 1996), pp. 169-71. This is an example of using theological beliefs to control the reading of scriptural texts. The appeal to a "secret will" of God behind the "revealed will" is but another example of the attempt to discover a God beyond the God of Scripture on the basis of a human ideal (the *dignum Deo*).

[6]Wright, *No Place for Sovereignty*, p. 151, admits that specific sovereignty leads to limited atonement.

[7]Augustine *City of God* 21.12. In his *Enchiridion* 103, Augustine wrestles with the tension that exists between the scriptural assertion that God wills everyone to saved (1 Tim 2:4) and the fact that not everyone will, in fact, be saved. His solution is twofold: (1) divine willing is understood as meaning that no human is saved unless God wills his or her salvation (this, of course, is not what the text says!); (2) "everyone" refers to all groups of people (racial, gender, vocational and so on), not to all individuals.

[8]John Piper, *The Justification of God: An Exegetical and Theological Study of Romans 9:1-23* (Grand Rapids, Mich.: Baker, 1983), p. 100.

[9]Jonathan Edwards expresses this view in one of his letters, which may represent his mature position. See *The Works of Jonathan Edwards,* ed. Edward Hickman (Edinburgh: The Banner of Truth Trust, 1974), 1:cxl.

[10]I will return to this criticism in 8.3.2.

[11]Calvin *Institutes* 3.21.6.

[12]Jerry L. Walls, *Hell: The Logic of Damnation* (Notre Dame, Ind.: Notre Dame University Press, 1992), p. 99.

[13]R. C. Sproul, *Chosen by God* (Wheaton, Ill.: Tyndale, 1986), pp. 32-33.

[14]See Bruce Reichenbach, "Freedom, Justice and Moral Responsibility," in *The Grace of God, the Will of Man,* ed. Clark Pinnock (Grand Rapids, Mich.: Zondervan, 1989), pp. 277-303.

[15]John Hick, *Evil and the God of Love,* rev. ed. (New York: Harper & Row, 1978), pp. 66, 174, finds this idea self-contradictory. Hick simply cannot accept the notion of gratuitous sin. He believes there must be a cause somewhere, and he places it squarely on the shoulders of the Creator.

[16]The concept of hereditary sin has many problems, but there is a core element of truth in it. For views of sin in general, see David L. Smith, *With Willful Intent: A Theology of Sin* (Wheaton, Ill.: Bridgepoint, 1994); and Ted Peters, *Sin: Radical Evil in Soul and Society* (Grand Rapids, Mich.: Eerdmans, 1994). On hereditary sin, see A. van de Beek, *Why? On Suffering, Guilt and God,* trans. John Vriend (Grand Rapids, Mich.: Eerdmans, 1990), pp. 143-48; C. Stephen Evans, "Salvation, Sin, and Human Freedom in Kierkegaard," in *The Grace of God, the Will of Man,* ed. Clark Pinnock; Gregory R. Beabout, "Does Anxiety Explain Hereditary Sin?" *Faith and Philosophy* 11, no. 1 (1994): 117-26; Hendrikus Berkhof, *Christian Faith,* trans. Sierd Woudstra (Grand Rapids, Mich.: Eerdmans, 1979), pp. 187-210; and Clark Pinnock and Robert Brow, *Unbounded Love: A Good News Theology for the 21st Century* (Downers Grove, Ill.: InterVarsity Press, 1994), pp. 57-66.

[17]The Eastern Orthodox are able to speak of a personal address between sinful persons and God. They have never affirmed the Augustinian understanding of sin. See John Meyendorff, "Humanity: 'Old' and 'New'—Anthropological Considerations," in *Salvation in Christ: A Lutheran-Orthodox Dialogue,* ed. John Meyendorff and Robert Tobias (Minneapolis: Augsburg, 1992), pp. 59-66.

[18]Karl Barth, *Church Dogmatics* 3/3, trans. Geoffrey W. Bromiley and T. F. Torrance (Edinburgh: T & T Clark, 1960), p. 357.

[19]See Richard A. Muller, *God, Creation and Providence in the Thought of Jacob Arminius* (Grand Rapids, Mich.: Baker, 1991), pp. 143-207; and Muller, "Grace, Election and Contingent Choice: Arminius's Gambit and the Reformed Response," in *The Grace of God, the Bondage of the Will,* ed. Thomas Schreiner and Bruce Ware (Grand Rapids, Mich.: Baker, 1995), 2:251-78. On Wesley, see Randy L. Maddox, *Responsible Grace: John Wesley's Practical Theology* (Nashville: Abingdon, 1994), pp. 55-56.

[20]It is also an issue for theological ethics. Nicholas Wolterstorff points out that the "divine command" theory of obligation suffers from internal inconsistencies if God is wholly unconditioned by anything external to himself, since the Bible attributes a wide range of speech actions including commanding, promising, asking, covenanting and so on. But if God is completely unconditioned, then we must radically reinterpret divine promising and covenanting, since the normal way of understanding these entails conditionality in God. See Wolterstorff, *Divine Discourse: Philosophical Reflections on the Claim That God Speaks* (New York: Cambridge University Press, 1995), pp. 97-103.

[21]James Daane, "Can a Man Bless God?" in *God and the Good,* ed. Clifton Orlebeke and Lewis Smedes (Grand Rapids, Mich.: Eerdmans, 1975), p. 166.

[22]Brümmer, *Speaking of a Personal God,* pp. 68-89; and David A. S. Fergusson, "Predestination: A Scottish Perspective," *Scottish Journal of Theology* 46 (1993): 457-78.

[23]See James Jorgenson, "Predestination According to Divine Foreknowledge in Patristic Tradition," in *Salvation in Christ: A Lutheran-Orthodox Dialogue,* ed. John Meyendorff and

Robert Tobias (Minneapolis: Augsburg, 1992), pp. 159-69. Of course, it remains an important question whether the theory of foreknowledge is consistent with humans having libertarian freedom.

[24]Divine election may be conditional whether one affirms that God predestines individuals on the basis of foreknown faith or whether one holds that election is of a corporate nature: we are elect in the Son. On these two views, see Jack Cottrell, "Conditional Election," in *Grace Unlimited*, ed. Clark Pinnock (Minneapolis: Bethany Fellowship, 1975), pp. 51-73; and William W. Klein, *The New Chosen People: A Corporate View of Election* (Grand Rapids, Mich.: Zondervan, 1990).

[25]Certain conservative evangelicals fail to see this and so attempt to draw a sharp line between the openness of God model and Arminianism. See chapter 5, note 113.

[26]See 6.5.

[27]Brümmer, *Speaking of a Personal God*, pp. 87-88, 75-76.

[28]See Vincent Brümmer, *The Model of Love: A Study in Philosophical Theology* (New York: Cambridge University Press, 1993), pp. 202-3.

[29]Brümmer, *Speaking of a Personal God*, pp. 68-89; and J. R. Lucas, *Freedom and Grace* (Grand Rapids, Mich.: Eerdmans, 1976), pp. 22-26, discuss the various understandings of "irresistibility." Brümmer says that the love of God is rationally irresistible because it is irrational to reject it.

[30]Regarding various theories as to how God makes salvation universally accessible, see my *No Other Name: An Investigation into the Destiny of the Unevangelized* (Grand Rapids, Mich.: Eerdmans, 1992), pt. 3.

[31]See Vincent Brümmer, *What Are We Doing When We Pray? A Philosophical Inquiry* (London: SCM Press, 1984), pp. 79-80.

[32]See Barth, *Church Dogmatics* 3/3, p. 247.

[33]See Jerry L. Walls, "Can God Save Anyone He Will?" *Scottish Journal of Theology* 38 (1985): 155-72. Walls discusses different views of sovereignty in relation to universalism and predestination.

[34]See Brümmer, *Model of Love*, p. 132.

[35]Paul Helm, "Grace and Causation," *Scottish Journal of Theology* 32 (1979): 102-3.

[36]The following discussion is indebted to William Abraham, *An Introduction to the Philosophy of Religion* (Englewood Cliffs, N.J.: Prentice Hall, 1985), pp. 149-51.

[37]See his insightful discussion in *Freedom and Grace*, pp. 2-5.

[38]See the discussion by Gijsbert van den Brink, *Almighty God: A Study of the Doctrine of Divine Omnipotence* (Kampen, Netherlands: Kok Pharos, 1992), pp. 237-39.

[39]Moreover, according to quantum physics, even billiard balls do not operate by strict determinism.

[40]This is the position of A. A. Hodge and C. Samuel Storms. See Storms's "Prayer and Evangelism Under God's Sovereignty," in *The Grace of God, the Bondage of the Will*, 1:230-31.

[41]For the Orthodox position, see Bishop Maximos Aghiorgoussis, "Orthodox Soteriology," and John Breck, "Divine Initiative: Salvation in Orthodox Theology," both in *Salvation in Christ: A Lutheran-Orthodox Dialogue*, ed. John Meyendorff and Robert Tobias (Minneapolis: Augsburg, 1992). According to the Orthodox, "synergy" does not mean there is some latent power in humans that cooperates in conversion. Rather, it is an attitude of openness in faith to God's saving grace. On the major agreement reached on, among other things, predestination between the Lutheran and the Reformed, see "The Agreement of Leuenberg," in *An Invitation to Action: The Lutheran-Reformed Dialogue Series III, 1981-1983*, ed. James E. Andrews and Joseph A. Burgess (Philadelphia: Fortress, 1984), pp. 65-73. On Wesley, see Maddox, *Responsible Grace*, pp. 141-56.

[42]See Jerry L. Walls, "The Free Will Defense, Calvinism, Wesley and the Goodness of God," *Christian Scholar's Review* 13, no. 1 (1983): 25.

[43]Lucas, *Freedom and Grace*, p. 14.

[44]Philip Edgcumbe Hughes, *A Commentary on the Epistle to the Hebrews* (Grand Rapids, Mich.: Eerdmans, 1977), pp. 206-22, helpfully discusses many of the church fathers on Hebrews 6:4-6. Unfortunately, he concludes that the author of Hebrews is only worried that some of those reading the letter might not be genuine believers in the first place and thus do not belong to God's people. Actually, one would hope that false believers in Christian congregations would be shown to be what they actually are so that genuine believers might not be harmed!

[45]For an exegetical study of this position, see I. Howard Marshall, *Kept By the Power of God: A Study of Perseverance and Falling Away* (Minneapolis, Bethany Fellowship, 1969); and Marshall, "The Problem of Apostasy in New Testament Theology," in Marshall, *Jesus the Saviour: Studies in New Testament Theology* (Downers Grove, Ill.: InterVarsity Press, 1990), pp. 306-24.

[46]Robert R. Cook suggests that even those who affirm libertarian freedom may claim that apostasy for Christians is impossible because God performs "radical soul-surgery" on believers that settles their dispositions. After all, most believers claim God will do this in heaven, so why not now? See Cook's "Apostasy: Some Logical Reflections," *Evangelical Quarterly* 65, no. 2 (1993): 148-49. I believe Cook has a point, but I do not believe our dispositions are settled, even by God, in an instantaneous fashion.

[47]These two thinkers are compared on this issue by William J. Abraham, "Predestination and Assurance," in *The Grace of God, the Will of Man*, pp. 231-42.

[48]This is in opposition to the popular evangelical teaching that saying a liturgical formula ("I accept Jesus as my Savior") or performing a religious ceremony (coming forward at an altar call) makes one a Christian. Such religious rites may or may not be the start of fellowship with Christ. A basic problem in this approach is that it tends to make salvation a thing or object that one possesses instead of seeing salvation as a relationship between persons.

[49]Eberhard Jüngel, *God as the Mystery of the World,* trans. Darrell Guder (Grand Rapids, Mich.: Eerdmans, 1983), pp. 170, 196-97.

[50]Hendrikus Berkhof, *Christian Faith,* trans. Sierd Woudstra (Grand Rapids, Mich.: Eerdmans, 1979), p. 476.

[51]See David Basinger and Randall Basinger, "The Problem with The 'Problem of Evil,'" *Religious Studies* 1 (March 1994): 89-97.

[52]On the freewill defense, see Alvin Plantinga, *God, Freedom and Evil* (Grand Rapids, Mich.: Eerdmans, 1977); and Michael Peterson, *Evil and the Christian God* (Grand Rapids, Mich.: Baker, 1982).

[53]For a helpful summary and evaluation of some of these views, see Michael Peterson, William Hasker, Bruce Reichenbach and David Basinger, *Reason and Religious Belief: An Introduction to the Philosophy of Religion* (New York: Oxford University Press, 1991), pp. 103-12.

[54]The most celebrated proponent of this view is Hick, *Evil and the God of Love.*

[55]See S. Paul Schilling, *God and Human Anguish* (Nashville: Abingdon, 1977), pp. 169-73.

[56]See Kristiaan Depoortere, *A Different God: A Christian View of Suffering,* Louvain Theological and Pastoral Monographs (Grand Rapids, Mich.: Eerdmans, 1995), pp. 47-48; and Schilling, *God and Human Anguish,* pp. 59-72.

[57]This shows affinity to the strong version of the principle of sufficient reason.

[58]Paul Helm, *The Providence of God,* Contours of Christian Theology (Downers Grove, Ill.: InterVarsity Press, 1994), p. 141.

[59]Jerry Bridges, "Does Divine Sovereignty Make a Difference in Everyday Life?" in *The Grace of God, the Bondage of the Will,* 1:209.

[60]John Calvin, *Concerning the Eternal Predestination of God,* trans. J. K. S. Reid (London: James Clarke, 1961), pp. 179-81.

[61]In his theodicy Calvin finally gives up on rational argument. After using circular reasoning, equivocation and name calling, he appeals to mystery. See Anna Case-Winters, *God's Power:*

Traditional Understandings and Contemporary Challenges (Louisville, Ky.: Westminster John Knox, 1990), pp. 73-80.

[62]Calvin *Institutes* 1.15.8.

[63]Helm, *Providence of God,* pp. 214-15.

[64]On these and other problems, see Bruce R. Reichenbach, "Evil and a Reformed View of God," *Philosophy of Religion* 26 (1988): 67-85. Of course, if God needs the world to express his nature, then creation is not out of grace and God would thus be "limited."

[65]Van de Beek, *Why?* p. 230.

[66]George Mavrodes, "Is There Anything Which God Does Not Do? *Christian Scholar's Review* 16, no. 4 (1987): 388.

[67]David Hume, *An Inquiry Concerning Human Understanding,* ed. Charles W. Hendel (New York: Bobbs-Merrill, 1955), p. 111.

[68]This misuse of Isaiah 55:8 and the illegitimacy of antinomies was discussed in 2.5.2.

[69]See William Hasker, "The Necessity of Gratuitous Evil," *Faith and Philosophy* 9, no. 1 (1992): 29-30.

[70]Helm, *Providence of God,* p. 137.

[71]See T. J. Gorringe, *God's Theatre: A Theology of Providence* (London: SCM Press, 1991), pp. 45-46; and Brümmer, *Speaking of a Personal God,* pp. 133, 139-44. Barth, *Church Dogmatics* 3/3, pp. 292, 365, rejects the freewill defense because it places the blame on the creatures, implying that evil arises out of God's good creation. He seeks to avoid this by speaking of the "Nothingness" and so emphasizing God's opposition to and victory over it in Jesus. However, it seems to me that Barth has not escaped making God culpable because the Nothingness arises from God's No. Furthermore, Barth here loses touch with personal categories.

[72]See Keith Ward, *Divine Action* (San Francisco: Torch, 1990), pp. 119-33.

[73]Peter van Inwagen, "The Magnitude, Duration and Distribution of Evil: A Theodicy," in his *God, Knowledge and Mystery: Essays in Philosophical Theology* (Ithaca, N.Y.: Cornell University Press, 1995), pp. 96-122. This excellent essay on the problem of evil is similar to my own.

[74]See George B. Wall, "A New Solution to an Old Problem," *Religious Studies* 15, no. 4 (1979): 519-22.

[75]W. S. Anglin, *Free Will and the Christian Faith* (New York: Oxford University Press, 1990), pp. 141-42.

[76]See Keith Ward, *Rational Theology and the Creativity of God* (New York: Pilgrim, 1982), p. 207; Michael J. Langford, *Providence* (London: SCM Press, 1981), pp. 118-20; van den Brink, *Almighty God,* pp. 251-52; and Brümmer, *Speaking of a Personal God,* pp. 142-44.

[77]Wall, "A New Solution to an Old Problem," pp. 511-30, provides one of the best discussions of this view (though he seems to value human freedom for its own sake rather than for love's sake).

[78]Hick, *Evil and the God of Love,* pp. 66, 69.

[79]See Frank G. Kirkpatrick, *Together Bound: God, History and the Religious Community* (New York: Oxford University Press, 1994), pp. 137-39; and Wall, "A New Solution to an Old Problem," p. 518.

[80]Gordon Kaufman, *Systematic Theology: A Historicist Perspective* (New York: Scribner's, 1968), pp. 302-3.

[81]See Kirkpatrick, *Together Bound,* pp. 90-92.

[82]See the helpful discussion in C. Stephen Evans, *The Historical Christ and the Jesus of Faith: The Incarnational Narrative as History* (New York: Oxford University Press, 1996), pp. 110-11, 165-69.

[83]Regarding why God sometimes but not always acts, see the helpful discussions by Ward, *Divine Action,* pp. 134-53; and Frank E. Tupper, *A Scandalous Providence: The Jesus Story of the Compassion of God* (Macon, Ga.: Mercer University Press, 1995).

[84]On gratuitous evil, see Peterson's *Evil and the Christian God;* Hasker, "The Necessity of Gratuitous Evil"; and van Inwagen, *God, Knowledge and Mystery,* pp. 115-21.

[85]See van den Brink, *Almighty God,* pp. 251-52.

[86]Two works that offer real-life situations in which the standard answers of exhaustive sovereignty are examined and ultimately rejected are Philip Yancey, *Where Is God When It Hurts?* (Grand Rapids, Mich.: Zondervan, 1977); and Penny Giesbrecht, *Where Is God When a Child Suffers?* (Hannibal, Mo.: Hannibal Books, 1988).

[87]See David Basinger, "Human Freedom and Divine Providence: Some New Thoughts on an Old Problem," *Religious Studies* 15 (1979): 505.

[88]D. J. Bartholomew, *God of Chance* (London: SCM Press, 1984), points out that randomness in nature can lead to the advancement of life as well as to deformity. With the concept of chance the sufferer is relieved of guilt or the burden of divine calling. I do not know whether God could have made a different natural environment that excluded hurricanes and earthquakes and still provided the needed air and water movements. We do know that in the present system this is not physically possible. Some believe that heaven will be such a hedonic paradise. Although the Scripture describes a place of incredible delight with some dramatic changes from what we presently experience, I am not sure precisely what the new heaven and earth will be like.

[89]Peterson, *Evil and the Christian God,* p. 111, maintains that for God to eliminate the ill effects of good natural resources would be to eliminate the natural order all together. Others go beyond this, claiming that natural evil is necessary for our growth as persons. For a critique of this last claim, see Gijsbert van den Brink, "Natural Evil and Eschatology," in *Christian Faith and Philosophical Theology,* ed. van den Brink et al. (Kampen, Netherlands: Kok Pharos, 1992), pp. 39-55.

[90]Plantinga, *God, Freedom and Evil,* p. 58, suggests that it is "logically possible" that demonic forces are to blame for natural evils. Others, however, go further and use this idea in developing a theodicy. See Anglin, *Free Will and the Christian Faith,* pp. 147-49; and Gregory Boyd, *God at War: The Bible and Spiritual Conflict* (Downers Grove, Ill.: InterVarsity Press, 1997).

[91]Anglin, *Free Will and the Christian Faith,* p. 153.

[92]The impotency of God is stressed by Rabbi Harold Kushner, *When Bad Things Happen to Good People* (New York: Schocken, 1981), and in the "fellow sufferer who understands" of process philosophy.

[93]The following is indebted to Shirley C. Guthrie, "Human Suffering, Human Liberation and the Sovereignty of God," *Theology Today* 53, no. 1 (1996): 33.

[94]Barth, *Church Dogmatics* 2/1, trans. Geoffrey W. Bromiley and T. F. Torrance (Edinburg: T & T Clark, 1960), p. 411.

[95]David Hume, *Dialogues Concerning Natural Religion,* ed. Nelson Pike (Indianapolis: Bobbs-Merrill, 1970), p. 169.

[96]Fyodor Dostoyevsky, *The Brothers Karamazov,* trans. Constance Garnett (New York: Random House, 1950), p. 287.

[97]See Brümmer, *Speaking of a Personal God,* p. 145; and Wolfhart Pannenberg, *Systematic Theology,* trans. Geoffrey W. Bromiley (Grand Rapids, Mich.: Eerdmans, 1991-1994), 2:166-67.

[98]Stephen T. Davis, *Logic and the Nature of God* (Grand Rapids, Mich.: Eerdmans, 1983), p. 108.

[99]The nature of "heaven" and the question whether both moral and natural evil will, by divine fiat, immediately cease to exist in such a state raises a number of significant problems: for example, why God does not *now* or did not originally create such a state. George B. Wall, "Heaven and a Wholly Good God," *Personalist* 58 (1977): 352-57; and Wall, "Other Worlds and the Comparison of Value," *Sophia* 18 (July 1979): 10-19, explore these questions without resolving them.

Those who affirm a compatibilistic definition of human freedom sometimes accuse proponents of libertarian freedom of being committed to believing that we will be able to sin in heaven. The compatibilist does not have this problem, since God will then ensure that all of our desires are only righteous desires. The problem for the compatibilist is to explain why God did not originally create us with only righteous desires.

A number of questions remain for proponents of libertarian freedom. Is the possibility of sin removed somehow? If so, is it removed instantaneously or progressively? In the eschaton will we continue to develop and renew our minds in the likeness of Christ? Will the process of sanctification go on? Will the presence of God so change us that we will have no further need of process and transformation? Will we all instantaneously arrive at Christlikeness in our individual and social lives? David Brown, "No Heaven Without Purgatory," *Religious Studies* 21 (December 1985): 447-56, argues that the traditional doctrine of purgatory is necessary because God always desires a free response involving complete self-acceptance from the individual and this requires a temporal purgatory for its complete achievement. Will heaven involve the abolition of human freedom so that we are not permitted to sin, or will it involve a process of transformation resulting in the confirmation of our character? Gary R. Habermas and J. P. Moreland, *Immortality: The Other Side of Death* (Nashville: Thomas Nelson, 1992), pp. 150-51, suggest that the glorification process involves the free choice to attain the state in which we are either unable to sin or consistently able not to sin. Perhaps our material freedom becomes so confirmed and pervasive that we freely never use our formal freedom to sin. One might connect this to the Eastern Orthodox notion of theosis, whereby we are incorporated into the divine nature (or image of Christ) and thus never desire to sin. Or perhaps the reason why God granted us libertarian freedom—to make the choice to enter into a loving relationship with God—will have been fulfilled and so there will no longer be need of it. Van Inwagen, *God, Knowledge and Mystery*, pp. 112-13, suggests that in heaven we shall have both the Beatific Vision and the memories of the hideousness of our existence prior to our restoration to God. Such knowledge will prevent us from sinning. But even should it be possible to sin in the eschaton, it may be that the effects will not then be so deleterious due to the work of Christ and the ministry of the Spirit in our lives.

Will all natural evil and suffering be automatically removed, or will our ability to cope with it and our acceptance of God's help be such that its negative effects are greatly lessened? At the least it would seem that there cannot be any natural evil that would result in the destruction of or irredeemable impairment of those in heaven. All such issues direct themselves to the divine wisdom. Was God wise to create and govern the world the way he has? I am not exactly sure what heaven will be like, nor do I understand why God delays bringing about the new heaven and earth. Admittedly, these issues need to be more fully explored. For some speculative possibilities, see van Inwagen, *God, Knowledge and Mystery*, pp. 113-15.

[100]Origen *On Prayer*, in *Origen: An Exhortation to Martyrdom, Prayer and Selected Works*, trans. Rowan Greer, Classics of Western Spirituality (New York: Paulist, 1979), p. 92.

[101]Calvin *Institutes* 1.17.3.

[102]Helm, *Providence of God*, p. 159.

[103]Paul Helm, "Prayer and Providence," in *Christian Faith and Philosophical Theology*, ed. Gijsbert van den Brink et al. (Kampen, Netherlands: Kok Pharos, 1992), p. 110.

[104]Storms, "Prayer and Evangelism," p. 224.

[105]Ibid., p. 228.

[106]Edwards, "The Most High: A Prayer-Hearing God," in *Works of Jonathan Edwards*, 2:115-16 (emphasis mine).

[107]Abraham Heschel, *The Insecurity of Freedom* (New York: Farrar, Straus and Giroux, 1966), p. 258. I believe Heschel to be speaking hyperbolically here because, strictly speaking, God's immanence in the world is not entirely dependent on us.

[108]Margaret Falls-Corbitt and F. Michael McLain answer this by affirming that God chooses to

respect our privacy in such a way that prayer becomes genuine disclosure of that which God would not otherwise know. See their "God and Privacy," *Faith and Philosophy* 9, no. 3 (1992): 369-86.

[109]On the importance of presenting reasons to God in biblical prayers, see Patrick D. Miller, "Prayer as Persuasion: The Rhetoric and Intention of Prayer," in *They Cried to the Lord: The Form and Theology of Biblical Prayer* (Minneapolis: Fortress, 1994).

[110]Very helpful on prayer as a vital element in a personal relationship with God are the following: Terence Fretheim, "Prayer in the Old Testament: Creating Space in the World for God"; and Paul Sponheim, "The God of Prayer," both in *A Primer on Prayer*, ed. Paul Sponheim (Philadelphia: Fortress, 1988); Vincent Brümmer, *What Are We Doing When We Pray?* Samuel E. Balentine, *Prayer in the Hebrew Bible: The Drama of Divine-Human Dialogue*, Overtures to Biblical Theology (Minneapolis: Fortress, 1993); van de Beek, *Why?* pp. 316-32; and Richard Foster, *Prayer: Finding the Heart's True Home* (New York: HarperCollins, 1992).

[111]Paul Helm caricatures this view of prayer as one that has God functioning like an old-fashioned switchboard operator, putting calls through if the line is open. He believes this view of prayer makes it a *force* that controls God. See Helm's "Asking God," *Themelios* 12, no. 1 (1986): 24.

[112]See especially Fretheim, "Prayer in the Old Testament"; Tupper, *Scandalous Providence*, pp. 274-80; and Heschel, *The Insecurity of Freedom*, p. 258.

[113]Peter R. Baelz, *Prayer and Providence: A Background Study* (New York: Seabury, 1968), p. 118.

[114]On this debate, see Eleonore Stump, "Petitionary Prayer," *American Philosophical Quarterly* 16 (April 1979): 81-91; David Basinger, "Why Petition an Omnipotent, Omniscient, Wholly Good God?" *Religious Studies* 19 (1983): 25-41; Joshua Hoffman, "On Petitionary Prayer," *Faith and Philosophy* 2, no. 1 (1985): 21-29; Eleonore Stump, "Hoffman on Petitionary Prayer," *Faith and Philosophy* 2, no. 1 (1985): 30-77; Michael J. Murray and Kurt Meyers, "Ask and It Will Be Given to You," *Religious Studies* 30, no. 3 (1994): 311-30; David Basinger, "Petitionary Prayer: A Response to Murray and Meyers," *Religious Studies* 31, no. 4 (1995): 475-84; Ward, *Divine Action*, pp. 159-66; and Brümmer, *What Are We Doing When We Pray?* pp. 47, 55-59.

[115]See Ward, *Divine Action*, p. 158; and Lucas, *Freedom and Grace*, pp. 37-40.

[116]See Balentine, *Prayer in the Hebrew Bible*, pp. 272-95; and Miller, *They Cried to the Lord*, pp. 325-27.

[117]David Basinger, a proponent of the risk model, disagrees with me on this point. See his "Practical Implications," in *The Openness of God*, by Clark Pinnock et al. (Downers Grove, Ill.: InterVarsity Press, 1994), p. 161. For discussion of this debate, see the references in note 114 of this chapter. Paul Helm, *Providence of God*, p. 159, believes the risk model of prayer makes us responsible for Auschwitz. (He prefers to place the responsibility on God's shoulders.)

[118]Ward, *Divine Action*, p. 166. See also the discussion in Boyd, *God at War*, pp. 203-5.

[119]Two helpful works on the means by which God guides are Garry Friesen, *Decision Making and the Will of God: A Biblical Alternative to the Traditional View*, Critical Concern Book (Portland: Multnomah, 1980); and Derek Tidball, *How Does God Guide?* (Grand Rapids, Mich.: Zondervan, 1991). Both authors propose the "wisdom model" with which I agree. However, both authors also seem to affirm exhaustive divine sovereignty in which God's will is never thwarted while also affirming that God has no exhaustive blueprint for our lives. Given their emphasis on the way of wisdom, it would seem that they should not affirm specific sovereignty.

[120]Hence some Christians' interest in interpreting circumstances as "open and closed doors" and their search for divine "signs."

[121]Curiously, Helm, *Providence of God*, p. 127, says that we "may" learn what God wants to

teach us. But given his belief in meticulous providence, he should say that we "will" learn whatever God wants to teach us at that particular moment—even if what God wants us to learn is that we are confused.

[122]Ibid., p. 130.

[123]Proponents of the no-risk model who write on divine guidance often fail to see this and thus make it sound as though we could miss the divine guidance God desired to give. But "missing" divine guidance can only occur in the risk model.

[124]Van de Beek, *Why?* p. 49.

[125]John Boykin, *The Gospel of Coincidence: Is God in Control?* (Grand Rapids, Mich.: Zondervan, 1986), critiques the common assumption that all circumstances are God's doing.

Chapter 9: Conclusion

[1]In fact, it should be noted that even the proponents of the openness of God do not agree regarding all the details I have proposed in this book.

Bibliography

Abraham, William J. *An Introduction to the Philosophy of Religion*. Englewood Cliffs, N.J.: Prentice Hall, 1985.

———. "Predestination and Assurance." In *The Grace of God, the Will of Man*, edited by Clark Pinnock. Grand Rapids, Mich.: Zondervan, 1989.

Adams, Robert Merrihew. "Must God Create the Best?" *Philosophical Review* 81 (1972): 312-32.

Aghiorgoussis, Bishop Maximos. "Orthodox Soteriology." In *Salvation in Christ: A Lutheran-Orthodox Dialogue*, edited by John Meyendorff and Robert Tobias. Minneapolis: Augsburg, 1992.

Albrektson, Bertil. *History of the Gods: An Essay on the Idea of Historical Events as Divine Manifestations in the Ancient Near East and in Israel*. Sweden: Gleerup, 1967.

Allison, Dale C., Jr. "Matthew 10:26-31 and the Problem of Evil." *St. Vladimir's Theological Quarterly* 32, no. 4 (1988): 293-308.

Alston, William. "Can We Speak Literally of God?" In Alston, *Divine Nature and Human Language*. Ithaca, N.Y.: Cornell University Press, 1989.

———. "Divine and Human Action." In *Divine and Human Action: Essays in the Metaphysics of Theism*, edited by Thomas V. Morris. Ithaca, N.Y.: Cornell University Press, 1988.

———. "Divine-Human Dialogue and the Nature of God." *Faith and Philosophy* 2, no. 1 (1985): 5-20.

———. "Functionalism and Theological Language." In *The Concept of God*, edited by Thomas Morris. New York: Oxford University Press, 1987.

Althaus, Paul. *The Theology of Martin Luther*. Translated by Robert Schultz. Philadelphia: Fortress, 1963.

Andersen, Francis I., and David Noel Freedman. *Amos: A New Translation with Introduction and Commentary*. The Anchor Bible, vol. 24a. New York: Doubleday, 1989.

Anderson, Bernhard W. "The Kingdom, the Power and the Glory." *Theology Today* 53, no. 1 (1966): 5-14.

Andrews, James E., and Joseph A. Burgess, eds. *An Invitation to Action: The Lutheran-Reformed Dialogue Series III, 1981-1983*. Philadelphia: Fortress, 1984.

Anglin, W. S. *Free Will and the Christian Faith*. New York: Oxford University Press, 1990.

Aristotle. *Eudemian Ethics*. In *The Basic Works of Aristotle*, edited by Richard McKeon. New York: Random House, 1941.

Aquinas, Thomas. *Summa Theologica*. Edited by Anton C. Pegis. 2 vols. New York: Random House, 1945.

Augustine. *City of God*. Translated by Marcus Dods. New York: Random House, 1950.

———. *Augustine: Confessions and Enchiridion*. Translated by Albert C. Oulter. Library of Christian Classics, vol. 7. Philadelphia: Westminster, 1955.

———. *On Free Will*. Translated by John H. S. Burleigh. *Augustine: Earlier Writings*. Library of Christian Classics, vol. 6. Philadelphia: Westminster, 1953.

———. *The Trinity*. Translated by John Burnaby. *Augustine: Earlier Writings*. Library of Christian Classics, vol. 8. Philadelphia: Westminster, 1955.

Baelz, Peter R. *Prayer and Providence: A Background Study*. New York: Seabury, 1968.

Bailey, Kenneth E. *Poet and Peasant and Through Peasant Eyes: A Literary-Cultural Approach to the Parables in Luke*. Combined ed. Grand Rapids: Eerdmans, 1990.

Balentine, Samuel E. *The Hidden God: The Hiding Face of God in the Old Testament*. Oxford: Oxford University Press, 1983.

————. *Prayer in the Hebrew Bible: The Drama of Divine-Human Dialogue*. Overtures to Biblical Theology. Minneapolis: Fortress, 1993.

Barr, James. *Biblical Words for Time*. 2nd ed. London: SCM Press, 1969.

Barrett, C. K. *The Gospel According to St. John*. 2nd ed. Philadelphia: Westminster, 1978.

Barth, Karl. *Church Dogmatics*. 4 vols. Translated by G. W. Bromiley and T. F. Torrance. Edinburgh: T & T Clark, 1956-1975.

Barth, Markus. *Ephesians: Introduction, Translation and Commentary on Chapters 1—3*. Garden City, N.Y.: Doubleday, 1974.

Bartholomew, D. J. *God of Chance*. London: SCM Press, 1984.

Basinger, David. "Biblical Paradox: Does Revelation Challenge Logic?" *Journal of the Evangelical Theological Society* 30, no. 2 (1987): 205-13.

————. "Can an Evangelical Christian Justifiably Deny God's Exhaustive Knowledge of the Future?" *Christian Scholar's Review* 25, no. 2 (1995): 133-45.

————. *The Case for Freewill Theism: A Philosophical Assessment*. Downers Grove, Ill.: InterVarsity Press, 1996.

————. "Divine Control and Human Freedom: Is Middle Knowledge the Answer? *Journal of the Evangelical Theological Society* 36, no. 1 (1993): 55-64.

————. *Divine Power in Process Theism: A Philosophical Critique*. Albany: State University of New York Press, 1988.

————. "Human Freedom and Divine Providence: Some New Thoughts on an Old Problem." *Religious Studies* 15 (1979): 491-510.

————. "Middle Knowledge and Classical Christian Thought." *Religious Studies* 22, no. 3 (1986): 407-22.

————. "Middle Knowledge and Divine Control: Some Clarifications." *International Journal for Philosophy of Religion* 30 (1991): 129-39.

————. "Omniscience and Deliberation: A Response to Reichenbach." *International Journal for the Philosophy of Religion* 20 (1986): 169-72.

————. "Petitionary Prayer: A Response to Murray and Meyers." *Religious Studies* 31, no. 4 (1995): 475-84.

————. "Practical Implications." In *The Openness of God: A Biblical Challenge to the Traditional Understanding of God*, by Clark Pinnock et al. Downers Grove, Ill.: InterVarsity Press, 1994.

————. "Why Petition an Omnipotent, Omniscient, Wholly Good God?" *Religious Studies* 19 (1983): 25-41.

Basinger, David, and Randall Basinger. "In the Image of Man Create They God: A Challenge." *Scottish Journal of Theology* 34 (1981): 97-107.

————. *Predestination and Free Will: Four Views of Divine Sovereignty and Human Freedom*. Downers Grove, Ill.: InterVarsity Press, 1986.

————. "The Problem with the 'Problem of Evil.'" *Religious Studies* 1 (March 1994): 89-97.

Battles, Ford Lewis. "God Was Accommodating Himself to Human Capacity." *Interpretation* 31, no. 1 (1977): 19-38.

Bauckham, Richard. "Only the Suffering God Can Help: Divine Passibility in Modern Theology." *Themelios* 9, no. 3 (1984): 6-12.

Bavinck, Herman. *The Doctrine of God*. Translated by William Hendriksen. Grand Rapids, Mich.: Baker, 1977.

Beabout, Gregory R. "Does Anxiety Explain Hereditary Sin?" *Faith and Philosophy* 11, no. 1 (1994): 117-26.

Beasley-Murray, George R. *John*. Word Biblical Commentary. Waco, Tex.: Word, 1987.

Beckwith, Francis. "Limited Omniscience and the Test for a Prophet: A Brief Philosophical Analysis." *Journal of the Evangelical Theological Society* 36, no. 3 (1993): 357-62.

Berkeley, George. *Alciphron*. In *Berkeley: Essay, Principles, Dialogues*, edited by Mary Calkins. New York: Charles Scribner's Sons, 1929.

Berkhof, Hendrikus. *Christian Faith: An Introduction to the Study of the Faith*. Translated by Sierd Woudstra. Grand Rapids, Mich.: Eerdmans, 1979.

Berkhof, Louis. *Systematic Theology*. 3rd ed. Grand Rapids, Mich.: Eerdmans, 1946.

Berkouwer, G. C. *Man: The Image of God*. Translated by Dirk Jellema. Grand Rapids, Mich.: Eerdmans, 1962.

―――. *The Person of Christ*. Translated by John Vriend. Grand Rapids, Mich.: Eerdmans, 1954.

―――. *The Providence of God*. Translated by Lewis Smedes. Grand Rapids, Mich.: Eerdmans, 1952.

Bertocci, Peter A. *The Person God Is*. New York: Humanities, 1970.

Bilezikian, Gilbert. *Christianity 101*. Grand Rapids, Mich.: Zondervan, 1993.

Bloesch, Donald G. *Essentials of Evangelical Theology*. 2 vols. New York: Harper & Row, 1982.

―――. *God the Almighty: Power, Wisdom, Holiness, Love*. Christian Foundations. Downers Grove, Ill.: InterVarsity Press, 1995.

Boer, Harry. *An Ember Still Glowing*. Grand Rapids, Mich.: Eerdmans, 1990.

Bonda, Jan. *The One Purpose of God*. Grand Rapids, Mich.: Eerdmans, 1997.

Bonhoeffer, Dietrich. *Letters and Papers from Prison*. New York: Macmillan, 1972.

Boring, M. Eugene. *Matthew*. The New Interpreter's Bible, vol. 8. Nashville: Abingdon, 1995.

Boyd, Gregory. *God at War: The Bible and Spiritual Conflict*. Downers Grove, Ill.: InterVarsity Press, 1997.

―――. *Trinity and Process: A Critical Evaluation and Reconstruction of Hartshorne's Di-Polar Theism Towards a Trinitarian Metaphysics*. New York: Peter Lang, 1992.

Boykin, John. *The Gospel of Coincidence: Is God in Control?* Grand Rapids, Mich.: Zondervan, 1986.

Breck, John. "Divine Initiative: Salvation in Orthodox Theology." In *Salvation in Christ: A Lutheran-Orthodox Dialogue*, edited by John Meyendorff and Robert Tobias. Minneapolis: Augsburg, 1992.

Bridges, Jerry. "Does Divine Sovereignty Make a Difference in Everyday Life?" In *The Grace of God, the Bondage of the Will*, edited by Thomas Schreiner and Bruce Ware. 2 vols. Grand Rapids, Mich.: Baker, 1995.

Brightman, Edgar S. *The Problem of God*. New York: Abingdon, 1930.

Bromiley, Geoffrey W., ed. *International Standard Bible Encyclopedia*. Rev. ed. 4 vols. Grand Rapids, Mich.: Eerdmans, 1986.

Brown, Colin, ed. *The New International Dictionary of New Testament Theology*. 3 vols. Grand Rapids, Mich.: Zondervan, 1975.

Brown, David. "No Heaven Without Purgatory." *Religious Studies* 21 (December 1985): 447-56.

Brown, Raymond E. "How Much Did Jesus Know?" *Catholic Biblical Quarterly* 29, no. 1 (1967): 9-39.

Brown, Robert F. "God's Ability to Will Moral Evil." *Faith and Philosophy* 8, no. 1 (1991): 3-20.

Bruce, F. F. *The Book of Acts*. Rev. ed. New International Commentary on the New Testament. Grand Rapids, Mich.: Eerdmans, 1988.

Brueggemann, Walter. *The Book of Exodus*. New Interpreter's Bible, vol. 1. Nashville: Abingdon, 1994.

―――. "The Costly Loss of Lament." *Journal for the Study of the Old Testament* 36 (1986): 57-71.

―――. *Genesis*. Interpretation. Atlanta: John Knox, 1982.

———. *To Pluck Up, to Tear Down: Jeremiah 1—25*. International Theological Commentary. Grand Rapids, Mich.: Eerdmans, 1988.

Brümmer, Vincent. *The Model of Love: A Study in Philosophical Theology*. New York: Cambridge University Press, 1993.

———. "Paul Helm on God and the Approval of Sin." *Religious Studies* 20 (June 1994): 223-26.

———. *Speaking of a Personal God: An Essay in Philosophical Theology*. New York: Cambridge University Press, 1992.

———. "On Thanking God Whatever Happens." *Journal of Theology for Southern Africa* 48 (September 1984): 3-12.

———. *What Are We Doing When We Pray? A Philosophical Inquiry*. London: SCM Press, 1984.

Brunner, Emil. *The Christian Doctrine of Creation and Redemption*. Translated by Olive Wyon. Philadelphia: Westminster, 1952.

———. *Christian Doctrine of God*. Translated by Olive Wyon. Philadelphia: Westminster, 1949.

———. *The Divine-Human Encounter*. Translated by Amandus W. Loos. Philadelphia: Westminster, 1943.

Burrell, David B. *Freedom and Creation in Three Traditions*. Notre Dame, Ind.: University of Notre Dame Press, 1993.

Buswell, J. Oliver, Jr. *A Systematic Theology of the Christian Religion*. 2 vols. Grand Rapids, Mich.: Zondervan, 1962.

Butin, Walker. *Revelation, Redemption and Response: Calvin's Trinitarian Understanding of the Divine-Human Relationship*. New York: Oxford University Press, 1995.

Calvin, John. *Commentaries on the First Book of Moses*. Translated by John King. 2 vols. Grand Rapids, Mich.: Eerdmans, 1948.

———. *Concerning the Eternal Predestination of God*. Translated by J. K. S. Reid. London: James Clarke, 1961.

———. *Institutes of the Christian Religion*. Edited by John T. McNeill. Philadelphia: Westminster, 1960.

Capon, Robert. *The Parables of Judgment*. Grand Rapids: Eerdmans, 1989.

Carlston, Charles E. "Matthew 6:24-34." *Interpretation* 41 (April 1987): 179-83.

Carman, John B. *Majesty and Meekness: A Comparative Study of Contrast and Harmony in the Concept of God*. Grand Rapids, Mich.: Eerdmans, 1994.

Carson, Donald A. *Divine Sovereignty and Human Responsibility: Biblical Perspectives in Tension,* 2nd ed. Grand Rapids, Mich.: Baker, 1994.

———. *Matthew*. Expositor's Bible Commentary, vol. 8. Grand Rapids, Mich.: Zondervan, 1984.

Carter, Ben. *The Depersonalization of God*. Lanham, Md.: University Press of America, 1989.

Case-Winters, Anna. *God's Power: Traditional Understandings and Contemporary Challenges*. Louisville, Ky.: Westminster John Knox, 1990.

Cassuto, U. *A Commentary on the Book of Exodus*. Translated by Israel Abrahams. Jerusalem: Magnes, 1967.

Chadwick, Henry. *Early Christian Thought and the Classical Tradition: Studies in Justin, Clement and Origen*. New York: Oxford University Press, 1966.

Childs, Brevard. *The Book of Exodus*. Old Testament Library. Philadelphia: Westminster, 1974.

Chisholm, Robert B., Jr. "Divine Hardening in the Old Testament." *Bibliotheca Sacra* 153 (October 1996): 410-34.

Chisholm, Roderick M., and Dean W. Zimmerman. "Theology and Tense." *Nous* 31, no. 2 (1997): 262-65.

Ciocchi, David. "Reconciling Divine Sovereignty and Human Freedom." *Journal of the Evangelical Theological Society* 37, no. 3 (1994): 395-412.

Clarke, W. Norris. *God, Knowable and Unknowable*. Edited by Robert J. Roth. New York: Fordham University Press, 1973.

———. *The Philosophical Approach to God*. Winston-Salem, N.C.: Wake Forest University Press, 1979.

Clines, David. "Yahweh and the God of Christian Theology." *Theology* 83 (1980): 323-30.

Cook, John G. "The Sparrow's Fall in Mt 10:29b." *Zeitschrift für die Neutestamentliche Wissenschaft und die Kunde der Alteren Kirche* 79, no. 1-2 (1988): 138-44.

Cook, Robert R. "Apostasy: Some Logical Reflections." *Evangelical Quarterly* 65, no. 2 (1993): 147-53.

Cottrell, Jack. "Conditional Election." In *Grace Unlimited,* edited by Clark Pinnock. Minneapolis: Bethany Fellowship, 1975.

———. *What the Bible Says About God the Ruler*. Joplin, Mo.: College Press, 1984.

Crabtree, J. A. "Does Middle Knowledge Solve the Problem of Divine Sovereignty?" In *The Grace of God, the Bondage of the Will,* edited by Thomas Schreiner and Bruce Ware. 2 vols. Grand Rapids, Mich.: Baker, 1995.

Craig, William Lane. *The Only Wise God: The Compatibility of Divine Foreknowledge and Human Freedom*. Grand Rapids, Mich.: Baker, 1987.

Cranfield, C. E. B. *Romans: A Shorter Commentary*. Grand Rapids, Mich.: Eerdmans, 1985.

Creel, Richard. *Divine Impassibility: An Essay in Philosophical Theology*. Cambridge: Cambridge University Press, 1986.

Crenshaw, J. L. "The Birth of Skepticism in Ancient Israel." In *The Divine Helmsman: Studies on God's Control of Human Events,* edited by J. L. Crenshaw and S. Sandmel. New York: KTAV, 1980.

Crockett, William, ed. *Four Views on Hell*. Grand Rapids, Mich.: Zondervan, 1992.

Cullman, Oscar. *Christ and Time*. Rev. ed. Translated by F. V. Filson. London: SCM Press, 1962.

Cunningham, David S. *Faithful Persuasion: In Aid of a Rhetoric of Christian Theology*. Notre Dame, Ind.: University of Notre Dame Press, 1991.

Daane, James. "Can a Man Bless God?" In *God and the Good,* edited by Clifton Orlebeke and Lewis Smedes. Grand Rapids, Mich.: Eerdmans, 1975.

———. *The Freedom of God: A Study of Election and Pulpit*. Grand Rapids, Mich.: Eerdmans, 1973.

Davies, Horton. *The Vigilant God: Providence in the Thought of Augustine, Aquinas, Calvin and Barth*. New York: Peter Lang, 1992.

Davis, John J. *Moses and the Gods of Egypt*. Winona Lake, Ind.: BMH Books, 1971.

Davis, Stephen. *Logic and the Nature of God*. Grand Rapids, Mich.: Eerdmans, 1983.

———. "Why God Must Be Unlimited." In *Concepts of the Ultimate: Philosophical Perspectives on the Nature of the Divine,* edited by Linda J. Tessier. New York: St. Martin's, 1989.

Depoortere, Kristiaan. *A Different God: A Christian View of Suffering*. Louvain Theological and Pastoral Monographs. Grand Rapids, Mich.: Eerdmans, 1995.

Dillon, Richard J. "Ravens, Lilies and the Kingdom of God: Matthew 6:25-33/Luke 12:22-31." *Catholic Biblical Quarterly* 53, no. 4 (1991): 605-27.

Dorner, Isaak August. *Divine Immutability: A Critical Reconsideration*. Translated by Robert R. Williams and Claude Welch. Fortress Texts in Modern Theology. Minneapolis: Fortress, 1994.

Dostoyevsky, Fyodor. *The Brothers Karamazov*. Translated by Constance Garnett. New York: Random House, 1950.

Dunn, James. *Jesus, Paul and the Law*. Philadelphia: Westminster, 1990.

———. *The Partings of the Ways Between Christianity and Judaism and Their Significance for the Character of Christianity*. London: SCM Press, 1991.

———. *Romans*. 2 vols. Word Biblical Commentary. Waco, Tex.: Word, 1988.

Eddy, Paul R. "Religious Pluralism and the Divine: Another Look at John Hick's Neo-Kantian Proposal." *Religious Studies* 30 (1994): 467-78.

Edwards, Jonathan. *The Works of Jonathan Edwards*. Edited by Edward Hickman. 2 vols. Edinburgh: The Banner of Truth Trust, 1974.

Edwards, Rem B. "The Pagan Dogma of the Absolute Unchangeableness of God." *Religious Studies* 14 (1978): 305-13.

Eichrodt, Walter. *Theology of the Old Testament*. Translated by J. A. Baker. 2 vols. Old Testament Library. London: SCM Press, 1961.

Ellison, H. L. *Exodus*. Daily Study Bible. Philadelphia: Westminster, 1982.

Evans, C. Stephen. *The Historical Christ and the Jesus of Faith: The Incarnational Narrative as History*. New York: Oxford University Press, 1996.

————. *Passionate Reason: Making Sense of Kierkegaard's Philosophical Fragments*. Bloomington, Ind.: Indiana University Press, 1992

————. *Preserving the Person: A Look at the Human Sciences*. Downers Grove, Ill.: InterVarsity Press, 1977.

————. "Salvation, Sin and Human Freedom in Kierkegaard." In *The Grace of God, the Will of Man*, edited by Clark Pinnock. Grand Rapids, Mich.: Zondervan, 1989.

Evans, G. R. *The Language and Logic of the Bible: The Earlier Middle Ages*. New York: Cambridge University Press, 1984.

Evans, James H., Jr. *We Have Been Believers: An African-American Systematic Theology*. Minneapolis: Fortress, 1992.

Fackre, Gabriel. *The Christian Story*. Rev. ed. 3 volumes. Grand Rapids, Mich.: Eerdmans, 1984.

————. "Divine Perseverance." In *What About Those Who Have Never Heard?* edited by John Sanders. Downers Grove, Ill.: InterVarsity Press, 1995.

Falls-Corbitt, Margaret, and F. Michael McLain. "God and Privacy." *Faith and Philosophy* 9, no. 3 (1992): 369-86.

Farley, Benjamin Wirt. *The Providence of God*. Grand Rapids, Mich.: Baker, 1988.

Farmer, H. H. *The World and God: A Study of Prayer, Providence and Miracle in Christian Experience*. Rev. ed. London: Nisbet, 1955.

Feldman, Seymour. "The Binding of Isaac: A Test-Case of Divine Foreknowledge." In *Divine Omniscience and Omnipotence in Medieval Philosophy: Islamic, Jewish and Christian Perspectives*, edited by Tamar Rudavsky. Boston: Reidel, 1985.

Fergusson, David A. S. "Predestination: A Scottish Perspective." *Scottish Journal of Theology* 46 (1993): 457-78.

Ferré, Frederick. "In Praise of Anthropomorphism." In *God in Language*, edited by Robert Scharlemann and Gilbert Ogutu. New York: Paragon House, 1987.

Ferré, Nels. *The Christian Understanding of God*. New York: Harper, 1951.

Feuerbach, Ludwig. *The Essence of Christianity*. Translated by George Eliot. New York: Harper/Torchbooks, 1957.

Fiddes, Paul S. *The Creative Suffering of God*. New York: Oxford University Press, 1988.

Finger, Thomas. *Christian Theology: An Eschatological Approach*. 2 vols. Scottsdale, Penn.: Herald, 1989.

Flint, Thomas. *Divine Providence: The Molinist Account*. Ithaca, N.Y.: Cornell University Press, 1998.

————. "The Problem of Divine Freedom." *American Philosophical Quarterly* 20 (1983): 255-64.

————. "Two Accounts of Providence." In *Divine and Human Action: Essays in the Metaphysics of Theism*, edited by Thomas V. Morris. Ithaca, N.Y.: Cornell University Press, 1988.

Flint, Thomas P., and Alfred J. Freddoso. "Maximal Power." In *The Concept of God*, edited by Thomas Morris. New York: Oxford University Press, 1987.

Forster, Roger T., and V. Paul Marston. *God's Strategy in Human History*. Minneapolis: Bethany House, 1983.

Foster, Richard. *Celebration of Discipline: The Path to Spiritual Growth*. Rev. ed. New York: HarperCollins, 1988.

———. *Prayer: Finding the Heart's True Home*. New York: HarperCollins, 1992.

Fretheim, Terence. *The Book of Genesis*. The New Interpreter's Bible. Nashville: Abingdon, 1994.

———. "Creator, Creature and Co-creation in Genesis 1—2." *Word and World,* Supplement 1 (1992): 11-20.

———. "Divine Foreknowledge, Divine Constancy and the Rejection of Saul's Kingship." *Catholic Biblical Quarterly* 47, no. 4 (1985): 595-602.

———. *Exodus*. Interpretation. Louisville, Ky.: John Knox, 1991.

———. "Prayer in the Old Testament: Creating Space in the World for God." In *A Primer on Prayer,* edited by Paul Sponheim. Philadelphia: Fortress, 1988.

———. "The Repentance of God: A Key to Evaluating Old Testament God-Talk." *Horizons in Biblical Theology* 10, no. 1 (1988): 47-70.

———. "The Repentance of God: A Study of Jeremiah 18:7-10." *Hebrew Annual Review* 11 (1987): 81-92.

———. "Suffering God and Sovereign God in Exodus: A Collision of Images." *Horizons in Biblical Theology* 11, no. 2 (1989): 31-56.

———. *The Suffering of God: An Old Testament Perspective*. Overtures to Biblical Theology. Philadelphia: Fortress, 1984.

Friesen, Garry. *Decision Making and the Will of God: A Biblical Alternative to the Traditional View*. Critical Concern Book. Portland: Multnomah, 1980

Geach, Peter. "Omnipotence." In *Providence and Evil* (Cambridge University Press, 1977). First published in *Philosophy* 43 (1973): 7-20.

———. *Providence and Evil*. Cambridge: Cambridge University Press, 1977.

Geisler, Norman L. *Creating God in the Image of Man? The New Open View of God—Neotheism's Dangerous Drift*. Minneapolis: Bethany House, 1997.

Gerish, B. A. "'To the Unknown God': Luther and Calvin on the Hiddenness of God," *The Journal of Religion* 53, no. 3 (1973): 263-92.

Giesbrecht, Penny. *Where Is God When a Child Suffers?* Hannibal, Mo.: Hannibal Books, 1988.

Giles, Kevin. "The Biblical Argument for Slavery: Can the Bible Mislead? A Case Study in Hermeneutics." *Evangelical Quarterly* 66, no. 1 (1994): 3-17.

Gilkey, Langdon. *Reaping the Whirlwind: A Christian Interpretation of History*. New York: Seabury, 1976.

Gill, Jerry H. *On Knowing God: New Directions for the Future of Theology*. Philadelphia: Westminster, 1981.

Gill, John. *The Cause of God and Truth*. London: W. H. Collingridge, 1855.

Goldingay, John. *Models for Interpretation of Scripture*. Grand Rapids, Mich.: Eerdmans, 1995.

Goldstick, D. "Could God Make a Contradiction True?" *Religious Studies* 26 (Spring 1990): 377-87.

González, Justo. *A History of Christian Thought*. 3 vols. Nashville: Abingdon, 1987.

Gorringe, T. J. *God's Theatre: A Theology of Providence*. London: SCM Press, 1991.

Gowan, Donald E. *Theology in Exodus: Biblical Theology in the Form of a Commentary*. Louisville, Ky.: Westminster John Knox, 1994.

Green, Joel B., Scot McKnight and I. Howard Marshall, eds.. *Dictionary of Jesus and the Gospels*. Downers Grove, Ill.: InterVarsity Press, 1992.

Gregory of Nyssa. *The Great Catechism*.

Gresham, John L. "The Social Model of the Trinity and Its Critics." *Scottish Journal of Theology* 46 (1993): 325-43.

Gunton, Colin E. *The Actuality of Atonement: A Study of Metaphor, Rationality and the Christian Tradition*. Grand Rapids, Mich.: Eerdmans, 1989.

———. *Christ and Creation*. Grand Rapids, Mich.: Eerdmans, 1992.

――――. *The One, the Three and the Many: God, Creation and the Culture of Modernity.* The 1992 Bampton Lectures. New York: Cambridge University Press, 1993.

――――. *The Promise of Trinitarian Theology.* Edinburgh: T & T Clark, 1991.

Guthrie, Shirley C. "Human Suffering, Human Liberation and the Sovereignty of God." *Theology Today* 53, no. 1 (1996): 22-34.

Habermas, Gary R., and J. P. Moreland. *Immortality: The Other Side of Death.* Nashville: Thomas Nelson, 1992.

Hall, Douglas John. *God and Human Suffering: An Exercise in the Theology of the Cross.* Minneapolis: Augsburg, 1986.

Hallman, Joseph M. *The Descent of God: Divine Suffering in History and Theology.* Minneapolis: Fortress, 1991.

Hamilton, Victor P. *The Book of Genesis: Chapters 1—17.* New International Commentary on the Old Testament. Grand Rapids, Mich.: Eerdmans, 1990.

Harkness, Georgia. *The Providence of God.* New York: Abingdon, 1960.

Harris, Murray J. *2 Corinthians.* Expositor's Bible Commentary, vol. 10. Edited by Frank Gaebelein. Grand Rapids, Mich.: Zondervan, 1976.

Hart, Trevor. *Faith Thinking: The Dynamics of Christian Theology.* Downers Grove, Ill.: InterVarsity Press, 1995.

Hartshorne, Charles, and William Reese, eds. *Philosophers Speak of God.* Chicago: University of Chicago Press, 1953.

Hasker, William. *God, Time and Knowledge.* Cornell Studies in the Philosophy of Religion. Ithaca, N.Y.: Cornell University Press, 1989.

――――. "The Necessity of Gratuitous Evil." *Faith and Philosophy* 9, no. 1 (1992): 23-44.

――――. "A Philosophical Perspective." In *The Openness of God: A Biblical Challenge to the Traditional Understanding of God,* by Clark Pinnock et al. Downers Grove, Ill.: InterVarsity Press, 1995.

――――. "Yes, God Has Beliefs." *Religious Studies* 24, no. 3 (1988): 385-94.

Hebblethwaite, Brian. "Some Reflections on Predestination, Providence and Divine Foreknowledge." *Religious Studies* 15, no. 4 (1979): 433-48.

Helm, Paul. "Asking God." *Themelios* 12, no. 1 (1986): 22-24.

――――. *Eternal God: A Study of God Without Time.* New York: Oxford University Press, 1988.

――――. "Grace and Causation." *Scottish Journal of Theology* 32 (1979): 101-12.

――――. "Prayer and Providence." In *Christian Faith and Philsophical Theology,* edited by Gijsbert van den Brink et al. Kampen, Netherlands: Kok Pharos, 1992.

――――. *The Providence of God.* Contours of Christian Theology. Downers Grove, Ill.: InterVarsity Press, 1994.

――――. "The Role of Logic in Biblical Interpretation." In *Hermeneutics, Inerrancy and the Bible,* edited by Earl Radmacher and Robert Preus. Grand Rapids, Mich.: Zondervan, 1984.

Henry, Carl F. H. *God, Revelation and Authority.* 6 vols. Waco, Tex.: Word, 1982.

Heschel, Abraham J. *The Insecurity of Freedom.* New York: Farrar, Straus and Giroux, 1966.

――――. *The Prophets.* 2 vols. New York: Harper & Row, 1962.

Hibbard, Billy. *Memoirs of the Life and Travels of B. Hibbard.* 2nd ed. New York: self-published, 1843.

Hick, John. *Evil and the God of Love.* Rev. ed. New York: Harper & Row, 1978.

――――. *An Interpretation of Religion: Human Responses to the Transcendent.* New Haven: Yale University Press, 1989.

Hiebert, Paul G. *Anthropological Reflections on Missiological Issues.* Grand Rapids, Mich.: Baker, 1994.

Hill, William J. *Search for the Absent God: Tradition and Modernity in Religious Understanding.* Edited by Mary Catherine Hilkert. New York: Crossroad, 1992.

Hillary of Poitiers. *On the Trinity.* In *Nicene and Post-Nicene Fathers,* edited by Philip Schaff. 2nd series. Grand Rapids, Mich.: Eerdmans, 1983.

Hoffman, Joshua. "On Petitionary Prayer." *Faith and Philosophy* 2, no. 1 (1985): 21-29.

Holmes, Arthur. *All Truth Is God's Truth*. Grand Rapids, Mich.: Eerdmans, 1977.

———. *Contours of a World View*. Grand Rapids, Mich.: Eerdmans, 1983.

Honeycutt, Roy L. *Exodus*. Broadman Bible Commentary, vol. 1. Nashville: Broadman, 1969.

Hubbard, David Allen. *Joel and Amos*. Tyndale Old Testament Commentaries. Downers Grove, Ill.: InterVarsity Press, 1989.

Hughes, Philip Edgcumbe. *A Commentary on the Epistle to the Hebrews*. Grand Rapids, Mich.: Eerdmans, 1977.

———. *Paul's Second Epistle to the Corinthians*. New International Commentary on the New Testament. Grand Rapids, Mich.: Eerdmans, 1962.

Hull, John M. *What Prevents Christian Adults from Learning?* Philadelphia: Trinity Press International, 1991.

Hume, David. *An Inquiry Concerning Human Understanding*. Edited by Charles W. Hendel. New York: Bobbs-Merrill, 1955.

———. *Dialogues Concerning Natural Religion*. Edited by Nelson Pike. Indianapolis, Ind.: Bobbs-Merrill, 1970.

Hunt, David P. "Divine Providence and Simple Foreknowledge." *Faith and Philosophy* 10, no. 3 (1993): 394-95.

Hunter, W. Bingham. *The God Who Hears*. Downers Grove, Ill.: InterVarsity Press, 1986.

Hurtado, Larry W. *Mark*. New International Biblical Commentary. Peabody, Mass.: Hendrickson, 1989.

Irenaeus. *Against Heresies*. In *The Ante-Nicene Fathers*, translated by Alexander Roberts and James Donaldson. New York: Christian Literature Company, 1896.

James, William. *The Will to Believe and Other Essays in Popular Philosophy*. New York: Dover, 1956.

Jenson, Robert W. *The Triune Identity*. Philadelphia: Fortress, 1982.

Johnson, Elizabeth A. *She Who Is: The Mystery of God in Feminist Theological Discourse*. New York: Crossroad, 1993.

Jones, Major. *The Color of God: The Concept of God in Afro-American Thought*. Macon, Ga.: Mercer University Press, 1987.

Jones, W. T. *A History of Western Philosophy: The Classical Mind*. 2nd ed. New York: Harcourt Brace Jovanovich, 1970.

Jorgenson, James. "Predestination According to Divine Foreknowledge in Patristic Tradition." In *Salvation in Christ: A Lutheran-Orthodox Dialogue*. Edited by John Meyendorff and Robert Tobias. Minneapolis: Augsburg, 1992.

Jüngel, Eberhard. *God as the Mystery of the World: On the Foundation of the Theology of the Crucified One in the Dispute Between Theism and Atheism*. Translated by Darrell L. Guder. Grand Rapids, Mich.: Eerdmans, 1983.

Kaiser, Christopher. *The Doctrine of God: An Historical Survey*. Westchester, Ill.: Crossway, 1982.

Kaiser, Walter, Jr. *Exodus*. Expositor's Bible Commentary, vol. 2. Edited by Frank Gaebelein. Grand Rapids, Mich.: Zondervan, 1990.

———. *Towards an Old Testament Ethics*. Grand Rapids, Mich.: Zondervan, 1983.

———. *Towards an Old Testament Theology*. Grand Rapids: Zondervan, 1978.

Kant, Immanuel. *Critique of Pure Reason*. Translated by Norman Kemp Smith. London: Macmillan, 1933.

Kapitan, Tomis. "Can God Make Up His Mind?" *International Journal for the Philosophy of Religion* 15 (1984): 37-47.

———. "Deliberation and the Presumption of Open Alternatives." *Philosophical Quarterly* 36, no. 143 (1986): 230-51.

———. "Providence, Foreknowledge and Decision Procedures." *Faith and Philosophy* 10, no. 3 (1993): 415-20.

Kaufman, Gordon. *God the Problem.* Cambridge: Harvard University Press, 1972.

————. *In the Face of Mystery: A Constructive Theology.* Cambridge: Harvard University Press, 1993.

————. *Systematic Theology: A Historicist Perspective.* New York: Scribner's, 1968.

————. *Theological Imagination: Constructing the Concept of God.* Philadelphia: Westminster, 1981.

Kelly, Douglas. "Afraid of Infinitude." *Christianity Today* 39, no. 1 (1995): 32-33.

Kierkegaard, Søren. *Christian Discourses.* Translated by Walter Lowrie. New York: Oxford University Press, 1939.

————. *Philosophical Fragments.* Translated by Howard Hong and Edna Hong. Princeton: Princeton University Press, 1985.

Kirkpatrick, Frank G. *Together Bound: God, History and the Religious Community.* New York: Oxford University Press, 1994.

Klassen, William. *Judas: Betrayer or Friend of Jesus?* Minneapolis: Augsburg Fortress, 1996.

Klein, William W. *The New Chosen People: A Corporate View of Election.* Grand Rapids, Mich.: Zondervan, 1990.

Kneale, W. "Time and Eternity in Theology." *Proceedings of the Aristotelian Society* 61 (1960-1961): 87-108.

Knierim, Rolf. "Cosmos and History in Israel's Theology." *Horizons in Biblical Theology* 3 (1981): 59-123.

Knight, Douglas A. "Cosmogony and Order in the Hebrew Tradition." In *Cosmogony and Ethical Order: New Studies in Comparative Ethics,* edited by Robin Lovin and Frank Reynolds. Chicago: University of Chicago Press, 1985.

Knight, Henry H., III. *A Future for Truth: Evangelical Theology in a Postmodern World.* Nashville: Abingdon, 1997.

König, Adriö. *The Eclipse of Christ in Eschatology: Toward a Christ-Centered Approach.* Grand Rapids, Mich.: Eerdmans, 1989.

————. *Here Am I: A Believer's Reflection on God.* Grand Rapids, Mich.: Eerdmans, 1982.

————. *New and Greater Things: Re-evaluating the Biblical Message on Creation.* Translated by D. Roy Briggs. Pretoria: University of South Africa, 1988.

————. "Providence, Sin and Human Freedom: On Different Concepts of Human Freedom." *"Freedom" Studies in Reformed Theology* 1 (1996).

Kretzman, Norman. "Goodness, Knowledge and Indeterminacy in the Philosophy of Thomas Aquinas." *The Journal of Philosophy* supp. 80, no. 10 (1983): 631-49.

Kuitert, Harry M. *Signals from the Bible.* Translated by Lewis B. Smedes. Grand Rapids, Mich.: Eerdmans, 1972.

Küng, Hans. *Does God Exist?* Translated by Edward Quinn. New York: Vintage, 1981.

————. *Theology for the Third Millennium: An Ecumenical View.* Translated by Peter Heinegg. New York: Doubleday, 1988.

Kushner, Harold. *When Bad Things Happen to Good People.* New York: Schocken, 1981.

Kuyper, Lester J. "The Suffering and the Repentance of God." *Scottish Journal of Theology* 22 (1969): 257-77.

Kvanvig, Jonathan. *The Problem of Hell.* New York: Oxford University Press, 1993.

La Croix, Richard R. "Omniprescience and Divine Determinism." *Religious Studies* 12 (September 1976): 365-81.

LaCugna, Catherine Mowry. *God for Us: The Trinity and Christian Life.* New York: Harper-Collins, 1991.

Ladd, George Eldon. *A Commentary on the Revelation of John.* Grand Rapids, Mich.: Eerdmans, 1972.

Lakoff, George, and Mark Johnson. *Metaphors We Live By.* Chicago: University of Chicago Press, 1980.

Land, Stephen J. *Pentecostal Spirituality.* Sheffield: Sheffield Academic Press, 1993.

Lane, William L. *Commentary on the Gospel of Mark*. New International Commentary on the New Testament. Grand Rapids, Mich.: Eerdmans, 1974.

Langford, Michael J. *Providence*. London: SCM Press, 1981.

Lee, Sang Hyun. *The Philosophical Theology of Jonathan Edwards*. Princeton: Princeton University Press, 1988.

Levenson, Jon D. "Cataclysm, Survival and Regeneration." In *Confronting Omnicide: Jewish Reflections on Weapons of Mass Destruction*, edited by Daniel Landes. Northvale, N.J.: Jason Aronson, 1991.

————. *Creation and the Persistence of Evil: The Jewish Drama of Divine Omnipotence*. Princeton: Princeton University Press, 1988.

Lewis, C. S. *God in the Dock: Essays on Theology and Ethics*. Edited by Walter Hooper. Grand Rapids, Mich.: Eerdmans, 1970.

————. *Miracles*. New York: Macmillan, 1974.

Liefeld, Walter. *Luke*. Expositor's Bible Commentary, vol. 8. Grand Rapids, Mich.: Zondervan, 1984.

Lindström, Fredrik. *God and the Origin of Evil: A Contextual Analysis of Alleged Monistic Evidence in the Old Testament*. Translated by Frederick H. Cryer. Sweden: CWK Gleerup, 1983.

————. *Suffering and Sin: Interpretations of Illness in the Individual Complaint Psalms*. Translated by Michael McLamb. Stockholm: Almqvist & Wiksell, 1994.

Long, Gary Alan. "Dead or Alive?: Literality and God-Metaphors in the Hebrew Bible." *Journal of the American Academy of Religion* 62, no. 2 (1994): 509-37.

Long, Steven A. "Personal Receptivity and Act." *The Thomist* 61, no. 1 (1997): 1-32.

Lovejoy, Arthur *The Great Chain of Being*. Cambridge: Harvard University Press, 1964.

Lucas, J. R. "Foreknowledge and the Vulnerability of God." In *The Philosophy in Christianity*, edited by Godfrey Vesey. New York: Cambridge University Press, 1989.

————. *Freedom and Grace*. Grand Rapids, Mich.: Eerdmans, 1976.

————. *The Future: An Essay on God, Temporality and Truth*. Cambridge, Mass.: Basil Blackwell, 1989.

Luther, Martin. *The Bondage of the Will*. Translated by J. I. Packer and O. R. Johnston. Old Tappan, N.J.: Revell, 1957.

MacMurray, John. *Persons in Relation*. London: Faber & Faber, 1961.

————. *The Self as Agent*. Atlantic Highlands, N.J.: Humanities, 1969.

Macquarrie, John. *God-Talk: An Examination of the Language and Logic of Theology*. New York: Harper & Row, 1967.

Maddox, Randy L. *Responsible Grace: John Wesley's Practical Theology*. Nashville: Abingdon, 1994.

Maritain, Jacques. *Existence and the Existent*. Translated by Lewis Galantiere and Gerald Phelan. New York: Random House, 1966.

Marshall, I. Howard. *Acts*. Tyndale New Testament Commentaries. Grand Rapids, Mich.: Eerdmans, 1988.

————. *Jesus the Saviour: Studies in New Testament Theology*. Downers Grove, Ill.: Inter-Varsity Press, 1990.

————. *Kept by the Power of God: A Study of Perseverance and Falling Away*. Minneapolis: Bethany Fellowship, 1969.

Mavrodes, George. "Adopting a Different Model of Sovereignty." *Perspectives* 12, no. 3 (1997): 12-15.

————. "Is There Anything Which God Does Not Do?" *Christian Scholar's Review* 16, no. 4 (1987): 384-91.

Mays, James L. "Prayer and Christology: Psalm 22 as Perspective on the Passion." *Theology Today* 42 (October 1985): 322-31.

————. *Psalms*. Interpretation. Louisville, Ky.: John Knox, 1994.

McCabe, Lorenzo. *Divine Nescience of Future Contingencies a Necessity.* New York: Phillips & Hunt, 1882.

———. *The Foreknowledge of God.* Cincinnati: Cranston & Stowe, 1887.

McDonald, H. D. *The Atonement of the Death of Christ: In Faith, Revelation and History.* Grand Rapids, Mich.: Baker, 1985.

McFague, Sallie. *Metaphorical Theology: Models of God in Religious Language.* Philadelphia: Fortress, 1982.

———. *Models of God: Theology for an Ecological, Nuclear Age.* Philadelphia: Fortress, 1987.

McGrath, Alister. *Luther's Theology of the Cross: Martin Luther's Theological Breakthrough.* New York: Basil Blackwell, 1985.

McLelland, Joseph C. *God the Anonymous: A Study in Alexandrian Philosophical Theology.* Patristic Monograph Series. Cambridge, Mass.: Philadelphia Patristic Foundation, 1976.

McLeod, Mark S. "Religious Plurality and Realist Christianity: Idolatry and the Testing of One's Faith." *Faith and Philosophy* 11, no. 2 (1994): 224-41.

Meyendorff, John. "Humanity: 'Old' and 'New'—Anthropological Considerations." In *Salvation in Christ: A Lutheran-Orthodox Dialogue,* edited by John Meyendorff and Robert Tobias. Minneapolis: Augsburg, 1992.

Middleton, J. Richard, and Brian J. Walsh. *Truth Is Stranger Than It Used to Be: Biblical Faith in a Postmodern Age.* Downers Grove, Ill.: InterVarsity Press, 1995.

Migliore, Daniel L. *The Power of God.* Philadelphia: Westminster, 1983.

Miles, Jack. *God: A Biography.* New York: Knopf, 1995.

Miller, Patrick D. "Prayer as Persuasion: The Rhetoric and Intention of Prayer." *Word and World* 13, no. 4 (1993): 356-62.

———. *They Cried to the Lord: The Form and Theology of Biblical Prayer.* Minneapolis, Fortress, 1994.

Moberly, R. W. L. "The Earliest Commentary on the Akedah." *Vetus Testamentum* 38, no. 3 (1988): 302-23.

———. *Theology of Biblical Prayer* (Minneapolis: Augsburg Fortress, 1994).

Molina, Luis de. *On Divine Foreknowledge.* Translated by and introduced by Alfred J. Freddoso. Ithaca, N.Y.: Cornell University Press, 1988.

Moltmann, Jürgen. *The Crucified God.* Translated by R. A. Wilson and John Bowden. New York: Harper & Row, 1974.

———. *Jesus Christ for Today's World.* Translated by Margaret Kohl. Minneapolis: Fortress, 1994.

———. *The Trinity and the Kingdom.* Translated by Margaret Kohl. New York: Harper & Row, 1981.

Morris, Leon. *The Apostolic Preaching of the Cross.* Grand Rapids, Mich.: Eerdmans, 1956.

———. *The Gospel According to John.* Rev. ed. New International Commentary on the New Testament. Grand Rapids, Mich.: Eerdmans, 1995.

Morris, Thomas V. *The Logic of God Incarnate.* Ithaca, N.Y.: Cornell University Press, 1986.

———. *Our Idea of God: An Introduction to Philosophical Theology.* Notre Dame, Ind.: University of Notre Dame Press, 1991.

———. "Properties, Modalities and God." *The Philosophical Review* 93, no. 1 (1984): 35-55.

Morrison, Wesley. "Is God 'Significantly Free?'" *Faith and Philsophy* 2, no. 3 (1985): 257-64.

Mozley, J. K. *The Impassibility of God: A Survey of Christian Thought.* New York: Cambridge University Press, 1926.

Muller, Richard A. *God, Creation and Providence in the Thought of Jacob Arminius.* Grand Rapids, Mich.: Baker, 1991.

———. "Grace, Election and Contingent Choice: Arminius's Gambit and the Reformed Response." In *The Grace of God, the Bondage of the Will,* edited by Thomas Schreiner and Bruce Ware. 2 vols. Grand Rapids, Mich.: Baker, 1995.

Murray, Michael J., and Kurt Meyers. "Ask and It Will Be Given to You." *Religious Studies* 30, no. 3 (1994): 311-30.

Norris, Richard A. *God and the World in Early Christian Thought: A Study in Justin Martyr, Irenàeus, Tertullian and Origen.* New York: Seabury, 1965.

North, Robert. *Teilhard and the Creation of the Soul.* Milwaukee: Bruce, 1967.

Nygren, Anders. *Agape and Eros.* Translated by Philip S. Watson. Philadelphia: Westminster, 1953.

Oden, Thomas C. *The Living God: Systematic Theology in 3 vols.* San Francisco: Harper & Row, 1987.

O'Leary, Joseph Stephen. *Questioning Back: The Overcoming of Metaphysics in Christian Tradition.* Minneapolis: Winston, 1985.

Origen. *Contra Celsus.* In *The Ante-Nicene Fathers,* translated by Alexander Roberts and James Donaldson. New York: Scribner's, 1913.

———. *On Prayer.* In *Origen: An Exortation to Martyrdom, Prayer and Selected Works,* translated by Rowan Greer. Classics of Western Spirituality. New York: Paulist, 1979.

Outler, Albert C. *Who Trusts in God: Musings on the Meaning of Providence.* New York: Oxford University Press, 1968.

Owen, H. P. *Concepts of Deity.* New York: Herder & Herder, 1971.

Packer, J. I. *Evangelism and the Sovereignty of God.* Chicago: InterVarsity Press, 1967.   •

———. *Knowing God.* 20th anniversary ed. Downers Grove, Ill.: InterVarsity Press, 1993.

———. "Paradox in Theology." In *New Dictionary of Theology,* edited by Sinclair Ferguson, David Wright and J. I. Packer. Downers Grove, Ill.: InterVarsity Press, 1988.

Padgett, Allen G. *God, Eternity and the Nature of Time.* New York: St. Martin's, 1992.

Pannenberg, Wolfhart. *Basic Questions in Theology.* 2 vols. Translated by George H. Kehm. Philadelphia: Westminster, 1983.

———. *Systematic Theology.* 2 vols. Translated by Geoffrey W. Bromiley. Grand Rapids, Mich.: Eerdmans, 1991-1994.

Paunak, H. Van. "A Semantic Survey of *NHM.*" *Biblica* 56 (1975): 512-32.

Pelikan, Jaroslav. *The Christian Tradition: A History of the Development of Doctrine.* 5 vols. Chicago: University of Chicago Press, 1971.

Pennings, Timothy J. "Infinity and the Absolute: Insights into Our World, Our Faith and Ourselves." *Christian Scholar's Review* 23, no. 2 (1993): 159-80.

Peters, Ted. *God as Trinity: Relationality and Temporality in Divine Life.* Louisville, Ky.: Westminster John Knox, 1993.

———. *Sin: Radical Evil in Soul and Society.* Grand Rapids, Mich.: Eerdmans, 1994.

Peterson, Michael. *Evil and the Christian God.* Grand Rapids, Mich.: Baker, 1982.

Peterson, Michael et. al. *Reason and Religious Belief: An Introduction to the Philosophy of Religion.* New York: Oxford University Press, 1991.

Pike, Nelson. "A Latter-Day Look at the Foreknowledge Problem." *International Journal for the Philosophy of Religion* 33 (June 1993): 129-64.

Pinnock, Clark. "Between Classical and Process Theism." In *Process Theology,* edited by Ronald Nash. Grand Rapids, Mich.: Baker, 1987.

———. *Flame of Love: A Theology of the Holy Spirit.* Downers Grove, Ill.: InterVarsity Press, 1996.

———. "God Limits His Knowledge." In *Predestination and Free Will: Four Views of Divine Sovereignty and Human Freedom,* edited by David Basinger and Randall Basinger. Downers Grove, Ill.: InterVarsity Press, 1986.

———. "God's Sovereignty in Today's World." *Theology Today* 53, no. 1 (1996): 15-21.

———. "Systematic Theology." In *The Openness of God: A Biblical Challenge to the Traditional Understanding of God,* by Clark Pinnock et al. Downers Grove, Ill.: InterVarsity Press, 1995.

———. *A Wideness in God's Mercy: The Finality of Jesus Christ in a World of Religions.* Grand Rapids, Mich.: Zondervan, 1992.

Pinnock, Clark H., and Robert C. Brow. *Unbounded Love: A Good News Theology for the 21st Century*. Downers Grove, Ill.: InterVarsity Press, 1994.

Piper, John. "Are There Two Wills in God? Divine Election and God's Desire for All to Be Saved." In *The Grace of God, the Bondage of the Will*, edited by Thomas Schreiner and Bruce Ware. 2 vols. Grand Rapids, Mich.: Baker, 1995.

————. *The Justification of God: An Exegetical and Theological Study of Romans 9:1-23*. Grand Rapids, Mich.: Baker, 1983.

Placher, William. *Narratives of a Vulnerable God: Christ, Theology and Scripture*. Louisville, Ky.: Westminster John Knox, 1994.

Plantinga, Alvin. *Does God Have a Nature?* Milwaukee: Marquette University Press, 1980.

————. *God, Freedom and Evil*. Grand Rapids, Mich.: Eerdmans, 1977.

————. *The Nature of Necessity*. Clarendon Library of Logic and Philosophy. New York: Oxford University Press, 1974.

————. "Prologue: Advice to Christian Philosophers." *Faith and Philosophy* 1, no. 3 (1984): 14-37.

Plantinga, Cornelius, Jr. "Social Trinity and Tritheism." In *Trinity, Incarnation and Atonement*, edited by Ronald J. Feenstra and C. Plantinga. Notre Dame, Ind.: University of Notre Dame Press, 1989.

Plato. *Laws*. In *The Dialogues of Plato*, translated by B. Jowett. 2 vols. New York: Random House, 1937.

Pollard, T. E. "The Impassibility of God." *Scottish Journal of Theology* 8 (1955): 353-64.

Pope, Alexander. *An Essay on Man*. In *The Selected Poetry of Pope*, edited by Martin Price. New York: Meridian, 1980.

Pratney, William. *The Nature and Character of God*. Minneapolis: Bethany House, 1988.

Prestige, G. L. *God in Patristic Thought*. London: SPCK, 1975.

Prior, A. N. "The Formalities of Omniscience." *Philosophy* 32 (1962): 119-29.

Purtill, Richard. "Fatalism and the Omnitemporality of Truth." *Faith and Philosophy* 5 (1988): 185-92.

Reichenbach, Bruce. "Evil and a Reformed View of God." *Philosophy of Religion* 26 (1988): 67-85.

————. "Freedom, Justice and Moral Responsibility." In *The Grace of God, the Will of Man*, edited by Clark Pinnock. Grand Rapids, Mich.: Zondervan, 1989.

————. "God Limits His Power." In *Predestination and Free Will: Four Views of Divine Sovereignty and Human Freedom*, edited by David Basinger and Randall Basinger. Downers Grove, Ill.: InterVarsity Press, 1986.

Rice, Richard. "Biblical Support." In *The Openness of God: A Biblical Challenge to the Traditional Understanding of God*, by Clark Pinnock et al. Downers Grove, Ill.: InterVarsity Press, 1994.

————. *God's Foreknowledge and Man's Free Will*. Minneapolis: Bethany House, 1985.

Richardson, Herbert W. *Toward an American Theology*. New York: Harper & Row, 1967.

Rigby, Cynthia L. "Free to Be Human: Limits, Possibilities and the Sovereignty of God." *Theology Today* 53, no. 1 (1996): 47-62.

Rogerson, John. "Can a Doctrine of Providence Be Based on the Old Testament?" In *Ascribe to the Lord: Biblical and Other Studies in Memory of Peter C. Craigie*, edited by Lyle Eslinger and Glen Taylor. JSOT Supplement 67. Sheffield: JSOT Press, 1988.

Sailhamer, John. *Genesis*. Expositor's Bible Commentary, vol. 2. Edited by Frank Gaebelein. Grand Rapids, Mich.: Zondervan, 1990.

Sanders, John. "God as Personal." In *The Grace of God, the Will of Man*, edited by Clark Pinnock. Grand Rapids, Mich.: Zondervan, 1989.

————. "Historical Considerations." In *The Openness of God*, by Clark Pinnock et al. Downers Grove, Ill.: InterVarsity Press, 1994.

————. "Idolater Indeed!" In *The Uniqueness of Jesus: A Dialogue with Paul F. Knitter*, edited

.

by Leonard Swidler and Paul Mojzes. Maryknoll, N.Y.: Orbis, 1997.

————. *No Other Name: An Investigation into the Destiny of the Unevangelized*. Grand Rapids, Mich.: Eerdmans, 1992.

————. "Why Simple Foreknowledge Offers No More Providential Control Than the Openness of God." *Faith and Philosophy* 14, no. 1 (1997): 26-40.

Sandmel, Samuel. *Philo of Alexandria*. New York: Oxford University Press, 1979.

Sarna, Nahum. *Exploring Exodus*. New York: Schocken, 1987.

————. *Understanding Genesis*. New York: Schocken, 1970.

Sarot, Marcel. "Omnipotence and Self-Limitation." In *Christian Faith and Philosophical Theology: Essays in Honour of Vincent Brümmer,* edited by Gijsbert van den Brink et al. Kampen, Netherlands: Kok Pharos, 1992.

Sawyer, John F. A. *Prophecy and Biblical Prophets*. Rev. ed. Oxford Bible Series. New York: Oxford University Press, 1993.

Schilling, S. Paul. *God and Human Anguish*. Nashville: Abingdon, 1977.

Schmitz, Kenneth L. "Created Receptivity." *The Thomist* 61, no. 3 (1997): 339-72.

Schreiner, Thomas R. "Does Romans 9 Teach Individual Election unto Salvation?" *Journal of the Evangelical Theological Society* 36, no. 1 (1993): 25-40.

Schwöbel, Christoph. *God: Action and Revelation*. Kampen, Netherlands: Kok Pharos, 1992.

Sennett, James F. "Is God Essentially God?" *Religious Studies* 30, no. 3 (1994): 295-303.

Senor, Thomas. "Divine Temporality and Creation *ex Nihilo*." *Faith and Philosophy* 10, no. 1 (1993): 86-92.

Sigountos, William, ed. *Four Views on Hell*. Grand Rapids, Mich.: Zondervan, 1992.

Smith, David L. *With Willful Intent: A Theology of Sin*. Wheaton, Ill.: Bridgepoint, 1994.

Sokolowski, Robert. *The God of Faith and Reason: Foundations of Christian Theology*. Notre Dame, Ind.: University of Notre Dame Press, 1982.

Soskice, Janet M. *Metaphor and Religious Language*. New York: Oxford University Press, 1985.

Sponheim, Paul R. *Faith and the Other: A Relational Theology*. Minneapolis: Fortress, 1993.

————. "The God of Prayer." In *A Primer on Prayer,* edited by Paul Sponheim. Philadelphia: Fortress, 1988.

Sproul, R. C. *Chosen by God*. Wheaton, Ill.: Tyndale, 1986.

Steuer, Axel D. "The Freedom of God and Human Freedom." *Scottish Journal of Theology* 36, no. 2 (1983): 163-80.

Stienstra, Nelly. *YHWH Is the Husband of His People: An Analysis of a Biblical Metaphor with Special Reference to Translation*. Kampen, Netherlands: Kok Pharos, 1993.

Storms, C. Samuel. "Prayer and Evangelism Under God's Sovereignty." In *The Grace of God, the Bondage of the Will,* edited by Thomas Schreiner and Bruce Ware. 2 vols. Grand Rapids, Mich.: Baker, 1995.

Stott, John R. W. *The Cross of Christ*. Downers Grove, Ill.: InterVarsity Press, 1986.

Strauss, James D. "God's Promise and Universal History: The Theology of Romans 9." In *Grace Unlimited,* edited by Clark Pinnock. Minneapolis: Bethany House, 1975.

Strimple, Robert B. "What Does God Know?" In *The Coming Evangelical Crisis,* edited by John H. Armstrong. Chicago: Moody Press, 1996.

Stuart, Douglas. *Hosea—Jonah*. Word Biblical Commentary. Waco, Tex.: Word, 1987.

Stump, Eleonore. "Hoffman on Petitionary Prayer." *Faith and Philosophy* 2, no. 1 (1985): 30-37.

————. "Petitionary Prayer." *American Philosophical Quarterly* 16 (April 1979): 81-91.

Stump, Eleonore, and Norman Kretzman. "Eternity." *Journal of Philosophy* 78 (1981): 429-58.

Suurmond, Jean-Jacques. *Word and Spirit at Play: Towards a Charismatic Theology*. Grand Rapids, Mich.: Eerdmans, 1994.

Swinburne, Richard. *The Coherence of Theism*. Rev. ed. New York: Oxford University Press, 1993.

————. *The Existence of God*. New York: Oxford University Press, 1979.

Tannehill, Robert C. "Israel in Luke-Acts: A Tragic Story." *Journal of Biblical Literature* 104, no. 1 (1985): 69-85.

TeSelle, Eugene. *Christ in Context: Divine Purpose and Human Responsibility.* Philadelphia: Fortress, 1975.

Thompson, David L. "The Godly and the Good Life in Biblical Thought." *Christian Scholar's Review* 22, no. 3 (1993): 248-66.

Tidball, Derek. *How Does God Guide?* Grand Rapids, Mich.: Zondervan, 1991.

———. *The Social Context of the New Testament: A Sociological Analysis.* Grand Rapids, Mich.: Zondervan, 1984.

Tillich, Paul. *Systematic Theology.* 3 vols. Chicago: University of Chicago Press, 1951, 1957, 1963.

Torrance, Thomas. *Space, Time and Incarnation.* New York: Oxford University Press, 1969.

Tozer, A. W. *The Knowledge of the Holy: The Attributes of God, Their Meaning in the Christian Life.* San Francisco: Harper & Row, 1978.

Tracy, Thomas. *God, Action and Embodiment.* Grand Rapids, Mich.: Eerdmans, 1984.

Tupper, E. Frank. "The Bethlehem Massacre—Christology Against Providence?" *Review and Expositor* 88, no. 4 (1991): 399-418.

———. "The Providence of God in Christological Perspective." *Review and Expositor* 82, no. 4 (1985): 579-95.

———. *A Scandalous Providence: The Jesus Story of the Compassion of God.* Macon, Ga.: Mercer University Press, 1995.

Van de Beek, A. *Why? On Suffering, Guilt and God.* Translated by John Vriend. Grand Rapids, Mich.: Eerdmans, 1990.

van den Brink, Gijsbert. *Almighty God: a Study of the Doctrine of Divine Omnipotence.* Kampen, Netherlands: Kok Pharos, 1992.

———. "Natural Evil and Eschatology." In *Christian Faith and Philosophical Theology,* edited by van den Brink et al. Kampen, Netherlands: Kok Pharos, 1992.

Van Huuyssteen, Wentzel. *Theology and the Justification of Faith: Constructing Theories in Systematic Theology.* Grand Rapids, Mich.: Eerdmans, 1989.

Van Inwagen, Peter. *God, Knowledge and Mystery: Essays in Philosophical Theology.* Ithaca, N.Y.: Cornell University Press, 1995.

———. "The Place of Chance in a World Sustained by God." In *Divine and Human Action: Essays in the Metaphysics of Theism,* edited by Thomas Morris. Ithaca, N.Y.: Cornell University Press, 1988.

Vanstone, W. H. *The Risk of Love.* New York: Oxford University Press, 1978.

Viney, Donald Wayne. "Jules Lequyer and the Openness of God." *Faith and Philosophy* 14, no. 2 (1997): 212-35.

Wall, George B. "Heaven and a Wholly Good God." *Personalist* 58 (1977): 352-57.

———. "A New Solution to an Old Problem." *Religious Studies* 15, no. 4 (1979): 511-30.

———. "Other Worlds and the Comparison of Value." *Sophia* 18 (July 1979): 10-19.

Wallis, R. T. "Divine Omniscience in Plotinus, Proclus and Aquinas." In *Neoplatonism and Early Christian Thought,* edited by H. J. Blumenthal and R. A. Markus. London: Variorum, 1981.

Walls, Jerry L. "Can God Save Anyone He Will?" *Scottish Journal of Theology* 38 (1985): 155-72.

———. "The Free Will Defense, Calvinism, Wesley and the Goodness of God." *Christian Scholar's Review* 13, no. 1 (1983): 19-33.

———. *Hell: The Logic of Damnation.* Notre Dame, Ind.: University of Notre Dame Press, 1992.

Waltke, Bruce. "The Creation Account in Gen. 1:1-3." *Bibliotheca Sacra* 132 (1975): 25-36, 136-44, 216-28, 327-42.

Ward, Keith. *Divine Action.* San Francisco: Torch, 1991.

————. *Holding Fast to God: A Reply to Don Cupitt.* London: SPCK, 1982.

————. *Rational Theology and the Creativity of God.* New York: Pilgrim, 1982.

Ware, Bruce. "An Evangelical Reformulation of the Doctrine of the Immutability of God." *Journal of the Evangelical Theological Society* 29, no. 4 (1986): 431-46.

Ware, Kallistos (Timothy). *The Orthodox Church.* London: Penguin, 1987.

Wenham, Gordon J. *Genesis 1—15.* Word Biblical Commentary. Waco, Tex.: Word, 1987.

Wesley, John. *The Works of John Wesley.* Edited by Albert C. Outler. Nashville: Abingdon, 1985.

Wilkin, Robert L. "Not a Solitary God: The Triune God of the Bible." *Pro Ecclesia* 3 (1994): 36-55.

Williams, Michael. "Crossing Lessing's Ditch." In *God and Man: Perspectives on Christianity in the Twentieth Century,* edited by Michael Bauman. Hillsdale, Mich.: Hillsdale College Press, 1995.

Windt, Peter Y. "Plantinga's Unfortunate God." *Philosophical Studies* 24 (1973): 335-42.

Wolfe, David L. *Epistemology: The Justification of Belief.* Contours of Christian Philosophy. Downers Grove, Ill.: InterVarsity Press, 1982.

Wolterstorff, Nicholas. *Divine Discourse: Philosophical Reflections on the Claim That God Speaks.* New York: Cambridge University Press, 1995.

————. "God Everlasting." In *God and the Good,* edited by Clifton Orlebeke and Lewis Smedes. Grand Rapids, Mich.: Eerdmans, 1975.

Wright, G. Ernest. *The Challenge of Israel's Faith.* Chicago: University of Chicago Press, 1944.

Wright, John H. "Divine Knowledge and Human Freedom: The God Who Dialogues." *Theological Studies* 38 (1977): 450-77.

————. "The Eternal Plan of Divine Providence." *Theological Studies* 27 (1966): 27-57.

Wright, N. T. *The Climax of the Covenant: Christ and the Law in Pauline Theology.* Philadelphia: Fortress, 1992.

————. *The New Testament and the People of God.* Christian Origins and the Question of God. Minneapolis: Fortress, 1992.

Wright, R. K. McGregor. *No Place for Sovereignty: What's Wrong with Freewill Theism.* Downers Grove, Ill.: InterVarsity Press, 1996.

Wynkoop, Mildred Bangs. *A Theology of Love: The Dynamic of Wesleyanism.* Kansas City, Mo.: Beacon Hill, 1972.

Yancey, Philip. "Cosmic Combat." *Christianity Today* 38, no. 14 (1994): 21.

————. *Disappointment with God: Three Questions No One Asks Aloud.* Grand Rapids, Mich.: Zondervan, 1988.

————. *Where Is God When It Hurts?* Grand Rapids, Mich.: Zondervan, 1977.

Young, Francis, and David F. Ford. *Meaning and Truth in 2 Corinthians.* Grand Rapids, Mich.: Eerdmans, 1988.

Index of Names and Subjects

accommodation, 33, 67-69, 156, 295 n. 115
Adams, Robert, 222
Alston, William, 25, 214
Ambrose, 268
analogy, 25, 286 n. 43
Anaximander, 26, 227
Anglin, W. S., 259, 264
anthropomorphism, 14, 19-23, 25-26, 52, 67-70, 144, 156, 187, 295 n. 105
antinomies, 34-37, 256, 289 n. 89
apostasy, 249-250
Aquinas, Thomas, 25, 152-53, 155, 165, 191, 199, 207, 214, 224, 227
Arminius, Jacob, 157, 164-65, 196, 244
Arnobius, 145
Aristotle, 27, 152, 174, 225
assurance, 249-251
Athanasius, 145
Augustine, 147-51, 154-55, 160, 165, 189, 214, 228, 241
Baelz, Peter, 273
Balentine, Samuel, 66, 294 n. 84
Barth, Karl, 21, 90, 108, 163, 165, 170, 185, 190-91, 226, 244, 265, 320 n. 95, 335 n. 71
Barth, Marcus, 183
Bartholomew, D. J., 336 n. 88
Basil, 145
Basinger, David, 14, 136, 164, 171, 323 n. 122, 338 n. 117
Bavinck, Herman, 22, 186
Beckwith, Francis, 296 n. 119
Berkeley, George, 25
Berkhof, Hendrikus, 163, 169, 184, 186, 193, 318 n. 74
Berkhof, Louis, 239, 244
Berkouwer, G. C., 115, 133, 327 n. 30
Bertocci, Peter, 227
biblical-classical synthesis, 141, 152-53, 163, 173
Bilezikian, Gilbert, 162
Bloesch, Donald, 29, 162, 187, 190, 289 n. 89, 305 n. 115, 318 n. 74
blueprint, 56, 127-28, 232, 275-76, 299 n. 172, 338 n. 119
Boer, Harry, 163
Bonhoeffer, Dietrich, 21, 106, 175
Boring, M. Eugene, 134
Boston personalism, 227, 299 n. 170, 316 n. 58
Boyd, Gregory, 14, 162, 183
Boykin, John, 163
Bridges, Jerry, 253
Brightman, Edger S., 227
Bromiley, Geoffrey, 22
Brown, Raymond, 134-35
Brown, Robert F., 316 n. 58
Brueggemann, Walter, 52, 58, 62, 80, 86
Brümmer, Vincent, 17, 31, 105, 163, 176, 179, 185, 209, 211, 215, 219, 239, 244, 316 n. 58
Brunner, Emil, 43, 157, 163, 175, 179, 185, 193, 225
Burrell, David, 288 n. 78
Buswell, J. Oliver, Jr., 162
Calvin, John, 24, 33, 67-69, 72, 81, 155-57, 160, 165, 212, 214, 217, 219, 238-39, 242, 250, 243, 269, 299 n. 6, 314 n. 23
Carneades, 23
Carson, Donald, 35-36, 222
Cassuto, U., 65
chance, 215-16, 327 n. 19, 336 n. 88
chaos, 41-42, 290 n. 13
Childs, Brevard, 58
Chisholm, Roderick, 319 n. 78
Ciocchi, David, 289 n. 89
Clarke, W. Norris, 164, 180
compatibilism, 154-55, 212, 219-21, 238-40, 251, 336 n. 99
Cook, Robert R., 334 n. 46
cooperating with God, 125, 138, 192, 272, 333 n. 41
Cottrell, Jack, 200, 202
Craig, William Lane, 130, 306 n. 129, 307 n. 147
Cranfield, C. E. B., 121-22
creation, 41-44
Creel, Richard, 196, 223, 320 n. 79
Cyril of Jerusalem, 164
Daane, James, 244, 295 n. 105, 303 n. 79
Davis, Stephen, 37, 162, 266
de dicto, 30, 178, 191, 199, 252, 285 n. 36, 316

n. 56, 316 n. 58, 320 n. 95, 326 n. 6
de facto, 192, 247, 265
de jure, 192, 247
demons, 263, 336 n. 90
Depoortere, Kristiaan, 190
de re, 30, 191, 199, 320 n. 95
Descartes, René, 190
determinism, 9-10, 59-60, 81-87, 102, 112-15, 120-22, 155, 195, 290 n. 8, 297 n. 152, 305 n. 114
dignum Deo, 33, 68, 152-53, 208, 291 n. 22, 295 n. 115, 331 n. 5
divine wisdom, questioning of, 46-7, 58, 182-83, 266-67
Dostoyevsky, Fyodor, 266
Dunn, James, 122, 304 n. 88, 304 n. 99
Eastern Orthodoxy, 164, 195, 223, 244, 248
Edwards, Jonathan, 218-19, 250, 270, 314 n. 23
Eichrodt, Walter, 62
election, 61, 102, 144-46, 164, 239
Erasmus, Desiderius, 153-54
Erigena, John Scotus, 151
eternity. *See* God and time
Eunomius, 145-46
evil
    gratuitous, 261-63
    moral. *See* sin
    natural, 263-64
    and no-risk, 253-57
    and risk, 257-68
Fackre, Gabriel, 162, 305 n. 115
faith, 246-49
Farmer, H. H., 169, 190
Fergusson, David, 244
Ferré, Nels, 227
Feuerbach, Ludwig, 20, 30-32
Fiddes, Paul, 48, 163, 235, 301 n. 49
Findlay, J. N., 28, 32
Finger, Thomas, 163
Flint, Thomas, 323 n. 122
foreknowledge, 52, 58-59, 67-75, 101-3, 129-37, 142-45, 148, 158, 164, 171, 194-206, 260, 268, 300 n. 30
Foster, Richard, 162
free will
    libertarian, 45-46, 142-45, 171, 194-95, 221-

24, 251-52, 336 n. 99 (*see also* compatibilism)
    material, 223-24, 336 n. 99
Fretheim, Terence, 21, 24, 44, 49, 53, 59-60, 64, 72-73, 79, 85, 163
future as partially indefinite, 73-75, 125-18, 132, 163, 231
Geach, Peter, 164, 229-30
Geisler, Norman, 67-68, 322 n. 112
Gerish, Brian, 154
God
    aseity of, 24, 28, 30, 242
    as conditioned by the world, 10, 11-12, 53, 62-66, 92, 98, 118-19, 142-46, 157, 164-65, 185, 203, 219, 244-45, 278-82
    dark side of, 293 n. 58, 298 n. 170, 316 n. 58 (*see also* God, impeccability of)
    faithfulness of, 48, 66, 125, 186-88
    for us, 24, 30, 153-54, 188
    freedom of, 121, 169-70, 184-88, 242, 316 n. 58, 322 n. 116, 328 n. 47
    hiddenness of, 21, 30, 79-81, 104, 153-56 (*see also* God, incomprehensibility of)
    holiness of, 79, 179-80 (*see also* God, justice of; wrath of)
    human knowledge of, 24, 26-34, 43, 145, 153, 173
    humiliation of, 88, 109-10
    immutability of, 67-9, 143-44, 147-49, 165, 186
    impassibility of, 142-45, 147-52, 155, 159, 165, 207, 292 n. 42
    impeccability of, 293 n. 58, 298 n. 170, 300 n. 15, 316 n. 58, 328 n. 47 (*see also* God, dark side of)
    incomprehensibility of, 21, 25, 29
    infinity of, 25, 28-34
    in himself, 24, 27, 30
    justice of, 75-79 (*see also* God, holiness of; wrath of)
    language about, 23-34, 285 n. 36, 295 n. 116 (*see also* accommodation; anthropomorphism, literal and metaphorical)
    and laws of thought, 190-91, 320 n. 95 (*see also* necessary truths)
    love of, 75-79, 87-88, 104-6, 109-11, 124, 158, 175-81

as omnicausal. *See* determinism
omnipotence of, 188-94, 199, 290 n. 8
omniscience of, 102, 132, 194-206
as personal, 12, 21, 26, 32-33, 38, 174, 314
    n. 22
plans of, 58, 64-65, 70, 120, 231-32
purposes of, 45, 50, 71
and reciprocal relations, 12, 44, 163, 180,
    190, 210-11, 258
as relational, 11, 24, 146
repentance of, 48, 63-5 66-75, 78, 144, 149,
    156
resourcefulness of, 50-51, 56, 92, 119, 122-
    23, 183, 230-35
as responsive, 71, 86, 96-98, 142-46, 158,
    162, 244, 269-72
self-limitation of, 224-28
sovereignty of, 11, 42-46 (*see also* provi-
    dence)
suffering of, 33, 49, 77-78, 105-6, 144-45
and time, 146, 148, 187, 319 n. 78, 322 n.
    116, 330 n. 82
vulnerability of, 51, 57, 77, 79, 92, 104-5,
    110, 162, 177-79, 181, 187, 258
wisdom of, 129, 181-84 (*see also* divine
    wisdom, questioning of)
as wholly other, 25, 26-34
wrath of, 75-78, 111 (*see also* God, holiness
    of; justice of)
Gorringe, T. J., 91, 129, 217, 224
Gowan, Donald, 59-60, 66
grace, 41, 48, 61, 109-11, 158, 245-46
Gregory of Nazianzus, 145
Gregory of Nyssa, 145
Gregory Thaumaturgus, 144
Gunton, Colin, 103, 163
hardening, divine, 59-60, 122-23
Harkness, Georgia, 227
Hasker, William, 14, 164, 170, 194, 201-2, 222
heaven, 336 n. 99
Hebblethwaite, Brian, 24 , 231
Helm, Paul, 25, 36, 67-68, 102, 160, 170, 218,
    222, 228, 247, 253-54, 256, 269-70, 275, 318
    n. 59, 326 n. 8, 338 n. 117, 338 n. 121
Henry, Carl F. H., 160
Heschel, Abraham Joshua, 21, 40, 73, 76-77,
    272

Hick, John, 28-31, 33, 202-3
Hilary of Poitiers, 23
Hill, William J., 164, 193
Hodge, A. A., 248
Hubbard, David Allan, 73
Hughes, Philip Edgcumbe, 334 n. 44
Hume, David, 20, 256, 266
Hunt, David, 200-201
Hunter, W. Bingham, 160, 294 n. 102
Irenaeus, 142-43
James, William, 229
Jenson, Robert, 145, 163
Jesus as revealer of God, 21, 26, 90-91, 115, 233
Johnson, Elizabeth, 163
Jones, Major, 163
Jüngel, Eberhard, 163, 250
Justin Martyr, 142, 165
Kaiser, Walter, 85
Kant, Immanuel, 27-28
Kaufman, Gordon, 22, 28, 30-31, 33, 260-61
Kierkegaard, Søren, 29, 31, 176, 190
Kirkpatrick, Frank, 31
Klassen, William, 98-99
Knight, Henry, III, 162
Knitter, Paul, 287 n. 57
König, Adriö, 23, 62, 82, 125-27, 163, 223
Kuitert, Harry, 187
LaCugna, Catherine Mowry, 163
Langford, Michael, 216
Lessing, G. H., 33
Lactantius, 145
Levenson, Jon D., 42, 45, 223, 298 n. 170, 316
    n. 58
Lewis, C. S., 163, 204
Lindström, Fredrik, 82-82, 298 n. 155, 303 n. 74
literal, 25-26, 286 n. 49
Lucas, J. R., 164, 210-211, 222, 226, 232, 235,
    247-48
Luther, Martin, 153-55, 165
Macquarrie, John, 22, 25
Maritain, Jacques, 231
Mavrodes, George, 256
McCabe, Lorenzo, 136, 202, 305 n. 125, 306 n.
    130
McFague, Sallie, 31
McGrath, Alister, 154
metaphor, 11, 15-16, 26, 72, 85-86, 285 n. 31

middle knowledge, 196-98, 262

Migliore, Daniel, 194

Mill, James, 203

Mill, John Stuart, 203

Miller, Patrick, 65

models, theological, 12, 15-19, 280

Moltmann, Jürgen, 62, 97, 104, 106, 163, 301 n. 43

Morris, Thomas, 291 n. 22, 316 n. 58

natural theology, 288 n. 76

necessary truths, 320 n. 95

Oden, Thomas, 163, 186

openness of God, 49, 53, 64, 66, 75, 97, 100, 178, 230-35, 283 n. 3

Origen, 143-44, 268, 286 n. 46

Packer, J. I., 22, 35-36

Pannenberg, Wolfhart, 163, 185, 330 n. 82

Pelikan, Jaroslav, 151

permission, 217-20, 255

Philo of Alexandria, 27, 29, 33, 67, 76, 173

Pinnock, Clark, 162, 318 n. 74

Piper, John, 218, 241

Placher, William, 320 n. 79

Plantinga, Alvin, 221, 320 n. 95

Plato, 27, 69, 145, 160, 173, 184, 186

Pope, Alexander, 212

potentia absoluta, 191

potentia ordinata, 191

prayer, petitionary, 53-54, 63-66, 100, 144, 153, 160-62, 222, 268-74

predestination, 120-21, 148-49, 152, 154-55, 157, 196, 240-41

presentism, 12, 52-53, 58, 72-75, 129-37, 163-64, 198-206, 324 n. 125

principle of plenitude, 242, 321 n. 97

Prior, A. N., 164

process theology, 161, 190, 207, 322 n. 113

prophecy, 74-74, 101-3, 125-26, 129-37, 205, 294 n. 102. *See also* future

providence

    general, 10-11, 127, 213-17, 243-44, 258-63, 271-74, 276-78

    meticulous and specific, 10, 54-55, 81-87, 112-15, 149, 160, 174, 211-13, 219, 232, 239, 253-57, 269-71, 275-76

Pseudo-Dionysius, 151

purgatory, 336 n. 99

Purtil, Richard, 164

relational theism, 12, 14, 140-42, 161-65, 167, 195, 207, 282

Rice, Richard, 130

salvation, 203, 238-51

Sarot, Marcel, 227

Scotus, John Duns, 25, 323 n. 119

Scotist view of incarnation, 103, 301 n. 42, 301, n. 43

sin, 47-49, 223-24, 239, 243, 253-59

slavery, 284 n. 14

Sokolowski, Robert, 34, 288 n. 78

specific sovereignty. *See* providence, meticulous

Sproul, R. C., 208, 234, 242

Storms, C. Samuel, 269-70

Stott, John R. W., 127

Strimple, Robert, 322 n. 112

Swinburne, Richard, 25, 164, 199, 222

synergism. *See* cooperating with God

Tannehill, Robert, 119

Tertullian, 143

Tillich, Paul, 159-60

Torrance, Thomas, 163

Tozer, A. W., 160

Tupper, E. Frank, 91, 93, 95, 100-101, 127

Tracy, Thomas, 25

Trinity, 175-76, 178, 184, 314 n. 23, 318 n. 63

trust, 45, 50, 62, 97, 105, 111, 113, 124-25, 267, 316 n. 58

van de Beek, A., 126, 128, 188, 233, 255, 276, 303 n. 77, 316 n. 58, 318 n. 74

Van den Brink, Gisbert, 190-92

Van Inwagen, Peter, 215, 258

Vanstone, W. H., 176-79

Walls, Jerry, 242

Ward, Keith, 164, 225-26, 229, 274, 318 n. 60

Ware, Bruce, 67-69

Ware, Bishop Kallistos, 164

Wesley, John, 157-58, 164-65, 196, 244, 250

William of Ockham, 25

Wolterstorff, Nicholas, 162, 295 n. 116, 332 n. 20

Wright, N. T., 107, 304 n. 99

Wright, R. K. McGregor, 296 n. 131, 331 n. 5

Xenophanes, 20

Yancey, Philip, 49, 116, 162

Zimmerman, Dean, 319 n. 78

Index of Scripture

Genesis
1, *41*
1—3, *209, 223*
1:26, *43*
1:31, 49
2—3, *94, 223*
2—4, *46*
2:7, *49*
2:9, *45*
2:17, *48*
2:18, *44*
2:20, *44*
3, *46, 223*
3:1, *46*
3:12, *47*
3:15, *48*
3:16-17, *112*
3:21, *48*
3:22, *47*
6:5, *49*
6:6, *49, 73, 156, 213, 230, 252, 255, 257*
6:7, *49*
6:8, *50*
9:11-12, *50*
9:15, *50*
12:1-3, *50*
12:2, *63*
12:3, *52, 62*
15:1, *50*
15:2-3, *50*
15:6, *50*
15:8, *53*
15:9-21, *51*
15:13-16, *51*
16, 51, 75
16:10, *51*
16:11, *51*
17, *51*
17:17-18, *51*

18, *74*
18:12, *51*
18:14, *51, 193*
18:16-33, *66*
18:19, *53*
18:22-33, *53*
22, *52, 74, 201*
22:1, *52*
22:5, *52*
22:8, *52*
22:12, *52*
22:15-18, *53*
25:5-17, *74*
25:23, *74*
27:27-40, *75*
32, *54*
32:24-30, *227*
37:6-9, *75*
37:10, *75*
37:28, *54*
39:2, *55*
42:22, *55*
42:25, *55*
42:28, *55*
43:23, *55*
45, *55*
45:4-9, *54*
45:4-5, *54*
45:5, *55*
45:7, *55*
45:9, *55*
50:19-21, *55*
50:20, *55*

Exodus
1—2, *92*
1:13, *56*
2:9-10, *56*
2:23-25, *57*
3, *57*
3—4, *205*

3:15, *57*
3:16—4:9, *132*
3:18, *58*
4:1, *58, 74, 205*
4:2-8, *79*
4:5, *58*
4:5-7, *205*
4:8, *58*
4:8-9, *58*
4:11, *81, 84*
4:14, *58, 213, 273*
4:22, *87*
5:1, *58*
5:2, *60*
5:22-33, *179, 256, 266*
7:5, *59*
7:17, *59*
8:2, *59*
8:10, *59*
8:13, *271*
8:22, *59*
8:31, *271*
9:2, *59*
9:14, *59*
10:1, *59*
10:4, *59*
10:7, *59*
14:4, *59*
14:8, *59*
15:31, *60*
19:4-6, *61*
20:4-6, *78*
20:5, *114*
32, *66, 74, 76*
32—34, *63*
32:7, *63*
32:9-14, *160*
32:10, *63, 271*
32:11-13, *63*
32:11-14, *271*
32:14, *73, 213*
32:31-34, *64*
33:3, *64*
33:4-5, *64*
33:11, *79*
33:13, *65*
33:15-16, *65*

33:18, *65*
33:18—34:7, *91*
33:19, *65*
33:23, *153*
34:6-7, *65, 78, 87*

Leviticus
19:9-10, *112*
19:18, *63*
19:34, *63*

Numbers
11:23, *193*
23:19, *20, 22, 68-70, 156*

Deuteronomy
1:31, *61, 87*
6:5, *63*
6:24, *62*
10:13, *62*
10:17-18, *77*
18:10-20, *63*
18:21-22, *70*
21:22-23, *104*
28—30, *84*
28:30, *84*
28:37, *84*
28:53, *84*
30:1-3, *84*
30:19-20, *79*
32:11-14, *61*

Judges
6:13, *265*
6:25, *276*
10:6-16, *77*
10:13-14, *77*
10:16, *78*

1 Samuel
2:30, *71*
8, *273*
13:13-14, *70-71*
15:11, *69-70, 73, 84*
15:29, *20, 22, 68-70, 73, 156*
15:35, *70, 73*
23:7, *87, 277*

23:9-13, *131*

2 Samuel
4:8, *87*
4:8-12, *277*
12:14, *71*
12:22, *71*
18:31, *87*

1 Kings
13:2-5, *126*
18, *79*

2 Kings
16:2, *84*
18—19, *79*
20, *70, 75*
20:1-6, *271*
20:5, *71*

2 Chronicles
20:32, *84*
25:2, *84*
28:1, *84*
32:31, *80*

Job
28:23-24, *129*

Psalms
13, *256*
13:1, *79*
22, *105, 302 n. 57*
22:16, *101*
44, *80*
47:7-8, *39*
74:12-17, *41*
91:11-12, *94*
104, *41*
135:6, *228*
139:1-6, *129*
139:4, *130*

Proverbs
15:1, *84*
16:9, *81, 84*
20:24, *84*

21:1, *81, 84*
26:4-5, *84*

Isaiah
1:10-15, *257*
6:9-10, *119*
25:6-9, *110*
26:19, *39*
29:15-16, *86*
29:16, *81*
40-55, *82*
40:18, *20*
40:25, *20*
42:6, *82*
42:7, *82*
43:13, *133*
44:6, *129*
45:7, *81-82*
45:9-13, *86*
46:5, *20*
46:9-11, *130*
46:10, *130*
47:5, *82*
49:6, *82*
49:9, *82*
49:15, *87*
51:16, *100*
53:11, *82*
55:8, *35, 88*
55:8-9, *20, 36*
61:1-2, *126*
65:1-2, *63*

Jeremiah
2:2, *87*
3:7, *74, 132, 205, 213*
3:19-20, *132, 205*
5:7, *74*
7:5, *74*
7:16, *272*
11:14, *272*
12:1, *80*
14:11, *272*
15:1, *272*
15:5, *73*
18, *86*
18:1-6, *39*

18:6, *81*
18:6-10, *213*
18:7-10, *86, 131*
18:8, *156*
26:2-3, *74*
31:3, *88*
31:15, *93*
32:35, *74, 213*
38:17-23, *74*

Lamentations
1:12, *126*
2:1, *126*
2:15, *84*
2:20, *84*
2:22, *126*
3:38, *83-84*
3:46, *84*
4:10, *84*
5:11, *84*

Ezekiel
8:6, *80*
12:1-3, *74*
13:5, *126*
18:14-20, *78*
18:20, *114*
23:32-34, *100*

Daniel
4:35, *228*

Hosea
1-14, *87-88*
6:1, *77*
6:4, *74*
11:1, *133*
11:8-9, *22, 68, 78*
11:9, *20*

Joel
2:13, *73, 78, 87*
2:28-32, *126*

Amos
1:13, *83*
3:6-7, *121*

3:6, *81-83*
3:7, *83*
4:1-6, *83*
5:18-20, *126*
7, *74*
9:10, *83*
9:11-12, *126*

Jonah
4:2, *70, 73, 78, 87*

Micah
3:4, *80*

Habakkuk
1:1-4, *80*
1:2-4, *266*
1:5-11, *80*
1:12-17, *80, 266*
2:2-20, *80*
2:4, *265*
3:2, *80*

Haggai
1:10-11, *85*

Malachi
3:1-2, *126*

2 Maccabees
7:28, *41*

Matthew
1—2, *92*
1:26-33, *92*
1:29, *92*
1:34, *92*
2:15, *134*
2:17-18, *93*
2:23, *134*
3:17, *91*
4:1, *94*
4:4, *112*
6:9, *91*
6:10, *114*
6:25-34, *112*
6:26, *39*

6:30, *112*
10:24-34, *113*
10:29, *39*
15:21-28, *96*
15:26, *96*
15:27, *97*
15:32, *96*
16, *95*
16:10, *95*
16:21, *95*
16:22, *95*
17:5, *96*
18:15-20, *98*
20:1-16, *243*
21:31-46, *110*
22, *110*
22:10, *111*
23:37, *115, 255*
24:2, *135*
25:14-30, *243*
26:21, *98*
26:39-44, *100*
26:39, *100*
26:54, *134*
27:42-43, *104*
28:18, *94*
28:20, *138*

Mark
1:2, *126*
2, *97*
6:5-6, *97, 228*
6:6, *97*
10:33-34, *134*
13:2, *135*
14:36, *100*
14:49, *134*
26:38, *136*
26:40-41, *136*

Luke
1:37, *193*
4:16-20, *126*
7:30, *103, 115*
8:9-15, *249*
8:43-48, *97*
8:48, *97*

9:31, *95*
12:1-12, *113*
12:20, *114*
13:1-5, *114*
15, *177*
15:1-2, *109*
15:20, *109*
17:3, *98*
21:6, *135*
22:20, *105*
22:21, *98*
22:24, *135*
22:31, *135*
22:42, *100*
22:44, *99*
23:34, *106*
24:19-26, *135*
24:21, *95, 104*

John
1:14, *26, 91*
4:23, *129*
9:1-5, *114*
11:24, *107*
13:4-17, *193*
13:21, *98*
13:26, *99*
13:27, *99*
14:9, *26, 91*
14:13-14, *272*
14:16-18, *138*
14:26, *138*
15:15, *169*
17:22-24, *103*

Acts
1:6, *107, 117*
2:16-21, *126*
2:23, *103, 129, 200*
4:28, *103*
6, *117*
9:22, *119*
10—11, *117*
10—15, *117*
10:2, *117*
10:4, *117*
10:16-17, *117*

10:34-35, *118*
10:44, *118*
10:47, *118*
11:2, *118*
11:18, *118*
13—14, *118*
13:32-33, *133*
13:45, *119*
13:46, *120*
14:5, *119*
14:19, *119*
15:1, *118*
15:2, *118*
15:7, *118*
15:15-18, *126*
15:28, *119*
21:11, *75*
26:5, *129*
28:25-28, *119*
28:28, *120*

Romans
1:16, *246*
3:29, *115*
4:17, *41*
5:1-11, *108*
5:3-5, *127, 267*
5:8, *267, 316 n. 58*
7:11, *48*
8:18-23, *235*
8:18, *267*
8:24-25, *235*
8:28, *127, 160, 192, 253, 263*
8:29, *127, 129*
8:31-39, *183*
8:35-37, *264*
8:35-39, *267, 316 n. 58*
8:38-39, *108, 128*
9—11, *120-23, 186*
9:6-13, *121*
9:15-16, *121*
9:19, *217*
9:20-21, *156, 186*
9:20-22, *122*
9:21, *39*
9:22, *122*

9:23-33, *122, 218*
10:1-13, *123*
11:2, *129*
11:7, *121*
11:11, *120*
11:11-27, *123*
11:25, *121*
11:26, *123*
11:32, *123, 129, 182*
11:33, *182*
11:33-36, *123*

1 Corinthians
1:24-25, *189*
1:24, *182*
1:25, *104, 182, 193*
3:9, *125, 272*
13:4-7, *181, 246*
13:5, *189, 193, 255*
15:25, *233*
15:27-28, *192*
15:28, *233*

2 Corinthians
5:18-20, *125*
5:18, *192*
6:1, *125*
9:14, *274*
10:5, *192*
13:7, *274*

Galatians
2:11-21, *119*
3:16, *127*
3:29, *127*

Ephesians
1:4, *101-2*
2:1-3, *238*
2:8-9, *237, 246*
3:10-11, *123*
4:30, *240, 249*

Philippians
2:6-7, *116*
2:7, *226*
4:6, *272*

Colossians
1:15-20, *26*
1:15, *233*
1:22-23, *249*
2:3, *129*
2:9, *26*
2:15, *234*

1 Thessalonians
5:8, *235*

2 Thessalonians
1:11, *274*
3:1, *274*

1 Timothy
2:4, *240*
4:10, *235*

2 Timothy
2:13, *186, 193*

Hebrews
1:1-2, *90*
1:3, *26*
2:10, *124*
2:18, *108, 124*
3:2, *124*
3:7-19, *124*
3:12, *124, 249*
3:13, *48*
4:1, *124*
4:6, *124*
6:4-6, *249*
6:13-20, *186*
6:13, *188, 193*
6:17-18, *125*
6:18, *193*
9:24, *108, 188*
10:34, *125*
11, *124*
11:3, *41*
11:6, *125*

11:16, *127, 129*
11:32-39, *125*
12:2, *125*
13:18, *274*

James
1:13, *193*
2:23, *174*
4:2-3, *271*
4:2, *97, 213, 222, 268*
5:14, *274*
5:16, *272*

1 Peter
1:2, *129*
1:20, *101, 129*

2 Peter
1:3-11, *249*
3:9, *240*
3:12, *126*
3:17, *129*

1 John
4:8, *175*
4:9-11, *124*
4:19, *248*
5:14-15, *272*

Revelation
5:1-14, *116*
13:8, *101-2*
16:14, *126*
17:8, *101-2*
21, *127*
21:1, *233*
21:1-2, *127*
21:1-4, *108*
21:4, *233*
21:22, *233*
21:25, *233*
22:3, *233*